Madagascar

PRAEGER LIBRARY OF AFRICAN AFFAIRS

The Praeger Library of African Affairs is intended to provide clear, authoritative, and objective information about the historical, political, cultural, and economic background of modern Africa. Individual countries and groupings of countries will be dealt with as will general themes affecting the whole continent and its relations with the rest of the world. The library appears under the general editorship of Colin Legum, with Philippe Decraene as consultant editor.

Already Published

Madagascar

NIGEL HESELTINE

PRAEGER PUBLISHERS
New York · Washington · London

Praeger Publishers, Inc.
111 Fourth Avenue, New York, N.Y. 10003, U.S.A.
5 Cromwell Place, London, S.W.7, England
Published in the United States of America in 1971
by Praeger Publishers, Inc.

Library of Congress Catalog Card Number: 70-79070

Printed in Great Britain

Contents

Contents

Figures

Acknowledgements

The author wishes to express his deep gratitude to Professor Hubert Deschamps, Professeur à la Sorbonne, Dr P. Radaody-Ralarosy, President de l'Académie Malgache, the Reverend J. T. Hardyman, FJKM, Missionary at Imerimandroso, and Monsieur Pierre Vérin, Directeur du Musée d'Art et d'Archeologie de l'Université de Madagascar, who have been kind enough to read the proofs of this book, and who have provided a number of valuable criticisms, corrections and suggestions.

A NOTE TO THE READER

The name of this country is 'Madagascar'. On its official note-paper appears 'Repoblika Malagasy', the translation being the Malagasy Republic, as the translation of 'République Française' is the French Republic. However, no one calls France 'French' on account of its official note-paper; thus no one should call Madagascar 'Malagasy', which is the adjective. A man is Malagasy, he speaks Malagasy, but he lives in Madagascar. It is thought by some that Madagascar changed its name on achieving political independence. This is not so, and the official name of the country is, as always, Madagascar.

Preface

The President of the Académie Malgache has much pleasure in presenting this book by Mr Nigel Heseltine, who for many reasons is something more than a friend.

Having in a sense followed the preparation of this book from the moment the author began, it is not difficult for me to state that this work has been thoroughly prepared, is of great interest, and is also very timely. In particular it enables one to realize how far we have progressed in the last twenty years, if one refers for example to the book by the Rev J. T. Hardyman, *Madagascar on the Move:* published in London in 1950.

It is interesting to note, on the one hand when one travels abroad that many educated people apparently do not know exactly where Madagascar is, while on the other hand it is astonishing to see the mass of published material, often valuable, which has appeared concerning Madagascar, written by Portuguese, French, British, Dutch, Norwegian, German, Italian, Russian and Malagasy scholars and authors. To mention only a few of these, one can quote the names of the Grandidier (father and son), the British missionaries who contributed to the 'Antananarivo Annual' (1875–1900). Since 1900 the publications of the Académie Malgache, since 1940 those of the Institut de la Recherche Scientifique de Madagascar, and since Independence those of the University of Madagascar, enable research workers to study the best authors— missionaries, scholars, administrators, economists, settlers, travellers, men of letters and artists.

During the past ten years a number of works have appeared in English—not always of the highest standard it is true—in Great Britain and in the United States, concerning Madagascar.

The present book is the work of Nigel Heseltine, a man of wide culture, who is both an economist and an agronomist, who came to us in Madagascar, originally from Ireland, after many years work in Africa, at the request of our Government. As economic adviser to the President of the Republic, he is in a 'front row seat' as an observer. He has travelled to every corner of Madagasar, he has seen much and read much.

Madagascar

'The style is the man himself'. This book is extremely readable, but it is tightly packed with information. It is for the educated reader, and is not entirely a popular presentation.

Written by a conscientious man, who has an encyclopaedic taste for documentation, this book will be indispensable for anyone undertaking the study of the history, geography, philology, ethnology, or the general scientific aspects of Madagascar.

One could, of course, find material for criticism in this book, and there might even be certain changes in a second edition, but in spite of these, this work owes its values to many original judgements formulated by the author, who is a man of action and good-will, and who has been an eye-witness of the events of the last ten years in Madagascar.

Whether one has curiosity or concern, Madagascar is an absorbing country. Moored like an aircraft carrier in the Indian Ocean of which great poets and great navigators have written in the past, and which still awaits its Camoens, (perhaps Russian or Japanese), the position of Madagascar in relation to Africa, has been flatteringly compared by some to that of Great Britain beside Europe or Japan beside Asia.

The eye cannot see itself, thus Madagascar needs the observations of a 'stranger' who is also a friend. Thus we must be grateful to a man, who at the summit of his career, has not remained in an ivory tower, but has worked for long in the field, and speaking Malagasy, has lived the life of the population, under the sky and on the soil of the country to which he is attached.

Thus, let us congratulate Nigel Heseltine, for his keen insight, and for whom the phrase 'international solidarity' is not simply a word.

Dr P. Radaody-Ralarosy
Président de l'Académie Malgache

x

Introduction

MADAGASCAR is a country set apart, but not only because it is an island. In a sense, all islands are peculiar. Some have inhabitants of a bizarre origin, like the Pitcairn islanders; some have peculiar animals, like the extinct dodo of Mauritius, or the marsupials and other indigenous fauna of Australia; St Helena was once covered with big trees related botanically to the daisy. Madagascar has all these elements and many others which set it apart, but with an important difference of its size which classes it, at approximately 380,000 square miles, as one of the largest islands of the world. Its population of Malayo-Polynesian origin, with some African admixture from imported slaves, arrived across the Indian Ocean within historic times, but sufficiently long ago for it to form a homogeneous society speaking one language, Malagasy. Its chief towns almost all occupy sites inhabited for two or three hundred years or longer.

Geologically, Madagascar appears as a stepping-stone attached to a mainly granite outcrop of the Karoo system which links southern Africa to India; and, for students of continental drift, the island appears to fit the east coast of Mozambique as well as West Africa fits Brazil. However, its separation from Africa is ancient, as far back as the Tertiary period, and this is reflected in the fauna and flora of Madagascar which shows special endemic features not found in present-day Africa. Thus, Madagascar split from Africa before the arrival of contemporary African animals and plants, while such species as it has in common with Asia are few and do not point to any more recent connection.

Such characteristics are shared by other islands and would not suffice by themselves to explain the individuality of Madagascar. It is probably the fusion of the population, the welding of many alien elements that have arrived at different times, which gives the impression of an entirely different environment to travellers arriving from the heterogeneous societies of Africa. Mauritius, which is smaller, has many of these characteristics; but, since the immigrations are much more recent, and since different racial policies have been followed by colonising agents, there has been virtually no fusion of the heterogeneous elements and the country is a very long way from becoming an integrated society.

Inevitably, the first impressions of a traveller to Madagascar are those on arrival, usually by air, in the capital city, Tananarive, situated at about 4,000 feet on the 'Hauts-Plateaux' (high plateau) or central mountain massif which runs from north to south of the island. Most travellers arrive either from Europe or from East Africa, and their first view of the land as the plane descends is of numerous rolling hills, coloured green or brown according to the season, wet (summer) or dry (winter). The hills are treeless, and the winding valleys contain small rectangles, that turn out to be irrigated paddy fields, sometimes climbing up the sides of the hills in terraces, as in the Far East. There are small villages of tall narrow red-brick houses with tiled roofs, and near the villages clumps of eucalyptus trees. The landscape could hardly be less like East Africa. Up to 1967, when the airport of Tananarive was at Arivonimamo, thirty miles distant, the traveller's first contacts were with the Malagasy countryside—the villages, rice fields, ox-carts, and large herds of long-horned cattle being driven into Tananarive for slaughtering. Now the airport is at Ivato and the short ten-mile run gives a similar but less varied view.

Except for those fortunate few who arrive by ship at Tamatave, with its coconut palms, mangroves, rickshaws and Chinese grocers, few travellers see anything other than the Hauts-Plateaux. Although one can hop by air with ease from Tananarive to a number of small towns all over the island by Air Madagascar, conscientious travel would require much time, individual transport and some introductions. This is all possible, but not for hurried travellers; thus, few foreigners, even residents, other than the specialists can claim to have travelled extensively in the interior of the island.

Time is required to travel in Madagascar, not only because it is large and because some roads are, for the time being, difficult, but also because of its exceptional variety. Although the people, numbering in all nearly 7 million (1970), speak closely-related dialects of one language, Malagasy, they vary in appearance and often there are great differences in dress and manner. The landscape is very varied: there are at least five major ecological regions in Madagascar, each having a different climate, special types of vegetation, and, in consequence, the manner of life of the population adapted to the special conditions.

The cool rolling hills of the Hauts-Plateaux change rather suddenly into an area of dense humid tropical forest which descends sharply to the east coast. From temperate uplands having a mean annual fainfall of about 47 inches, the traveller moving east will reach within sixty miles a zone where there is practically no dry season and the rainfall may exceed 120 inches per annum. To the west of the Hauts-Plateaux is a huge area of savannah grassland, derived by fire from dry deciduous forest, which has a dry season of seven to eight months. Here are found most of the cattle, estimated to total between 10 and 12 million head. In the extreme south, between Fort Dauphin and Tuléar, is a large area of sclerophytic bush dominated by endemic *Euphorbiaceae* and species such as the *Dideriaecea* which exist nowhere else in the world and resemble closely the giant cacti of the Arizona desert. It was here that the aepyornis lived, a giant ostrich-like bird, similar to but larger than the moa of New Zealand. Broken eggs of the aepyornis (which became extinct in historic times) are found easily in valleys of the south, such as the Linta.[1] The fifth and smallest region, the Sambirano in the north-west, is a delightful place, shadowed by the highest mountain in Madagascar, Tsaratanana (9,347 feet). In this micro-climate grow pepper, cacao, coffee, sugar cane, and a perfume plant, ylang-ylang, with flowers on its curiously bent and tortured branches that scent the whole island of Nosy-be.

The people and their mode of life in these various climates are also different, although speaking dialects of one language and presenting a general cultural unity. The tall narrow red houses of the Hauts-Plateaux, with their steep tiled or thatched roofs and balconies, are not found elsewhere. On the east coast, the houses are rectangles built of plaited bamboo and stand on stilts, very much like certain Indonesian villages. On the west coast, the houses are huts built of *vondro* (reeds) roofed with fronds of palms (*Hyphaenae shatan, Borassus spp.*), and they resemble African villages. An inhabitant of Imerina, the central region of the Hauts-Plateaux, could be set down in Java and no one would take him for anything but an Indonesian. A Javan—and many Malays— would pass quite unnoticed in the streets of Tananarive. On the west coast, the Sakalava cattle owners are big men, with little that is oriental about their appearance: their faces, their physique and even their songs show some African admixture. On the east coasts are populations such as the Betsimisaraka, and the smaller

3

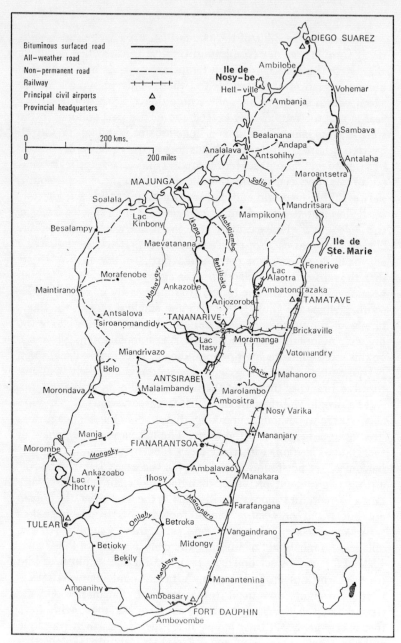

Map 1. Communications system in Madagascar

tribes such as the Antaifasy and Antaimoro, who have a pure Malayo-Polynesian appearance and show certain cultural features, such as their houses built on stilts, their looms and other implements. Here there has been Arabic influence, which has left traces in pockets of Muslims at Vohipeno and ancient manuscripts in the Malagasy language written in Arabic script, but there has been no African penetration. Many of the fruit-trees and edible plants growing here are familiar to those who have lived in the Far East: the bread-fruit, anonas and letchis among the fruits, and the taro or coco-yam growing on the edge of the rice fields.

Penetrating any region for the first time, the traveller to Madagascar has the impression of intense activity, similar to what is seen on the West African coast, but completely absent over huge areas of the African savannah, and more particularly in the European-settled countries of Central Africa. Tananarive displays a refreshing absence of 'town-planning', and is strongly criticised by many Europeans whose sense of 'order' is outraged by the multiple activities of a closely-packed town of nearly 400,000 inhabitants. Everywhere are small shops and artisans observing no early closing or any other regulation. Booths and stalls along the edges of the market are rigged like those in Europe in the Middle Ages. At night, stalls and small shops are lit by flickering oil lamps or bright pressure lanterns. They are thronged with people buying, haggling, selling, eating and drinking. Country people who have come a long way to sell their goods sleep on the ground around the great central market, the Zoma, in the centre of the town, waiting for daybreak and customers. The streets, not only of Tananarive but also of other small towns, are thronged with a mixture of ox-carts, bicycles, hand-carts, huge trucks, 'deux-chevaux' taxis and private cars. Many cars show signs of recent but minor damage. There are few pavements and pedestrians push against the wheeled traffic.

This is very unlike the 'town-planned' but empty stretches like Cairo Road in Lusaka, from which the inhabitants disappear at five in the afternoon, their only resource the barrack known as a 'beer hall' somewhere in their locations, far from areas of European habitation. In no town in Madagascar is there such a thing as a 'residential quarter'. There has never been a 'European quarter' in any Malagasy town: General Galliéni, the conqueror and first Governor-General, had the wisdom to forbid such a venture when certain of his entourage suggested it, and Malagasy and European have lived side by side ever since. A large house may have a huddle of little houses near it. Its back-yard may give on to a rice field still existing in the town. Tananarive is a hilly island surrounded by rivers—the Ikopa, the Sissaony, the Mamba and others. There is little room for houses, land is expensive and gardens tend to be very small. The houses rise in terraces one above the other on the hilly slopes. Penetration up and down is by tortuous stone staircases. It is a town vividly alive from early morning till far into the night. The movement to and fro, the shops large and small, the booth eating-houses and restless transport are all signs of economic activity.

Transport facilities are abundant on most of Madagascar's roads. The 'taxi-brousse' is often a Renault 1000 with fifteen to twenty seats, or a Peugeot 403 pick-up with seats arranged in the back. On to this climb the country people with their baskets of produce, chickens and geese, and they move off towards the local market uninhibited by any 'road traffic commissioner'. The empty roads of Central Africa, where people can wait for up to three days for a lift to some nearby town, are unknown in Madagascar.

This unusually integrated society has a strong French stamp in towns such as Tananarive, Tamatave or Antsirabe. Malagasy and French are the two official languages, but Malagasy is very much the national language. Thus, within the administration, documents are written in French but meetings are held in Malagasy, except where a French official is present. Malagasy officials speak to one another in Malagasy on the telephone but write their memoranda in French. The gendarmes have specifically French kepis but speak only rudimentary French. The churches, even small village ones, resemble nineteenth-century French rural churches but the service is in Malagasy. The larger shops within the towns stock mainly French products, not because others are unobtainable but because these are familiar to the public. Advertisements of products well known in France appear on the walls. Education beyond a certain standard is in French, and all secondary and university teaching is in French, although many students take Malagasy as a subject in their baccalauréat examination and some as a special subject at university. The reading public reads French books, and in the larger towns there are excellent bookshops stocking the latest publications. France has left more than cultural ties. It can be said that the cultivated Malagasy cherishes his French culture, although he has access to two cultures, so that his French education makes him more aware of traditional Malagasy cultural values. The keenest students of Malagasy language and culture are often those who have been highly educated in the French system and may even have lived several years in France. Once outside the towns, however, there are few signs of France other than the familiar blue and white signposts on the main roads. The villages, and even the smaller towns, are wholly Malagasy, and not a word of French will be heard in the streets.

As soon as one leaves the tarred road, even on the outskirts of Tananarive, one finds ancient villages that have altered hardly at all as a result of European influence. In fact, Europeans rarely are seen in such villages and their appearance excites curiosity and sometimes mistrust, even within sight of the capital city. Tananarive is ringed by the ancient capitals of rival minor monarchies which were gradually subdued by the Merina monarchy in the eighteenth century. Alasora, Ambohimanga, Ambohidratrimo, Ambohimasimbola, all within ten miles of the city, were once capitals of small kingdoms. Flying over the Hauts-Plateaux, the traveller sees numerous circular moats, sometimes surrounding villages, sometimes surrounding nothing but rough vegetation on the tops of hills. These are *hadivory*, or defensive fortifications, moats fifteen feet deep or more, usually showing interesting relics of trees from the vanished forests that once surrounded these villages. Fortified villages once occupied all the hilltops around Tananarive, but now they contain only clumps of wild sisal, guava bushes and coarse grass. During the nineteenth century, when the Merina monarchy established law and order over wide areas, and especially after the French conquest in 1896, most of the hill-top villages moved down nearer their rice-fields and water supply in the valley. Sometimes, a few ancient houses still remain inhabited. These fortified hill-top villages are cited as an Indonesian heritage, although their situation is similar to the hill-top *ksars* in North Africa and ancient Mediterranean hill towns found from Spain to Turkey.

Entering one of these villages, usually by a rough cart-track which runs through high red walls, the traveller finds himself in a compact community of tall narrow houses, all orientated north-south, so that the afternoon sun strikes the balconies shading the west windows, while a windowless wall faces the east against the cold winter south-east trade winds. The larger villages often have two churches of identical design facing one another—one Catholic and the other Protestant. Hidden among the houses may be sacred stones still used for sacrifices, and on summits of the highest hills, even within sight of Tananarive, there are sacrificial stones, where one can often see fresh feathers and blood of recent sacrifices of chickens. It is taboo for a European to walk across such places. Dogs are absolutely taboo near tombs and within the royal palaces of the former Merina monarchy. These sacrifices are often offered to the Vazimba, the legendary aboriginal inhabitants, as on the summit of Andringitra to the north of the new international airport of Ivato.

Suspicious curiosity will always give place to welcoming smiles when the traveller greets the villagers, and especially if he speaks even a few words of Malagasy. Curiously enough, one asks permission to enter a house by using the Kiswahili word '*Haody?*', or 'May I enter?', although the answer, 'Come in', will be in Malagasy, '*Mandrosoa*'; '*Karibu*' will be heard only on the west coast, where a number of Kiswahili words have entered the Malagasy language.

The tall red houses have a large number of tiny rooms. The living-room may well be on the first floor, reached by a steep narrow staircase. In the floor of one of the ground-floor rooms there will be a trap, leading to a cellar, the *lavabary*, lined with clay and waterproof, in which the year's supply of paddy is stored. The bedrooms are on the first or even the second floor, since the Merina do not care to sleep on the ground floor. The windows will have not glass but heavy wooden shutters that are tightly closed at night. The rooms have rough wooden furniture, tables and chairs, made by local carpenters, and beds with mattresses stuffed with dried grass. The cooking is done in a little shed outside in the yard, the smoke escaping through the chinks in the roof. The little courtyard in front of the house usually has benches against the west wall for sitting in the afternoon sun, and one or two fruit trees, almonds or peaches, sometimes a tree-cassava (*Manihot glazowii*) from which the leaves are plucked and chopped to be cooked with fat pork. A deep well has often been sunk to supply the household.

In many of the villages there are one or two larger houses with fine balconies, set behind walls of red pounded clay sometimes twelve to fifteen feet high. These are houses belonging to middle-class families; they rarely live in them, since the descendants are usually in Tananarive. Within the walls and near the house there is a huge rectangular block of masonry, the family tomb or vault, in which members of the family have been buried for perhaps two hundred years. Such houses often belong to the many heirs of noble or high bourgeois families—andriana or hova are the names of these two castes—and it would be very difficult for a stranger to buy one of these houses unless the agreement of many members of a scattered family could be obtained. The upper classes have largely abandoned the countryside for the capital, where they hold posts in the administration and business, while the villages, which they still own as absentee landlords, together with large areas of the land are inhabited by their former slaves, the andevo, who are darker in colour and have crinkly hair showing African admixture. The straight-haired brown-skinned Merina of pure Malay descent do not, in general, intermarry with anyone showing the slightest signs of African blood.

At night, after sundown, there is no sign of life in such villages. The shutters are tightly closed, all are inside the house, and if a rare figure is met out after dark, he is likely to be running for fear of evil spirits. No one sits outside his front door after dark, and there is little visiting. A Merina proverb warns the traveller against arriving in a village after dark for 'he will be welcomed only by the dogs', and it is advisable to start early and arrive in good time when touring off the main roads. However, the Merina peasant is up well before sunrise and moves off with his carts and his animals in the dark, shouting greetings to his neighbours at four in the morning.

On the coasts it is quite different, and life goes on outside the houses and in the villages far into the night. The climate is a good deal warmer than on the Hauts-Plateaux and it is pleasant to enjoy the cool night air. Moreover, the houses do not lend themselves to tight shuttering. On the east coast, the wooden houses on stilts have fine smooth floors of tropical hardwood. The walls woven from flattened laths of bamboo allow air to pass through, and the roof, tightly woven of ravenala (the 'travellers tree' of botanic gardens), while keeping off the frequent rain, insulates the rooms from heat. Here furniture is at a minimum and one sleeps on thick raffia or reed mats which are rolled up in the day. The inhabitants usually sit on the floor on other mats while conversing or eating. The whole aspect of the houses within and without is almost exactly like certain countries of the Far East. The Chinese store-keeper in these villages is well-assimilated, and marriages between Malagasy and Chinese are frequent and successful. The inhabitants sit on their balconies far into the night, visit each other and walk about without fear. Songs are heard, and drumming, quite unlike the complete silence of the tall brick houses of the Hauts-Plateaux. The west coast is similar, with a rather intense night-life in the villages, but the design of the houses is much simpler and the floors are of beaten earth. Sleeping in such a house at night, one hears crickets rustling in the roof of palm fronds. On the east coast it is the loud croaking of frogs in the rivers and lagoons that sounds all night.

On the west coast, the Sakalava villages are isolated in the middle of great rolling grassland savannahs, the small houses surrounded by a stockade of stakes and the older villages shaded by large mango trees. The east coast is far more thickly populated; about 30 per cent of the population of Madagascar live in a thirty mile wide strip running along the east coast from north to south. Some villages are huge agglomerations of two to three thousand people. The houses, still all facing north-south, are grouped round a much larger house, the *trano-be*, or big house, the residence of the village headman.

Even within the larger towns, and certainly outside them, the dress of the Malagasy has remained curiously specific. Around Tananarive, and even in its streets, men wear the *malabar*, a long *djellaba* of brightly checked flannelette, a *lamba* or shawl wrapped around their shoulders, a broad-brimmed straw hat on their heads, and they are often barefoot. The older women still dress in a long white dress, with the white *lamba* around their shoulders, and carry a parasol. Well-to-do women wear elegant white silk *lambas* draped with taste in the traditional style, and also carry parasols, since a pale complexion is rather prized. On the west coast, men and women wear the *lamba hoany*, identical with the Malayan *sarong*, or the Swahili *lambas* of East Africa. As in East Africa, these have predominant colours: the Sakalava wear red, the Comoriens wear red, yellow and brown, while on the east coast the *sarong* is often blue. All bear a motto, as in East Africa, such as '*Firenena man-*

droso no harena' ('The nation advances to riches'). In the extreme south, the Antandroy herdsmen walk through the spiny cactus-like bush, herding their cattle, wearing only the *salaka*, or loin-cloth, with a pointed helmet-like straw hat on their heads and carrying a long spear.

Invited into the house of an educated upper-class Merina in Tananarive, a European will see hardly anything unfamiliar. The houses in the capital are more elaborate versions of the tall brick houses of the villages. They have the same balconies, but the rooms are larger and the living room is on the ground floor. The kitchen is often in a courtyard. Inside, the visitor will be shown into a parlour with a polished wooden floor of local timber (often *nato*—a *sapotaceae* from the forests to the east). The furniture is very much as it would be in a small provincial town in France. On the wall are usually large portraits of parents or grandparents, some framed diplomas, and religious pictures of Catholic or Protestant inspiration according to the family's allegiance. Many upper-class families of Tananarive are Protestant—the London Missionary Society (LMS) converted the Queen in 1869 and thus it was fashion-able to be Protestant—while the Catholics, and particularly the Jesuits, concentrated on the lower classes; but today these dis-tinctions are blurred. The visitor will be served French aperitifs or even whisky, although the Merina drink very little. It is when the meal is served that the visitor will find strange dishes.

The Malagasy, as the Chinese and other oriental peoples, often place all dishes on the table at the same time. The European habit of serving separate courses, with a long wait between each, strikes them as tedious. A very large bowl of rice occupies the centre of the table. With this may be served a stew of meat cooked with ginger and aromatic leaves, meat in sauce, grilled fish or fish in sauce, or chicken or duck, cut up and cooked in broth. Lumps of pork fat cooked with chopped cassava leaves—*ravintoto*—is a delicacy. Everyone has a small bowl of broth made from other leaves which he sips while eating. Often the only drink will be rice-water, or water boiled after the remains of the rice have been allowed to burn in the bottom of the pot. This is the *ranovola* or *ranonapango*, which is drunk hot and is very refreshing. Drunk in the bush it has the advantage of being safe, since it has been boiled. The visitor may be served wine, and fruit finishes the meal. Many Merina do not care for coffee, and tea is never drunk.

The standard of education in such a household may well astonish a visitor. The tradition of education in Madagascar is already ancient, and owes much to missionaries, both Protestant and Catholic, as far back as the early nineteenth century. In the Malagasy language English words, assimilated as *sekoly* for school, *pensily* for pencil, *solaitra* for slate and *boky* for book, are an eloquent reminder of the work of the London Missionary Society from 1820 onwards. There are many women doctors and lawyers, and not only among the Merina. The first doctors were trained by English missionaries as far back as the 1880s; and, although the French conquerors made some of them resit their examinations after 1896, the work of the Tananarive Ecole de Médicine was vigorously expanded by the French administration.

The colonisation of Madagascar differed materially in methods and results from that of neighbouring African countries. Firstly, the French conquest of 1896 was the take-over of an organised political state, similar to the British annexation of the Indian states in the nineteenth century. The Merina monarchy had extended a territorial administration over practically the whole of the island by the middle of the century; it had established diplomatic relations with England and France and had signed a commercial treaty with the United States in 1883. The first embassy of the Merina monarchy was received by Queen Charlotte, wife of George IV, in 1817, and an engraving of the event hangs in the former royal palace in Tananarive. The French conquest was a very different matter from the penetration of vast areas of Africa only recently occupied by semi-nomadic tribes. No West African state, even the vanished Sudanic empires of Ghana, Bornu or Mossi, had as permanent a hold on its subjects as the Merina monarchy which was finally overthrown in 1896.

Even then, the elite was preserved by the French administration so long as it was loyal, and this perpetuated the Merina domination, rather as Lugard's policy of indirect rule perpetuated the declining Fulani emirates in Northern Nigeria. As late as 1960, the year of political independence, 60 per cent of all secondary educational establishments were sited in and around Tananarive. This imbalance is now substantially redressed and lycées exist in all the provincial headquarters. The Merina elite provided a substantial basis for an indigenous administration, and accounts for a high percentage of senior administrative staff today. The decolonisation of Madagascar was thus a transfer of power to an educated minority, which provided a comparatively smooth transition, despite genuine inter-tribal stresses between the inhabitants of the Hauts-Plateaux and the less-favoured population of the coastal districts. In 1970 the educational system of Madagascar, closely patterned on the French structure and staffed at lycée and university level largely by French expatriates, turned out more than 1,500 bachéliers and 5,000 BEPC*, while the University of Tananarive had more than 4,000 students. These figures may be compared with the situation of Zambia at independence in 1964, with approximately 800 'school certificates' in the whole country, and less than a hundred university graduates (many of them educated in South Africa) for a population of 3·7 million.

The educated elite was inherited from the former Merina monarchy. Thus Madagascar is a country which has a history before colonisation, similar to the colonised countries of the Far East. Though much of this history is oral tradition which has been written down by Europeans, such as the *Tantara ny Andriana* ('Tales of the Kings'),[2] it nevertheless enables us to list the chronology of the Merina, Sakalava, Betsileo and other monarchies, and trace the evolution of the unification of the island under the sovereigns of Tananarive and the order of contacts with the outside world. Less clearly, the inscribed traditions refer to the successive immigrations of Malayo-Polynesian peoples and enable some idea to be formed, though very imprecisely, of the routes of their penetration into the island's interior. These historical fragments contain many unsolved references, such as those concerning a primitive population inhabiting the forests before the arrival of the major waves of immigrants. These aboriginals, or Vazimba, have left traces, not only in legend but in their inviolable tombs, found in many places, and in the traditions of their ability as magicians. They present some familiar features, similar to those found in other countries. Their physical appearance is now distorted, they are magicians, the ancestral guardians of the soil. However, certain noble Merina families claim descent from the Vazimba, and it is known that some early kings in the fifteenth century married Vazimba princesses on arrival in the Hauts-Plateaux.

There are no clear traditions of the arrival of a sea-people in

* Brévet d'Etudes du Premier Cycle.

13

a Kon-Tiki-like expedition across the Indian Ocean, though the ancestors may have come in huge outrigger canoes, like the Arawa in which the Maoris are known to have reached New Zealand. The Malagasy language is sufficiently evolved as a coherent, but separate, stem of the Malayo-Polynesian languages for it to have developed for a long time in situ. The people themselves present many different strains, the majority deriving from the Malayo-Polynesian area. It would seem that, when the ancestors of the Hawaiians and Tahitians moved east, the proto-Malagasy moved west. However the details of the peopling of Madagascar remain a mystery, which considerable anthropometric and archaeological research, today hardly begun, might perhaps elucidate.

In whatever order they may have arrived, the Malagasy have been great assimilators of one another and the historical traditions all speak of considerable mixing between Merina and Betsileo, Sakalava and Betsileo, Merina and Sihanaka, and so on. Such mixing is less evident today, when a strong feeling of race inhibits intermarriage and a rather well-defined caste system prohibits marriages between social classes in certain tribes, especially among the Merina. Paradoxically, a Merina upper-class or bourgeois family will prefer a son or daughter to marry a European than to marry outside the social caste. Marriages with Europeans, especially between French and Malagasy, have been common since the conquest, and the *métis* (half-castes) are usually absorbed without any difficulty. Many French fathers recognised and educated their offspring and others married the mothers legally. The Malagasy widow of a former French Governor was in 1970 a respected citizen of Tananarive, and others of mixed descent have been ministers and ambassadors. The mixing of Europeans and Malagasy has gone on so easily that no one ever pauses to think of the race of his neighbour. The atmosphere is very unlike certain African countries, where Europeans and Africans are always race conscious, and is due basically to a policy of assimilation inaugurated by General Galliéni and imposed, though with occasional set-backs, by successive French administrations.

This policy of assimilation did not prevent the French commercial interests from having a very definite control of all important sectors of the Malagasy economy. Structures were laid down on the familiar metropolitan-colonial pattern, which continues to exist, sometimes with few modifications, today. The implantation of 'comptoirs coloniaux', such as the Société Marseillaise or Société Lyonnaise, laid down patterns that did not evolve in the direction of decentralisation and a withdrawal from retail trade as did those of the United Africa Company in West Africa. Madagascar was also marked out as a country for European settlement, and a small number of settlers established coffee-plantations on the east coast and farms around Lake Alaotra on the edge of the Hauts-Plateaux. However, there was never a well-defined area of settlers such as the White Highlands of Kenya, or what were the 'white lowlands' of Morocco around Meknès and Fez. Apart from some tobacco farmers in the hot valley around Miandrivazo to the west of the Hauts-Plateaux and in the valley between Mampikony and Port Bergé to the north of Majunga, few settlers became prosperous. Capital seems to have been short and the number of settlers was never great. But as late as 1956 the colonial administration contemplated settling French small farmers in the highlands of the Ankaizina, north-east of Majunga.

Though the economy is agricultural and almost all the export income is derived from this source, the range of products exported is surprisingly wide. Twenty agricultural products account for 85 per cent of total exports by value, with robusta coffee and vanilla together accounting for more than 40 per cent. This variety is a result of the wide variations in climate and rainfall over the five major ecological regions of the island. Rice is the basis of practically all peasant farming. A farmer in almost every region will have a hectare more or less of irrigated paddy field, a few cattle and some dry farming of cassava, maize, sweet potato and beans. Poultry are always kept, and ducks and geese are found in large flocks. Curiously, the Malagasy words for geese, *gisa*, and the Sakalava dialect word *duk-duk* seem to be derived from English, but such numbers of these birds are kept that one is reminded of Chinese duck-farms in the Far East.

The huge numbers of cattle, almost two for every inhabitant, are found mainly on the great savannahs of the west and north-west. Madagascar is as disease-free as Australia or New Zealand, having no foot-and-mouth disease, no rinderpest, no brucellosis, no East Coast fever, no tse-tse fly and thus no trypanosomiasis. Also, unlike Africa, Madagascar has no large carnivores, so that the only danger is from well-organised cattle-thieves, against whom the government has waged vigorous campaigns since independence. Among certain tribes, such as the Sakalava, the Bara or the Antandroy, cattle are the object of veneration, just as they are among the Fulani or the Masai. The cattle are all large long-horned zebus and have a much finer conformation than the nondescript Masai or Wakamba cattle of East Africa. The Malagasy word for cattle, *omby*, is derived from the Kiswahili *ngombe*, and the traditions all speak of numbers of wild cattle on the island when the first immigrants arrived. The Merina kings hunted wild cattle (*baria*) 150 years ago, and some are said to survive between Belobaka and Ankavandra on the western edge of the Hauts-Plateaux. Cattle are the object of sacrificial slaughter, especially in connection with burial rites, and the Mahafaly tombs in the south are decorated with the horns of up to fifty oxen slaughtered when a notable was buried.

The small farms, especially on the Hauts-Plateaux, provide what is necessary for simple living, and the peasant lives in a reasonable balance with his available resources. His standard of living, in the province of Tananarive, is not far from that of the peasant of Spain, Southern Italy or Greece. In fact, he lives better than those unfortunates perched at 4,500 feet on the edge of the Central Appenines, who, though only a hundred miles from Rome, live off a flock of goats and sheep, the brush-wood they can cut and a slender crop of wheat on a corner of soil among the limestone. The Appenine peasant has a long snowy winter. The peasant of Imerina has the cool south-east trade wind for five months of the year, but these are the months when the sun shines continuously from the moment when the morning mists are dispelled, about seven o'clock. Arabica coffee may suffer from frost once in five years at 5,000 feet between Antsirabe and Ambatolampy, but it will grow again and give abundant fruit. There is no word for snow in Malagasy except *fanala*, which appears to refer only to the white crystals of frost. Snow falls every few years on some mountain top, and 20 inches are said to have been photographed by a forestry officer on the top of Andringitra (8,638 feet) to the south of Fianarantsoa in 1961. There is nothing like the regular snowfalls on the Drakensberg mountains in South Africa, or like the eternal snow of Kilimanjaro, farther to the north and nearer the Equator.

The Merina peasant has his house of two or more storeys, built of brick and roofed with tiles, unless he is very poor and can afford only thatch: the quality of the roof is an index of prosperity. He has one or more hectares of paddy field, which will give him from 1·5 to 2·0 tons of paddy per hectare. The colluvial soils around the paddy fields are planted with cassava, sweet potatoes, some maize, beans and leafy vegetables for stewing in the broth. The cassava is used as a reserve when there is insufficient rice or when the rice—the basic and preferred foodstuff—has been sold for cash. His livestock include all the fowl of the farm-yard—hens, ducks and geese—some pigs, and sheep which are tethered to graze on the edge of the paddy fields or in the middle after the harvest. Cattle roam the neighbouring bare hills, grazing rough grass, or are tethered like the sheep. The peasant's fuel supply comes from a few eucalyptus planted round his house, which are regularly coppiced. The advantage of the eucalyptus, or at least of the *var. robusta* and *rostrata* which are the dominants on the Hauts-Plateaux, is that, when cut back to their stumps, they quickly sprout multiple poles again.

The Betsimisaraka peasant on the east coast lives on the edge of the humid tropical forest and on land gained with difficulty from the forest. In his country it rains for eleven months in the year to a total of 120 inches, with a short halt in the month of October. As in other high-rainfall tropical areas of the world, almost everything grows without effort. He has rudimentary rice fields, since he does not have to work out elaborate methods of canalising or storing water like the Merina or Betsileo on the Hauts-Plateaux. He often sows rice broadcast, and does not bother to make a nursery and transplant. Coco-yams, sweet potatoes, cassava, bananas, various fruits and almost anything he likes to plant grows luxuriantly. Often he is merely content to cut or burn a section of forest and plant mountain rice among the ashes. This habit of *tavy* or *kapa-kapa* is discouraged by the administration but is still practised as the Malagasy form of shifting-cultivation or bush-fallowing. Most important of all, he has a cash crop, which he crops rather than cultivates, robusta coffee or cloves. Vanilla, which requires more effort, is also a valuable crop, but over-production has been a problem.

Cattle do not do well on the wet east coast, particularly cattle brought down from the Hauts-Plateaux. Some years ago, the French administration introduced Asian buffaloes, which were kept for some years in quarantine on the island of St Marie under the supervision of a Malagasy veterinarian, Dr Rajaofera, but were later transferred to the region around Tamatave. However, they did not flourish and their few descendants are kept with difficulty by the local veterinary service.

The Sakalava in the dry grassland-savannahs of the west coast can pay for any service he requires with his cattle. Thus the minimum of cultivation required for his rice-supplies may be paid for with an animal, and the construction of his house, which means going far off to cut timber for the walls and grass for the roof, may also be paid for in the same way. His standard of living is comparable rather to that of the Masai or Fulani than to that of any contemporary group in Europe.

This equilibrium—where some elements of the population may be undernourished but where no one dies from hunger, where there is usually a sufficient minimum supply of money derived from the sale of paddy, coffee or cattle, for basic needs—maintains the peasant of many regions of Madagascar in balance with his surroundings. It does not press home to him any urgent needs, except the slow attraction of consumer goods, and it does not seem to be conducive to changing his habits. Here is found both the obstacle to development and a favourable terrain for economic change. The peasant on the Hauts-Plateaux is already living in an organised society, as are the Tsimihety farther north, the Betsimisaraka, and the smaller tribes, Antaifasy-Antaimoro, of the east coast. He has a history and a social structure, together with an exchange economy. This is very different from some regions of Central or East Africa, where loosely-knit tribes have arrived recently and have few roots in the area. At the present time, communications are sufficiently widespread in Madagascar, whether by radio or word of mouth, that these rural populations are aware of standards of living elsewhere. The highly-organised popular transport system of the rural areas of Madagascar means that much of the population is constantly exposed to the attraction of consumer goods and of the higher standard of living in the small towns. The first effect may be that he sells paddy which formerly he ate, so that he falls back on an inferior foodstuff, cassava. The second effect may well be that he increases his rice production by using fertiliser and improved tools. This is already happening. Or he may go further and raise the productivity of his livestock. This society is apparently in equilibrium, but not all the elements are static at present.

On the other hand, the closely organised society of the villages, directed by the *Fokon'olona*, presents a barrier against penetration by new ideas or customs. The village council or *Fokon'olona* (recognised by a government decree of July 24, 1962) is formed by the notables of a village whose inhabitants descend from a common ancestor. It has a function of social solidarity, especially in the face of a natural disaster. It maintains order and cleanliness in the village, helps the authorities to find and arrest criminals, and is particularly active in running down cattle thieves. This communal basis, found all over Madagascar though most strongly developed on the Hauts-Plateaux, is a structural advantage for development, but acts at the same time as a conservative force, filtering and hindering new ideas and practices.

This organised society has lived in contact with outside influence for at least as long as the coast of West Africa, and with more enduring results. Madagascar was on the main sea route from Europe to the Far East until the opening of the Suez Canal— that is, for about four hundred years. Although the first recorded contact with the West is the shipwreck of a Portuguese vessel in the bay of Ranofotsy in 1527, contacts were frequent, both on the east and on the west coasts. Before that, Madagascar participated in the movements of other maritime peoples over the Indian Ocean. Arab navigators arrived early; they had an important settlement at Vohémar on the north-east coast from which they sent their settlers towards the south to Vohipeno, where a handful of Malagasy Muslims still survive. The Arab contribution to the Malagasy language is significant, not for the number of words but for their quality. Thus the Malagasy word for 'write' is '*manoratra*', which contains the Arabic root '*surat*.' Paper is '*taratasy*', from Arabic '*karatasy*'. The names of the days of the week, *Alahady, Talata, Zoma*, are all taken from Arabic, as is the lunar month used by the Malagasy. The Arabic methods of divination by arranging beads in a rectangular pattern are used by the *mpisikidy*, the soothsayers, today in Madagascar, and their influence on local magical practices is extensive. The Muslim religion is represented by the Comoro island and Pakistani minorities, and there is also a very small indigenous Malagasy Muslim community centred on Vohipeno on the south-east coast.

Certain tribes, such as the Antakarana in the extreme north, have been influenced by Muslim customs.

It is thought probable that Indian and even Chinese navigators, who certainly reached the East African coast around Mombasa, also reached Madagascar. A French missionary, E. Vernier, reported Lacadive islanders being shipwrecked at Antalaha in 1930. They remained several weeks and then returned home. Arab-style dhows or *boutres* still sail between the Comoro islands and the north-west ports. In the past they also came from Zanzibar, and farther afield.

The contacts with the European world before the eighteenth century were limited to sporadic landings of Portuguese, French and Dutch navigators, mainly on the south coasts. Flintlock guns were introduced by the Portuguese during the seventeenth century. Sporadic settlements were installed by the French at Fort Dauphin from 1642 onwards, and the British attempted settlement in the Bay of St Augustin, south of Tuléar, where boats put in on their way to the Far East. These populations appear to have fused completely with the local inhabitants, and tradition gives the Vezo, the fishing tribe of the south-west coast, some Portuguese blood.

Trade between occasional ships and the towns on the coast continued sporadically, but it was not until the beginning of the nineteenth century that France finally occupied the island of Ste Marie and also other places on the east coast, including Tamatave. At this time, Britain began to take an interest in Madagascar, mainly as a result of the Napoleonic Wars. This interest was exercised in a very personal manner by the British Governor of Mauritius, Farquhar, who appears to have used the Merina king, Radama I, as an instrument of policy, and to have supported Radama's pretensions to sovereignty over the whole of Madagascar, which he proclaimed in 1817 with British recognition. This brought him into conflict with French territorial claims, but France, immediately after the Restoration, was not in a position to take up the challenge. Farquhar having persuaded Radama in 1815 to open Tananarive to foreigners, a major cultural and technological penetration took place, whose influence lasted throughout the nineteenth century. There was, in particular, the creation of the first Protestant mission by two English missionaries, Jones and Griffiths; the arrival of English and French military instructors, Hastie, Brady and Robin, who reformed the Merina army; as well as the work of a number of artisans, such as Cameron, a weaver from Manchester, which resulted in the inauguration of many artisan activities around Tananarive.

These contacts increased rapidly throughout the nineteenth century, stimulated by an Anglo-French rivalry for influence over the monarchy. The result was a more rapid opening up of Madagascar to Western techniques and habits than was the case for many African countries. At the time of the French conquest in 1896, Madagascar was by no means terra incognita. While no explorers such as Livingstone or René Caillé wrote and captured the popular imagination concerning Madagascar, numerous records existed already in 1896. As far back as 1661, Etienne de Flacourt had published a detailed account of Madagascar, while in the eighteenth century travellers such as Mayeur, who penetrated Imerina in 1777, and Dumaine, who published an account of his travels in 1792, had left detailed and often accurate accounts of the country.[3]

The most remarkable traveller of them all was Alfred Grandidier (1836–1921), who made more than twenty journeys through Madagascar between 1864 and 1870. The remainder of his life was devoted to writing and publishing thirty-eight folio volumes, profusely illustrated, covering every aspect of Madagascar, including its geography, ethnography, history, natural history, sociology and economy. This remarkable work remains an indispensable source of information. Grandidier was a truly scientific explorer and possessed the scientific background and the private means that enabled him and his son Guillaume to complete this encyclopedia of Madagascar.[4]

The early missionaries left travel journals during the nineteenth century, many of them preserved in the *Antananarivo Annual*.

Madagascar was penetrated by Europeans more easily than the interior of Africa, and certainly personal relations were more easily established. The Christian missionaries, both Protestant and Catholic, despite inevitable hardships and setbacks, had an immediate and lasting effect, which is very evident today. Indeed, the missionaries have done more than any administrative intervention to shape present-day educated people in Madagascar.

Contacts with the West have been more constructive in their effects on Madagascar than on any other newly-independent country. An educated elite has been created which has taken the government in hand; the traditional values of Malagasy society have been largely preserved. There is no feeling of inferiority or hostility towards Europeans. The relations with France, the former colonial power, present many unusual positive features that deserve close comparative study with similar situations in other ex-colonies. On balance, Madagascar possesses many factors favourable for an economic 'take-off', in the quality of its population, its climate, geography and natural resources. The factors inhibiting and favouring such a change will be examined in greater detail, beginning with a more detailed description of the physical environment which makes up the subcontinent of Madagascar.

1. The Land

On the map, Madagascar appears as a fragment of Africa, rather as the British Isles appear as a part of Europe, separated by a recent and fairly shallow channel. At its closest point, Cape St André, Madagascar is only 190 miles from the Moçambique coast; and, farther north, the Comoro islands, themselves of volcanic origin and containing an active volcano, appear as a series of stepping stones with Africa. The connection with Africa is, however, more remote than it would appear, and the relationship is in no way similar to that of the off-shore European islands with the Continent.* In fact, the relationship of Madagascar to Africa has much more in common with the relationship between Australia and the mainland of South-East Asia, including a very distinct endemic flora and fauna. No aboriginal human population, similar to the Australian aborigines, is known to have existed, but the population itself has a highly original origin, being basically Malayo-Polynesian.

The origin of Madagascar has interested those who follow Wegener's theory of continental drift and the outline of the west coast appears to fit as neatly into the Moçambique coast as Brazil does into the Gulf of Guinea. Other geological evidence has been put forward for this theory of drift, which would have had Madagascar detach itself from the African land-mass and move gradually, perhaps since early Tertiary times, into its present position.[1] An examination of the recently published map of the floor of the Indian Ocean[2] shows a trough 13,000 feet deep to the east of Madagascar, the Mascarene Basin, out of which rise the volcanic peaks of Tromelin, Réunion and Mauritius. A trough more than 10,000 feet deep lies between the west coast and the submarine Moçambique Plateau, with yet another trough 13,000 feet deep between it and the Natal coast. To the south of Madagascar

---

* If the sea-level were lowered 1,000 metres (3,250 feet), as in a bathymetric map prepared by the Prince de Monaco, no land bridges appear between groups of Mascarene islands now separated, and none between Madagascar and Africa. See Renaud Paulian, *La Zoogéographie de Madagascar et des Iles mascareignes*, Tananarive 1961.

lies another plateau joined irregularly with the Mid-Oceanic Ridge, the great range of submarine mountains that crosses the Indian Ocean midway north and south. Thus the country is separated enough from Africa to be considered a minor subcontinent. The area of Madagascar is approximately 230,000 square miles; it is about 980 miles long and 360 miles wide at its greatest width; no mountain is higher than 10,000 feet but it has a chain of central highlands whose peaks vary between 6,500 and 9,200 feet. It is held by many geologists to be a fragment of the vanished continent of Gondwana, together with Southern India, Southern Africa, South America and Antarctica. The endemic flora and fauna of the island have relationships with living forms of other continents, and by no means all of these are with Africa. Affinities exist among plants and animals with India and with South-East Asia, while some plant species are shown by plant geographers to exist in such widely separated spots as Madagascar, Patagonia and New Guinea.

> In general the flora of Madagascar and its neighbouring islands may be described as of African affinity with a strong Asiatic and Pacific element. This is well illustrated in Madagascar itself. The proportion of endemic species is high, perhaps 85 per cent, but many of them are related to African species and what is called the African element may account for about one quarter of the whole. . . . At the same time it may be doubted whether the floristic relation with Africa is as strong as should be expected from the proximity of the two areas, and the presence of so many non-African types raises problems of its history which are of great interest.[3]

The origin of Madagascar is thus known in its general relationships, and it is also known to be a very ancient island, having been totally separated from Africa since the early Tertiary period, which dates its isolation back some 20 million years. Apart from the unexplained presence of a very few African animals, such as the crocodile, potamochère, guinea-fowl and a fossil dwarf hippopotamus, the Malagasy fauna consists of species not found elsewhere, although having species in common with the other Mascarene islands. This group, including Madagascar, Réunion, Mauritius, Rodriguez, the Comoro islands, the Seychelles and smaller islands or atolls such as Aldebra, Tromelin and Europa, forms a biogeographical subregion. This tendency towards endemism, which is typical of island biology, is best known from the Mauritius dodo, a giant flightless pigeon which became extinct through being eaten by seventeenth-century Dutch settlers. Other flightless birds existed on all the larger Mascarene islands and all are now extinct, though not for the same reason.[4]

Madagascar is an assymetric island, as the cross-section shows in Figure 1, page 26. The east coast is considered to be of faulted origin[5] and the physiography of the island, with the gradual slope up from the west to the maximum heights which then fall very sharply to the east coast, shows that the basement complex has tilted, and is probably still tilting, down into the Moçambique Channel and up from the Indian Ocean. The watershed between the Indian Ocean and the Moçambique Channel lies not more and often much less than 100 miles from the east coast. The rivers which run to the west coast have a long steady fall, and finish with broad alluvial valleys as they cross wide sedimentary plains to the Moçambique Channel. Those that run east have precipitous falls, sometimes of 3,000 feet in 12 to 20 miles, and cross a narrow sedimentary plain to end in lagoons with their mouths blocked by sand-bars at the Indian Ocean.

The basement complex, either uncovered or decomposed, accounts for two-thirds of the land surface of the island,[6] but it is by no means a homogeneous mass, and, in its geology and geomorphology, Madagascar shows the same extreme diversity and originality as in other fields. The greater part of the basement complex is formed from gneiss, a metamorphic rock derived from granite. Various degrees of metamorphosis are present, ranging from pure granite outcrops to all degrees of transformation. This mass of gneiss-granite is pierced by a series of more or less ancient eruptive rocks, diorites, gabbros and pegmatites, and appears to have been subject to strains and pressure that cause the structures and faulting generally to run north-south.

The 'Gondwana' deposits, which begin with the Permian-Carboniferous, are closely related both to the Karoo system of Southern Africa and to similar formations in Southern India. These Karoo deposits are not exclusively continental, as they appear in Southern Africa, and the types of sedimentation, as well as fossil evidence, shows that the Moçambique Channel, although not complete, was already in existence as a gulf or an estuary at

Madagascar

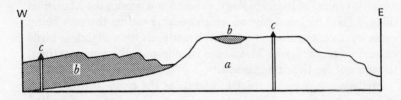

Fig. 1. Schematic section across Madagascar (Wellington after H. Besaire). (a) granite-gneiss; (b) sedimentary; (c) recent volcanics

Fig 2. Madagascar: geological divisions (Wellington).

(a) granite-gneiss
(b) continental Karoo sediments
(c) upper (marine) Karoo and later sediments
(eruptive rocks not shown)

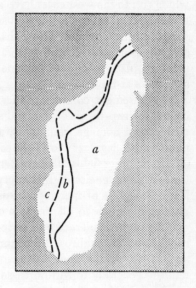

this remote date. However, fossil evidence—in particular the rich and varied collections of dinosaur fossils, similar to those appearing elsewhere in the Cretaceous, as in South America—again seems to indicate that the break with Africa was not yet complete. These dinosaur remains are sometimes found in pits, where large bones can be picked up by hand, and they are among the best-known Madagascar fossils. One such pit occurs just off the main road, about 30 miles south of Majunga. The sedimentary deposits are far more extensive and varied on the west than on the east coast, although a general picture of the geological structure of Madagascar shows a central mass which is a fragment of the African basement complex, tilted and rising towards the east and surrounded by sedimentary deposits of variable width. The sediments to the west consist of large masses of sandstone and a band of limestone running north-south along the coast. Travellers recognise these strata immediately, since the tracks crossing the sandstone contain large patches of sand difficult to cross in the dry season, while the limestone areas have roads with a broken-up surface, unpleasant to negotiate. Among other prominent fossils in the sandstone are trunks of fossil trees of large dimensions, which may often be seen lying alongside the track.

Although it appears that the sea advanced and retreated during the whole of the Tertiary period, leaving shore-lines sometimes 250 feet above present sea-level, it does not seem that the sea ever totally submerged the whole island. Variations in sea-level are particularly evident on the north-west coast, where shore-lines and terraces are found on the lower valleys of rivers from 10 to 130 feet high. In the alluvial plains of the large rivers such as the Marovoay, Betsiboka and Mahavavy in the neighbourhood of Majunga, deposits of oyster shells are found 100 feet above present sea-level. In the big estuaries in the same region there are drowned valleys or fjords 165 feet deep, notably in the Bay of Narinda, which was an Arab port two hundred years ago and which may once again become an important deep-water port if present plans are implemented. These drowned valleys show a sinking of the west coast, corresponding to the rise of the eastern mountain chain.[7]

The evolution of Madagascar is therefore as complex as the variety of its geology would suggest. The geological map shows an extraordinary number of formations and of outcrops. Almost

27

every mineral one can think of appears to be present, though mainly as samples. As in other countries, geological research in Madagascar has consisted in the past of mapping the surface formations, and it is only since 1964–65 that prospection has been undertaken using modern techniques of 'remote sensing' and, in particular, geophysical and geochemical techniques. At the same time, much research has been carried out over large areas of the island since 1946. The Commission d'Energie Atomique (French atomic energy agency) carried out extensive surveys in the centre, south and west, and set up prospectors' camps which remained for long periods in different regions. The Société Malgache des Petroles (SPM) invested some 12,000 million Malgache francs (FMG) ($US 43·6 million)* in prospections which proved negative. In 1968, research and prospection for petroleum was being undertaken by a number of companies, particularly in the off-shore regions north of Majunga. Prospection for ground-water in the south-west, financed by the United States, was carried out from 1964 with positive results, and a further survey was undertaken in this region, using advanced geochemical techniques, by experts financed by the United Nations Special Fund. All this has added very considerably to our knowledge of the mineral resources and development potential of Madagascar (see chapter 8).

PHYSIOGRAPHY

The best-known physical feature of Madagascar is the so-called 'Hauts-Plateaux', the central highlands on which Tananarive is situated (at 4,100 feet). To the observer, these present no aspect of a plateau; however, what geographers call 'concordant heights' are evident among the landscape of numerous rounded hills. These hills are themselves dominated by high mountains of volcanic origin, of which one, Ankaratra (8,655 feet) is conspicuous to the south-west of Tananarive and plays a dominant role in the weather of the capital. The other parts of the plateau are made up of a great variety of geological material which reacts differently to erosion and gives rise to quite different landscape and soil-types. The surface of the plateau is thus very much broken up, with deep

* After the 1969 devaluation of the Malagasy franc (FMG), $(US)1.00 equalled 275 FMG, and £1 equalled 660 FMG.

valleys, high mountains and some wide alluvial or lacustrine plains.

The central highlands of Madagascar have been justly described as a 'museum' of the results of erosion under tropical climates of an ancient basement complex, rising in places above 8,000 feet.[8] The road which runs south from Tananarive for more than 375 miles before turning west towards Tuléar passes a great variety of landscapes, ranging from alluvial plains to rounded hills covered with laterite crusts and to mountain peaks rising to sharp rocky points. The highest points are much nearer the eastern seaboard than the west, and heights of nearly 6,000 feet occur within 60 miles of the Indian Ocean, while, to the west, rivers fall in regular valleys and end in large alluvial estuaries. Coming from the west, one has to cross some three-quarters of the island before the descent to the Indian Ocean begins. This assymetry is found not only in the relief but also in the distribution of population, which is concentrated on the east coast, where about 30 per cent of the total population live, and on the central highland region around Tananarive and Fianarantsoa.

Volcanic activity, both ancient and recent, has given rise to important outcrops and has considerably modified the landscape of the central highlands. There are three main groups of mountains of volcanic origin in Madagascar. The highest mountain in the island, Tsaratanana (9,449 feet) is a great outcrop of gneiss and granite, considerably eroded, but covered in part by volcanic eruptions of Pleistocene and recent origin. A chain of recent volcanic cones appears in the region to the south of Tsaratanana known as the Ankaizina, which has an important agricultural potential. Ankaratra is a more ancient, probably Tertiary, volcano, but eruptions appear to have continued until recent times, and extinct cones with crater lakes are found near Antsirabe. The volcanic material erupted from Ankaratra has created, especially to the east and south of the mountain, zones of fertile soil and high agricultural potential, Betafo and Antsirabe, where the late eruptions occurred. A large lake, extending to the north of Antsirabe, existed in Quaternary times and layers of volcanic eruptive material appear sandwiched in between the alluvial deposits. The last volcanic strata lie immediately under the alluvions in which have been found the subfossil remains of an extinct fauna of great interest. These include the giant flightless bird, the aepyornis, which existed until perhaps three or four hundred years ago in the extreme south of the island; its eggs, much bigger than ostrich eggs, can still be picked up in the valleys of this area. Remains of mullerornis, a smaller but still large flightless bird, of a dwarf hippopotamus and of a giant lemur are also found in the vanished lake of Antsirabe. It is almost certain that all these animals survived well after the arrival of man on the island—that is, until very recent times.

The most recent volcanoes are found around Lake Itasy, about 60 miles to the west of Tananarive. These form part of the Ankaratra system, but cover a much smaller area (290 square miles for Itasy and 1,540 square miles for Ankaratra). Geologists recognise two types of volcano here: the Hawaiian, or 'calm' type, and the Vulcanien, or 'explosive'. The cones have very steep slopes and there are numerous crater lakes. It appears that eruptions may have occurred here within the last few hundred years; some writers held these responsible for the massive destruction of the forests of the central highlands, although it seems that man-made bush fires are the real reason.

The most ancient volcanic complex is that of the Androy in the extreme south of the island, where the eruptions are dated as occurring in the Cenonian period with basaltic outflows resembling those on the west coast. No craters are found here.

One of the most conspicuous physical features of Madagascar is the rift valley running north-south to the east of Tananarive, which contains the Lake Alaotra area, again of high agricultural productivity. This valley has been caused by a fairly recent subsidence which some writers link with the period of formation of the great rift valleys of East Africa. The lake lies at an altitude of 2,497 feet between two cliffs 2,300 feet higher to the west and 1,600 feet higher to the east. The lake was also much larger in comparatively recent times and shore-lines appear 260 feet above the present water-level. Earth tremors are frequent here since it would appear that this particular subsidence is still going on.[9]

Madagascar has numerous large rivers, since the central highlands act as a powerful watershed, fed by the moisture-laden prevailing south-westerly trade winds blowing from the Indian Ocean for seven to eight months of the year. The crystalline impermeable rock of which the central mountain mass is composed determines the permanent flow of these streams, even during the long dry season extending from May to November over the western two-thirds of the island. The rivers flowing to the Indian Ocean all have a rapid fall as they cross the faulted eastern mountain barrier. Some of these falls are spectacular, and one of the highest is that of the Sakoleona behind Nosy Varika, well south of Tamatave, where the river falls a sheer 1,950 feet. A traveller going on foot from the central highlands to the east coast will follow streams and rivers that fall along steep steps and disappear for a time into deep canyons before suddenly levelling off among the foothills and the coastal plain.

On the west coast, the rivers broaden out into great alluvial valleys such as the Mangoky, the Tsiribihina, the Betsiboka and Ikopa, which, if they existed in the Far East, would each harbour several million inhabitants practising irrigated agriculture. In Madagascar, as in Africa, this sort of valley was practically uninhabited until very recent times. Of the great river valleys of Africa, only the Nile was settled, and this below the Fifth Cataract—that is to say, outside the area of purely African settlement and well within the Arab cultural and technical zone. Rivers like the Niger, the Congo, the Rufiji and the Zambezi are only sporadically settled, and dams have been constructed almost exclusively for hydro-electric power supplies. In Madagascar, these great valleys present almost similar technical problems of water control; it is only since 1960 that developments have been undertaken, financed mainly by the Fonds Européen de Développement (FED—Common Market Development Fund) to install large irrigated settlement schemes on the Mangoky, primarily for cotton cultivation, with schemes on less important rivers, the Fiherenana and the Taheza south of Tuléar. A vast agricultural potential remains to be exploited on a series of rivers spreading out over wide alluvial plains between Tuléar and Majunga. The drainage of these alluvial basins is often difficult, and gives rise to large lakes alongside the rivers, lying close to abandoned beds of the rivers not far from the sea coast. The largest are Lake Kinkony, near the Mahavavy south of Majunga, and Lake Ihotry, near the Mangoky, with a chain of smaller lakes on the north and south banks of the Tsiribihina. Lake Kinkony has a curious fish population, since the waters are slightly saline, and species of both fresh- and salt-water fish are found here, including some endemic species. This lake provides prosperous fisheries, and dried and smoked fish from here reaches the Tananarive market 375 miles distant. Lake Ihotry is more remote but is well-known to naturalists because of the large population of pink flamingoes (*Phoeniconiaias minor*), the same breed as those found on Lakes Naivasha in Kenya and Manyara in Tanzania.

These rivers are, of course, a considerable obstacle to motor traffic. A traveller going north-south on the west coast relies on ferries to cross the large rivers, but these ferries cannot function well in the dry season, when there is too little water and they get hung up on sand-banks, while in the rainy season the floods are such that they cannot operate at all. On the east coast there are even more rivers and lagoons to cross—for example, sixteen ferries between Tamatave and Maraontsetra, 220 miles to the north— but, since there is no pronounced rainy season, the water level is constant and the ferries function all the year round. Water supplies become a problem in Madagascar only as one approaches the ex- treme south-west and south, where the rainfall falls off very sharply, with an average of 12 inches per annum immediately behind Tuléar and much lower averages farther south. Since a limestone band runs along the entire west coast and approaches the sea in the south-west, there is practically no surface water and within this band deep wells are necessary. On the south coast beside the sea at Faux-Cap, sweet potatoes are grown as a main food crop, irrigated only by the heavy dew provoked by the sea breezes.

Although the relief determines to a considerable degree the climate of the major ecological regions of Madagascar, the climate itself is to a great extent the result of the weather prevailing in the Indian Ocean, with some seasonal influence from the tropical disturbances coming from East Africa. The predominant maritime influence is responsible for the high regularity of rainfall over the greater part of the land surface of Madagascar, which is thus considerably favoured in comparison with Southern Africa or much of East Africa where the rainfall reliability is rather low. In Central Africa, rainfall reliability increases as one goes north from Botswana, Rhodesia and South Africa towards the Equator. The reliability of rainfall in the western regions of Madagascar, which have a long dry season from May to November, is comparable to the reliability in Northern Zambia and Katanga.

CLIMATE

The climate and meteorology of Madagascar have been thoroughly studied over a period of at least thirty-five years, but, even before 1930, individual observations were carried out by serving army officers, missionaries and others. Meteorological data of a fragmentary nature dates back over a hundred years (since 1860). The observatory of Tananarive was erected in 1881 by the Jesuit fathers of the Catholic mission; it was destroyed by shell-fire during the French conquest of Tananarive in 1896, but it was rapidly restored and has continued its work without interruption since then. It is now attached to the university but is still under the direction of the Jesuit fathers, and the present director, is also a Jesuit priest. The observatory supplies regular data on seismology, geomagnetism and meteorology, and has recently been equipped by the United States to study the variation and frequencies of fields of radio emissions. The Service Météorologique de Madagascar[10] was established in 1926 and now operates a network of stations, including marine stations on the islands of Europa and Tromelin.

Weather in Madagascar is dominated by the south-easterly trade winds blowing from an area of high pressure, or anticyclone, in the Indian Ocean. This is roughly similar to the effect of the south-westerly winds blowing from the Atlantic anticyclone that dominate the weather of Western Europe. As in the Atlantic, the tropical anticyclone in the Indian Ocean moves north and south with the sun: that is, it follows the sun in its apparent course when the zenith moves north to the tropic of Cancer in the northern summer and south to the tropic of Capricorn in the austral summer. In the austral winter, the anticyclone spreads west and covers a part of Madagascar, lying between 20° and 25° latitude south; thus from June to August the greater part of the island has a prevailing cool south-westerly wind.

In the austral summer the anticyclone descends until it lies at about latitude 33° south, and the barometric pressure falls over the whole of Madagascar. The effect of the south-west winds is thus much diminished and confined locally to parts of the east coast, while the prevailing winds, and particularly those which bring abundant rain, blow mainly from the north and north-west. It seems that Madagascar receives the tail-end of the Indian monsoon, although its effect is not considered to extend farther south than the Seychelles. It is probable that the main influence is the southward expansion of the mass of warm equatorial air at this season, which provokes the rainy season in Madagascar. These rains, marked by violent tropical thunderstorms and sometimes by cyclones or hurricanes blowing in from the direction of Mauritius in the Indian Ocean, last from December to April over the greater part of Madagascar: all except the narrow eastern coastal band between the mountains of the highlands and the sea, where oceanic influences determine an annual rainfall of more than 120 inches spread over at least eleven months of the year.

Three main air-masses determine the climate of Madagascar.[11] The first is that provoked by the great anticyclone over the Indian Ocean, which is responsible for the moisture-laden (average 75 per cent humidity) south-east trade wind. The South Atlantic anticyclone also influences the weather. It acts from the south, where air-masses move from west to east and are much less stable than the trade wind, taking the form of a series of depressions and anticyclones, influenced by currents of cold and humid air coming up from the Antarctic. Lastly, the Equatorial air-mass acts from December to April, provoking violent tropical storms and heavy rainfall. It is this that provides Madagascar's rainy season.

The most dramatic feature of the Madagascar weather is the cyclones or hurricanes occurring from the end of January to the beginning of March. The paths usually followed by cyclones are shown in Figure 3, page 35, and normally these originate in the Indian Ocean, move due west and curve south. Their destructive effects are marked when this southward curve causes them to hit Mauritius or Réunion or when the curve carries them southwards or south-eastwards over the land-mass of Madagascar. These cyclones consist of winds blowing at speeds up to and exceeding 110 miles per hour, accompanied by torrential rains. Rainfall may exceed 25 inches in twenty-four hours, and great damage is done to houses, trees, crops and roads. Very occasionally cyclones strike Madagascar while still moving due west; such cyclones are catastrophic, as was that of 1927, which caused great destruction in Tamatave. In 1959 the downward curving cyclone hit Tananarive and caused extensive flooding of the town by the overflowing of the Ikopa and Sissaony rivers. Since then, the dykes containing these rivers, originally constructed by Andrianampoinimerina, King of Imerina from 1782 to 1810, have been considerably heightened and strengthened. The hurricanes that hit Mauritius or Réunion may then turn south in the intervening 300 miles of sea and miss Madagascar. Thus the cyclone 'Carol', which caused great damage in Mauritius in 1960, did not touch Madagascar. As 'Carol' uprooted trees estimated as being six hundred years old among the remains of the climax forest to the south-west of Mauritius, such disastrous hurricanes may be said to have approximately this frequency. This climax forest, known as 'La Forêt de la Machabée' (Corpse Forest), has

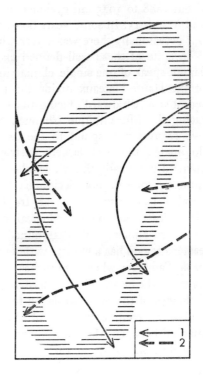

Fig. 3. Average paths of cyclones affecting Madagascar

1. normal paths
2. exceptional paths

as its dominant species various *Sapotaceae* which have developed a remarkable system of intertwined roots above the surface of the ground, which appear to anchor them against cyclones.

Many of these cyclones disappear into the southern Indian Ocean and all that is heard is the navigation warning on the Tananarive radio. They are similar to hurricanes and typhoons that hit the coasts of India, China and the southern United States, and have a similar origin in a confrontation between an intertropical front and a cold air stream. As the 'eye' of the cyclone moves comparatively slowly, at about 12 m.p.h., warning can be given by radio well in advance, but this does not help those who live in houses made of local materials such as bamboo and palm-fronds. From 1888 to 1945, all cyclones occurred between December 15 and March 15. In some years there were as many as five cyclones, but occasionally there was a year without any.[12]

In spite of these well-defined external climatic influences, we cannot speak of one single climate in Madagascar. The mountains of the Hauts-Plateaux divide the island into two main climatic regions: a 'windward', facing the Indian Ocean, and a 'leeward', facing the Moçambique Channel. Speaking very broadly, these two regions correspond to the two main vegetation types that dominated the now largely destroyed climax forest that once covered practically the whole island. The windward region has a humid, tropical, non-deciduous type of rain-forest, while the leeward has a dry, deciduous, tropical forest.[13] In between these are at least four major ecological sub-regions and a whole series of micro-climates, all determined by altitude and relief. The eastern region has a climate with an abundant and regular rainfall, as at Tamatave where 120 inches of rain fall on an average of 239 days in the year. The western region, which is not under the influence of the moisture-laden trade winds, has a warmed, drier and more continental type of climate. The dry season is very marked between May and November and the rainfall diminishes sharply towards the south.*

*	inches	days
Majunga	65	88
Maintirano	36	73
Morondava	29	49
Tuléar	14	32

The climate of the Hauts-Plateaux is that of the western region modified by altitude: that is, a dry season from May to November, but with lower average temperatures and a much wider range of day temperatures. The observatory at Tananarive stands at an altitude of 4,292 feet and its mean annual rainfall is 54 inches of which, on average, 92 per cent falls on 105 days between November and April. The breaking of the rains is rather variable. Usually, there is a brief storm called locally 'la pluie des mangues' ('mango rains'), a short spell of rain lasting two or three days around October 14, at the time when the mangoes are ripening on the west coast and in the north. There is a further dry period until the rains break at the end of November or the beginning of December—a series of thunderstorms and heavy rains. These usually occur in the afternoon; it is rare to wake up in the morning and find it raining. Lightning is a hazard on the Hauts-Plateaux and all houses of any size carry a lightning conductor. Deaths from lightning are frequent—in an average year, sixty people are killed by it.[14] The irregular beginning of the rains delays the transplanting of rice in the numerous cultivated valleys of the Hauts-Plateaux. The paddy fields are prepared, and the rice plants are waiting in the nurseries, but nothing can be done until the first rains set the springs flowing again at the head of each valley.

The proximity of the east coast further modifies the climate of Tananarive during the dry season, since the trade wind accumulates moisture-laden clouds over the mountains to the east of the town. Thus, morning fogs are common and one awakes to see the former royal palace, high over the town, floating above the clouds. During the morning the clouds lift, and the winter day is a period of almost Californian sunshine over the town, although one can see the bank of clouds stationary over the mountains to the east. Sometimes, the clouds advance and a cold unpleasant drizzle falls, similar to the 'chiperones' which fall in the dry season around Mount Mlanje in Malawi. The variations in day temperature in Tananarive are considerable, and within twenty-four hours the temperature may vary by as much as 10 to 15 °c. The mornings can be cold in the dry season in Tananarive, and one sees the inhabitants shivering in their cotton clothes with 7 to 8 °c in July. Frost is rare in Tananarive, but frequent in Antsirabe about 100 miles to the south, where the lowest recorded temperature is −8 °c in August 1915. Above 6,500 feet ice forms readily, and hoar-frost may be seen in the hollows. Snow is not unknown but is very rare.

In the extreme south of the island, the region south of a line drawn between Tuléar and Fort Dauphin, long dry periods occur between irregular rainstorms and drought-years are not uncommon, such as that which occurred in 1943. In this region, the Madagascar locust (*Nomadacris semifasciata*) breeds and large swarms may sometimes be met, although nothing like as important or widespread as the desert locust or the red locust in Africa. An effective control service has prevented any serious outbreaks in recent years. The rainfall in this zone varies from 14 inches per annum at Tuléar to less than 2 inches per annum in a narrow coastal band running southwards from Tuléar to Tsihombe.

This is a region of extensive cattle keeping, the population relying for subsistence on meagre crops of maize, sorghum and sweet potato irrigated by dew along the sea coast. It is a cattle area perhaps for the same reasons as are the drier parts of West and East Africa: it is not really livestock country, but nothing but livestock could be raised in such a climate. A remarkable feature is the very abrupt transition of both climate and vegetation in passing over the watershed to the east near Fort Dauphin, where there is a total change from the semi-arid to the humid tropical forest in a distance of five miles.

All these climates of Madagascar are favourable to human occupation, and, since the control of malaria, Europeans can live well in all parts of the island. One no longer hears of sudden deaths from fevers among Europeans, as was the case with the first arrivals in the nineteenth century. Tananarive, where most Europeans live, has been described by doctors as a 'faux bon climat': like all regions of altitude in the tropics, it does not suit all Europeans. Some experience sleeplessness and loss of appetite, while women find a disturbance of the rhythm of menstruation. It may trouble those suffering from cardiac disturbance. In the evening, a European tends to become rapidly tired around seven o'clock and the climate is certainly more tiring, perhaps because of the great diurnal variations of temperature, than the climate of Salisbury or Lusaka on about the same latitudes. On the other hand, the maximum temperature in Tananarive very rarely exceeds 32 °C (maximum recorded, 34 °C in 1904) and the nights are always cool so that air-conditioning is quite unnecessary. Winter is a pleasant season for, although a wood fire is welcome in the evening, the sun shines strongly in the daytime.

VEGETATION

The traveller flying from East Africa passes over the Comoro islands and his first sight of Madagascar will be the coast around Majunga. A few minutes later he will see huge expanses of bare rolling hills, with only slight remains of gallery forest or patches of woodland on slopes or summits of hills. He will be struck by the moorland aspect until the plane starts to descend towards Tananarive, when he will begin to see small plantations. These turn out to be eucalyptus, an imported species from Australia.

The destruction in recent historic times of the climax forest that covered practically the whole of Madagascar is as complete as the destruction of the Mediterranean forest on nearly all the coastal mountains from Spain to Syria. The Malagasy forest was destroyed later than that of the Mediterranean, and man-made fire has here replaced goats and sheep as the principal agents preventing regeneration. Over most of the Hauts-Plateaux the destruction of woody vegetation is now irreversible, and a fire-climax has been established of low-grade grasses such as *Aristida sp.* with heather-like plants, *Philippia* and *Helichrysum*, which give these mountains their moor-like appearance.

It is considered that this total destruction, without even the stage of regeneration of bush or maquis that normally follows the destruction of forest, is due to the ecological instability of much of the Malagasy forest.[15] It is thought that the present flora evolved under more humid conditions and that the climate has become progressively drier since the Quaternary period. This would correspond to the dessication of the Sahara, where a savannah type of vegetation has largely vanished since the end of the last glacial period in Europe—that is, during the past ten thousand years. There appears to be some correspondence between the main glaciations of the northern hemisphere and the so-called 'pluvials' or periods of high rainfall in Africa. These have been studied particularly in East Africa,[16] where one of them was named 'Gamblian' after evidence was found on the farm of a Mr Gamble in Kenya. While the climatic variations in recent geological times have been less thoroughly studied in Madagascar, there is evidence of similar high rainfall periods occurring in cycles related to, but perhaps not entirely corresponding with, those of East Africa. These wet periods gave rise to the great Quaternary lakes of Madagascar—the large lake north of Antsirabe, the lake that covered the plain on which Tananarive now stands and a much larger Lake Alaotra.

With a drier climate, much of the Malagasy forest adapted to a high rainfall might have been displaced by floristic associations better adapted to a long dry season had Madagascar been joined to Africa. In Africa it is known that the humid Equatorial forest has at times had a much greater northward and southward extent than today. Where drier conditions prevail, and where fire is applied each year in Central Africa, the association known as 'miombo' (*Brachystegia, Isoberlina spp.*), which covers much of Angola, Katanga, Zambia and Tanzania, has replaced it. These *Leguminosae* are absent from the Malagasy flora, and there has thus been no association of trees able to form a similar fire-climax after the destruction of the primary forest, except for very limited pure stands of 'tapia' (*Uapaca clusiaca*) seen to the west of Tananarive and to the south along the road to Fianarantsoa, whose appearance recall the sudano-guinean savannah of West Africa.

The tropical rain forest of the narrow band of high rainfall along the east coast has not suffered in this way; where it is locally destroyed for shifting cultivation of mountain rice, a secondary association of low trees, bamboos and bushes appears immediately, which is fairly rapidly replaced by regenerated forest from which only a few of the slowest-growing species of the primary forest (such as ebonies and pallisanders) are absent. Two-thirds of the island, however, experiences the long dry season of five to seven months. The climax forest of the Hauts-Plateaux has been almost completely destroyed but the very small remains show that it was a rich association with many large broad-leafed trees. Degraded fragments of the climax forest near Tananarive have been preserved because of religious or cultural associations: around the former royal palace of Ambohimanga, 12 miles north of Tananarive, and at Baybay where some venerated tombs exist. The dry deciduous forest of the west coast regenerates locally after burning, but repeated burning gives a distinct fire-climax dominated by widely spaced palms (*Borassus sp.* and *Hyphaenae shatan*). The sclerophytic cactus-like bush of the extreme south appears well-adapted to its extreme climate and regenerates well after destruction.

The flora of Madagascar is highly original, as might be expected on a geologically old island. It presents many of the characteristics of an island flora, a high degree of endemicity not only of genus but of entire families and a marked localisation of certain associations. A problem arises from the relationship of the Malagasy flora to that of other regions. Although African affinities are important,[17] the Indo-Malay affinities are important in a high proportion of taxonomic groups. A remarkable series of generic and even specific affinities are found, particularly with New Caledonia,[18] Australia, New Zealand and South America. These affinities are all the more interesting since they often occur for species which do not exist in intervening territories (Africa and Indo-Malaya), thus suggesting parallel evolution from very ancient stocks.

Madagascar is therefore not a 'continental' island in the sense that the British Isles or New Guinea are continental islands—that is, detached fairly recently from a neighbouring continent with which it shares the main characteristics of the flora and fauna. Neither is it an 'oceanic island' of an extreme kind, such as St Helena or even New Zealand. Its biological affinities show that Madagascar has been attached at various times to both Africa and to Asia, but these links are already so ancient that we must also add South America. The land bridges thus presuppose an arrangement of the land masses of the world that would bear little or no relation to present continents.

For purposes of establishing the origins of Malagasy flora and fauna, we need go no further back than the definite detachment of the island from the African continent; this is already quite far enough, beginning in the Cenonian zone of the Upper Cretaceous, which takes us back at least twenty million years. This is the period when chalk was being laid down in England and Northern Europe.[19] The complete break as a result of the formation of the Moçambique Channel is held to have occurred during the Tertiary period, but authorities are divided as to when exactly during this period it occurred. Since this puts the separation of Madagascar in an era when the Alps and the Himalayas are being formed, when placental mammals suddenly appear and the flowering plants (*Angiosperms*) are established as the dominant group, it is not surprising that Madagascar's flora and fauna present highly original and archaic features.

The floristic regions of Madagascar correspond to the major climatic divisions: a 'windward' region, receiving the moisture-laden winds from the Indian Ocean during most of the year, and a 'leeward' region, with a dry season lasting from five to seven months.[20] These two major divisions correspond to the former extent of the tropical rain forest and dry deciduous forest climaxes. Of these, the eastern floristic sub-region extends from the coast to an altitude of approximately 2,600 feet, the central highlands sub-region from 2,600 to 6,500 feet and the areas of montane forest from 6,500 feet upwards. The tropical rain forest of the east coast has large virtually intact areas; the limited montane zones are confined to a few mountain-tops, as in East Africa; and the forest cover of the central highlands has largely been destroyed.

The western region has two major floristic sub-regions: the dry deciduous forest of almost all the west coast, which formerly extended to cover large areas of the central highlands below 3,900 feet and the sclerophytic, highly original and endemic associations of the semi-arid south-west of the island. Within the western region there is an important micro-climate, the Sambirano, an area of somewhat degraded humid tropical forest on the north-west coast. This occurs as a result of local orographic rainfall produced by the massif of Tsaratanana (9,337 feet). This region, though small, is economically important since the production of cacao, pepper, coffee and other tree and fruit crops is quite highly developed.

In spite of the extensive destruction, large areas of forest remain in Madagascar, in both the east and the west of the island. The area under true forest, as opposed to secondary bush, is about 15,000 square miles, less than 10 per cent of the total land surface. However, considerably larger areas are covered with bush or remnants of forest in various stages of destruction. Two-thirds of the remaining true forest is found in a narrow band running north-south, between the east coast and the central highlands, while the finest stands are found in a compact mass extending from the Point à Larée, opposite the island of Ste Marie, around the bay of Antongil, to Antalaha to the east of the massif of Tsaratanana. This largely untouched forest belt contains large trees 75-100 feet high, often with a superficial root system not unlike the formation found in the remains of the primary forest of Mauritius. It is a forest growing on a multitude of small hills and is crossed only by narrow winding paths. No road crosses it and there are few villages. The sparse population of the forest is among the most isolated and primitive of Madagascar, living mainly on cooked bananas and wild yams, with little rice and very little meat except for protected animals such as lemurs which they hunt. Madagascar's rivers are poor in indigenous fresh-water fishes,* and the large rivers that rush down waterfalls and steep valleys in this forest provide little in the way of food. The only exchanges with the economy outside the forest are sales of wild honey, which is carried in kerosene tins for as much as three days to be sold in the first villages at the eastern edge of the forest.

This tropical rain forest is extremely rich in a wide variety of species. There may be more than a hundred different kinds of tree in an area of a few hundred square yards. It is thought that this floristic richness is because the forest lies on an ancient geological formation, which has suffered no submergence under the sea or other disturbance. The east coast of Madagascar has probably been facing the sea since very remote times; therefore the vegetation would not have suffered from marked climatic changes. Similar considerations are held to apply to the rain-forest of the Amazon and the Congo basin, which also lie on ancient geological formations that have been undisturbed for millions of years and have thus allowed the evolution of a very rich and varied flora.[21]

The Malagasy rain forest differs from the rain forest of Central Africa in having a lower average height (80 to 100 feet) and by the absence of the giant trees sometimes seen towering above the African forest. Orchids and other epiphytes are very numerous. It is not easy to walk in the forest, partly because of the very hilly country on which it grows and also because of the dense under-brush. Along the water-courses grow the largest trees and a very varied collection of palms. It is estimated that there are in Madagascar perhaps 900 species of orchids, of which at least 700 are endemic, and more than 200 species of palms, of which more

---

* Many species of exotic fresh-water fish have been successfully introduced, including trout (high up on Ankaratra), tilapia, black bass and carp.

than 90 per cent are endemic. Many fine tropical hardwoods exist in the forest, but their density per acre is much lower than in the forests of West Africa. Since even in the rich forests of Africa comparatively few species of hardwoods are exploited commercially, there is even more limited exploitation in Madagascar, where hardwoods belong to endemic genera and species quite unknown on the world market. Thus, in private houses, one sees very fine floors and furniture made by local carpenters from these timbers. It is doubtful whether the Malagasy rain forest would stand the type of exploitation practised in African forests, since the stands are widely scattered and conditions of regeneration of valuable species are unknown. Experiments carried out by the Forest Service in planting lines of pure stands of valuable species such as *Canarium ramy* are as yet inconclusive.

The rain forest, when cut for shifting cultivation and bush-fallowing for mountain rice, regenerates into a secondary bush known as 'savoka' dominated by the 'travellers tree' (*Ravenala madagascarensis*), a relation of the banana which has found its way into botanic and ornamental gardens all over the world. It is so called because the traveller can extract drinkable water by cutting into the soft trunk below the main stems, and it has become part of the national seal of the republic. This savoka will regenerate into a secondary forest if left undisturbed, but if it is burned it degenerates further into a prairie of ferns and heath-like plants growing on completely leached and degraded soils unfit for cultivation. Some of the best partridge ('francolin') shooting in Madagascar is available for those willing to push through these thickets with a good dog.

The dry deciduous forest of the western part of the island seems at first sight to resemble the forest remaining in the drier regions of Africa. However, the west of Madagascar has a less severe dry season than East or Central Africa. The flora is far more varied than the miombo fire-climax that dominates Central Africa from Angola to Tanzania, and the *Leguminosae* that dominate this monotonous forest (*Brachystegia* and *Isoberlina spp.*) are absent from Madagascar. Magnificent baobab trees are particularly noticeable in the forest that lies between Morondava and Belo-sur-Tsiribihina. It is interesting that four species of baobab exist in Madagascar as against one only in Africa, which has led some authorities to name Madagascar as the centre of origin of these conspicuous trees.* This forest also contains some fine hardwoods, though they are very spaced out and are unlikely to support heavy cutting. A number of small sawmills exist here and there on the west coast, cutting for local consumption, and it is probable that anything more extensive would lead to rapid destruction of this forest.

Before 1940 parts of the west coast, and in particular the regions north and south of Morondava, produced quantities of maize for export by bush-fallowing. The forest was cut and burned for maize culture under shifting cultivation, which produced extensive destruction, since this was followed by annual burning to give grazing for the very large cattle population. More than two-thirds of the ten million or so cattle of Madagascar are found to the west of the central highlands. Fire is applied annually and, if one flies over this region at the end of the dry season, the sky may be darkened by the many bushfires, in spite of official attempts at control. This type of destruction is irreversible and gives a very open savannah dominated by large isolated palms, *Borassus madagascarensis* and *Medemia nobilis*, the *Borassus* being a close relative of the West African toddy-palm, with a similar bulge high up on the trunk. A smaller palm resembling the doum palm of the sudano-guinean formations in Africa (*Hyphaenae shatan*) is used for construction of houses, and another conspicuous isolated tree is the sakoa (*Sclerocarya caffra*), which gives a small black edible fruit. It must be admitted that the destruction of this forest leaves a very fine grassland dominated by *Hyperhenia rufa*, and *Heteropogon contortus*, both good pasture when young, and it is difficult to persuade the cattle-owners not to burn but to make hay or grow forage crops, however good this technical advice may be.

This forest on the west coast changes its composition as one goes south, showing more species adapted to the semi-arid climate of the south-west. After the baobabs, one sees other trees with curiously swollen trunks—*Pachypodium*, *Euphorbiaceae* of very varied kinds—and finally the sclerophytic bush dominated by the cactus-like *Didieraceae* in the extreme south. This last association is probably one of the most original in the world and is composed

---

* The Madagascar baobabs are *Adansonia za*, *A. grandidieri* and *A. madagascarensis*; one species only is found in Africa, *A. digitata*, which appears to have been introduced to Madagascar.

of a very high proportion of endemic species. An extreme example is the palm with a triangular stem (*Neodypsis decarii*), which grows only on a few square miles on the watershed between the east and west just behind Fort Dauphin and nowhere else in the world.

The high mountains of Madagascar have their own peculiar flora. While there is nothing corresponding to the dense bamboo forests of East African mountains, such as the 'impenetrable forest' on the borders of Uganda and the Congo, some mountain bamboo thickets are found, as on the mountains of Tsaratanana and Ibity at 7,500 and 8,500 feet. Bamboos are conspicuous in the degraded savoka bush dominated by the travellers tree on the east coast. The remains of montane forest existing at altitudes above 4,500 feet is held to be a relic that has evolved under a wetter climate. This type of forest can be well observed from the track passing through it between Mandritsara and Andilamena, and consists of small closely-packed trees, sometimes with a dense undergrowth, and often covered with long lichens. This forest has a silvery look when seen from a distance, due to the lichens, and is destroyed almost totally after one burning, without any regeneration, except the heath-like plants (*Philippa spp.*, *Helichrysum spp.*).

FAUNA

The flora of Madagascar is highly original and varied, but this is apparent only to specialists; what strikes the traveller most is the absence of trees on the central highlands. The fauna is equally original but the number of species is much smaller. It is certain that the Malagasy animals evolved before the emergence of today's African fauna. There are no antelopes in Madagascar, no elephants, no lions or other large carnivores, except the local fossa, a creature the size of a large dog, belonging to the genus *Viverridae* and thus related to ferrets and weasels rather than cats. The most conspicuous mammals—that is, wherever a substantial forest remains —are the lemurs, but there are a number of small inconspicuous mammals of great interest to zoologists. These include an endemic family of insectivores, the *Tenrecidae*, with at least ten genera and thirty species, which many zoologists regard as one of the most primitive mammals; its closest relative is the solenodon of the West Indies.

There is still much discussion as to how and when the Malagasy fauna reached the island, and the question of land bridges with Africa across the Moçambique Channel has not yet been satisfactorily elucidated by geologists. Some zoologists state that the existing fauna probably require none; that is, animals now found in Madagascar have evolved in situ and in isolation from ancestors that entered from other continents not later than the Tertiary.[22] The existence of dinosaurs on Madagascar in the Mesozoic may have required a land bridge, since the abundant examples found among Malagasy fossils belong to species found elsewhere in the world.

Like other large islands, such as New Guinea, Madagascar is very poor in fresh-water fishes, which extend very little beyond continents and recently-detached continental islands like Britain. Many of the endemic fish on Madagascar have a certain salt-tolerance and are found in brackish lakes such as Lake Kinkony; thus it would appear possible for them to have crossed salt-water gaps. In common with the large islands of the West Indies, Madagascar has no poisonous snakes, though snakes are seen everywhere. No one takes much notice of them, although the large brightly coloured snakes which are conspicuous in the forest are regarded with respect and some suspicion. A very large snake, the do (*Acrantophis madagascarensis*), related to the boa constrictor of South America and with no intervening relatives on the African continent, lives in holes in the forest, and the feathers and bones of small animals can be seen scattered outside its entrance.

The birds of Madagascar are very distinctive, although the bird fauna as a whole is poorer than that of East Africa and many families of birds that occur there are not found in Madagascar. Thus there are no ostriches, cranes, vultures, hornbills, barbets, starlings or representatives of many other families. There are, however, four Asiatic tropical genera not represented in Africa, and some other birds which are thought to have Oriental relationships.[23] The bird fauna is very limited on the almost treeless Central Highlands, but is richer in the dry deciduous forest of the west and in the undisturbed parts of the eastern rain forest. Walking along forest paths well away from human habitation, the eastern forest comes alive with lemurs and numerous birds, but near roads or villages it is silent and empty.

The best-known family of Madagascar animals is that of the

lemurs. Here again the relationships with other continents appear to show the long isolation of the island, since the lemurs of tropical Africa and Asia are directly related to one another, but those of Madagascar belong to a separate evolution.[24] Fossil lemurs are found in rocks in Europe, but outside Madagascar only very few species have survived, such as the galagos in the African forests and the loris in Asia. In Madagascar there are more than twenty distinct species, nearly all of them highly localised, another characteristic of an island fauna. Thus a species may be confined to a comparatively small area of forest and be found nowhere else in Madagascar. They range in size from lemurs the size of mice to those as big as a quite large monkey. Some are nocturnal and never seen; others are conspicuous in undisturbed forest. Although they swing and climb trees like monkeys and have a similar curiosity, their faces are like those of foxes and not at all ape-like. The best-known, which is sometimes found as a pet in Europe, is *Lemur catta*, which has a black and grey ringed tail and can be tamed. The lemurs are strictly protected animals in Madagascar and it is forbidden even to keep one as a pet; unfortunately they are hunted for food by scattered forest populations, who (it must be admitted) have little else in the way of protein in a country where there is little game.[25]

Other better-known curiosities are the chameleons, which may have originated in Madagascar and which are regarded with great respect by the inhabitants, and the coelacanth, which is caught from time to time near the Comoro islands. This fish, which has survived for about three hundred million years and existed long before the dinosaur, is still caught two or three times a year by Comorian fishermen, and is called by them '*kombessa*'.

The fact that very few African animals are found in Madagascar again brings up the problem of how animals arrived on the island. There exist a bush pig of the African genus *Potamocherus*, the African crocodile (*C. niloticus*) and a species of guinea-fowl (*Numidia mitrata*). The pig is called *lambo* in Malagasy, a word related to the Malay word *lambu*, ox. Thus the first immigrants, knowing the ox in their native Indonesia, must have found the bush pig already on the island. However, it is not found in sub-fossil deposits of lakes such as the vanished lake of Antsirabe, where remains of the dwarf hippopotamus are found, and the mystery of how it was introduced remains. The crocodile has two names: *voay*, of Malay origin, and *mamba*, which is its Kiswahili name; the guinea-fowl is called *akanga* which is also a Kiswahili word.

The sub-fossil remains have a dwarf hippopotamus—not the same as the pygmy hippo found in West Africa—which was abundant in Madagascar in fairly recent times. In fact, oral tradition of a beast called *Lalomena*, even around Tananarive on the Ikopa river, would seem to indicate that the hippo survived till well after the arrival of the ancestors of the Malagasy. The other sub-fossil remains give us the picture of a much more varied fauna than appears today. One can imagine Madagascar, some two or three thousand years ago, almost entirely covered with dense forest, with numbers of huge lakes and with great swamps in valleys which are today covered by paddy fields. The lakes and swamps must have had large populations of pygmy hippos and crocodiles, with great flocks of water-birds which even today are numerous on open water. In the forests were giant flightless birds, several species of aepyornis, taller than the ostrich, and of muller-ornis, slightly smaller. There were many more lemurs than today, including representatives of about ninety species known only from fossils. One of these at least was a giant compared with present-day lemurs.

None of these animals which had evolved for millions of years in situ solves the problem of how the pig and the crocodile arrived more recently from Africa. The pig may have been introduced by man, and the crocodile may be able to cross salt water, since the mouths of rivers are sometimes infested by both sharks and crocodiles. The Zambezi is reported to shoot out masses of tree-trunks brought down by floods for long distances into the Moçambique Channel, and the skeleton of an elephant is reported (by the Madagascar Meteorological Service) to have once been washed up on the island of Europa where a meteorological station is maintained midway between Moçambique and Madagascar. As regards the hippo, which does not belong to the evolutionary period of other Madagascar mammals, the island of Celebes, another diverse old island, once had a dwarf endemic elephant, standing about six feet at the shoulder, and a dwarf buffalo.[26]

Whatever its origins, the Madagascar fauna is primarily a forest fauna, and the destruction of the forest has restricted it to certain remote areas, except for animals such as the bush pig which prey on crops. To see animals at all requires time and patience and willingness to penetrate forest reserves on foot. Hunting for large animals in Madagascar is limited to the bush pig and the crocodile. Pig require a large number of dogs to get them out of cover, and the usual party consists of two guns, two men with spears and fifteen to twenty small village dogs. Pig must be hunted very early in the morning and will sometimes charge when cornered. There appear to be two species, having separate names in Malagasy, *lambo sohihy* and *lambo an' ala* (that is, bush pig and forest pig). Crocodile have been so much hunted for their skins that they are rarely seen, although there are reports nearly every year of people being attacked while wading in rivers or bathing. A common Malagasy wood-carving represents an ox caught by the nose by a crocodile which is pulling it into the water. They can still be hunted by anyone willing to spend half the night in a boat on the rivers of the east and west coasts. The most agreeable shooting in Madagascar are many species of duck and teal on lakes and swamps, and partridges (francolin) and the African snipe, which is especially abundant along the east coast. As in Africa, game will only be found in company with someone from a nearby village who knows where to go, and the hunter must be prepared for many hours of walking or wading for a small but sometimes quite varied bag.

The mountainous nature of the country, the impermeable granite watershed that is the central core of the island and the prevailing south-easterly winds from the Indian Ocean have determined the wide variety of climates within Madagascar. These in turn give rise to varied and often magnificent scenery. The mountains of the Hauts-Plateaux often recall some of the finest country of East Africa, where, as in Madagascar, the traveller can pass in a few hours by road from a dry to a wet tropical climate or climb from sea level to several thousand feet. It is this climatic diversity that determines the agricultural production patterns of Madagascar, and it is the ancient geological isolation of the island that is responsible for the originality of its flora and fauna.

2. The People : Origins to 1800

ALTHOUGH no precise historical record can be reconstructed of the manner in which Madagascar received its population, nor of the order in which the different elements arrived, enough data exists for certain conclusions to be drawn.

The origin of the Malagasy language is unquestionably Malay-Polynesian, as is the ethnic origin of the greater part of the population. There are numerous resemblances between Malagasy, Malay and other languages of the same family, even Maori of New Zealand. The numerals and basic words are almost identical in many of these languages. Other ethnic and cultural elements have been supplied by immigrants from Africa and Arabia, but these are all subordinated to a Malayo-Polynesian cultural and linguistic unity. The homogeneity of the Malagasy language and culture, in spite of local variations of dialect and custom, is in striking contrast to the heterogeneity of the neighbouring African territories. The complete fusion that has operated to weld the different components would appear to indicate a fairly long period of settlement, since this unity existed already at the time of the first accounts of Madagascar by European visitors in the sixteenth and seventeenth centuries.

This cultural fusion compares with a certain ethnic diversity that is only partial, and a number of contrasting physical types are clearly distinguished among the Malagasy. Two scientific studies have examined the morphological characteristics of the population.[1] The evidence of these researches shows that a number of distinct racial types coexist in Madagascar, ranging from individuals who resemble closely Malays or Javanese, with long straight hair, pale brown skins and light bone-structure, to a type resembling both Bantu and Melanesian, with crinkly hair, dark skins, thick lips and flat noses. Between these two types is an intermediate group, with paler skins, curly hair, thick lips and nostrils less pronounced than the Bantu. This mixed group is held to be the most widespread. As regards blood groups and the Rhesus (Rh) factor, the Malagasy appear to be midway between Indonesians

Map 2. Ethnography of Madagascar

Note: This 'ethnographic' map shows grouping of populations to whom there is reference in the text. It is not a map of 'tribes' as stated by some writers on Madagascar. In fact tribes in the sense that they are found in Africa, of peoples of different origins, speaking mutually unintelligible languages, and with very different customs, do not exist in Madagascar.

It would be more correct to call these groupings 'clans'. All groups in Madagascar speak mutually-intelligible dialects of one common language, Malagasy. The only exception on this map are the Comorians, immigrants from the Comoro Islands, who are of Afro-Shirazi origin similar to Zanzibaris, and who speak a dialect of Kishwahili.

Apart from this one exception, the groups shown on the map, belong to one ethnic group, and have basically similar customs.

and Africans. Sickle-cell anaemia occurs fairly widely in Madagascar, although said to be absent from Indonesia.[2]

It is known from tradition and from linguistic and cultural evidence that an unspecified number of immigrations took place, probably during the first millenium AD and certainly prior to the sixteenth century when the first European accounts speak of established populations. Deschamps argues that the proto-Malagasy must have left their country of origin in the Malayo-Indonesian archipelago after the introduction of iron,* which he estimates at between 300 BC and AD 200, and before the introduction of the Hindu religion into Indonesia, from the second to the fifth century. However, Hindu penetration was far from uniform in Indonesia and large areas remained untouched by it. Thus the first proto-Malagasy emigrations may well have been later, and could have been around the eighth century or later. Elaborate tombs, standing stones or menhirs (*tsangambato*) and fortified hill-villages, which were all to be found in prehistoric Indonesia, are still features of today's landscape in Madagascar. The Malagasy language shows archaic features that have been lost in modern Malay; indeed, it would not be too far-fetched to say that Malagasy is related to Malay in the same degree that Icelandic is related to English. The migrations must have taken place in large outrigger canoes, similar to the Arawa in which the Maori immigration to New Zealand is known to have taken place, capable of transporting two hundred people. Whatever route they took—and this must be examined in relation to prevailing winds and currents—they must have crossed at least 3,500 miles of open sea, which is an exploit as incredible as the peopling of Easter Island by Polynesians.

In determining the make-up of the Malagasy nation, it is necessary to examine the question of whether the island was uninhabited when the first immigrants arrived from the East. Some archaeological research has been carried out in Madagascar, but mainly

* The social position of the blacksmith varies sharply between regions. Among the Merina, iron working is confined to the highest social class— '*an'ny Andriana ny vy*' ('iron is for the nobleman'). A commercial register reveals that jewellers, lapidaries and tinsmiths all belong to noble families. However, among the Masikoro, a sub-group of the Sakalava living between the Onilahy and Mangoky rivers, the *tamby* (smiths) are pariahs, excluded from society and unable to marry outside their caste. Henri Lavondes, *Bekoropoka: Quelques aspects de la vie familiale et sociale d'un village malgache*, Paris 1967.

since 1962.[3] Excavations have been carried out on sites on the north-west and east coasts and on the Hauts-Plateaux, but relate to settlements later than the tenth century. In the absence of widespread excavations on many sites, it is only possible to say that, until now, no remains of fossil man have been found, nor stone implements nor bronze objects, although interesting connections with Indonesia and Africa have been observed. At the earliest of the sites examined, it has been shown that man coexisted with sub-fossil animals now extinct, including the dwarf hippopotamus (*Hippopotamus lemerlei*), a giant lemur, and mullerornis, a flightless bird like the dodo of Mauritius. These negative conclusions indicate that, in the absence of any archaeological evidence, Madagascar appears to have been uninhabited at the time of the first migrations of populations from the Far East.

The existence of a primitive population, the Vazimba, is attested from numerous traditions and place-names, and even from the name of an ethnic group still living among the Sakalava of the west coast.[4] Many countries have such traditions, including Britain and Ireland where the 'fairies' and 'little people' seem to relate to a Bronze Age population displaced by Celtic immigrants. In Africa, the pygmies are a living witness of the truth of legends which give them a much wider distribution than their forest refuges today. The Wanderogo of the forests of the Aberdare Mountains of Kenya are another such group. In the Malay peninsular and in the Melanesian islands, groups of primitives displaced by the ancestors of present-day populations still survive in the interior.[5] Thus there is nothing exceptional in the existence of Vazimba in Madagascar: the question to resolve is to what race did they belong, where did they themselves come from.

The primitives of whom legends survive in many countries have certain common traits. They are feared and revered and sometimes their magic is considered stronger than that of the immigrants. Often they speak a strange unknown language. Marriage with one of their women may bring disaster, as many folk-tales concerning fairy-women relate: *Ondine* is a literary monument to such beliefs. These characteristics point to the primitives' having belonged to a different race from that of the immigrants.

The Vazimba have some of these features, but also more important and significant differences. Two hypotheses are held by writers on this people: one, that they were of African origin; the other, that they were in fact proto-Malagasy, the survivors of an earlier immigration than the more massive waves of people that arrived after them.

The theory of African origin[6] is based on the Bantu consonance of the name Va- or Ba- Zimba, *Ba* or *Wa* being the Bantu prefix meaning men or 'people'; the word Zimba (even if we exclude *simba*, since there were never lions in Madagascar) also has an African consonance. It may also be argued that, although the Bantu do not appear ever to have been sea navigators but rather to have confined themselves to their coasts, even in West Africa, it cannot be impossible that winds and currents deposited African fishermen on the west coast of Madagascar. The Malagasy crocodile (*Crocodilus niloticus*), the same beast as infests African rivers, is one of the very few African animals to be found among the Malagasy fauna. It was almost certainly not introduced by man, since crocodiles are not normally regarded as useful domestic animals. If the crocodile can have crossed by unknown means the 180 miles of sea from Moçambique, it is not impossible that men in canoes should also have done so.

The rival theory that the Vazimba were in fact proto-Malagasy, is also possible. There is another possible etymology of the name, this time authentically Malagasy. The word *simba* in modern Malagasy means 'broken' or 'spoiled'. Thus the word can take on the sense of abandoned or degraded, and can be applied to a relic or something that has been displaced as primitive by a new wave of immigration.[7] Therefore, the name Vazimba was perhaps not that of a race but referred to people who may have been the survivors of earlier, less successful, immigrations, those who had been conquered and displaced by tribal wars, individuals expelled from their social group and escaped slaves. As regards the last, we know that many Malagasy brought as slaves to Réunion and Mauritius in the eighteenth century did escape and lived the life of bandits in the forests of the mountainous interior of those islands. A possible parallel might be found in the sedentary population of the Sahara oases, the Hartani (plural, Haratin), who, while having a substratum of negroid Sudanese and North African–Mediterranean, have received over the centuries Zenata refugees, negro slaves and escaped semi-Hamite prisoners.[8]

The most persistent oral accounts of the Vazimba are in Imerina, the country inhabited by the Merina. The first Merina immigrants encountered Vazimba installed in and around present-day Tananarive as they entered this region for the first time, coming up from the coast.[9] Antananarivo was then called Analamanga ('the blue forest') and was inhabited by Vazimba. The Merina chief Andriamanelo (1540–75) 'used iron to attack the Vazimba of Antananarivo. He conquered them because their arms were clay points fixed in bamboos, while he, having discovered iron, forged spears capable of piercing the skin and killing.'[10] Analamanga was finally taken from the Vazimba by Andrianjaka (1610–30), but the Vazimba chiefs were allowed to retain certain fiefs and privileges. Intermarriage occurred, and certain noble Merina families today claim Vazimba ancestors.

Although the Vazimba were displaced, they were absorbed rather than expelled. But their survival took the form of a cult practised by the population. Their tombs became places of pilgrimage to which people went to ask favours or seek cures. Oxen, sheep and cocks were sacrificed on mountain tops, or on their tombs. The Vazimba were (and are) supposed to haunt certain springs and rocks (*vatom-bazimba*). These rocks were anointed with fat, honey and blood to obtain favours. Today bottles, fruit and other offerings will be found around certain stones or springs. In the 1930s a French district commissioner of Ambohidratrimo, ten miles north of Tananarive, attempted to suppress the cult of the Vazimba Queen Ranoro who had drowned herself with her child in the Ikopa in the sixteenth century. In the face of determined opposition, the administration had to yield and allow the cult to continue.

Certain conclusions can be drawn from these details. Firstly, the Vazimba in Imerina do not seem to have been complete strangers to the Merina immigrants. We hear of no difficulty of communication and there seems to have been no reluctance to intermarry. The Vazimba were (and are) recognised as the 'lords of the soil' and, when dispossessed, were given other land. The present-day 'Vazimba' on the west coast are Malagasy in every way and speak Sakalava dialect as do their neighbours. In favour of the African hypothesis, it would seem probable that the proto-Malagasy spent some time on the African coast, or that certain elements established themselves there. One sign is the outrigger canoe, a purely Malayo-Polynesian object, that can be seen in a crude form on the coast between Dar es Salaam and Mombasa. Among other Indonesian elements are the quadrilateral house built on stilts and the large circular fishing net of the Malay or Malagasy type.

The names of all domestic animals in the Malagasy language are taken from Kiswahili, except for certain animals like the dog and the crocodile that have both Malay and Kiswahili names.* It does not seem that the immigrants coming by sea encumbered themselves with domestic animals, although they probably brought many plants, such as coconut, coco-yams and sugar cane, which have Malay names. The first immigrants may not have brought women with them, for it is curious that the word *vahini*, which means 'girl' in Tahitian, a related Malayo-Polynesian language, has an equivalent in Malagasy *vahiny*, which means 'stranger' or 'guest' (in Tahitian, stranger is *menahini*). This might mean that the first women came as strangers or guests among an already-established population of male immigrants who had sent home for wives of their own race.

The sea-routes by which the Malayo-Polynesian peoples reached Madagascar may be estimated by a study of the prevailing winds and currents of the Indian Ocean. Certain winds and currents in the southern and central part of the Indian Ocean would carry them westwards from Indonesia, while the reversal of winds and currents with the monsoon season in the northern part would enable them to return. Study of the winds and currents of the Indian Ocean (Maps 3 and 4, pages 58–59) shows the existence of one constant current, the south Equatorial current flowing east-west at all seasons, and one seasonal current, the Equatorial counter-current flowing west-east from November to March. The south Equatorial current originates south of Java and strikes the east coast of Madagascar. After the explosion in 1883 of the island of Krakatoa situated between Java and Sumatra, fragments of pumice stone were washed up on this coast of Madagascar. The south-east

*		*Malagasy*	*Kiswahili*
	Cattle	omby	ngombi
	Sheep	ondri	kondo
	Goat	osi	mbozi
	Fowl	akoho	koko
	Dog	alika/amboa	mbwa
	Crocodile	voay/mamba	mamba
	Guinea Fowl	akanga	akanga
	Cat	saka	paka

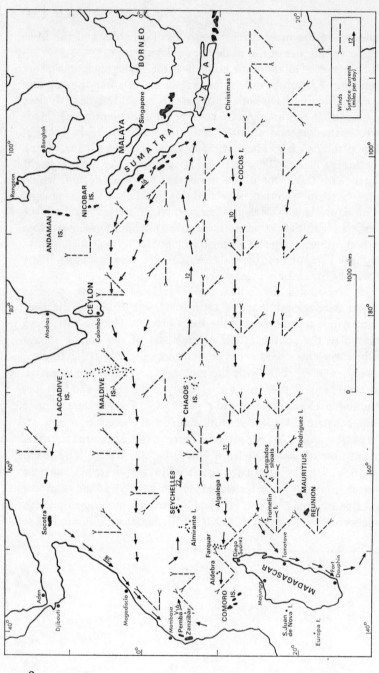

Map 3. Indian Ocean: January winds and currents

Source: Atlas of Pilot Charts, South Pacific and Indian Oceans, us Oceanographic Office, Washington 1966

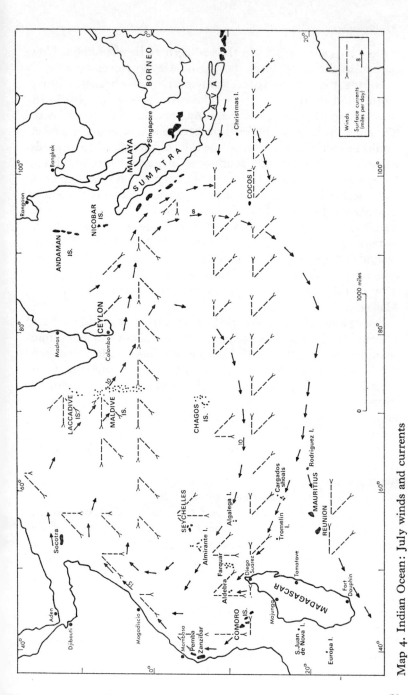

Map 4. Indian Ocean: July winds and currents

Source: Atlas of Pilot Charts. South Pacific and Indian Oceans, US Oceanographic Office, Washington 1966

trade winds are constant in the southern Indian Ocean but blow particularly strongly during the period May to November.

During those months the south-west monsoon causes heavy rainfall and storms over India. The currents flow in a clockwise direction and the Somali current flows at a speed of seven knots. Thus a ship leaving Madagascar between May and September would be carried north-east by the Somali current, and eastwards towards Ceylon by the south-west monsoon current. From Ceylon to Sumatra the distance is not too great and the Andaman and Nicobar islands provide stepping-stones. Between November and March the north-east winter monsoon, a cold wind coming from the winter-bound Asian landmass, causes the same currents to flow in an anti-clockwise direction. The Somali current turns around and becomes the north-east monsoon drift. At this season, therefore, a ship leaving Ceylon is carried by winds and currents west to the coast of Somalia and south towards the north of Madagascar.[11]

Sea communications with the East African coast would not have presented problems. The average distance is about 250 miles from coast to coast, and the Comoro islands are almost midway between the Moçambique coast and the north-west of Madagascar. Currents in the Moçambique Channel are variable but are not as strong as those in the Indian Ocean. The south-east trade wind blows from April to October, but north and north-east winds blow from November to March.

While no historical evidence exists to enable us to say with any certainty which routes the proto-Malagasy took in their Kon-Tiki-type expeditions across 3,500 miles of open sea, there are clearly two possibilities, determined by the direction of winds and currents. The distance between Java and Madagascar is enormous; it is still one of the longest airflights over open sea. However we know that the Polynesian navigators were not intimidated by great stretches of unbroken ocean, and Hawaii and Easter Island represent journeys from Indonesia at least as formidable as that to Madagascar.

We do not know from what point in Malaya or Indonesia the proto-Malagasy departed, or even if they came from different islands. We are somewhat in the position of those who study the Etruscans, another sea people; it is known that they came from the coast of Asia Minor, but the exact location is not known. Whatever the point of departure, there appear to be two possible routes for outrigger sailing canoes: the south Equatorial current running east-west and the Equatorial counter-current running west-east from May to October; and the Somali and monsoon currents, along the African and Indian coasts, running east-west from May to October and west-east from November to April.

The Polynesians sailed as far east as they could, possibly, according to the theory of Thor Heyerdahl, reaching South America. Recent studies of chromosome botany show that the varieties of sweet potato cultivated by the Maori of New Zealand came directly across the Pacific from its country of origin, Peru, and not from Brazil via Africa, where it was introduced along with cassava, groundnuts and maize by the Portuguese.[12] It is probable, therefore, that the proto-Malagasy sailed as far west as they could, using similar techniques of navigation.

Records of navigation in ancient times in the Indian Ocean have come down to us. The Alexandrine Greek documents describe the *Journey in the Erythrean Sea* (first century AD) which appears, in describing 'Azania', to refer to the Somali and East African coast. There is mention of an island, 'Menouthias', which may be Zanzibar or Pemba. Ptolemy, in his *Geography* (second century AD), assessing the accounts of Greek navigators, also mentions 'Menouthias', giving as bearings 5° of longitude north-east of Prason—a cape on the coast of Moçambique—and 12° 30' latitude, which would be very near the port of Diego-Suarez in the north of Madagascar. A number of Arab and Chinese texts describe navigation in the Indian Ocean and appear to describe the East African coast—'Zendj'—and a large island—'Komr'. Arab and Chinese accounts of navigation in the south-west Indian Ocean[13] speak not only of an island which may be Madagascar but also of what appear to be Indonesian navigators, with settlements on the Madagascar coast from which they departed for marauding expeditions. Thus the Indonesian immigrations may have continued over a long period, of even a thousand years, and have been maintained by trading relations.

While we cannot speak of specifically Arab settlements on the coast of Madagascar, in the way that we can of Zanzibar, Malindi or Mombasa on the East African coast, there appears to have been an important Islamic penetration in the Middle Ages which left settlements that persisted until the arrival of the first European visitors in the seventeenth and eighteenth centuries. These Arab settlers left important traces in the language, such as the names of the lunar months and days of the week, and in divination and magical practices, but they left remarkably little religious influence. Existing Moslem communities in Madagascar today are of either Comorian or Pakistani (Ismaeli) origin.

The settlers of the late Middle Ages were the Antalaotra and the Iharaniens, known from accounts of early European visitors and from excavations, particularly those carried out at Vohémar on the north-east coast. The Antalaotra ('sea-people' in Malagasy) were traders from the Comoro islands, a mixed population of Arab, Malagasy and African origin, who still speak a dialect of Kiswahili containing many Arabic and Malagasy words and maintain the Muslim religion, dress and customs. Trading posts were established by them on the north-west coast;* ruins can still be seen of walls and tombs, among which fragments of pottery are found. These trading posts appear to have been fortified, rather like the early European forts placed on the West African coast. At the time when the first Portuguese navigators began to visit Madagascar, these cities were still flourishing; Tristão da Cunha destroyed Nosy Manja in 1506. Luis Mariano, a Jesuit priest with the Portuguese, left a detailed account of these posts and of their trade with East Africa.[14]

The Iharanians are known from excavations carried out at Vohémar, and in particular from the examination of skeletal material from their tombs, which contain many objects including pottery from China, glass from Persia and assorted jewellery. This material appears to have belonged to a Muslim population, and examination of the skeletons shows a mixed population with a strong African (Bantu) strain, similar to that of the present-day inhabitants of the Comoro islands. Immediately to the north of Vohémar are a small group, the Onjatsy, who claim Arab descent and are renowned as fortune-tellers. It is from this region that an emigration took place, recorded in oral tradition to the south of this coast, where a small population of Malagasy Muslims, the Antaimoro, still live, mainly in the valley of the Matitana and in the town of Vohipeno. They have conserved the '*sorabe*' or

* At Mahilaka or Antseranantalaotra, literally 'port of the Antalaotra', in the bay of Ampasindava, Nosy Manja and on a number of small islands.

'great writings', which is written in Malagasy but using Arabic script on paper specially manufactured locally and roughly bound in ox-hide. Many of these books have been examined and have been found to contain magic formulae and prayers, but two books are kept secret and have never been read by historians.[15] The Arab immigrants seem to have been fairly completely absorbed by the coastal Malagasy tribes such as the Antaimoro and Zafiraminia; certainly, they have left far fewer traces than on the East African coast or in the Comoro islands. The Arabs, who established them-selves as traders on the north-west coast and who planted the great baobab tree still standing in the middle of Majunga, were not absorbed. Probably this was because the local Malagasy tribe, the Sakalava, were themselves semi-nomadic cattle people and not agricultural sedentaries like the east coast tribes. The traders remained in constant communication with their towns on the East African coast. The statements of many medieval Arabic writers concerning this coast—the writings of Masudi, Edrisi and the *Chronicles of Kiloa*—contain references which enable an assessment of the early Arabic influences on Madagascar to be made.[16] However, the uncertainty surrounding names, and es-pecially the name of Madagascar, which was not used by Arabic writers, makes it difficult to be certain as to which territory is described.

The most obvious relics of Arab influence are the names in Malagasy for the days of the week.* A more curious borrowing was the names of months, before the introduction of the French names which are now used in their Malagasy forms. The Arabic names of the months used by many Malagasy until quite recently were in fact the names of the constellations of the zodiac. Flacourt, an early French traveller to Madagascar of the seventeenth century, states that the people on the south-east coast among whom he lived knew the names of the constellations of the zodiac and used them in divination.[17] The names of the constellations were used

* Malagasy	Arabic	English
Alahady	El-ahad	Sunday
Alatsinainy	El-etnen	Monday
Talata	El-t'late	Tuesday
Alarobia	El-arba'e	Wednesday
Alakamisy	El-chamis	Thursday
Zoma	El-dsuma	Friday
Asabotsy	Es-sabt	Saturday

two hundred years later in the interior of the island for the names of the months. These were, of course, lunar months, and the names used varied, according to nineteenth-century missionaries, from one region to another. Thus *Adaoro* (January 15 to February 15) is *Az-tzauru*—Taurus; *Asorotany* (March 15 to April 15) is *As-saratanu*—Cancer. It is possible that the adoption of astrological terms, since these were not the names of the months used by the Arabs themselves, was connected with the Malagasy doctrine of *vintana* (destiny or fate), based on the identification of lucky and unlucky days by the *mpsikidy* (soothsayer). This name appears to derive from the Arabic *sichr*, which denotes anything of a magical character, including charms and incantations. The *mpsikidy* is essentially concerned with counter-charms against black magic emanating from *mpamosavy* (sorcerers), and he is therefore a 'white' magician. The Arabic names of the signs of the zodiac were also used for groups of days in any given month, almost certainly in relation to *vintana*. Thus the 1st to 3rd days were called *Alahamady* (Aries), the 20th and 21st days *Alakaosy* (Sagittarius).

The Malagasy word for music, *mozika*, appears to derive from the Arabic *musiqa*, and it is probable that some of the musical instruments in use in Madagascar before the arrival of Europeans, who brought others and profoundly influenced Malagasy music were of Arabic origin. Thus the clarinet, *anjomara* in Malagasy, is *az-zamara* in Arabic; *sobaba*, a flute, is *subbab*. Terms referring to books and writing also appear to be derived from Arabic, and include *taratasy* (paper) from *qartas*, and *soratra* (writing) from *surat*, meaning a line or a verse of the Koran. *Sary* (a picture or drawing) may come from the Arabic *zura*, form or image.[18]

This rather special contribution is entirely divorced from any religious influence. The Malagasy seem to have been little interested in the Muslim religion, compared with the speed and enthusiasm with which they adopted the Christian religion, in both Catholic and Protestant teachings, when it was introduced in the nineteenth century. The Arabic contribution, however, has had a profound influence on everyday life in Madagascar, given the importance of divination and of auspicious and inauspicious days to the great majority of the population, including many educated people.

The degree of African influence in Madagascar is less easy to assess and must be examined carefully, especially in relation to the import of slaves which persisted until the French conquest. Whether there was ever any significant free immigration of Africans into Madagascar is doubtful, though not impossible. Certainly, there were African crews on Arab boats sailing between the East African coast, the Comoro islands and Madagascar. There were substantial populations speaking *cafr* (probably Kiswahili) on the west coast when Luis Mariano SJ visited it in the seventeenth century.* The Makoa, a distinct tribe in the north-west of Madagascar who spoke a language related to Chinjanja and Tomboka in Malawi, were probably of almost pure African descent; a tribe of the same name exists to this day around Nampula in northern Moçambique. However, since the names 'Makoa' and 'Masombiki' were synonomous for 'slaves' until the end of the nineteenth century, it would be unwise to assume much free immigration from Africa. The only Kiswahili speakers in Madagascar today are Comoro island immigrants. The Makoa have completely lost their language and are now Malagasy monoglots. If any other African languages were spoken by immigrants, these have also been completely absorbed in the unity of the Malagasy language.

No scientific comparative study exists of the techniques and characteristics found in Madagascar that are common either to Indonesia or to East Africa. Few scholars can be deeply acquainted with such a wide field of knowledge; most writers tend to be specialised and are thus influenced in their interpretation of the cultural make-up of Madagascar. Deschamps gives what is probably the most complete comparative list, but himself states that the only complete scientific comparative study relates to musical instruments.[19] Of these, those of Indonesian origin include the *valiha* (a guitar made from a hollow bamboo tube), a xylophone and a cone-shaped drum, while those from Africa include rattles, a violin on a calabasse and various drums.

Techniques introduced from Indonesia include irrigated terraced paddy fields (the most striking), the outrigger canoe and certain fishing methods, types of houses raised on stilts (pilotis), depilation of the body hair (both sexes), the forge made of pistons

---

* Mariano was acquainted both with the Malagasy language and with that of the East African coastal tribes.

in two tree-trunks and the loom used for weaving raffia cloth which is an exact copy of the Indonesian loom. African characteristics are the cattle-cult, with cattle as a sign of riches and importance, the marks cut by owners in cattle's ears, some articles of clothing (the 'toga' or *akanjo*) and some types of pottery.

Plants and animals have been introduced from both Indonesia and Africa. It would appear that Madagascar had no ancient methods of agriculture, since it was probably uninhabited when the immigrants from Indonesia first arrived. There are no known traces of Palaeolithic or Neolithic civilisation on the island, and it appears that no cereal was cultivated in Madagascar before the introduction of rice from Indonesia. The oldest food-crops appear to be Bambara groundnut (*Voandzeia subterranea*), from Africa; cocoyam (*Colocasia antiquorum*), from Asia; plantain (*Musa paradisiaca*), banana (*Musa sapientium*), beans (*Phaseolus spp.*), arrowroot (*Canna edolis*) and yams (*Dioscorea alata*), from India and Indonesia. Yams and Bambara groundnuts regressed as food-crops with the introduction of cassava, sweet potatoes, groundnuts, maize and Lima beans, all of South American origin and introduced by the Portuguese to Africa probably in the fifteenth century.[20] The balance of crops and agricultural techniques is of Asian rather than African origin,* if we except local cultivation of maize on the west coast and of sogho and millet in the extreme south, both introduced from Africa. The cattle-cult, however, would appear to be strongly influenced by African practice, and many of the traditional attitudes are similar, though usually less well-developed, to those of the Nilotic, Hamitic and Fulani cattle peoples.

The most obvious source of African influence must be found in the massive and continuous importation of African slaves that continued until slavery was officially abolished by Resident Laroche in 1896, immediately after the French occupation. It is probable that the first to introduce slaves into Madagascar were the Arabs from East Africa. Portuguese travellers in the sixteenth century speak of boats coming from Mombasa and Malindi to buy slaves.[21] There was certainly a two-way traffic, and Malagasy slaves were

---

* In contrast to the names of domestic animals, nearly all derived from Kiswahili words (see note on page 57), names of plants are almost all of Indonesian origin: sugar-cane, *fary*; coconut, *voanio*; beans, *tsara-maso*; rice, *vary* (?Sanskrit); roots, *ovy*; banana, *fontsy;* etc.

taken by Arabs, Portuguese, Dutch and British, especially during the eighteenth century, and sold to Ile de France, Bourbon and Cape Colony and also transported to the Caribbean and North America.

The Malagasy themselves imported slaves from the African coast and enslaved each other as a result of inter-tribal wars, and the same Arabs who bought Malagasy slaves on one part of the coast disembarked Makoa and other African slaves elsewhere on another part of the coast. It is impossible to estimate the number, but, over the two hundred years that the trade flourished, it must have been considerable.

Slavery leads to mixing of races, although it gives rise to rigid taboos concerning marriage. The African slaves were used as concubines by the Malagasy, exactly as their white owners used them in Brazil or the United States. The results have been precisely similar, and there is an admixture of African blood amongst many Malagasy today, which comes from sexual intercourse with female slaves. Those having African blood are, of course, hedged off by marriage taboos among certain tribes, especially the Merina of the Hauts-Plateaux. In general, those of apparently pure Malayo-Polynesian descent, who resemble closely the Javanese, do not intermarry with anyone showing signs of African blood. This is interpreted rather by hair-types than by the colour of the skin. The Merina prize long straight black hair and look for crinkly hair as a sign of slave descent. They attach less importance to darkness of complexion. These taboos are far less operative among the populations of the west coast, where there is a substantial proportion of Makoa or Masombiki descent.

The intermingling of Indonesian and African cultures is shown strikingly in the systems of parentage, marriage interdictions, inheritance, customs and the place of residence after marriage. A recent study describes these as 'On the one hand, a very general structural affinity with the systems of the Malayo-Polynesian area, on the other, resemblances on points of detail . . . with Central and East Africa. In other words, an Indonesian basis with a strong African colouring.'[22] This statement is broadly true of the mingling of the various techniques and cultural factors: the basis is essentially Indonesian, with points of detail arising from African contacts. However it is the 'profound unity in the broad essentials, extreme diversity in the details',[23] that has struck almost every student of Madagascar.

Thus unity has been confirmed, and in many ways pushed even further, by the last wave of influence and immigration—that of the Europeans. Here again the first visitors were seafarers and often shipwrecked sailors. The Portuguese appear to have discovered Madagascar as a result of a storm off the Cape of Good Hope that dispersed the squadron of Pedralvares Cabral (who had succeeded Vasco de Gama). Blown out to the Indian Ocean, he touched a coast which he believed to be that of Moçambique, but on sailing north he found that it was a large island. In 1502 a Portuguese map drawn by Cantinho shows this large island as 'Madagascar'. This island had already been placed on the globe of Martin Behaim, but had not, apparently, been seen by any European.

The name of 'Madagascar' is first mentioned by Marco Polo, although he certainly never visited the island and his references appear to refer rather to Mogadiscio on the coast of Africa. The name of 'Madagascar' was used by Europeans from the seventeenth century, after a brief period when the island was called the 'Ilha de San Lourenço' after its official 'discovery' by a Portuguese squadron under Dom Francisco de Almeida on February 1, 1506. The Arab navigators knew Madagascar as 'Komr' or 'Bouki'. The name given by the earliest Indonesian immigrants is of course unknown, but the first European missionaries do not report the Malagasy using the name 'Madagascar' for the country. Instead they used a phrase (still used in conversation) '*izao tontolo izao*', 'the whole world'; or sometimes '*ny anivon 'ny riaka*', 'in the midst of the waters'. Radama 1, King of Imerina (1810–28), had engraved on his silver coffin, which lies in the tombs of the royal family beside the Palace of Manjakamiadana in Tananarive, '*Tompo'ny anivon'ny riaka*', 'lord of what is in the midst of the waters'—that is, the island of Madagascar.[24] Another possible origin of the name may be found in early contacts with the Portuguese coming from the coast of Moçambique on their way to India, who began to obtain supplies of food and water in Madagascar, especially on the south-east coast. Early accounts in the seventeenth century of such contacts speak of a bay, Ranofotsi, where their ships moored, in the country of the Matacassi (Antanosi, today), which may have given rise to the names Madecasse or Malagasy for these people, which were afterwards applied to the whole population.[25] The Portuguese navigator Tristan d'Acunha visited Réunion island in 1507 and in 1528, to which he gave the name of Mascarenhas island; thus the group of Réunion and Mauritius is still called in French 'Les Iles Mascareignes'.

There were a number of shipwrecks at this period. One, in 1527, cast ashore on the south-west coast 600 men who were never recovered and were either massacred or absorbed by the population, which to this day points out ruins of stone walls and caves attributed to the Portuguese. The Portuguese attempts at penetration, accompanied by the conversion of an Antanosi prince who subsequently returned to the faith of his ancestors when faced with a hostile population, lasted from 1613 to 1619. The Jesuit priest Luis Mariano was present for the whole of this period, at the end of which the Portuguese abandoned the idea of religious conversion and settlement and were content to maintain trading relations as a staging post on their sea-route to the Far East.

On March 1, 1598, the Dutch took possession of the uninhabited island to which they gave the name of Mauritius, and they began to visit Madagascar on their way from the Cape to the Far East. Their main concern was to obtain supplies of food and slaves for their island. They were exploiting the forests which then covered Mauritius, especially to extract ebony, and they were entirely dependent for manpower on slaves, most of whom were captured or bought on the Malagasy coast. Throughout the seventeenth century Mauritius was used by the Dutch at intervals as a staging post on the Far East route, but was occupied only intermittently. They finally abandoned the island in 1712, by which time they had extracted a great deal of ebony from the forests and had killed and eaten all the dodo, the large flightless bird distantly related to the pigeon. The ships of the British East India Company continued all through the seventeenth century to take on supplies at various points on the east coast of Madagascar, but principally in the Bay of St Augustin to the south of Tuléar in the south-west.

Charles I considered sending a British expedition to Madagascar in 1636, to establish a colony under Prince Rupert of Bavaria. The poet Thomas Herbert had described Madagascar as being rich in every kind of metal, and a legend of the riches of the island was prevalent in England at this time. A further appeal for settlers for the island containing gold, silver, pearls and precious stones was published in 1640,[26] and a more detailed description, issued in 1644, urged the establishment of a Protestant colony in Madagascar.[27] In fact, in 1644, 120 English men and women, under a certain John Smart, arrived in the Bay of St Augustin and constructed a fort as a first step to a colony. The local inhabitants urged their aid against tribal enemies, which the colonists were unwise enough to refuse. As a result, they were murdered and starved out and twelve survivors left for home a year later; one of them, Waldegrave, published a refutation of the glowing account given in 1644, saying that the mines did not exist and that the country was barren, with a horrible climate.[28] The survivors left behind them only a ruined fort and a large cemetery. The myth of fabulous riches in Madagascar had been finally exploded in Britain.

This period of first contacts with Europeans ends with the first and unsuccessful French settlement, which, however, survives as the town of Fort Dauphin in the extreme south-east, named in honour of the future Louis XVI by an agent of the French Compagnie des Indes Orientales in 1643. An earlier attempt at settlement near Mananjary had failed; many of the settlers had either been massacred or died of fever. In 1648 the company sent a governor, Etienne de Flacourt, a well-educated man, who arrived with more settlers and two Lazarist fathers sent by St Vincent de Paul.

This settlement lived in a state of constant war and pillage with the Antanosy. The two priests died and the settlers lived behind a stockade from which they emerged only to raid the countryside for supplies. In 1653 Flacourt tried to leave for France; before leaving, he erected a pillar on the shore on which was engraved: '*O advena, lege monita nostra tibi tuis vitaeque tua profutura. Cave ab incolis. Vale.*' (O new arrival, read our warning, and it will save your life. Beware of the inhabitants. Farewell.) This ship was wrecked but another took Flacourt off. He left behind two more priests, who had just arrived, and Pronis, who had been the first of the company's settlers in 1643 and who now returned. Flacourt is remarkable not for his work as a settler but for two books he wrote on his return to France, which were the first scientific accounts of Madagascar and contain material which is still valuable today: the *Histoire de la Grande Isle de Madagascar* (1658) and a *Dictionnaire de la langue de Madagascar*. The history remained for one hundred and fifty years the only source of reliable information on Madagascar, and its historical value today is still great.

The fortified settlement of Fort Dauphin continued to receive reinforcements. A serious attempt at colonisation of the east coast took place in 1667, when a force was landed consisting of a lieutenant-general, the Marquis de Montdevergue, two trading directors, a procuror-general, eight traders, settlers and four infantry companies; in all ten ships and about two thousand people. Supply difficulties were the reason for considerable trade in foodstuffs along the coast and for the first known European penetration of the interior. A supply column of local levies headed by nineteen French went up the valley of the Maningory to Lake Alaotra at the end of 1667, but were driven back by the Sihanaka. These penetrations added considerably to European knowledge of Madagascar, but their warlike character prepared the way for the complete severance of contacts in the eighteenth century and certainly built up much hostility among the Malagasy.[29]

The Marquis de Montdevergue was recalled in 1669 by Colbert, Minister of Finance to Louis XIV, as a result of internal political disputes between colonists and the company, and he died in prison at Saumur. Many of the leading personalities left for India, and the company obtained from the King a discharge of its responsibilities for Madagascar. The Antanosy continued their attacks, the settlers fought among themselves or died of fever, and finally the sixty-three survivors, who could no longer leave the stockade without being murdered, spiked their guns, burned the buildings and fled to Ile Bourbon (Réunion).

The consequences of this attempt, which lasted thirty years, to establish a French settlement in Madagascar, were, apart from the genuinely scientific work of Flacourt, the setting up of a French colony on Bourbon and the beginning of a claim to sovereignty over Madagascar. This claim was founded on concessions in Madagascar granted to the Compagnie des Indes Orientales by the French crown, on the basis of which a theoretical annexation of Madagascar by France was declared on July 14, 1665. The abandoning of Fort Dauphin in 1674 made no difference to these claims to what had been termed the 'Ile Dauphine', and they constituted the legalistic arguments put forward in the nineteenth century during events leading to the eventual annexation at the conquest of 1896. With the departure from Madagascar, French colonising efforts in the Indian Ocean, and many of the individuals concerned with Madagascar, were now concentrated on India and also on Ile Bourbon.

The end of this period of shipwrecks, pioneers' stockades, fevers and cemeteries, saw a virtual abandoning of Madagascar by the European colonising powers during most of the eighteenth century. The riches of this mountainous island had been, at that time, found to be illusory. The inhabitants were already sufficiently organised to resist European aggression. Other continents provided much richer and more immediate prizes for France, England and the Netherlands, in India, Indonesia, America and the Antilles. The eighteenth century was a period of continued internal expansion by the two dynamic peoples of Madagascar of that time, the Merina and the Sakalava, but it was also one of frequent outside contacts. However, these contacts were chiefly with pirates who, throughout this century, made Madagascar a base for their activities, similar to North Africa or the Antilles.

It may be that piracy was a continuation of the sea-going tradition of the Malagasy ancestors, for the Malagasy themselves participated very actively in the piratical activities of Europeans based on the coasts of the island. A number of these pirates had been chased out of the Atlantic by the navies of France and Britain. Their tactics were generally to install themselves on the east coast of Madagascar, but with the complicity of the local inhabitants, unlike the earlier attempts at orthodox colonisation. Their prey was mainly the European maritime traffic with the East, passing via the Cape of Good Hope and Madagascar on its way to India, Indonesia and China, but also the Arab traders between South Arabia and East Africa. The pirates were nearly all English, French and American; they include Caracciolo, Thomas Tew, Burgess, La Buse, Howard, Misson, Thomas White, and the notorious Captain Kidd* who was hanged in 1701.[30]

The pirates integrated themselves with the Malagasy where they established themselves on the coast, and intermarriage, often with the daughters of local chiefs, produced a race known as the Zana-Malata (derived from the French 'mulâtre', half-caste). One

---

* Captain William Kidd originated in the Bahamas. He was commissioned to fight the pirates off Madagascar, but became a pirate himself, and was hanged in New York in 1701. See Charles Johnson, *A General History of Pirates*, London 1724.

of these was the chief Ratsimilaho, who united the Betsimisaraka into one kingdom. His half-sister Betia*—perhaps as a result of her love affair with Corporal Louis Labigorne of the French Compagnie des Indes—ceded Ste Marie to the French in 1750 as their first permanent settlement in Madagascar. (The inhabitants of Ste Marie automatically possessed French citizenship throughout the whole colonial period.) The European pirates were largely suppressed after an English squadron under Commodore Matthews was sent against them in 1721, but by the end of the century the Zana-Malata were organising regular raiding expeditions against the Comoro islands and the East African coast. Their ships were the dug-out canoes of the east coast, capable of carrying up to fifty men; the long racing canoes still to be seen on the east coast at Nosy-Varika and farther south are perhaps the descendants of these dug-outs. To this period belongs the drama of Robert Drury, an English seaman who was shipwrecked on the south coast of Madagascar in 1702 and remained for fifteen years a captive. He was taken off by a visiting ship in 1717 and returned on a slaving expedition in 1718, leaving on the same ship in 1720. His book, *Madagascar, or Robert Drury's Journal during Fifteen Years of Captivity on that Island*, contains a roughly phonetic vocabulary of the Malagasy language.

The eighteenth century was thus a period of considerable contacts, though none too legal, with the outside world. Numerous Europeans lived on the coast of Madagascar and left descendants. Many Malagasy served in the crews on marauding expeditions to the neighbouring Mascarene islands and the African coast. The slave traffic grew throughout this period, in particular with Ile Bourbon and Ile de France, where arabica coffee, introduced since 1720, assured considerable prosperity before the introduction of sugar-cane. It was an ideal period for European adventurers, and of those who survived fever and assassination by the locals, Benyowski is the best remembered. This Austrian citizen of Polish origin had been a prisoner of the Russians and claimed to have escaped from Kamchatka. He established himself in the Bay of Antongil and founded a settlement called Louisbourg, from which he eventually proclaimed himself 'Emperor of Madagascar'. His name reappeared in 1937, when a Polish mission, which had

* Betia, literally 'the one who loves much', is usually incorrectly spelt as Betty.

come to Madagascar to study the possibility of settling Polish
Jews in the Ankaizina, brought up the name of Benyowski in one
of their reports as proof of an historical connection between
Poland and Madagascar.

In spite of the apparent confusion and sporadic nature of these
contacts with Europeans, this period of one hundred and fifty
years did much to determine the future development of Madagascar. Little material remained of these contacts except flintlock
guns, powder and shot, but these arms enabled energetic local
chiefs to extend their authority and to become local 'kings'. It
was from Madagascar that French settlers finally colonised the
neighbouring Mascarene islands, and it was the growing prosperity
of these islands, with their cash crops, that sent the settlers back
to Madagascar to trade in food supplies and slaves. The Arab
trading settlements on the north coast disappeared without a
trace, but the European trading posts on the east coast became the
modern towns of Tamatave, Mananjary and Fort Dauphin.

Although little in the way of material objects remained, much of
the Arab and European contribution filtered through the eastern
forest and up on to the Hauts-Plateaux where the Merina were
beginning to consolidate their kingdom on the great rice plain
of the Betsimitatatra around Tananarive, and to absorb their
neighbours. Although the outside world knew practically nothing
of the existence of the Merina, a people already better-organised
and culturally more evolved than the coastal tribes, the Merina
had by this time received the art of writing from the coastal Arabs
and a number of European goods, including firearms.

The Napoleonic Wars transformed the Mascarenes into a strategic zone, with the capture of Ile de France and Ile Bourbon (now
to become Mauritius and Réunion) from the French by the British
and with the occupation of Tamatave by Commodore Lynn of
the British navy in 1811. This intensification of Anglo-French
rivalry in the area, paralleled by the rise of Imerina under a
remarkable organiser, King Andrianampoinimerina (1745–1810)
prepared the way for the great invasion of western technology and
religion of the early nineteenth century, culminating in the French
conquest of 1896.

3. The Society

MANY EUROPEAN WRITERS have sought to underline the differences among the various elements of the population of Madagascar, often termed 'tribes'. Examination of the socio-cultural character of these groups shows an underlying unity of custom and belief, with a marked differentiation in detail natural among peoples who were, until the colonisation, separated by great distances and politically divided under many local rulers.[1] There is first the unity of language. All Malagasy speak the same language with dialectical differences no greater than those existing between Sicilian and Tuscan speech, or Gascon and standard French. There is an underlying unity of ancestral religious beliefs and practices. All believe in one supreme being, who has various names such as *Zanahary* and *Andriamanitra* (literally, 'the scented lord'), all believe in the immortality of a soul and in a life after death. All believe that the ancestors watch over the living, and thus burial rites are carried out with particular care, and tombs are sacred places. There is also belief in spirits dwelling in springs and wells and in the forest. There are many taboos, again highly individual according to locality. These are known as *fady*, and may mean that a village may not work on a certain day, or that men or women may not do certain work. In Imerina, no one will hand an egg directly to another person but will place it on the ground for him to pick up. A Merina of a certain caste will not clear away dog's excrement, even with a broom. In certain parts of the forest one will be told by the guide not to whistle. One must not urinate near a paddy field. Dogs must not be allowed to walk near a tomb. Dogs and pork meat must not be introduced into any of the *rova*, the former royal palaces of the Merina kings.

The idea of sacrilege is contained in the violation of the prohibitions laid down by the ancestors, or the failure to perform obligations imposed by them. From this comes the fear of 'blame' (*tsiny*) for any action of nonconformity, or sometimes for an innovation. The misfortune which comes as a result of going against the customs of the ancestors, or from any aggressive or anti-social act, is known as the *tody*.*

The burial customs of the Merina have attracted much attention among foreign writers. Family tombs are conspicuous objects in Imerina. They are large square constructions, and vary from old grass-grown humps, scarcely distinguishable, to elaborately carved structures with blind doors and windows. Near Tananarive, and especially in the suburb of Ambatobe, are large cemeteries of such tombs, all different; one walks through narrow streets, between dozens of blind edifices.

According to Malagasy beliefs, although the dead have disappeared from this world, they lead a new existence in the next and remain in touch with their descendants, controlling their obedience to traditional customs, giving them advice and showing their displeasure by appearing to them in dreams. The dead are invoked by prayers and sacrifices, and the dead and the living thus form a single society in constant contact. Amongst the Merina there is a saying concerning the family tomb: 'One house only for the living members of a family, and one tomb only for the dead.'[2] The worst thing that can happen to a Malagasy is to be excluded from being buried in the family tomb. This ban of excommunication would be passed by the members of the family only for some terrible crime against tradition. Death, unless from old age, was for long considered the result of sorcery or a punishment of God (*Zanahary*) or of the ancestors for want of respect or transgressing a taboo. This is the main reason for the multitude of taboos that bind the lives of Malagasy. All over Madagascar are found standing stones, some erected in memory of a notable event, others in memory of an ancestor who could not for some reason be buried in the land of his fathers. These funerary stones are 'cenotaphs', providing a soul with a resting place and thus preventing its wandering.

There are strict rules in Imerina as to who can be buried in the great family tomb. Sons, and daughters who were unmarried or who married and had no children, can be buried together with their fathers. Married women with children are buried in the tombs of their husband's family. Burial rites among the Merina have

* A Malagasy proverb says: '*Ny tody tsy misy fa ny atao no miverina*' ('There is no *tody*, but what you do to others they will do to you in return.')

changed since 1900 under the influence of church missions, and are coming more to resemble Western practices. Normally the body is washed in cold water and placed on a new rush mat in the north-east corner of the house, called the *zoro firazanana*, the corner of the ancestors. Before burial it is clothed in a white shirt and wrapped in a shroud of red silk, the *lambamena*. The men of the family wrap the body very tightly in the *lambamena*. Formerly, numbers of cattle were sacrificed and eaten during the funeral ceremonies, and on tombs amongst the Mahafaly in the south can be seen the horns of dozens of cattle that have been slaughtered at a burial. It is considered that the cattle follow the dead man into the next world.

The family will watch over the body laid on its mat in the house for two or three days, sitting in line on several rows of chairs. A visitor enters and stands in front of the seated family, after saluting in a particular formula; he makes a short speech of praise for the dead person and adds his condolences for the family. He then makes a small gift of money and sits with the family facing the body for a few minutes as a sign of respect. The funeral procession, when the body wrapped in the *lambamena* is carried to the tomb, is accompanied by funeral songs. The door of the tomb is opened an hour or so before the burial, and members of the family go in with a candle. No one except the family can enter the tomb. Around the tomb the women sing funeral songs, and then a senior member of the family pronounces the funeral oration, thanking all those who have come and speaking of the qualities of the dead person. After the burial, the mourners disperse and everyone washes his hands and face in running water to wash off the touch of death.

Formerly, when someone died during a festival or from an infectious disease such as smallpox or far away from the ancestral tomb, he received a temporary burial and was later exhumed for reburial in the family tomb. Thus the bodies of all the Malagasy soldiers killed in the First World War were exhumed and brought back to Madagascar at government expense. In Imerina there is a ceremony known as *famadihana*, or exhumation, which has attracted much attention from foreigners. Briefly, the body is taken out of its tomb, wrapped in a new shroud or *lambamena* of silk that covers the old one, taken in procession with music, singing and rejoicing and then replaced in the tomb. A feast is held and there is much eating and drinking. The *famadihana* occur in the winter, the dry season, and are a joyful festival. These exhumations may occur five years or later after the death. Where they have been delayed and only bones remain, the principal bones—skull, tibias, femurs—are collected in a little box. The day and hour of these exhumations is always indicated by the *mpanandro*, or wise man.

Tombs vary in different parts of Madagascar, and may be in caves or among rocks or sometimes in trees, but the basis of the cult of the dead has an underlying similarity, even if the details vary.

These customs have been christianised, and the Catholic and Protestant Churches have wisely decided to associate themselves (unofficially) with the strongest-rooted belief of the Malagasy. Even under the colonisation, no French district commissioner could touch a local tomb without causing a riot. Galliéni displaced the remains of the Merina kings from Ambohimanga to the royal palace in Tananarive, but this was at a time when the conquest had smashed the established Merina society. In 1938 the French government brought back the remains of the last queen, Rana-valona III, from Algiers where she had died in 1917, and buried them with appropriate ceremonies within the walls of the former royal palace.

Christianity has taken deep roots among the Malagasy. Over most of the country, both Catholic and Protestant churches are organised more as parishes than as isolated missions. On the central highlands of Imerina, Catholic and Protestant churches, often of identical design, face one another, rather as they do in some Irish villages. Protestants are predominant in Imerina,*

* The following statistics for various Christian cults appeared in the Malagasy Official Gazette for 1968:

	Adherents	Churches or places of worship	schools
Catholics	1,400,000	5,000	918
Fiangonan'i Jesosy Kristy eto Madagascar (FJKM)	1,030,000	5,161	386
Lutherans	252,000	1,400	250
Episcopalians	39,600	400	50
Seventh-Day Adventists	20,770	87	40

There were estimated to be about 3,200,000 Christians in a population of nearly 7 million.

Catholics in the Betsileo and on the east coast, while Norwegian Lutheran missionaries have been active for about a hundred years around Morondava and Belo-sur-Tsiribihina on the west coast. In the South, at Ford Dauphin and at Edjeda, the American Lutheran mission runs two excellent hospitals. The old rivalry and bitterness between Protestants and Catholics, which had a political tinge at the time when Britain and France were competing for influence in Madagascar, has died down very considerably, and the ecumenical spirit of Pope John XXIII has been widely observed in a rapprochement between the two major groups, which has been marked since 1962.

However, there are still wide regions very little touched by Christianity, where ancestral beliefs and practices are unchanged. This is true particularly of small villages encountered deep in the rain forest of the east coast, where ceremonies around standing stones in the centre of the village, accompanied by appropriate sacrifices, are the only religious practices seen. There are large zones in the south and west where churches exist, but where, for want of clergy, services are rare. Pastors and priests are sometimes itinerant, saying offices in a different church every few days, and good work is performed by catechists, who lead prayers in the absence of the clergy.

The Catholic Church was in a condition of inferiority to the English-dominated Protestant churches in Madagascar until the French conquest in 1896. Catholic church services thus tend to be unusually original in Madagascar, perhaps as a result of entering into competition with Protestant services, especially as regards hymn-singing (highly appreciated by the Malagasy), long sermons and extempore prayers that appear in no known Catholic liturgy. Mass tends to vary from one church to another, very much at the whim or fantasy of the priest. Since there are fewer priests than churches, much latitude is left to the catechists, and long homilies and improvised prayers precede the arrival of the priest, punctuated by hand-clapping to signal when the congregation should kneel or stand.

While in 1970 the Cardinal-Archbishop and several bishops were Malagasy, the influence of numerous resident French priests remains strong, especially that of the Jesuits, the largest single body. Among the Protestants, there remained in 1969 none of the old type of English missionary, though English missionaries

79

remained as teachers in theological colleges and schools. Among the Norwegian Lutherans, a number of Norwegian pastors still remained.

The churches are all active in running schools, and are making an indispensable contribution, in close collaboration with state schools. There is neither conflict nor competition in Madagascar between state and church schools, and there have been none of the disputes or sudden take-overs of church schools such as have been seen in certain African countries since independence.

At the same time, the state preserves a rigorous impartiality in matters of religion, in accordance with the constitution. The President and the government show an equal respect to Protestant and Catholic churches, and to the Muslim religion practised by several thousand Comoro islanders and Pakistanis together with very small numbers of Malagasy on the south-east coast around Vohipeno. Respect for the beliefs of another person is ingrained in the Malagasy character, and anything like fanaticism is usually foreign to them. Thus, representatives of a very wide number of sects have been welcomed and continue to work without interference in Madagascar, provided they observe the law and maintain political neutrality.

Ancestral beliefs are still practised by many educated Christians. A wise man, or *mpanandro*, will be called to advise on the siting of a house or a new tomb, and on the days which work should be started or the house occupied. The *mpanandro* will also fix the day on which a couple should be married.

Both white and black magic exist in Madagascar. The *mpanandro* is 'white', as is the *ombiasy*, who is a soothsayer and healer, prescribing powders and infusions of medicinal plants—an art of which certain Malagasy have a profound knowledge. The *ombiasy* practises a form of geomancy to foretell the future, often arranging beans in a square geometrical pattern (*sikidy*). He is highly respected as a wise man. Black magic is practised by the *mpamosavy* (witch) in ceremonies performed at night on or near tombs. Such persons circulate at night, sometimes naked but covered with grease so that they cannot be seized. Dances are performed on tombs at certain phases of the moon. The *mpamosavy* are much feared in Imerina, and precautions are taken by burying certain powdered plants at the entrance to properties to prevent their coming in. The *mpamosavy* are often concerned in cases of poisoning, and can introduce medicinal plants into food which cause temporary or permanent madness.

No ceremony is complete in Madagascar without music, and Malagasy music is original and considerably developed. Its origins are no doubt oriental, as are the basic musical instruments, the *valiha* or guitar of which the strings are stretched around a bamboo, and certain drums. But many other instruments have been introduced: the flute by the Arabs (*sobaba*, from Arabic *subbab*), various kinds of xylophones on the west coast, from Africa, and, from the eighteenth century onwards, trumpets, clarinets, the accordion and the harmonium.

Song and music is a vigorous small industry, since the numerous local troupes are much in demand for official ceremonies, family feasts and local dances. Songs vary from the purely traditional, usually melancholic, pentatonic, to those showing Western influences, melodies and harmonies derived from Protestant hymns, eighteenth-century dances brought in via the Creoles of Réunion, American negro spirituals or up-to-date dance tunes.

The Malagasy have a highly developed tradition of comic songs, which require an accurate knowledge of the language to be appreciated. Others take the form of mocking songs exchanged between groups of young men and girls; or again the young women are going to fetch water and the young men tease them. Sentimental love-songs, often with most beautiful melodies, are very popular.

The typical troupe, the *mpihira-gasy* or 'Malagasy singers', consists of about fifteen men and women, some of the men playing trumpets, accordions, clarinets and drums. The leader begins by a vigorous speech in the best 'fair barker' style, which may be mocking or patriotic according to the occasion. The band then begins full blast, followed by the singers, who dance in measured figures, not unlike eighteenth-century European dances, while they sing. Harmony is highly developed, many songs being sung by two or three young girls, singing descants in minor thirds. The sharp true voices of Malagasy women recall in some ways the 'bitter-sweet' songs of women of the Eastern Mediterranean.

Although the Malagasy family is nominally patriarchal, women have an outstanding position, especially among the Merina of the Hauts-Plateaux. Among the other peoples of Madagascar a similar trend can be observed wherever education is making real progress, and it can be said that the development of the character and sense of responsibility of women is an essential part of Malagasy society. Among the Merina, women have undergone considerable intellectual development as a result of education. The maturity and balanced personality of these women is shown in a tendency to dominate within the family. This trend springs from the structure and organisation of the Malagasy family.

A boy has, in the eyes of his parents, a higher level of importance than a girl. He is honoured and served by the female members of the family and undertakes only 'noble' tasks. A certain respect and consideration is shown to a boy, because he is a male. A girl participates in the work of the household from the time she is very young, and she is closely associated with her mother in all the activities of the household. Malagasy families are large and, at a very early age, a little girl will be looking after her younger brothers and sisters. She will be directly responsible for their well-being, carry them on her back like a little mother and look after their education until they go to school. The little girl thus takes responsibility and develops her powers of decision from a very early age. The mother relies on her daughters for carrying out certain well-defined tasks—cooking, cleaning the house and looking after the youngest children.

Thus the assurance of Merina and other Malagasy women, whose evolution is being accelerated by a rise in their standard of living, can be accounted for by this training within the family. As a result, the women appear intellectually free, are well able to face up to difficulties and are open to all kinds of knowledge. They have a certain facility in learning and in acquiring culture, and they appear to have a strong desire to succeed when they undertake courses of study.

These positive aspects of the position of women in Madagascar are to some extent counteracted by certain rigid attitudes which they inherit regarding their relations with men. As a result of her education within the family where the boy is her superior and is served and looked after by her, a woman who has attained a high level of education may still feel a certain inferiority with respect to a man having the same, or even a lower, level of education as herself. Thus, a conflict may arise within a family, with the woman feeling herself bound to give respect to the man as the head of the family but refusing at the same time to be subordinate to him intellectually. This may be expressed by a certain aggressiveness, especially in discussion. In many Merina families the woman appears to dominate the man and to take all major decisions concerning the house and the children. The weekly or monthly pay-packet is usually handed over entirely to the woman, who meets all expenses and allows her husband what she feels is necessary for his needs.

Women will certainly play an increasing role in public life in Madagascar, which already has many prominent women lawyers, doctors, teachers and businesswomen. As education transforms the social structures of the coastal peoples, a similar tendency appears, and already among these peoples, where women were subordinate a few years ago, intellectually active women are emerging to take part in the direction of many affairs. This does not tie in with the point of view of many Malagasy men, who still regard the woman as a delicate object, an element of prestige within the family and quite unfitted for certain matters. However, the emergence of women as powerful personalities and as leaders had begun before the conquest, and has continued with the spread of education and the intellectual development of women who have benefited from Western knowledge. The Malagasy woman, with her dynamism, her courage and her intellectual capacity, represents a very considerable capital for the future development of the country.

Education has transformed Madagascar in the present century, but this is also because the Malagasy seized on education with an avidity not always seen elsewhere. The rapid spread of education and the intellectual level quickly achieved by many Malagasy, both men and women, after the introduction of Western methods of education was not merely because this was the policy firstly of the missions and later of the French colonial administration. In fact, the latter, in common with other colonial governments, had considerable doubts as to the wisdom of rapid educational development. The rapid spread has been due mainly to the intellectual capacity of the Malagasy people and to their facility for absorbing and utilising Western knowledge. In this they resemble more than a little the Japanese, and it is interesting to note that an article published in 1913, which described the rapid absorption of

Western technology by the Japanese,* was the spark which lit a whole political movement, seen first in the Vy, Vato, Sakelika (vvs)† students 'plot' of 1916, but growing into the beginnings of a movement for national independence over the next thirty years.

The development of education in Madagascar during the nineteenth century, from the introduction of the first schools in Tananarive by the LMS missionary Jones in 1820, is a matter of history, and is described in Chapter 4, below. It was once again General Galliéni who laid the foundations of an education programme which continued until independence in 1960. Very soon after the conquest, a Director of Education was appointed by the General, and, at the time of Galliéni's departure in 1905, there were already many schools operated by the administration, apart from the mission schools. Galliéni himself stated: 'The question of education exerts such a strong influence on the political and economic condition of a country that it is impossible for the higher administration to be indifferent to it'. He thus appears to have attached the same importance to education as Lugard did to land communications in British colonies.

Galliéni's successors did not have exactly the same ideas concerning the number of Malagasy who should be trained or the level to which they should be brought. Access to French schools, established primarily for French residents' and officials' children, was limited to children of those Malagasy who had acquired French citizenship by assimilation under the Decrees of 1909 and 1930. This education was expensive, and the Malagasy were thus under a considerable disadvantage. Access to higher education was limited by the small numbers admitted to the lycées (secondary schools).

The establishment of several thousand settlers in Madagascar and the organisation of the colonial administration, together with the attitude of Europeans of that time towards the advancement of colonial peoples, did not favour the advancement of Malagasy beyond a certain point. While a small elite, which studied in French lycées in Madagascar and took degrees in universities in France, was allowed to develop, there was no question of admitting any significant number of Malagasy to senior posts. Training

* See Chapter 5. This article, by Ravelojaona greatly impressed the Malagasy intellectuals of the time, who felt that it could also happen in Madagascar.

† 'Iron, stone, shoots' in translation.

institutes were run for forty years after Galliéni's departure to provide competent 'middle grade' Malagasy employees for the administration and for business.

This was the chief function of the écoles régionales, of which the most important was the Ecole Myre de Villiers in Tananarive, which trained Malagasy middle-grade civil servants. These regional schools were reorganised by the Decree of October 1933 concerning official education in Madagascar. Under this, education for Malagasy was divided into three stages. First, there was elementary schooling, including the teaching of French. Second, there were regional schools, themselves having two branches: preparation for further special education; and preparation of specialised workers for employment in industry, commerce and by settlers (trade schools). Third, there was the Ecole Myre de Villiers, which trained candidates for the colonial civil service in Madagascar and industrial apprentices. In this school the subjects taught were French, Malagasy, geography, mathematics, natural science, chemistry and physics. In spite of apparent barriers, there were a significant number of Malagasy in French lycées by 1938, when the Lycée Galliéni in Tananarive had 250 Malagasy and 392 French pupils. In 1947 the figures for the same establishment were 438 Malagasy and 392 French pupils.

In line with the new colonial policies laid down at the Brazzaville Conference of 1944 presided over by General de Gaulle, the Medical Academy founded by the Protestant missions in 1886 was transformed into a School of Medicine (the first in the French Union) in 1946, and a School of Law and a School of Agriculture were opened in Tananarive in the same year. In that year, the official schools numbered 1,074, with 120,000 pupils, and the mission schools had 93,000 pupils. Secondary school pupils for the whole country had increased from 1,782 in 1930 to 3,297 in 1946, though these were still concentrated in and around Tananarive.

In 1951 a Conseil Consultatif de l'Enseignement with substantial Malagasy representation was set up by Governor-General Bargues; this was followed by a Decree in November 1951, again reorganising the educational system, this time with the aim of abolishing as far as possible the division between French and Malagasy systems as practised in the respective schools. Under this reorganisation the regional schools became cours complémentaires, a form of preliminary secondary schooling, while the

Madagascar

Ecole Myre de Villiers, became a collège administratif, with six sections—teacher training, medicine, judiciary, post office, technical and administrative—for preliminary training, with a view to government or private employment in specific jobs. Under this reform, the same examinations were established for Malagasy and French, but the accent was still on the training of 'middle-grade' civil servants, who could not rise beyond a certain grade.

At independence, the main problem was the excessive concentration of secondary and further education in and around Tananarive, which had favoured the Merina and effectively barred the coastal peoples from rising in any numbers to responsible posts. Thus decentralisation of education at all levels has been the major objective and lycées have been rapidly created in all provinces.

In 1964 the objective of the First Five-Year Plan concerning the percentage of school attendance for the whole population had been set at 52·8 per cent for 1968 and in 1967 this percentage had already been reached. The number of educational establishments and pupils are shown in the table below.

	1965–66	*1966–67*	*1968–69*
Primary Schools	2,652	2,934	3,527
pupils	491,693	536,443	598,488
Secondary Schools (lycées)	11	12	12
pupils	11,089	12,578	13,762
Collèges d'enseignement général:	52	58	72
pupils	7,540	8,373	10,913
University of Tananarive			
students (Malagasy)	2,385	3,107	3,430
(French)	528	499	530
Teacher training colleges			
lower	7	7	7
trainees	205	250	300
higher	2	2*	2
trainees	408	421	570

(*Source: Rapport sur l'Activité du Gouvernement*, Présidence de la République, Tananarive 1967 and 1969.)

* The two Ecoles Normales at Tananarive train 'cadres B'; the Institut National Supérieur de Recherche et de Formation Pédagogique, created with UNESCO assistance, trains 'cadres A' who teach in lycées.

Apart from decentralisation of schooling to cover all provinces, government policy is to reform what is taught in schools and how it is taught, and to step up the training of Malagasy teachers, so as to be less reliant on French technical assistance, in 1968 reinforced by Canadian volunteer teachers.

The reform of primary schooling, based on full use of the Malagasy language—which was felt to be more in line with the economic and social realities of the country—was carried out in 1965. Pupils who stop their schooling at this level have less use for French. However, in secondary and higher education, French is used, and Malagasy can be taken as a special subject either in the baccalauréat or as part of an arts degree in the faculté des lettres.

The University of Madagascar was created immediately after independence and grouped already existing faculties of law, agriculture and medicine. It should be noted that these faculties trained students for the first parts of degree courses which were continued in France, and that only in 1968 was a move in progress towards complete training in such disciplines in Madagascar. Although the number of Malagasy studying in French universities is diminishing, in 1967 there were still 186 students (of whom 79 were girls) studying in France. Of these, 13 were medical students, 13 dental, 15 pharmacy, 12 agronomy, and 52 in various higher technical fields. The University of Madagascar was created almost entirely with funds supplied by France, and the teaching staff in 1968 included 105 French and 47 Malagasy. The buildings are fine but not exaggeratedly luxurious and are situated on hills to the east of Tananarive, near the observatory. The government party, the Parti Social Democrate (PSD), has done much to raise funds and has constructed a large students' hostel. Technical training is carried out in a large number of institutes. Teachers are trained in the Ecole Normale Nationale de l'Enseignement Technique in Tananarive, with a similar institute in Diego-Suarez. Schools of public works, telecommunications, maritime engineering, mechanical engineering and a number of others have been created or enlarged since 1960.

Many of the problems found in organising education in developing countries appear in Madagascar. Present teaching curricula are still based largely on those of France, although in France

87

reforms are taking place and much questioning is going on concerning the future orientation of its schools and universities. With a comparatively high rate of intake into secondary and higher education, Madagascar should be able to supply trained people in considerable numbers within a very few years. Whether these can be absorbed within the economy is a matter for the orientation of present development programmes, but already the problem of finding jobs for a quite large number of intelligent and well-trained persons of both sexes is beginning to arise in Madagascar. Their satisfactory absorption will be necessary if social strains and future political unrest are to be avoided. Their absorption will depend on the rate of expansion of the economy, and on how fast new industries and new services can be established within the resources of the nation. But there should be no pessimism concerning this output of well-trained young people who provide a capital which may well produce considerable economic change within Madagascar; trained Malagasy may also to go work in neighbouring countries.

Medical degrees were the first university qualifications to be acquired by Malagasy; the first Malagasy graduated from the University of Edinburgh in 1881 Under French colonisation, the work of training local medical personnel was carried on, although the graduates of the Ecole de Médécine at Befalatanana in Tananarive were only locally qualified; their degree did not allow them to practise outside Madagascar. A small number of Malagasy did, however, study medicine in France and obtain degrees there which put them on an equal footing with French doctors in government service. A corps of Malagasy midwives was created under Galliéni, and during his administration very considerable progress was made in creating a national health organisation, with the help of French army doctors. These officers have played a dominant part in creating and staffing the health services of Madagascar, and in 1968 there were still many army doctors serving in the country. Madagascar was the first French colony to organise its medical service. At Galliéni's departure in 1905, his health service had created 38 hospitals, 56 dispensaries, 35 maternity units and 11 leper hospitals.

At the time of the colonisation, malaria was a fatal disease, and accounted largely for the high infant mortality which kept population growth at a very low rate.* From 1948, when intensive programmes of control were undertaken, together with prophylactic administration of quinine and related anti-malarial drugs, the mortality rate fell sharply. The rapid rise in the growth-rate of the population dates from the anti-malarial campaign. Leprosy is still an endemic problem, and in 1966 there were in Madagascar 31,101 known lepers, of whom 18,913 were receiving treatment and 2,341 were clinically cured but still under observation. Here again certain French army doctors have played an important part in organising and running leprosaria, but the work of certain missions—such as the leper hospital run by the Capuchin fathers at Ambanja (with a lay mission doctor), and that at Manankavaly run by the Protestant missions—has been most important. Malagasy doctors themselves took a lead in organising local voluntary assistance, headed for many years by the late Dr Raharijaona, and have received aid from various international bodies. Leprosy, which can today be cured by the timely administration of certain drugs, remains a social problem, since cured lepers will not be readmitted to their villages. Schemes have therefore been undertaken to create new villages and settle cured lepers on land of their own, again with international help for equipment and supplies. Bubonic plague was endemic at the time of the colonisation and reappeared sporadically for many years. In 1965 only ten cases were known to have occurred.

Health problems in Madagascar concern especially preventative medicine, and priority was given under the First Five-Year Plan to improving control of leprosy, tuberculosis and venereal diseases. Together with these preventative programmes, health education has been spread in rural districts by teams of women trained in nutrition, the Equipes féminines d'éducation nutritionnelle (EFEN), and nutrition education has been introduced into courses run for other disciplines in Tananarive. Mother and child health clinics have been established in all parts of the country and in 1965 gave 874,000 prenatal and 657,000 postnatal consultations.

The Plan had as an objective the creation by 1968 of 15,000 new hospital beds over and above the 14,150 beds existing in 1963. This objective was reached at 100 per cent in the urban zones, and

* Comparative figures for infantile mortality for 1925: Paris, 86 to 89 per 1,000; Tamatave, 300 per 1,000; Tananarive, 159 to 177 per 1,000.

at 95 per cent in the rural districts. A total of 14,800 new hospital beds had been created by 1968.

Public Health Services (Situation in 1970)

	Number	Beds
Main hospitals and specialised centres	11	5,395
Small hospitals, medical centres, and midwifery centres	478	11,176
Bush dispensaries	113	391
Total	602	16,962
Leper colonies	16	
Specialised dispensaries	16	
X-ray posts	62	
Mobile health teams	11	
Mother and child protection centres		
(main)	6	
(secondary)	16	
Health groups (with MCH functions)	625	

Personnel

Doctors	514	Dentists	14
Pharmacists	34	Midwives	650

At the time of the French conquest, Madagascar, unlike the African colonies, possessed not only a highly developed body of customary law but a written code of laws.[3] Of these the most important was the 'Code of 305 Articles of March 29, 1881', which had classified the principles of law handed down from the past, while improving them and arranging them in order. The history of organised law in Madagascar begins with the *kabary* (edicts) of Andrianampoinimerina (1782–1810), as related in the *Tantara ny Andriana*, or Royal Chronicles. The king brought together a mass of customs and usages already in being; since there existed no other written documents of customary law.

The traditional laws and customs of Madagascar show the same unity as is found in other aspects of Malagasy culture. Among the characteristics originating in Asia are held to be the predominance of patrilineal descent, taboos against endogamy, legal freedom of women, adoption as a frequent practice and the collective property rights of the extended family. Deschamps considers that in certain parts of the country African customs have been brought in with slaves from Moçambique, such as the rights of the maternal uncle and some survivals of matriarchy. [4]

The codified laws of 1881 were those of Imerina, for at that time the Merina monarchy held sway over nearly all the other peoples of Madagascar. Article 263 of the 'Code of 305 Articles' states that customs which have been in use for a long time and which are still applied have the same force as the present written laws. This principle is still widely applied in the present period of codification and creation of a unified body of Malagasy law. In 1960 a commission was set up by the government, charged with preparing the Civil Code of Laws. The government's desire is to obtain a system of legislation which is both simple and up-to-date, and at the same time to introduce a uniform system of laws for the whole country. The commission has therefore been instructed to study and collect all customs and usages now in force among the different peoples of Madagascar and to codify the civil law contained therein and the procedures. A commission on commercial law and a comission for the reform of crimminal law have also been set up, as also a commission to establish exact translations of legislative texts into Malagasy and to fix the judicial vocabulary.

The basis of Madagascar's social structure is the *fomba*, or customs, which are rigorously prescribed so that it is absolutely clear to anyone what he may and may not do in all circumstances of his life. Taboos are called *fady*; these are what he must on no account do, without running the risk of incurring the displeasure of the ancestors or of God himself. These customs and interdictions are the framework of everyday behaviour.

It appears that Andrianampoinimerina, in his *kabary* which first codified the traditional law, wished to define all the legal questions that appeared to him to be fundamental to the lives of his people. Thus he wished to regulate the organisation of the family, to protect his subjects and to install some kind of judicial organisation. First, therefore, he regulated marriage, defining the consent of the couple, the *vodiondry** or gift made at the time of the engagement, repudiation or divorce and polygamy. He defined paternal authority and laid the foundations of Merina practice concerning wills and succession. He organised the distribution of and titles to land and the rules of procedure in cases of disputes about land. Various degrees of judgement were laid down,

* Literally, 'sheeps' rump'.

although in the last resort it was the king (or queen) who uttered the final judgement. Following his edicts, certain fundamental principles appear throughout all the written codes which later classified the *kabary* of Andrianampoinimerina; the authority of the *ray aman-dreny* (the fathers and elders), the cohesion of the extended family, the legal freedom of women, the juridical survival of the personality in succession and the flexibility of the marriage bond.

Over the next sixty years (1830–90) seven written texts appeared, each adding to and rounding out the earlier ones. While the kings borrowed the idea of codified laws from the Continent, it is clear that they were also strongly influenced by Anglo-Saxon legal principles, and above all by the pragmatism of Anglo-Saxon law whereby a great part is made by the decisions of judges. In the royal archives are to be found a number of translations of law books and essays on English law, while in 1885 Tacchi prepared a small compendium of English law for the use of the royal house.* Legislation concerning landed property was inspired by the Torrens Act of Australia, and on the proposal of Laroche, the French Resident, Queen Ranavalona III introduced a law of March 9, 1896, by which titles to land could be legally recognised after a court decision had confirmed, after examination, the claim of the occupant to ownership.

The powers of the judiciary emerge clearly from legal decisions made between 1837 and 1896. Justice is a function of the state and is exercised by officials representing the royal authority. Justice thus stems from the sovereign and judgements are made in his name. The role of the judge is to correct by his sentence a disequilibrium in society which has been caused by the transgression. Judgement had a sacred character as emanating from the sovereign which made it inviolable and indisputable.

After the French conquest, it was declared by a Decree of December 1, 1900, that the 'Code of 305 Articles' was applicable over the whole territory of Madagascar. At the same time it was stated that France would respect Malagasy law and customs except where, as with slavery and recognition of castes, these were contrary to certain principles. In fact the French administration applied only the Merina law, through assessors in local courts

* He also wrote *Tacchi's Money Tables*, published in Tananarive in 1890.

who were all Merina. At the same time it was declared that all French laws existing at the time of the conquest would apply to Madagascar. Thus, so long as there were two classes of citizens, there were two systems of law. All French citizens and assimilated citizens under the Decrees of 1909 and of 1930 were judged in French tribunals under French laws. The Malagasy were judged in 'native courts' under the Merina laws, and could furthermore be sentenced summarily by a district commissioner, as being subject to the restrictions of the 'indigénat' or second-class status.

In 1961 the commission set up to prepare the Civil Code conducted a nation-wide enquiry into the customs relating to the rights of the person and of the family. At the same time it was explained that this enquiry was to establish common features and arrive at a uniform practice and not to perpetuate local differences. A vast amount of material has thus been collected, and the task is to produce a uniform code, which at the same time preserves the beneficial effects of sixty years' association with French law.

Modern law has become familiar to Madagascar since the establishment of French courts in 1896. Under a decision of the Tananarive Court of Appeal, and confirmed by a decree of 1909, judges could apply French law wherever Malagasy law appeared to be insufficient or non-existent. Since many Malagasy have thus lived according to two sets of statutes, a number of problems have arisen since independence. An attempt to resolve these was made in 1961 by the passing of a new law concerning the 'civil status', which set up uniform procedures for establishing declarations and obtaining certificates of births, deaths and marriages.

This duality is seen in respect of persons, whereby the Malagasy law holds that a person may be patrilineal or matrilineal according to the custom of his people, and also by giving legal force to the claims and responsibilities of what anthropologists call the 'extended family'. Within this extended family, authority is exerted by the eldest son of the eldest branch. In general, any individual is subject to a whole range of taboos and interdictions, and the family can subject him to discipline of which the worst punishment would be 'rejection from the family tomb'. The basic social bond is the right to be buried in the same tomb. This is preserved even among people who have migrated far from their native village.

Children are, in a certain manner, the property of the extended family and it is common to see children, particularly of a large family, distributed and brought up by uncles and aunts and grandparents. Traditional Malagasy society does not attach the same importance to legitimacy and affiliation as do Western jurists; thus in traditional custom the child belongs to the whole extended family and not only to a father and mother.

The rights of property are far more the rights of the extended family than those of any one individual, but many Malagasy living outside their community of origin have acquired a 'Roman' conception of property. Thus, several systems of land tenure exist side by side. Land registration, as a result of a court decision, has been in operation since the Law of 1896. The decree of September 28, 1926, confirmed the right of ownership to land if proof of occupation prior to 1896 could be established. Such land is registered in the central land registry office (Service des Domaines), which issues title deeds, and the Service Topographique demarcates the property with official boundary stones. This procedure was also applied to certain large concessions granted to individuals and companies during the French colonial period. Over very large regions outside Imerina, customary land tenure systems have the force of law and are administered by village chiefs and councils of elders (*fokon'olona*). The greater part of all land in Madagascar is held to be state land ('terrain domanial') and is administered by the central land registry office in the Ministry of Agriculture.

Modern civil law has transformed and supplanted many traditions and customs, particularly where Malagasy living in towns far from their place of origin are concerned. There is a slow dissolution of the clan, and the small Western-style restricted family begins to become more important where these more sophisticated people base their lives on a small family unit.

The government is in the process of establishing a Civil Code which, so far as possible, will be a harmonious synthesis of the major systems of customary law but which will apply a uniform system to the whole country. The principles guiding this codification are that it should be original and authentically Malagasy, that it should be uniform, modern, simple and easy to understand. It is intended that the code shall be accessible to the people through clear editions in the Malagasy language, which is the task of the linguistic commission preparing the exact equivalent in Malagasy of juridical terminology.

The comparatively high degree of organisation existing within Malagasy society is quite striking. This arises partly because of the linguistic and underlying cultural unity of the nation and partly because of its Asiatic origins. It may be assumed that the first immigrants came from organised societies and that they preserved the essential structures. The stability arising from this organisation is seen not only within the family unit but also within the village community, where many of the traditional functions concerning maintenance of order, division of land, cleanliness of streets and so on existed before the French conquest and have been utilised by all administrations since then. There exist, of course, important local variations in the nature and degree of such social organisation, and customs and usage are by no means uniform; but a basic sense of order and a degree of homogeneity have considerably assisted the work of evolving an efficient territorial administration.

4. State and Politics : 1800-1896

THE HISTORY of the development of political unity in Madagascar sometimes appears as if it were the exclusive work of the Merina. This is partly because their expansion is the best-documented, since they were in close contact with Europeans, particularly missionaries, who were prolific writers.

However, the Sakalava peoples established an expansionist feudal-type monarchy in the sixteenth century, nearly two centuries before Radama I, and rapidly imposed over two-thirds of the country the first political organisation that Madagascar had seen, beyond petty kingdoms. The prestige of the Sakalava semi-divine kings has come down to present times and the funeral ceremonies of descendants of their royal and princely families, who are buried in *doany* situated on *mahabo* or small hills, continue with great pomp for many days. Hereditary guardians watch over these tombs from one generation to the next.

The origin of the Sakalava royal families appears to have been among the small tribes of the south-east, around Fort Dauphin (the Antambahaoka, Antaimoro, Antaisaka, Antaifasy, Zafisoro and Antanosy.) Traditions speak of the founders of the dynasties of the Sakalava, Bara, Mahafaly and Antandroy as recent immigrants who brought in new ideas of royalty and political organisation. It is interesting to speculate whether the last wave of Malayo-Polynesian navigators, bringing more advanced techniques and a superior intellectual development, was enabled to impose itself as a monarchy and nobility on more primitive earlier arrivals. It was the south-east that had seen much Arab and Islamic influence prior to the fifteenth century by the Sunnite ancestors of the Antaimoro, emigrating from their earlier settlements at Vohémar.

It was from among these tribes that the Sakalava dynasty of the Maroserano originated. Under King Andriandahifotsy ('the white man'), they expanded rapidly, establishing the kingdom of Menabe which extended at his death (about 1685) from Mangoky river to the north of Maintirano. His successor, Andriamandisoarivo, continued this advance and occupied all the west coast up to Majunga and Marovoay, thus gaining control of ports and of trade with the outside world. This enabled him to acquire arms and ammunition of a higher standard than those of the scattered populations who opposed him. At his death about 1710, the Sakalava kingdoms of Menabe and Boina controlled all the vast but sparsely-populated western zone of Madagascar, their frontiers being the shifting boundaries of the other organised kingdoms of the Merina. Sihanaka, Betsileo and Masikoro.

The nineteenth century is divided, for Madagascar, into three periods. The first saw a rapid penetration of European religion and technology in Imerina as a result of the political unification of the Merina under Andrianampoinimerina (1787–1810) and continued by Radama I (1810–28). The second period saw an extreme xenophobic reaction under Queen Ranavalona I (1828–61). This was followed by increasing French penetration of the Merina state, which culminated in the conquest of 1896.

Andrianampoinimerina enlarged the Merina kingdom from an area extending to about twenty miles around Tananarive until it included the greater part of the Hauts-Plateaux, absorbing all the feudal rulers of the Merina tribe and also the Betsileo kingdoms to the south. He was not only a conqueror but also a considerable organiser, and thus he laid the foundations of the Merina state which provided the leverage for future European penetration of Madagascar. His conquests were assured by considerable purchases or firearms and by his talent for organising an elite corps (*tsindranolahy*). Disposing thus of a small but well-armed and disciplined force, he was able rapidly to subdue or secure the allegiance of his neighbours. In addition, he secured new economic resources by land reclamation and the annexation of valleys, which greatly increased supplies of rice. Many of the great drainage canals which still serve the plain of Betsimitatra around Tananarive were first designed and dug during his reign. For this he obliged freemen to furnish free labour, and the corvée (*fanompoana*) was widely used to secure the execution of public works. The corvée, subsequently used by the French colonisers for road-building and other public works, was thus not a colonial invention, as has often been claimed. Forced labour represents a forced capital formation similar to a levy on monetary capital; at that time it was the only method available to rulers for mobilising the sole capital available, the underemployed manpower resources.

The organisation of the state used existing structures but gave them the greatly increased authority of the king. Andrianampoini-merina was an absolute ruler, but he utilised public meetings (*kabary*) at which, through stylised speeches, he explained his intentions, obtained the acclamation of the people and gave them a sense of participation. These *kabary* remain an integral part of public life in Madagascar today, and are used by all public figures, from the President of the republic to rural mayors. The *kabary*, illustrated freely with the proverbs (*ohabolana*), in which the Malagasy tradition is rich, are given with a certain fixed style. Questions are put for the acclamation of the crowd, which replies; advice is given, the deity is invoked, the ancestral customs are illustrated as being respected. The style of former rulers is still used today under the republic.

The family organisation or clan (*foko*) had its council of elders, the *fokon'olona*, which regulated the affairs of the village, especially those concerned with the apportionment and use of land. Villages in the fragmented feudal society of Imerina were derived mainly from individual family groups, and the inhabitants were thus of one clan of *foko*, under the authority of a 'squire' (*tompomenakely*). The conquests of Andrianampoinimerina put an end to this anarchy and, by centring the principle of authority on himself instead of on the local *tompomenakely*, he laid down the hierarchy of obedience which was most marked under the Merina monarchy and constitutes today an essential part of the Malagasy character. The *fokon'olona* was given responsibility for maintaining public order and for executing the king's decisions as declared in his *kabary*. It organised the corvée for public works and had the power of arrest of petty criminals. Many of these powers have been redefined and confirmed by the republican government by an ordinance of 1962.

The king's immediate counsellors were twelve wise men chosen from those who had helped him in his rise to power, while a wider council of seventy *vadin-tany* ('husbands of the land') chosen from all free castes acted as roving inspectors and judges of the king. The army ensured the maintenance of this power, and was organised by periodic levies of freemen, centred on a small permanent force. These territorials shared the booty resulting from conquests. Slaves (*andevo*) were excluded from the army.

The economic basis was secured by land distribution, and by undertaking reclamation through mobilisation of labour under the corvée. The king declared himself sole owner of the land: 'The land is mine' ('*Ahy ny tany*'). Much redistribution was undertaken to ensure that each family produced a maximum of rice. He appears to have aimed at the eventual unity of Madagascar, declaring 'the sea is the limit of my paddy field' ('*ny riaka no valamparihiko*'), but he was intensely suspicious of the Europeans on the coast and forbad their installation in Tananarive. His main source of monetary income appears to have come from the sale of slaves to the Mascarene islands.[1] These were captives of his military expeditions against his neighbours, and were thus probably Betsileo and Sihanaka, since his conquests had annexed these two tribes. The Malagasy slaves had long had a reputation for indocility, and often escaped into the interior of the Mascarenes where they lived as bandits and raided the plantations to which they had been sold. The income from the sales of slaves served largely to buy guns and ammunition, which were furnished by French, Comorian and Creole traders on the coast.

His successor, Radama I, was chosen by him from among twenty-four children. It was under Radama that Madagascar was truly opened up to European penetration. He not only consolidated and expanded the territorial conquests of his father, but he also introduced European techniques, which he much admired. His reign saw a massive penetration of English Protestant missionaries who, in addition to the Gospel, introduced a number of skilled artisans. These years saw the beginning of entirely new building techniques and of a number of artisan industries and, most important of all, the introduction of reading and writing, when the Malagasy language was finally written in Latin characters.

The background to these changes was the strategic importance gained by the Mascarene islands as a result of the Napoleonic Wars. In 1810, Britain had seized the French possessions, Ile Bourbon and Ile de France, and Tamatave was taken in 1811. The Treaty of 1814 restored Ile Bourbon, now called La Réunion, to France but Britain kept Ile de France, which took its old Dutch name of Mauritius. The governors of Mauritius, especially Sir Robert Farquhar, who had served in the East Indies, followed various independent lines. Communications with London took several months, and the anti-French feeling stirred up during the Napoleonic Wars appears to have incited these officials to combat French interests in Madagascar.

The picture is rather familiar. Throughout the nineteenth century, local representatives of colonial powers were annexing and presenting their reluctant governments with a fait accompli, often when public opinion at home was opposed to any further colonies. Farquhar's policies were not unlike those of Lugard, eighty years later. He began by refusing to return the French trading posts on the east coast of Madagascar, which had been seized after the Treaty of Paris in 1814, and by attempting to establish one himself in the Bay of Antongil, where Benyowski had reigned some years before as 'Emperor'. Although the British government ordered the return of these posts in 1816 and refused its support for a British post, Farquhar resolutely continued his own colonial policy. The rise of the Merina state had been fully reported to Farquhar, and he acted brilliantly to exploit it, using the monarchy as his agent to secure further control of Madagascar. His Creole agent in Mauritius, Barthélémy Huet de Froberville,* kept him fully informed on events in Madagascar, and another agent, Chardenoux, was sent in 1816 to bring two brothers of King Radama to Mauritius for education.

Farquhar followed up his advantage by sending a one-man military mission in the person of Sergeant James Hastie, formerly of the Indian army. The reorganisation of the Merina army and its weapons and techniques was one of the first results of the new contact with Europeans. But French rivalry intervened: a former soldier in Napoleon's army, from Réunion, Robin, became Radama's secretary and was a principal agent of the introduction of the Latin alphabet. In 1820 there were three sergeants around the King, the third being a Jamaican half-caste, Brady, also an army instructor.

Radama's two young brothers had been received with particular care by Farquhar in Mauritius, and had received part of their education under the care of Hastie, then the Governor's private secretary. The British thus created a favourable impression in the mind of Radama, and this opened the way to further contacts.

Radama was determined to continue the conquests of his father

---

* De Froberville was the author of *Le Grand Dictionnaire de Madagascar*, a detailed description of the country in five volumes. This remained in manuscript form in the British Museum until 1963, when the *Bulletin de Madagascar* began to publish an edition prepared by Jean Valette and Flavien Ranaivo.

Andrianampoinimerina, and extend the Merina kingdom to the sea coast. For this he needed arms and military instructors, and these could be obtained only by increased contacts with Europeans. In a *kabary* given in Tananarive, he explained his project to the people, following the practice of his father. 'This is why I shall bring in the Europeans. I tell you, my people, I am going to create an army. The foreigners will instruct our soldiers and make them the horns of the country and of the state. They will bring us cannon, guns, powder, flints and bullets, and it is with these that we shall create our country and our state.'[2] Farquhar, on his side, was given an opportunity by the recently-enacted Abolition of the Slave Trade Act, 1807. If the Foreign Office would not support him in his earlier attempts to oust the French from their trading posts on the east coast and install British agents in their places, they could not oppose him if he carried out the provisions of a recent Act of Parliament which had the weight of public, and especially of Protestant, opinion in Britain behind it. Farquhar thus proposed to Radama to supply him with the arms and instructors which he needed, if, in return, he would sign a treaty abolishing the export of slaves from Madagascar. At this time the slaves were exported to Réunion and Mauritius from the east coast, which was still controlled by a number of Betsimisaraka chiefs, and in particular the Zana-Malata, who carried out their annual slave-raiding expeditions on the Comoro islands and East Africa, and also traded in Malagasy slaves with the planters of the Mascarene islands. Radama was not in any way in control of this coast, but Farquhar's tactics were to give him the force necessary to bring it under control, and thus finally open Imerina to the outside world.

The negotiations had been begun by the Mauritian trader, Chardenoux, sent by Farquhar to persuade Radama to send his brothers to Mauritius. In 1817 Hastie was given definite instructions by the Governor and arrived in Tananarive, where he was well received by Radama; Hastie noted in his diary that he spent most of each day with the King.[3] The signature of this treaty was a politically delicate matter for Radama, since it went against the interests of a number of notables who earned large revenues from the sale of slaves. On the other hand, the class of freemen, the hova, among whom were small traders and artisans and who were sometimes themselves sold into slavery, would support the abolition of this trade.

Many *kabary* or public meetings were held between August and October 1817, some of the meetings gathering 5,000 people, and the treaty was finally signed at Tamatave on October 23. It would appear that Radama convinced the notables that the advantages of greatly increased trade with the outside world would outweigh the loss of revenues from slave exports. Farquhar agreed on behalf of the British government to pay an annual subsidy of two thousand pounds in lieu of compensation, and some of this may have been used to persuade influential opponents. The total subsidy was stated as an annual payment of 1,000 dollars in gold, 1,000 dollars in silver, 100 barrels of powder, 100 guns, and uniforms. In the text of the treaty Radama was declared 'King of Madagascar', being thus officially recognised by Britain as the de jure sovereign of the whole island.

Farquhar went on leave in 1817, and his replacement, General Hall, refused to pay the subsidy; thus, on Farquhar's return in 1820, new negotiations were necessary. Hastie was again sent to Tananarive in 1820, this time with the title of British Resident. Apparently he was able to convince the King that, in any case, the British navy would prevent the resumption of slave exports, and a new treaty was signed on October 11, 1820. In one of the clauses, the British government undertook to educate twenty young Malagasy.

The period of military reorganisation and conquest now began in earnest, with Hastie as the principal instrument, aided by the other two sergeants, Robin and Brady. The first expedition to the east coast had enabled Radama to install a garrison in Tamatave in 1817, and Imerina was opened to the outside world. The occupation of Tamatave, which had been a French trading post until 1811, caused the French government to reoccupy the island of Ste Marie in 1821 with a small force under Sylvain Roux, who had been the French agent in Tamatave at the time of its evacuation. The pattern of colonial penetration is thus a familiar one. Arms were supplied to Radama to reinforce his own position, and he found himself temporarily committed to Britain in the face of what appeared to be French countermoves.

The three sergeants were promoted generals, and Hastie combined the position of British Resident with that of commanding

officer of the newly-organised Malagasy army. This was transformed from a band of armed irregulars operating only in the dry
season into a force of 14,000 men organised in six brigades, together with 600 artillerymen and 600 engineers.[4] The army was
trained on parade-grounds such as Mahamasina (where the sports
stadium now stands in Tananarive), given shooting-practice, and
the corps of officers was organised. Equipped with guns and cannon left over from the Napoleonic Wars, the army had no equivalent opponent in Madagascar, and Radama was able rapidly to
expand his power over most of the island.

The Sakalava feudal-type monarchy contained elements of
social instability inherent in a transhumant cattle people, occupying vast almost uninhabited spaces. Moving freely across empty
country, the bonds uniting the subjects to the king were fragile and
fighting between rival candidates broke out on the death of each
king. Thus the Merina, a small minority occupying the central
highlands but bound together in a social and military organisation
under a series of dynamic rulers, were able effectively to subdue
those peoples with a less stable economic and political base. Their
first conquest of the Sakalava kingdoms, carried out by Radama I
in 1822–24, was facilitated by disputes over the succession of the
lately deceased king of Menabe, Mikala.

Military posts, with Merina governors, were established in
the outlying provinces, at Fort Dauphin, Tamatave, Mahabo and
Marovoay. These settlements also acted as trading posts for
imported goods. The western kingdom of the Sakalava was subdued in 1824, and the King, Andriantsoli,* took refuge with the
Sultan of Zanzibar. Radama's last expedition, in 1825, captured
Fort Dauphin from its skeleton French garrison of five soldiers
and subdued the greater part of the south-west. By 1825, therefore,
the plan of Farquhar had succeeded. The greater part of Madagascar was under the rule of his protégé, the Merina King, Radama,
and the French had been evicted from all their posts on the east
coast except Ste Marie. Hastie, who had led several of these
expeditions, was elevated to the high rank of '12 Honours' (12
Voninahitra) under the Malagasy version of his name, Rainihasy,
before he died in Tananarive in 1826.

Parallel to this military expansion was the no less remarkable

* He subsequently became Sultan of Mayotte in the Comoro islands.

penetration of Imerina by the missionaries sent by the London Missionary Society (LMS). At one of the earliest meetings of the directors of the LMS, held in 1796, the possibility of a mission in Madagascar was discussed, and the society used its agents in Cape Colony and Mauritius to gather information about the island. Farquhar, as part of his plan, wrote to the LMS before 1817, urging them to undertake missionary work in Madagascar and promising them his support. He thus ensured support for his own activities from the influential section of Protestant public opinion which had secured the abolition of the slave trade.

The story of the first penetration is sad, but indicates clearly the personal bravery of missionaries, entering with their families into unknown tropical countries, with no protection against tropical diseases and none of the comforts and amenities that Europeans in the tropics today take for granted. In November 1818, the Reverend David Jones of the LMS landed with his wife and child at Tamatave. In January 1819, the Reverend Thomas Bevan landed with his wife and child, to find that Mrs Jones and her child had died of fever and that Jones was seriously ill. The Bevan's child died on January 20, Bevan himself on January 31 and his wife on February 3. Thus, within a few weeks of landing, five out of the six members of the two missionary families had died.[5] Jones survived the fever (probably the malignant form of malaria) and went to Mauritius to recruit his strength. This courageous and dedicated missionary returned to Madagascar with Hastie in September 1820, and was received along with the British Resident by King Radama in Tananarive. This time there was an immediate result of his mission, and the King, after hearing why he had come, sent a letter to the directors of the LMS, saying: 'I request you to send me, if convenient, as many missionaries as you may deem proper, together with their families, if they desire it, provided you send skilful artisans, to make my people workmen as well as góod Christians.'[6]

This opened the first phase of missionary work among the Merina, which lasted until the death of Radama in 1828 and the complete change of policy under his successor, Queen Ranavalona. Between 1820 and 1830 the LMS produced some remarkable results; in all, they sent fourteen missionaries. Six of these were ordained ministers and eight were missionary artisans. The artisans included a tanner, a carpenter, a blacksmith, a cotton-spinner and a printer, and it was these skills that rapidly secured a solid position for the LMS mission in Tananarive.

The dynamic qualities of the Merina people were seen not only in their military conquests but in the technology they used for organising their expansion. Now in contact with Europeans, through the east coast, they were eager to adopt other techniques and proved to be apt pupils. In a short time building techniques on the Hauts-Plateaux were transformed, and a number of artisan industries sprang up. An exchange economy already existed as a result of the transformation of external trade. The bartering of slaves against arms and ammunition was no longer possible following the application of the treaty of 1820, and trade in foodstuffs, mainly rice and cattle, began to develop. Regular trade between Tamatave and Tananarive grew up after the conquest by Radama, and a number of small industries and distilleries were created on the coast. The opening of the country to the outside world was rapid, but was greatly facilitated by the avidity with which the Merina seized on Western technology. In a short time, Radama was able to organise in and around Tananarive corporations or guilds of people skilled as stone-cutters, tin-smiths, sawyers and leather-workers. Before his death in 1828, these guilds are said to have included 4,000 members.[7]

No less remarkable was the rapid introduction after 1820 of education in the Western sense, with the active support of Radama. The Reverend David Jones, the sole survivor of the attempted settlement in Tamatave (1817–19), opened the first school beside the Palace of Andafiavaratra in Tananarive in December 1820. There were three pupils, and though parents were at first reluctant to send their children, Radama gave active encouragement, visiting the schools and distributing prizes. By 1824 there were 1,000 pupils; at Radama's death in 1828, there were 2,300 pupils, of whom one third were girls, in twenty-three schools.[8]

The first problem was to reduce the Malagasy language to writing and to establish an orthography. When the missionaries arrived, Radama had four secretaries, men from the south-east coast who could write Arabic, and the little written material that existed in Malagasy was written in Arabic characters. Sergeant Robin taught the King to write the Latin alphabet, and Radama immediately decided that Malagasy would be written in this script. The next problem was the spelling, since Robin used French pronunciation and the missionaries used English. Apparently, they compromised and agreed that Malagasy should use English consonants and French vowels, however approximately. The work of translating the Gospels into Malagasy was begun by the LMS missionaries in 1823, and, by 1827, 4,000 Malagasy could read and write.[9] New laws were now written down and fixed to the door of the royal palace. Printing followed rapidly, again introduced by the LMS. The first printing-press arrived in 1827, although the artisan printer died before its arrival, and the apparatus was set up by Cameron in 1828. The first spelling books and readers were printed at once, as well as Gospel tracts. Permission to preach in Malagasy had been given to the LMS missionaries by Radama in 1824. By March 1830, an edition of 3,000 copies of the New Testament had been printed and certainly contributed to the survival of the Christian religion during the years of repression that followed under Queen Ranavalona.

Two Europeans, one Scots and the other French, were responsible for the introduction of nearly all the important techniques at this period. James Cameron, the son of a tax-collector in Dunkeld, Scotland, came to Madagascar as an artisan-missionary in 1825 and worked first at Ambatonakanga, in Tananarive, as a builder for the LMS. It was he who first introduced the burned clay brick, whose use was to transform the aspect of Tananarive, at this time entirely composed of tall narrow wooden houses with steep pointed roofs. With constant cutting and burning, the forests were receding to the east, and bricks provided an easily available substitute. Cameron had considerable mechanical ability and he constructed simple machinery as well as a number of buildings.

The death of Radama in 1828 produced a complete change of policy regarding the Christian religion and relations with foreigners; there began a period of xenophobia and isolation that lasted for more than thirty years. The technological introductions, however, were not lost and were carried on largely by Jean Laborde, a Frenchman, who arrived in Madagascar after being shipwrecked on a voyage from India in 1831. His mechanical, technical and organising ability was greater even than that of Cameron, and, under the extreme repression of succeeding years, he was able not only to maintain European technology in Imerina but to expand it very greatly. The sudden reversal of policy also put a temporary end to British influence and saw a new French penetration, this time carried out by astute traders and technologists such as Napoléon de Lastelle and Jean Laborde. The swing towards France also assisted eventual penetration by Catholic missionaries and was decisive for the future of Madagascar. Although the British missionaries returned in 1863, and although they converted Queen Ranavalona II and members of the Merina aristocracy, they proved unable to counteract French policy which had been greatly helped by the prestige of individuals such as Laborde during the isolationist period under Ranavalona I.

On Radama's death, the reaction was rapid and brutal. The swing to isolation was a defence against foreign penetration and domination, similar to that in Morocco, Japan and China, which also tried to preserve their political independence during the period of colonial expansion by cutting off contacts with the outside world. Ranavalona I was the first queen to rule in Imerina, and therefore the royal advisers took on a new importance. Having been chosen as a wife for his son by Andrianampoinimerina, Ranavalona considered herself bound to carry on his policy of expansion and at the same time to maintain the traditions of Merina society. Her immediate adviser, Rainitsimindrana, an old man who had been a close companion and councillor of her father-in-law, represented the traditionalists who had been disturbed by the rapid innovations and the influx of foreigners encouraged by Radama.

The advisers appointed a particular companion for the Queen, known as the *mpitaiza Andriana*, literally someone 'who looks after the Queen as if she were a child'. A number of these companions succeeded each other, some of them being murdered, and gave place to a series of hereditary prime ministers. These prime ministers gradually took over the real power of government as representatives of an oligarchy of the andriana, or Merina nobility. From 1828 until the French conquest of 1896, four queens reigned, with a brief reign by a king, Radama II (1861–63), who was assassinated by the oligarchy. The prime minister was usually the husband of the queen. The exact inter-relationship of the royal family, in which the succession was determined by the choice of the oligarchy, and the family to which the prime ministers belonged is complex. The queens enjoyed almost complete freedom in their choice of what were, in effect, male concubines, not being bound even by the rigid rules of caste that applied to the nobility.

The oligarchy that emerged after the death of Radama I was drawn from families whose economic interests had been damaged by his policies of suppressing the slave trade and introducing foreign commerce. As they came to power with Queen Ranavalona, and since she is said to have been a credulous, dogmatic and energetic woman, they appear to have rapidly convinced her that only a complete reversal of policy, including a return to the religion of the ancestors, could preserve the country from foreign domination. Her reign was thus marked by a continued territorial expansion which eventually covered the whole island and a rejection of foreign contacts and trade. This did not prevent the Queen utilising a small number of foreigners, all French, who assisted in implementing her policies.

In November 1828 the Queen notified Robert Lyall, who had arrived to succeed Hastie as British Resident, that she did not recognise him and that she repudiated the treaties of 1817 and 1820 concerning the slave trade. Lyall was attacked, significantly, for allegedly having ridden a horse into the village where a royal talisman* was kept, and he was forced to leave the country. The slave trade was rapidly restored, and in 1829 the Queen signed a contract with two French traders already established on the east coast, de Lastelle and de Rontaunay, giving them wide monopolies and assuring them a supply of slaves in return for certain payments. This had the effect of rapidly reducing trade in British goods and of concentrating foreign trade in the hands of the oligarchy, using de Lastelle as their agent.[10] In 1836, the Governor of Mauritius, Sir William Nicolay, wrote to a Malagasy embassy then on its way to Europe: 'Since the accession of the Queen, British trade has fallen to half of what it was at the time of King Radama.'[11] This reduction was embarrassing for Mauritius which, with the growth of the sugar-cane plantations that occupied most of the good land on the island, was obliged to import cattle and rice to feed its growing employed population. Madagascar was the only convenient source of supply, but the oligarchy around the Queen now organised trade in these commodities so that it all passed through their hands. It appears that the Queen granted a

---

* The royal talismans (*sampy*) were called 'idols' by the Christian missionaries. They were small wooden objects, having a personality, and held to protect the kingdom. They were given guardians and were carried at the head of the army on campaign and in all state processions.

monopoly to twelve members of the royal family for the export of cattle from Tamatave.[12]

This policy of concentrating external trade in the hands of Malagasy notables and using a few foreigners as agents of national economic policy was the first step towards resisting threats of foreign intervention. France unwisely chose this moment to re-assert its presence on the east coast. Count de Villèle, who was related to large plantation owners on Réunion, became a minister to Charles x of France and sent Commandant Gourbeyre to re-occupy Tamatave, which the French had abandoned in 1811, calling on the Queen to 'recognise the historic rights of France on the east coast of Madagascar'. Gourbeyre landed with Senegalese troops and destroyed Tamatave, following which he occupied other points farther north. At the same time, another French naval force landed the deposed king of the Sakalava* and attempted to use him to provoke a rising of the tribes of the west coast against the Merina monarchy. Thus Ranavalona appeared fully justified in her policy of reducing contacts with foreign powers. It was only the Revolution of 1830 in France, and the fact that Louis-Philippe wished no trouble with Britain, that caused the French government to order Gourbeyre to withdraw from the points he had occupied on the east coast.

The reaction against the British missionaries followed rapidly. While religious meetings were attended by large crowds in Imerina, it is estimated that genuine conversions had been few. There were perhaps two hundred convinced Christians in Tananarive in 1830 belonging to the Protestant confession. The Catholics were not yet present in Imerina, although Msgr de Solages, Apostolic Prefect of Réunion, had attempted to go up to Tananarive from the coast, without the Queen's permission, in 1832; he had died, abandoned by his porters and without food, at Andevorante on the coast. Catholic missions were established in the islands of Ste Marie and Nosy-be, already under French occupation, and unsuccessful attempts were made to found missions among the Sakalava.

The British missionaries might well have been obliged to leave Madagascar with Lyall. They were saved for a few years by the

* Andriantsoli in 1832 had become Sultan of Mayotte, one of the Comoro islands, with French support. He ceded Mayotte to France in 1841.

ability of their artisan, Cameron, to make soap. The Queen
called them together in the house of the senior missionary to hear
a communication. Here the Queen's messengers thanked the
missionaries for what they had done, and informed them that
the Queen wished to know if there was anything else they could
teach the Malagasy people. Apparently they answered that there
were still many things to be taught, including the Greek and
Hebrew languages.[13] The Queen's answer was that she did not
care for the teaching of languages that nobody spoke but that she
wished to know whether the missionaries could teach her people
how to make soap. A kind of Malagasy soap existed (and is still
on sale in markets) in the form of black balls made of ashes and
certain leaves, bound together with tallow, but the Queen found
European soap much superior. The missionaries asked for a week
in which to reply to the Queen and handed over the technical
problem to Cameron. At the end of the week, the messengers
returned and Cameron handed over two bars of quite good soap.
The queen then granted the missionaries leave to continue with
their schools and religious teaching, on condition that Cameron
taught a number of young noblemen to make soap. It was under-
stood that the permission would expire when the young men had
learned to make good soap, but this apparently took five years,
during which time new schools were opened and the first converts
were baptised in Tananarive in 1831.*

Although in 1831 a royal *kabary* reasserted the liberty to practise
the Christian religion, as allowed by Radama, it appears that
religious meetings became identified with political opposition to
the Queen and the oligarchy. These meetings spread over
Imerina; many thousands of people attended and there was much
public discussion. This was enough to alarm a despotic government. In 1832, an edict forbad slaves to learn to read and write,
and in 1834 this prohibition was extended to anyone not belonging
to government service. In 1832 baptisms were no longer authorised
and in 1835 the Malagasy were forbidden to adopt the Christian
religion. The missionaries were expelled and the last two left
Tananarive in July 1836. The artisans also left and Cameron went

---

* Dr Livingstone (as quoted by the Reverend T. T. Matthews): 'If
young missionaries for Africa would spend one half the time they have to
spend over Latin verbs in learning how to make a wheel-barrow or mend
a waggon, it would be infinitely more useful to them afterwards.'

to work in Cape Colony, where he remained until his return to Madagascar in 1863.

The departure of the missionaries was followed by the burning of all the Bibles and religious tracts that could be found. Some of the ancient manuscripts written in Arabic script and containing magical formulae were also burned at this time. The official policy was a return to strict orthodoxy and the religion of the ancestors. However, the practice of prayer-meetings, hymn-singing and Bible-reading merely went underground, and meetings were held in remote places or secretly in houses, even in Tananarive. Political resistance against the monarchy thus became identified with Protestant Christianity, and it is significant that many of the future leaders of political movements for independence during the period of French rule belonged to the Protestant Merina upper-class. Repression of Christians rapidly became severe; the first martyr was killed in 1837, a woman called Rasalama. Thereafter, many others were either killed or sold as slaves. Five who had escaped visited England and appeared at a public meeting of the LMS at Exeter Hall in 1839 before returning to Mauritius to work among Malagasy who had been taken there as slaves. Other Christians were burned alive in Tananarive or thrown from a cliff below the royal palace.

Pressure from outside on the Merina monarchy continued, in the form of sporadic attacks by French and British forces on the coasts. The need for food supplies compelled the traders of Réunion and Mauritius to buy from Madagascar. In the face of monopolies and the complete ban on the presence of foreign traders in Tananarive, they directed their ships to parts of the coasts far removed from the direct military control of the Merina. This encouraged the local chiefs to seek French and British support against the central monarchy, and created constant instability. It was to counteract these moves that Ranavalona sent an embassy to Britain and France in 1836. Lord Palmerston, who received them in London, proposed an agreement that would allow free trade, establish a British consul in Tananarive and allow the navy to use Malagasy ports in repressing the slave trade. The Malagasy refused in particular to allow foreign traders to establish themselves in Tananarive, admitting that if they allowed this their own traders would lose their profits.[14] No agreement was signed. In Paris, Louis-Philippe treated their mission as a simple good-will visit.

The French continued to encourage various chiefs and minor rulers on the west coast to cede them territory that was technically controlled by the Merina, and, in the face of continued provocations, the Queen finally notified the surviving European traders on the coast that the laws of the country, particularly in respect to the manufacture and sale of alcohol, which was theoretically forbidden in Madagascar, would be rigorously applied. There followed the equivalent of the Chinese 'Opium War' (also of this period); an Anglo-French naval expedition appeared off Tamatave in 1845 in response to appeals by twelve British and elven French traders. Commandant Romain-Desfossées and Captain William Kelly took the traders on board, bombarded the town and landed a force* which was repulsed by the Malagasy. This force left behind twenty dead, their heads cut off and stuck up on spears as a warning to others.[15] The immediate result of this was that the Queen issued an edict putting a stop to all foreign trade, and in particular to furnishing any supplies to Réunion and Mauritius. Madagascar was now officially cut off from outside contacts and lived in more or less complete isolation until 1853. The traders of the Mascarene islands continued to put in ships at remote villages on the west coast, such as Soalala, to take on cattle and rice.

The policy of economic independence encouraged the creation of local industries, and from 1831 until 1857 it was the French technician, Jean Laborde, who created what was, for the epoch, a remarkable industrial complex at Mantasoa, some thirty miles east of Tananarive. The son of a blacksmith of Auch in south-west France, he was picked up by de Lastelle after being shipwrecked on the east coast on a voyage from India on a treasure-hunting expedition. De Lastelle, a Breton from St Malo, had become the commercial agent of the Merina oligarchy, serving as their intermediary for the sale of cattle and rice and operating his own sugar mill and distillery supplied by his plantations near Mananjary. De Lastelle sent Laborde to Queen Ranavalona, who employed him to manufacture guns for the army. Needing more abundant supplies of iron, Laborde set up a small blast furnace at Mantasoa, where there was an abundant supply of fuel from the forest and water-power from the river, and where iron was locally available. The royal government is said to have mobilised 20,000 men in a

* Commanded by Lieutenant (later Rear-Admiral) Albert Heseltine, RN.

giant corvée to build the factories, which subsequently employed a thousand workers, a huge number for the period.

The blast furnace and iron works were only a beginning. Laborde apparently used the *Manuels Roret*[16] and other technical publications and created an industrial town at Mantasoa which he named Soatsimanampiovana (literally, 'the beauty that does not change'). Here a wide range of articles was manufactured, including guns and ammunition, shells, swords, glass and pottery, bricks and tiles, lime, charcoal, sulphuric acid, dies, soap, silk and lightning-conductors. The latter are essential in Imerina during the violent tropical storms of January to March. Laborde built a new palace for the Queen in 1839, the Manjakamiadana; it was built entirely in wood, around a central tree-trunk 130 feet high which took 5,000 men to haul it from the forest to Tananarive. In 1868–69, this same palace was encased in stone, in the form it has today, by Cameron after his return to Madagascar from Cape Colony. De Lastelle and Laborde were considered members of the oligarchy and assimilated to the Merina nobility. Laborde received '15 Honours' (15 *Voninahitra*), which was the highest grade, and both of them lived in customary marriage with Malagasy ladies of high rank. Laborde's house still stands, a little below the Palace of Andafiavaratra, the family residence of the former prime ministers and now the presidential offices.

The period of comparative isolation ended as a result of two events. In 1848, the revolution in France that led to the establishment of the government of Louis-Napoleon abolished slavery in Réunion and contemplated a complete withdrawal from the French-occupied posts on the west coast of Madagascar, where Europeans had been killed in a rising in Nosy-be in 1849. In 1852, the Prime Minister, Rainiharo, who had been commander-in-chief of Radama's army, died, and was succeeded by his son, Rainivoninahitriniony, who succeeded him as Prime Minister and the Queen's 'consort'. This family thus became hereditary 'mayors of the palace'; Rainilaiarivony, the brother of Rainivon-inahitriniony, was Prime Minister and 'consort' of three queens from 1864 until the French conquest of 1896.

With the abolition of slavery in Réunion, the oligarchy lost its remaining external market for slaves and was forced to consider the reopening of external trade as an economic alternative. De Lastelle and Laborde used their considerable influence with the

Queen and her son, Prince Rakoto (subsequently King Radama II).[17] The Queen was concerned at the lack of security of the coasts, where clandestine supply ships from the Mascarene islands landed arms for the local chiefs and encouraged subversion against the Merina garrisons. In his letter to the Malagasy embassy of 1836, the Governor of Mauritius had observed that the Merina government would find it difficult to maintain its sovereignty over the coastal regions without the benevolent neutrality, if not active support, of the naval powers, Britain and France. The Queen demanded, as the price for reopening external trade, an indemnity of 15,000 piastres (nearly £16,000) to be paid by those responsible for the attack on Tamatave by the Anglo-French naval expedition of 1845. The Chamber of Commerce of Réunion and Mauritius traders offered her even larger sums for exclusive privileges. In 1853 the ports were reopened officially to foreign shipping after payment of the indemnity of 15,000 piastres, apparently only by Mauritius.[18] European traders were explicitly confined to the coast; the large profits derived from the supply of cattle and rice and the retailing of imported goods thus remained in the hands of the Merina oligarchy, and in particular in those of the family of the Prime Minister.

The first European trader to re-enter Tananarive did so through having won the favour of the Queen by lending her a ship to carry supplies to the Merina garrison at Fort Dauphin. This was Lambert, a French trader already established in Mauritius, which he had supplied with rice and cattle and also with 'indentured labour', for which he went as far afield as Zanzibar and Moçambique. As a result of his service to the Queen, he obtained her permission to come to Tananarive. He arrived at Laborde's house in Mantasoa in June 1855, accompanied by a 'Monsieur Hervier', who was in fact Father Marc Finaz, the Apostolic Prefect of Nosy-be, disguised as a layman.

The establishment of a Catholic mission in Tananarive had been a main objective of the Jesuits from their base on Réunion where Msgr Dalmond, responsible for Madagascar since 1837, had printed vocabularies of the Betsimisaraka and Sakalava dialects of Malagasy in 1842, and extracts from the Old and New Testaments in the Sakalava dialect, for use in their small missions on the west coast. Father Finaz had been sent by Father Louis Jouen, Apostolic Prefect of Madagascar, who had succeeded Msgr Dalmond in 1854. Jouen had received a letter from Prince Rakoto, in which he said: 'I ask you to tell me in which year and month the expedition will arrive in Madagascar'.[19] These contacts with France were apparently an attempt to secure French support to overthrow the government of Queen Ranavalona and their discovery led to her renewed expulsion of foreigners in 1857.[20]

Father Finaz was introduced to the Queen by Lambert as his secretary and made a considerable impression by various objects he had brought with him, which included daguerreotypes, balloons and a musical box. He said the first mass ever in Tananarive in July 1855, at which were present Prince Rakoto, Lastelle and Laborde and four Malagasy.[21] Lambert's mission was directed mainly at Prince Rakoto, who was considered the most likely successor to the Queen, and in June 1855 the Prince signed a secret agreement known as the 'Charte Lambert', by which, in return for French support, Lambert was promised very important concessions. These included the creation of a company which would have the right to mint money, process monopolies over mineral resources, exemption from all customs dues and immense land grants.

Louis-Napoleon, now Emperor, and allied with Britain in the Crimean War, proposed to the British government that they should share in the future company. The British representative was the Reverend William Ellis of the LMS, who had been twice refused permission by the Queen to go up to Tananarive and who had been in Tamatave since 1853. It would appear that he was in fact an agent of the British government in this affair. On his arrival in Tananarive, he is said to have 'violently reproached' Prince Rakoto.[22] The British missionaries were bitterly opposed to the Catholics in Madagascar, and the tone of the references in their writings to this religion is remarkably severe.[23] Certainly, Ellis would not have forgiven the Prince for attending mass. The immediate result of this dispute with the Prince was that the Queen was informed not only of the 'Charte Lambert' but also of the plot to overthrow her with French assistance.

There followed a savage repression of 'sorcerers' and Christians, since it appears that the survivors of those converted by the LMS group from 1820–32 formed an effective underground resistance and used prayer-meetings for political ends. Laborde returned to Tananarive, accompanied this time not by a priest but by an Austrian lady, Ida Pfeiffer.[24] Rakoto, Laborde and Lambert conspired to place Rakoto on the throne by a coup d'état, but the Queen was more rapid than they. In 1857 all Europeans, including Lastelle, Laborde, Lambert, Finaz and another Catholic priest, Father Webber,* were expelled from Madagascar. Laborde's workers took the opportunity of smashing up all his factories and machines at Mantasoa, and the ruins remain there to this day.

It seems reasonably certain that Ellis denounced Lambert to the Queen and certainly he was very antagonistic to Laborde. Lambert, on his return, had secured much of the capital necessary for the formation of the 'Compagnie de Madagascar, foncière, industrielle et commerciale' and had brought many presents. Ellis probably found himself without the necessary resources to carry out his mission to secure British participation and thus overthrew the plan by denouncing the plot.[25] He succeeded in holding up French penetration and the establishment of a Catholic mission in Tananarive only briefly, since the Queen died in August 1861, having nominated Prince Rakoto as her successor.

The reign of Radama II, the name under which Prince Rakoto came to the throne, was short but the change in policy was immediate and complete. Under Ranavalona, contacts with the outside were kept to a minimum, territorial expansion had continued with the conquest of nearly the whole territory of Madagascar and a rigid orthodoxy and adherence to ancestral customs and religion had been imposed by force. Under Radama, the country was thrown open to foreigners, captives taken in recent wars were sent back to the Sakalava and other coastal peoples, who now sent delegations to thank the Merina king, and complete liberty of religion once again allowed the Christian missionaries to operate.

Fathers Webber and Jouen returned to Tananarive in 1861

* Fr Webber sj had arrived by passing as the assistant to a Dr Milhet Fontarabie from Réunion who had successfully operated on Rainijohary, co-Prime Minister, for a cancer of the nose. It was Rainijohary who banished the Europeans, submitting Laborde to the '*tangena*', or poison ordeal, practised on a chicken representing him. He exempted the doctor and Fr Webber, who however followed the others. Fr Webber was the author of a French-Malagasy dictionary and established the first Catholic printing house in Tananarive under Radama II.

while the Reverend William Ellis returned in 1862 bringing money subscribed by British supporters of the LMS for the construction of four churches in memory of the Malagasy martyrs murdered under Ranavalona. Jean Laborde returned in the same year as French Consul, and obtained the King's signature on the 'Charte Lambert', giving the proposed company important monopolies and concessions in return for dues of 10 per cent to be paid to the King. Lambert himself was sent to France as Malagasy Ambassador, to obtain the recognition of Radama as King of Madagascar and to organise the operation of the company. This recognition was secured by a treaty signed with France in September 1862 which for the first time recognised internationally a king of the whole of the island. This treaty contained clauses that were similar to the type of agreements imposed on China at the time of the establishment of the foreign concessions and the regime of capitulation in Tsien-Tsien, Shanghai and elsewhere, and not only undermined the economic independence of the country but affected seriously the commercial interests of the oligarchy. The Prime Minister and his brother managed to include a clause (article 21) stipulating that the treaty would not come into force until it was ratified a year later, thus gaining time. It is reasonably certain that this treaty was one of the main reasons for the assassination of Radama by the oligarchy in 1863.

The British were more modest, or certainly more subtle, and were content with a charter signed by a trader called Caldwell, which, by its vagueness, could have been dangerous to Malagasy interests, but which apparently merely permitted Caldwell and his associates to trade and buy land in Madagascar. The British Consul, Thomas Packenham, is said to have proposed to Radama that the British government buy from him the concessions granted under the 'Charte Lambert' for 25 million francs ($US 7·5 million) out of which an indemnity or compensation was to be paid to Lambert of one million francs.[26] Packenham remained as Consul for more than twenty years, and appears to have been considerably more effective as a British agent than Ellis, although one English missionary refers to him as 'the degenerate son of a noble sire, married to a low French-Creole woman'.[27] This vituperation arises, no doubt, as much from the fact that Packenham was a Catholic as from differences in policy with Ellis.

The sudden opening of Madagascar to foreign penetration

certainly invited Franco-British intrigues for influence in securing markets and concessions. This was aggravated by the rivalry between Protestant and Catholic missionaries, the Protestants not having forgiven Radama for having organised the clandestine visit of Father Finaz to Tananarive in 1857. If the oligarchy had accepted the treaty with France of 1862, this was mainly because it recognised, for the first time, the existence of a Malagasy government with authority over the whole island and appeared to renounce French pretensions to a 'protectorate' over part of the west coast opposite their possessions such as the island of Nosy-be.[28] However, the treaty, and in particular the 'Charte Lambert', went absolutely against the economic interests of the oligarchy. The fortunes of the Merina aristocracy depended no longer on the slave trade, which had practically ceased to exist in that part of the Indian Ocean since its abolition in Réunion in 1848. But their occupation of the posts of army commander or local governor gave them trading privileges and the right of requisition of goods and services. The family to which the prime ministers belonged was dependent for its wealth on its control of monopolies such as that created by Ranavalona for the supply of rice and cattle to the Mascarene islands. All these privileges appeared seriously threatened by a treaty which would allow the free establishment and competition of foreign traders. The succession of a king who appeared to have a certain spirit of independence was an unwelcome change after more than thirty years of rule by a queen who could be more or less influenced by members of the oligarchy. No longer could a consort be put into her bed as their agent. Worse still, Radama II brought with him a number of young male favourites, the *menamaso* ('red eyes'), chosen for other qualities, and who did not belong to the families of the oligarchy. Radama is said to have amused himself with these favourites away from the palace, in a stone house specially built for such parties.

The oligarchy, and especially the family of the Prime Minister, organised the assassination of Radama some eight months after his coronation in 1862. The person of royalty was still sacred in Imerina, and a popular agitation was necessary as a justification before they could act. This took the form of a collective possession or hysteria, known as *Ramanenjana*, a kind of epidemic of convulsions which spread through Imerina and was explained as the companions of Queen Ranavalona come back from the dead to re-establish the old traditions. At this moment Radama II informed the Prime Minister and his brother, the Commander-in-Chief, that he intended introducing the practice of duelling not only between individuals but also between villages. This caused great scandal and was later held by the notables to justify his assassination, which was preceded by the killing of many of his *menamaso* favourites and culminated in his being strangled in the palace with a silken cord, since the blood of royalty was sacred and could not be shed.

Radama was the last king of Madagascar, and, until the French conquest of 1896, three queens reigned, all of them married in one way or another to the Prime Minister. On the same day that her husband was assassinated, Rabodo, the chief wife and cousin of Radama, was proclaimed queen, taking the name of Rasoherina, and was forced by the Prime Minister and his brother to sign what was practically a constitution. This document laid down that the wishes of the sovereign could no longer become law and that sentence of death could no longer be proclaimed without the agreement of the 'chiefs of the people'. An immediate revision of all treaties not yet ratified was stipulated, thus bringing the French treaty into question. The family of the Prime Minister thus imposed its own interests and ensured that henceforth the monarch would be a mere figurehead. For the remainder of the period of the Malagasy monarchy, it was the Prime Minister who governed.

The new Queen, faced with the choice between the Prime Minister and his brother Rainilaiarivony, chose the latter, and with her support he was able to stage a military coup d'état in the modern manner which overthrew his brother. Rainilaiarivony installed himself as Prime Minister and Queen's consort on July 14, 1864. He remained in power, as effective ruler of the country, until the conquest of 1896.[29]

By any standards he was a remarkable statesman, and his position for the next thirty years as virtual ruler of independent Madagascar, now internationally recognised but caught between French and British colonial expansion at its peak, is itself no mean achievement. He had a curious childhood, for, although the son of Prime Minister Rainiharo, consort of Queen Ranavalona, he was excluded from the family for having been born under a destiny (*vintana*) held by the sorcerers to be 'too strong'. His father therefore had the ends of two of his fingers cut off and he

5—M * *

was brought up outside the family.[30] He succeeded in learning to read and write and he built up a small business while still an adolescent. His father recognised his ability, and by the age of twenty-four had made him private secretary to the Queen, with '13 Honours'. Rainilaiarivony was closely associated with Laborde, from whom he learned much, and he sought the company of foreigners, also to learn from them what he could. He remained apparently under the orders of his brother, who had succeeded his father as Prime Minister, until he felt himself strong enough to come out into the open.

His position required consolidation, more especially as the foreign treaties and the reintroduction of Christianity did not have the full support of all the notables of Imerina. The first step was an adroit swing against French pressure and towards Britain. Thus, in 1866, the 'Charte Lambert' was publicly burned on the beach at Tamatave; a treaty had been signed with Britain in 1865 guaranteeing liberty of religion and forbidding the slave trade. A clause in this treaty, allowing British subjects to own property in Madagascar, did not appear in the Malagasy text. A similar treaty was signed with the United States in 1867. The abrogation of the 'Charte Lambert' cost the Malagasy government 1,200,000 francs (£350,000) in compensation to France. This, and the arrogant attitude of a certain Count de Louvières, turned the Prime Minister against France, in spite of Laborde's efforts to prevent a rupture. A new envoy, Garnier, succeeded in obtaining in 1868 a Franco-Malagasy treaty with almost the same text as the treaty with Britain.

The Prime Minister thus turned away from French Catholic influence towards British Protestantism, especially after the death of Queen Rasoherina in 1868. He chose as her successor the second wife of Radama II, a former pupil of the Protestant mission, who was crowned as Ranavalona II. She and the Prime Minister were baptised and married according to the Protestant rites, with the Bible present and without showing the royal talismans, in Tananarive on February 21, 1869. The Prime Minister, in adopting the Christian form of marriage, could not follow the Malagasy custom that recognised polygamy. He was thus obliged to renounce his wife Rasoanalina (also his cousin) by whom he had had nineteen children. He had no children by any of the three queens whom he married in succession.

This 'conversion' was followed by the burning of the royal talismans or 'idols' in September 1869. This was hailed by certain missionaries as a 'conversion of the Malagasy as a nation to God', but it would appear that its significance was mainly political. The burning of the talismans, which began with the famous '*Ikelimalaza*', the most revered of the twelve royal talismans of Imerina, took place without any reaction on the part of the population, despite the importance formerly attached to these objects, which had been held to be the guardians of royalty and which were always carried in procession with special guards.[31] This indicates that the minds of the people must have been carefully prepared. In fact, the new Queen and the Prime Minister took advantage of a genuine increase in Christian conversions to make Protestant Christianity virtually the state religion. In one year, the number of Protestants had quadrupled, and officials imposed on the inhabitants the obligation to build churches in villages and also to attend long services on Sunday. Accounts are given of people being driven into church by the equivalent of the English beadle of the seventeenth century, and kept there for many hours. Ten Protestant preachers were appointed governors of districts in Imerina.

These moves against paganism created a favourable impression upon the Britain of Queen Victoria and helped to counteract French penetration. By officially putting himself at the head of the Protestant movement, the Prime Minister cleverly prevented it becoming the political underground opposition it had been during the repression of Ranavalona I. It is none the less surprising that an attack on traditional religious beliefs, such as the burning of the talismans, went so smoothly. Probably, these talismans were only marginal to the main religious beliefs of the Merina; had any attempt been made to violate tombs, or modify burial customs and the cult of the ancestors, the reaction would have been violent. Even today, if a tomb has to be displaced to allow a new road to be built, it can be carried out only after elaborate ceremonies.

The public religious changes were followed by important legal reforms, and for the first time the laws of the country were printed and appeared in codified form.* The legal reforms concerned marriage and family obligations. Polygamy was officially abolished

* *Code of 101 Articles*, 1868, followed by the *Code of 305 Articles*, 1881.

and unilateral divorce (in the Muslim manner, a husband could repudiate his wife by thanking her and telling her to go, and often did so if she was barren) was replaced by a legal procedure before a tribunal. Custom was respected in the punishment laid down for sorcery and the prohibition of marriage across social caste lines. These laws were printed in the Malagasy language and copies distributed to provincial governors and officials. In 1878 three main tribunals were established for administering justice. A corps called the *sakaizambohitra* ('friends of the villages') was constituted; it was made up of old soldiers appointed to villages to ensure that the laws were obeyed and to keep a local register of births and deaths, the *Bokimpanjakana* ('book of the government'), in which deeds and agreements were also registered. This served to keep the *tompomenakely* (feudal 'squires') in check and ensured a minimum of uniformity in the administration throughout the kingdom, without the interposition of local leaders. It was a move to hasten the disintegration of feudal society by eliminating what remained of local feudal authority. The *menakely* were often appointed by the government as the official preachers of the villages and officiated in the churches on Sunday. These services were looked upon by the population as merely another form of corvée; they referred to the Sunday services as '*fanompoam-pivavahana*' (literally, 'prayer fatigue').

The use the regime made of the Protestant religion as a political instrument cannot be entirely blamed on the British missionaries. Whatever certain LMS enthusiasts thought in London, those on the spot were doubtful of the spiritual effects of such a policy. They were, however, much concerned by what appeared to them to be the 'barbarous' aspects of Malagasy society, in particular the existence of slavery and of a form of sexual morality entirely different from their Western conceptions. The Malagasy family was, and is, essentially patrilineal among the Merina, although variations of lineage occur among other tribes.[32] The male head of the family had a chief wife (*vady-be*) and often younger lesser wives (*vady-kely*), officially until the legal abolition of polygamy under the legal reform of 1868 and unofficially thereafter. Slave women were kept as concubines, as in other countries, and accompanied their master on journeys. Andrianampoinimerina had twelve wives and twenty-four children. A rigid caste system governed marriage and inheritance. The nobility (andriana) were divided into several different castes, the highest according to their degree of relationship with the royal family. Among the bourgeoisie (hova) there were also distinctions of caste, while the slaves (andevo), having African or captive blood, were completely excluded and their children were regarded as andevo, even if the father was noble. These caste distinctions were expressed in special forms of salutation, which subsisted until recently; they have been vigorously combated by the republican government, which at one time put up placards urging the use of a single salutation, '*salama tompoko*'.

These 'barbarisms' disturbed the missionaries, and discussion of them occupies considerable space in their writings. But the missionaries' influence on Malagasy society was none the less profound and enduring. Following the conversion of Queen Ranavalona II and the Prime Minister, a massive wave of conversions, estimated at 16,000 in one year, followed.[33] These included the Queen's personal astrologer and the guardians of the royal talismans, now unemployed. In the face of considerable opposition from the Reverend William Ellis, other sects entered the mission field: in Imerina, Lutherans from Norway, who remain active, especially on the west coast; the Friends, or Quakers (whom the LMS did not oppose), and the American Lutherans, who set up an excellent hospital, which still exists today, at Fort Dauphin. Penetration of other provinces began, and the Catholic mission of the Jesuit Fathers, seeing themselves excluded from the royal family and the nobility by the British Protestants, made considerable progress among the country people of Imerina and pushed rapidly southwards to the Betsileo. Violent comments on their progress appear in the Protestant missionary writings. In 1872, a bishop, Msgr Cazet, was placed at the head of the Catholic mission. However, Protestantism remained the ruling-class religion, except for a few noble families opposed to the Prime Minister who became Catholic to show their political opposition.

An immediate and tangible result of the return of the missions was the reopening of the schools, which had been suppressed in 1835, and the introduction of Western medicine for the first time. The medical pioneer was Dr Andrew Davidson, a Scotsman trained at Edinburgh University, who opened the first hospital in Madagascar at Tananarive (Andohalo, beside the royal palace) in 1862, with the Prime Minister laying the foundation stone. Davidson was not only an outstanding medical missionary, assisting the LMS group, but from the start undertook the training of Malagasy doctors and midwives. In 1864, also under the auspices of the London Missionary Society, Davidson opened a second and larger hospital at Analakely (the building still stands though it is no longer used for the same purpose). To this was attached the first medical school, called the Medical Missionary Academy, which trained the first Malagasy doctors, who practised in the hospital and in Tananarive privately. Among these appears the name of Dr Ralarosy, whose descendant, Dr Paul Radaody-Ralarosy was Director of Public Health until his retirement in 1969.

Davidson wrote, in Malagasy, a number of textbooks for use in training, covering anatomy, physiology and therapeutics.* He later became Professor of Tropical Medicine at the University of Edinburgh, was responsible for sending Andrianaly and Rajaonah to Edinburgh, from which they returned in 1880 as the first Malagasy doctors to hold European degrees. These two men were first trained in the small medical school which Davidson created in his hospital at Analakely in Tananarive. The school was later transferred to Befalatanana and is today the Faculty of Medicine of the University of Tananarive.

Rajaonah was an outstanding personality in fields other than medicine, and became known as a preacher touching on social and political questions and as a writer in a periodical, *Mpanolotsaina* ('Counsellor'), which appeared in Tananarive from 1882. Son of a high dignitary of the crown, Rainandriamampandry (who was later executed by General Galliéni for resistance to the French conquest), Rajaonah became involved in a plot engineered in 1893 by Rajoelina, the son of the Prime Minister, aiming at overthrowing his long dictatorship. Rajaonah was condemned to death but had his sentence commuted to exile in Ambositra in the Betsileo country.

The medical school turned out a series of remarkable doctors and laid the foundation of the high standard of medicine practised today in Madagascar. Some of these doctors produced original scientific work, such as the doctoral thesis of Dr Rasamimanana, who graduated from the University of Lyon in France in 1891,

---

* *Anatomy, Fampivelomana, Physiology, Therapeutika*, and a book of 640 pages, *Aretina sy fanasitranana*—'Illness and Cure'.

concerning the physiological effects of the *tangena*, or ordeal by poison. The thesis of Dr Ramisiray, a descendant of Andrianampoinimerina, presented on his graduation from the Faculty of the University of Paris in 1903, concerning the pharmaceutical and therapeutic properties of Malagasy medicinal plants, was another highly original contribution. The Ecole de Médecine in Tananarive continued to train doctors over five years of study; throughout the colonial period, they were entitled to practise only in Madagascar, until the school's absorption by the University of Tananarive as an internationally recognised Faculty of Medicine.[34]

The spread of education from 1862 was extremely rapid and has had lasting effects in Madagascar. Schools and medical facilities were confined to the Hauts-Plateaux, concentrated around Tananarive, with some activity among the Betsileo in Fianarantsoa, the main town (whose name means 'good learning'). This contributed further to consolidating the Merina as the dominant people but created problems for the future by the wide gap which now appeared in the intellectual standards of the Merina as compared with the remainder, and in particular the coastal peoples. This gap persisted down to independence in 1960 and great efforts have had to be made by the republican government to redress the imbalance by rapidly creating schools in the provinces. The high standard of education in Madagascar today is due to the great impetus given by the missions, both Protestant and Catholic, before the conquest of 1896, and to the major importance attached by the French colonial administration to education.

The Malagasy government gave full support to education, which was theoretically declared compulsory in 1876, although the necessary facilities were lacking for this to be enforced. The *Antananarivo Annual* giving educational statistics for 1882 stated that there were 146,521 pupils registered. The LMS then had 818 schools and the Catholic Missions 192.[35] Primary schools in 1894 are stated to have had 164,000 pupils, two thirds of whom were in Imerina with the remainder in the Betsileo and on the east coast.[36] In 1862 the LMS had created a teacher training school in Tananarive, followed in 1899 by a secondary school. The Catholic Mission founded the Collège Saint Michel, also a secondary school, in 1888, and it is estimated that about a hundred pupils a year were coming out of secondary schools in the 1890s, with sufficient education and knowledge of French and English to permit them to take degrees in European universities. Thus, in the field of education, Madagascar was at this time equal to, and even in advance of, certain European countries.

Printing presses established by both Catholic and Protestant missions enabled a steady stream of publications in Malagasy, English and French to appear. The *Antananarivo Annual* was a well-produced review containing very diverse articles written by missionaries. These are first-hand accounts of Malagasy language, folk-lore and customs and contain many fascinating accounts of journeys on foot and in canoes to the interior of the country. The first periodicals appeared, including the *Mpanolotsaina* in which Dr Rajaonah wrote, the *Teny Soa* ('Good Word') of the LMS, the *Sakaizon'ny Tanora* ('Friend of the Youth') of the Society of Friends and *Resaka* ('what is Told') of the Catholics.

While credit is due to the missionaries for this expansion, which was astonishing for the epoch and not paralleled by anything at all similar in Africa, it was the dynamism of the Merina people that made it possible. Missionaries have worked elsewhere with equal zeal but with disappointing results. The Merina had already seized on the elements of Western technology introduced by Cameron and by Laborde, and numerous artisans now practised these crafts. Similar crafts had been introduced into other countries but without stimulating any marked expansion of handicrafts. The Merina and many other Malagasy tribes have special manual dexterity which lends itself to small industries. Handicrafts of a high quality are found throughout the island, while the more sophisticated arts of painting and sculpture have flourished under the impetus of the Institut des Arts Appliqués in Tananarive. In the same manner the Merina seized eagerly on the intellectual awakening which was offered them by the teachers and doctors brought in by the missionaries.

It is not surprising, therefore, that in the latter part of the nineteenth century Madagascar presented most of the attributes of an organised state. Not only was there a central administration, with its provincial antennae and codified laws, but also a system of communications by porters and runners, a rudimentary postal service and the beginnings of a monetary system. It was unfortunate that this should have evolved at a time when the colonial expansion of the Western powers was reaching its apogee. Whether

Madagascar would have reached its present level of development without colonial intervention is another question. Certainly, the domination of the Merina over the other tribes would not have gone unchallenged indefinitely. A parallel with Ethiopia suggests itself, where the dominant Amhara have maintained their rule, with various difficulties, over disparate tribes far more heterogeneous than the Malagasy.

The consolidation of the state under the dictatorship of Rainilaiarivony was carried out in the face of a growing menace of foreign intervention. France in particular, after its defeat by Germany in the Franco-Prussian war and the amputation of Alsace-Lorraine, was expanding rapidly in Africa and the Far East. The 1871 Paris Commune appeared as an attempt by the working-class to seize power as the middle-class had seized power in 1789. The regime that followed its savage repression wavered under Thiers between a right-wing republicanism and a return to the monarchy under the Comte de Chambord as a Bourbon legitimate monarch. It is not necessary to be an astute interpreter of history to see how these internal tensions influenced the external expansion of the conquest of Indochina, Tunisia and vast expanses of West Africa. The influx of immigrants into Algeria, a colony since 1829, was greatly augmented by those who refused to live in Alsace-Lorraine under German rule. Whether Bismarck encouraged French colonial expansion to reduce their military pressure in Europe, as is claimed by some French historians, is also a question.

It was at this period that French pressure on Madagascar began to grow. It is claimed that two main pressure groups acted to push the French government towards intervention in Madagascar: the Catholic parties, who considered that their Church was put in an unfavourable position by the influence exerted by the British Protestant missionaries on the Merina ruling classes; and the inhabitants of Réunion, who considered Madagascar as a natural source of supplies and as an outlet for the growing population of a small island. [37] As early as 1845, the colonial assembly of Réunion had sent a memorial to Louis-Philippe, stating that they hoped to found an important settlement in Madagascar. France had maintained vague legalistic claims to Madagascar since the establishment of the ill-fated garrison of Fort Dauphin in the seventeenth century. They had permanent settlements in two small islands, Ste Marie and Nosy-be, and from the latter had at various times negotiated phantom 'protectorates' over the neighbouring Sakalava tribes, especially during the reign of Louis-Philippe. These were the same tactics as employed by other colonial powers and there appeared no reason why they should not succeed. However, an internationally-recognised state, which had sent embassies to European powers, was not to be invaded and annexed like the Upper Volta or Niger. There was not even the excuse that Madagascar was a Muslim country, with a history of Christian crusades to justify a take-over, as in the Maghreb.

France thus sought legalistic pretexts for intervention, of which the first was the inheritance of Jean Laborde. Venerated by the Malagasy, and especially by the Queen and the Prime Minister, Laborde had died in 1878. He had built himself a house which he left, with a considerable amount of real estate, to his two nephews. One of the heirs proposed to sell part of the land at Andohalo, near the palace, to the Catholic mission. Although this transaction eventually succeeded, and the Catholic cathedral today stands on this land with the archbishop's palace beside it, it will be remembered that the Malagasy government had always resisted any claim that land could be owned freehold by foreigners. This was the reason for the repudiation of the 'Charte Lambert' and the reason why the relevant clause in the charter negotiated with Britain at that time had been left untranslated into Malagasy. The Prime Minister now refused, under the newly-codified laws of 1881, to authorise the inheritance of Laborde's nephews. In leaving his property to his French nephews, Laborde had disinherited his two sons, born of his Malagasy common-law wife.

The second pretext for French intervention was provided by the action of two British missionaries, W. C. Pickersgill and John Parrett, a printer; while touring the north-west coast opposite Nosy-be, they persuaded the local Sakalava chiefs to hoist the red and white Merina flag. Ever since their occupation of Nosy-be, which dated from 1840, France had attempted to arouse the Sakalava tribes against the Merina. Agreements with individual chiefs, which has led to very little real influence, constituted what were known as the 'historic rights' of France in this area. This was therefore a fresh source of conflict with the Merina government which claimed sovereignty over the whole island. The French consuls, three of whom succeeded each other rapidly between

1881 and 1882, adopted a very aggressive tone towards the Prime Minister, and one of them departed so far from normal protocol as to summon the Malagasy Foreign Minister to his house, claiming that various original documents concerning the Laborde inheritance were so precious that they could not leave the consulate. A French gun-boat commanded by Captain Timbre completed this operation of 'gunboat diplomacy' by causing the Merina flag to be lowered on the coast opposite Nosy-be. The Prime Minister reacted to this aggression by sending an embassy led by his nephew, the Foreign Minister, to Paris, London and New York. This mission succeeded in obtaining international recognition of the sovereignty of the Queen over the whole of the island of Madagascar, and this was stated in communications from both the United States and British governments.[38]

It appears that there existed at this time a certain understanding between France and Great Britain over the influence to be exerted in Madagascar. Since 1881, Britain had been engaged in the annexation of Egypt and needed a certain neutrality from France. France continued an active 'gunboat diplomacy'; the next attack was made by Admiral Pierre-Joseph-Gustave Pierre in 1883 who bombarded a number of Merina garrisons on the north-west coast, shelled Majunga, and three weeks later attacked Tamatave and neighbouring posts. He proclaimed a state of seige at Tamatave and ordered all foreign consuls to leave within forty-eight hours. The British consul, who was still Thomas Packenham of whom the British missionaries had had such a low opinion twenty years earlier, died before the ultimatum expired. This attitude to its subjects caused the British government to issue a vigorous protest through its ambassador in Paris and Admiral Pierre was recalled.* Pierre died on the homeward voyage, but he was succeeded by Admiral Galiber, who bombarded Vohémar and sent a raiding party ashore. This party was actively resisted by the Merina troops and by the population, but many villages were destroyed. Sporadic attacks by small French forces continued and the ports were blockaded by the French navy. The Merina government expelled all French citizens from Tananarive

* It seems extraordinary to relate that, in independent Madagascar, a street in Tananarive (in which the British embassy was situated until 1963) is still called Rue Admiral Pierre. Very few Malagasy today have any idea of what the Admiral actually did.

and they retreated to the coast. Even the Catholic missions were left in the hands of a small number of Malagasy Catholics.

Queen Ranavalona II died in 1883. The Prime Minister chose as her successor a girl of twenty-two, from a branch of the family considered as under a curse because twins had been born to it.[39] He promptly married her and she was crowned as Ranavalona III amid considerable patriotic manifestations.

Hostilities with France were brought to an end largely as a result of the fall of the government of Jules Ferry in 1885 over the expedition to Tonkin in Indo-China. There had been popular manifestations in Paris against the Tonkin operation, and the new government sent plenipotentiaries to meet the Malagasy delegates in Tamatave. These emissaries were Rainizanamanga, a son of the Prime Minister, and Digby Willoughby, formerly a colonel of the Zululand Regiment, who had been appointed Commander-in-Chief of the Merina army in 1883. Willoughby had organised a successful resistance to French aggression south of Tamatave together with the Governor, Rainandriamampandry.*

The negotiations in Tamatave led to a treaty, signed on December 17, 1885, that gave France a virtual protectorate over Madagascar while leaving the Queen nominally responsible for internal administration. The treaty provided for Madagascar to be represented by France in its external relations, and for a French Resident with a military escort to be installed in Tananarive. French residents were allowed to hold leaseholds of property for ninety-nine years, and Diego-Suarez was to become a French military base.[40]

The Merina government was also condemned to pay an indemnity of 10 million francs (about $US 1·2 million). To raise this sum, the Prime Minister employed as an adviser Thomas Kingdon, a British citizen, who had arrived in Tananarive as an employee of the Protestant mission. Kingdon proposed to negotiate a loan of 20 million francs ($US 2·4 million) in London, at 7 per cent, in return for the concession of the import and export customs, which were to be farmed out to him. He was also to be allowed to set up a bank in Tananarive. The French Resident, Le Myre de Villiers,

---

* Willoughby's later career was unfortunate; he was convicted of embezzlement on his return from a mission to France in 1888, and exiled by the Prime Minister. Rainandriamampandry was executed by Galliéni in 1896.

persuaded the Prime Minister to break his contract with Kingdon and introduced the Comptoir National d'Escompte de Paris, which was set up as the first bank in Madagascar and made the necessary loan against the indemnity. Kingdon was later involved in the plot of 1893 against the Prime Minister and was banished. The expression '*vola kandaonina*' ('Kingdon's money') passed for a time into the Malagasy language to signify false money, since Kingdon had caused to circulate Mexican piastres cut into small pieces, at the same value as other silver coins recognised by the government.

A telegraph line was laid by French engineers between Tamatave and Tananarive, but the most lasting monument to this period of the protectorate was the construction of the French Residency, afterwards the Governor-General's Palace and now the French embassy, which was completed in 1892. This has been called unkindly a 'replica of a provincial prefecture'; certainly, the Renaissance style architecture does recall this type of French official building, but time has mellowed the brickwork, and the narrow windows and mansard roof look well against the background of the bald Imerina hills. The architect, Jully, was commissioned by the French Ministry of Foreign Affairs to design a building which would give an exact idea of French civilisation to the Merina and enhance French prestige. Jully had never been overseas, but when he arrived in Tananarive in 1889 he showed qualities similar to those of Jean Laborde. The Queen still reigned in her Palace on the top of the hill, and the French Resident had a house much more modest than those occupied by the LMS. Jully was obliged to organise everything, from labour to supplies, and timber was dragged from the forests and brick-kilns set up on the site.

The period of more than ten years that followed the signature of the treaty of 1885 has been called by some writers the 'phantom protectorate'. It was a period of continuing tension between France and Madagascar and of numerous incidents. France intended to transform the somewhat vague control provided for under the treaty into a real protectorate of the kind established in Tunisia in 1881, while the Prime Minister made every effort to preserve the status quo. The French Resident was considered to have the right of control over all external affairs of the government and to maintain a military escort, theoretically limited to fifty men. Vice-Residents were installed in six of the principal towns and a number of French citizens received large concessions of land, which they were usually unable to occupy.

The last few years of the monarchy saw a struggle of the Prime Minister on the one hand to retain his authority against the pretensions of the French Residents, and on the other to hold off the growing opposition of the Malagasy themselves. Some areas remained only nominally subject to the Merina monarchy, represented by isolated military posts under a 'governor', linked by a rudimentary system of communications, and sometimes succeeding in levying taxes or tribute. Thus the Bara people, warriors and cattle-raiders, submitted to the Merina occupation of Ihosy, but continued their expansion to the west, founding a new capital at Ankazoabo in 1838. Almost the entire arid south, inhabited by Antandroy and Mahafaly, remained independent of Merina rule, while the Antanosy, the origin of many dynasties and themselves in part of Arab descent, remained a source of trouble for the Merina whom they eventually expelled in 1883. The Merina returned in 1885, but their authority over Fort Dauphin, where a French Resident was by then installed, was nominal.

The long dictatorship of Rainilaiarivony had given rise to considerable political resistance, and bands of *menalamba*, or outlaws, operated even in Imerina, to the south of Tananarive in the Vakinankaratra. In 1887 the Prime Minister's nephew, the Foreign Minister, and in 1893 his son, were accused of plotting against him, and were exiled. Outlying provinces began to revolt, and raids were carried out by the Sakalava and Bara on Merina garrisons. In 1894, although Kingdon had already been exiled, the 'Mexican piastre scandal' finally broke, since a number of Europeans, including Kingdon, had bought Mexican silver piastres at 2·70 francs and resold them in Tananarive at 5·0 francs. These were being used as currency and the consequent devaluation caused great discontent among those who had been defrauded. The Prime Minister was obliged to declare these piastres illegal tender, and to throw all the blame on Kingdon, now out of the country.

During the nineteenth century, the rulers of Madagascar did not coin their own money, except for one or two trial mintings that were not followed up. Various European and American coins, obtained by trading in the Indian Ocean, were used for exchange purposes. The chief of these were the Spanish piastre, which circulated widely in the Indian Ocean, and, from about 1885, the French five-franc silver piece.[41] Only silver coins were used to any great extent—though, on the west coast, some gold pieces circulated and were highly sought after for jewellery—and, as there was no small change, the piastre was cut into as many as 720 small pieces (*variraiventy*), most of which had specific names in Malagasy. (These names are listed in *Tacchi's Money Table*.[42]) French coinage was issued at the time of the Conquest in 1896 and remained in circulation until 1925, when an issuing agency, the Banque de Madagascar, was created. This bank issued specifically Malagasy currency but was subject to the direct control of the French Treasury. In 1945 this Malagasy currency was converted to the CFA franc, equivalent at first to 1·70 and from 1948 to 2·00 metropolitan French francs. This was replaced in 1963 by the franc malgache, or FMG, issued by the Malagasy Institut d'Emission, with 50 FMG equivalent to one French franc; Madagascar remained a member of the franc zone. In the markets or shops, Malagasy give prices in units of five francs, or *ariary* (a relic of the old silver five-franc pieces); thus, an item costing 20 FMG is stated to cost 'four *ariary*'.

In 1890, a Franco-British convention was signed, recognising the 'French Protectorate' over Madagascar in exchange for the acceptance by France of the British Protectorate over the Sultanate of Zanzibar. This clearly showed the Prime Minister that, in spite of all the British missionaries had told him, he could no longer count on any British support to resist a French take-over. French policy was now influenced considerably by the representatives in Parliament of rich sugar planters from Réunion, and it was Brunet, Deputy for this island, who secured unanimous support of his resolution introduced in June 1894 to 'uphold this government in its efforts to maintain our position and our rights in Madagascar, to re-establish public order, protect our citizens, and secure respect for our flag'.

The French consul proposed the evacuation of French nationals supposedly threatened, and on October 14, 1894, Charles Le Myre de Villiers, a former Governor of Cochin-China, who had already served as French Resident to Madagascar, returned to the island with a draft treaty establishing a true protectorate. The Prime Minister made counter-proposals, which were themselves a return to the treaty of 1885, and on October 27 Le Myre de Villiers

lowered the flag on the French Residency and ordered the evacuation of all French citizens. As soon as this was known in France,
the French Parliament voted the necessary funds for a military
expedition to Madagascar. In December 1894 Tamatave was
occupied, followed early in 1895 by Nosy-be, Ampasindava,
Diego-Suarez and Majunga. An army of 15,000 men was landed
at Majunga under the command of General Duchesne, who had
had experience of campaigns in Algeria and Tonkin. This force
contained Algerian and Senegalese troops and a battalion of the
Foreign Legion.

As the objective was Tananarive, some 375 miles to the south,
it was necessary for the army to transform the footpath into some
kind of a road, since 5,000 Lefebre carts had been provided for
the supply column. This road began in the mangrove swamps of
the Betsiboka and Ikopa rivers, which enter the sea at Majunga,
and the expeditionary force soon suffered very considerable losses,
not from military action but from malaria and dysentery. In the
whole campaign, only 25 soldiers were killed in action, but
5,756 European and 3,550 Algerian troops died of disease and
twelve ships were needed to repatriate the sick.

Facing the French force was the Merina army of 45,000 men,
which still had two British instructors, Shervinton and Graves.
The Merina artillery put up an effective resistance and a series of
battles were fought as the Merina troops retreated from one
strong point to another towards Tananarive. While it is stated by
several writers[43] that the Merina military resistance was ineffective,
it is certain that it was organised, and isolated actions, such as the
offensive mounted by General Rainianjalahy against the French
at Andriba when they were more than half-way to Tananarive,
show that there was considerable fighting spirit. This was again
shown in the armed resistance that continued for many years
after the conquest. The defeat of the Merina forces was due to
superior armament and organisation of the French forces and not
to any collapse of the government.

To overcome the delays caused by continued sickness and the
slow progress of the road construction, General Duchesne
organised, on September 14, 1895, a flying-column of 4,000 men
with a mule convoy and twenty-two days' supplies. On September
30 began the battle of Tananarive, which was however more
symbolic than violent. An eyewitness reported that the French

forces first knocked out the Merina artillery outside the town and occupied the observatory of the Jesuits to the east. A Merina battery opened fire on the French, who replied by landing five melinite shells in the courtyard of the Royal Palace, killing many people who were gathered there. 'This brought matters to a crisis. At about three o'clock the Malagasy flag was hauled down from the top of the palace, after which not another shot was fired. Half an hour afterwards some native officers were seen carrying out a white flag to the French lines, submission was rendered and the war was at an end.'[44]

The treaty the Queen signed the next day, on October 1, was practically the same as the document presented by Le Myre de Villiers; it established a Protectorate under which France took over external relations, received the right to station occupation forces and to control internal affairs. The Queen and the court were maintained but the Prime Minister was put under house-arrest at his country place.* A new Prime Minister was appointed, from the same oligarchy which had for so long governed the country.

The instructions of the French government at this time were to avoid as far as possible any change in the existing structures, and to be extremely reserved in dealing with the non-Merina population'. It was intended that, under the Protectorate, a system of indirect rule should function, thus enabling France to govern using the administrative machinery already in existence.

However, the popular resistance continued. The defeat of the monarchy was interpreted as a result of its conversion to Christianity and its abandonment of the religion of the ancestors. Armed insurrection broke out at Arivonimamo, 35 miles west of Tananarive, where a force of 2,000 men seized the town and killed the Merina governor. William and Lucy Johnson, two British members of the Friends' mission, and their child were also murdered. It appears that this attack was part of a plot by a secret society, the Zanakantitra, to murder those whom they regarded as traitors for having accepted defeat and occupation. This band of 2,000 men was to assemble in Tananarive on a Friday, market day, with arms hidden under their clothes, and, at a pre-arranged signal, to rush the Royal Palace, the French Residency and the

---

* Rainilaiarivony was then over seventy. During the rebellion of 1896, he was exiled to Algiers, where he died four months later.

European quarter at Faravohitra. The plot misfired through a quarrel in which two Merina officers were killed, and this precipitated the attack on Arivonimamo. French troops were immediately sent west, and the plot came to nothing.[45]

In January 1896, Hippolyte Laroche, a former prefect, with no overseas experience, a Protestant and a liberal, was appointed Resident-General and made the Queen sign a new treaty in which the word 'Protectorate' disappeared and she was forced to recognise 'the taking possession of Madagascar by France'. Laroche's instructions were still 'carefully to avoid any action which might unnecessarily weaken the authority of the Queen over the population subject to her'. However, three governments succeeded each other in France between 1895 and 1896, and the instructions given to Laroche were imprecise and often contradictory.

Laroche continued the friendly relations with the Queen which General Duchesne had established, and contemporary accounts speak of receptions at the Palace and the Residency, where the young Malagasy princesses made a considerable impression on the French officers of the garrison. The Queen is even rumoured to have had a 'weakness' for Laroche, although the British missionary Matthews calls him 'a noble-minded Christian gentleman'.[46] He was attacked by the Catholics for being a Protestant, and accused of being 'in the pay of Lord Salisbury' because of his friendly attitude towards British missionaries. He was unpopular with the French Creole colonists because of his friendly relations with the Malagasy and was even criticised for beginning to learn the language.

His departure was precipitated by the insurrection against the French occupation that broke out in many districts at the end of the rainy season in March 1896. Armed bands killed French settlers and cut communications. A number of members of the aristocracy and the administration set themselves at the head of these resistance forces. Authority broke down rapidly all over the island when the insurrection spread to other tribes such as the Sakalava, for whom the defeat of the Merina was a liberation for themselves. Laroche's last act was to issue a law abolishing slavery in Madagascar, which automatically liberated about one third of the population and whose sudden effects were a considerable embarrassment to his successors, including General Galliéni.

A law was passed in the French Parliament on August 6, 1896, declaring Madagascar and its dependencies a French colony. On September 28 General Joseph Simon Galliéni took over with full military and civil powers. His instructions from the French Prime Minister, André Lebon, were as follows: 'Madagascar is now a French colony, and the system which consisted merely in exercising a protectorate over the dominant race is now set aside. The authority of the sovereign power must now be applied by the authority of the chiefs of each separate tribe'. This amounted to instructions to put an end to the power of the Merina monarchy, and to the dominance of the Merina people over the other tribes of Madagascar.

The expansion of the Merina, remarkable for such a small population, but facilitated by their social cohesion, sound agricultural base, and their ready absorption of European technology, was thus never complete over the whole of Madagascar. In 1895, much of the west, the south, and the south-east corner, were independent of the control of the Merina military posts. The authority of the Merina monarchy may be said to have been complete over two-thirds of Madagascar, comprising the most important economic and most populated regions. But it was in fact the conquest and administrative organisation carried out by Galliéni which achieved the first political unity of Madagascar. His arrival marks the beginning of the colonising action of France, which was to continue for the next sixty-four years.

5. State and Politics : 1896-1960

THE COLONISATION of Madagascar began with a period of extensive military action against the resistance that had developed over large areas of the island, following the capture of Tananarive by French forces under General Duchesne and the few months of 'protectorate' under Laroche. At the time of his arrival, General Galliéni found that the French forces held only a few of the main towns, that the countryside on the central highlands was in the hands of the resistance, and that communications for anything but a strongly-armed column had been cut. In Imerina the resistants were at first spoken of as *fahavalo*, or 'enemies', but soon came to be called *menalamba*, or 'red shawls', since they coloured their white *lambas* with red earth as a camouflage. The *menalamba* had existed as small bands of outlaws during the latter years of the rule of the deposed Prime Minister, Rainilaiarivony, and consisted partly of men in opposition to the government. They were now, in the words of an eye-witness, 'led by fanatical sorcerers and such like, and their object was to drive not only the French but all white men of whatsoever nationality out of the country and restore the old political and religious regime'.[1] The Zanakantitra* had destroyed a large number of churches and schools, about 750 in all, of which 500 were connected with the London Missionary Society. The resistants claimed that while they had worshipped the gods of the ancestors they had been independent, but that since the introduction of 'praying to the white man's ancestor, Jesus Christ' they had lost their freedom. The nationalists not only fought French military forces but also conducted a general attack on European missions. Local resistance movements developed rapidly among tribes previously wholly or partially independent of the Merina monarchy—the Sakalava, Bara, Antandroy and Antambaoka.

The immediate task of Galliéni was therefore to put an end to the state of anarchy and to establish an effective military occupation

* Zanakantitra, literally 'children of the old one', a noble family which had voluntarily become hova (or bourgeoisie) in exchange for grants of land under the monarchy.

that would control the whole country. For this he had available 7,000 French troops. He refused an offer of reinforcements from outside, except for a fresh battalion of the Foreign Legion; two battalions of Malagasy troops were raised on the east coast and in the Betsileo country.

In analysing the subsequent military operation, it is necessary to apply objective and purely military criteria. This operation was envisaged by France as a preliminary to the re-establishment of an organised state, though this time under French rule. In assessing the effects, economic and social, of the colonial experience on Madagascar (or indeed on any country), careful analysis is necessary, above all applied to the period in which the events recorded took place. A military operation, by definition, results in the killing of people on both sides. Unless one is prepared to condemn all military actions as immoral, which is a quite logical point of view, it is difficult and often illogical to condemn all or part of specific military operations. Much of the writing about this period comes from memoirs of French officers and officials. To them, the resistance was the unjustified action of uncivilised people, against whom strong repressive measures were fully in order. Their moral judgement is therefore exerted on the assumption that they were right and that the resistants were morally wrong. In a smaller number of books, written either by Malagasy or by liberal foreigners, the French military action is condemned on the assumption that the colonial intervention was morally wrong. Writing now some years after independence, it is probable that such value judgements are a waste of time, and it is safer to assume that in a military action, especially where the two sides are not evenly matched, there will be killing and individual acts of unjustifiable brutality.

In this operation Madagascar was fortunate in having Galliéni in charge of affairs. He was by any standards a remarkable man, not only as a soldier but more especially as an organiser and administrator. His career, which began as a cadet officer in the Franco-Prussian War, reached its climax when, as military governor of Paris in 1914, he mobilised the Paris taxis to carry troops and thus helped stop the German advance at the first battle of the Marne. He belongs to an exceptional category of military men— of whom Napoleon, Galliéni's inspiration, is the outstanding example—who transformed their conquests from a purely military operation by efficient administrative and economic organisation. (Lord Lugard is a similar British example.) Galliéni was of Italian descent on his father's side. His father left Italy to enter the French army, inspired no doubt by the Napoleonic ethos and also by the growing movement for independence in Italy. He married a Frenchwoman from Saint-Béat in the Pyrenees, and it was here that their son, Joseph Simon, was born in 1849. While a cadet at St Cyr, Joseph was drafted at once into the army on the outbreak of war against Prussia in 1870, and it was then that he met Kitchener, the future British field-marshal, who had left the Royal Military Academy, Woolwich, without permission in order to participate in the Franco-Prussian War on the side of the French. Their friendship was to last for the rest of their lives. Galliéni was a prisoner of the Prussians for seven months, and on his release was posted to Réunion where he remained for three years. Here, close to Madagascar, he learned much about that island, then still independent. His subsequent career brought him considerable experience of colonial wars, notably in Senegal, French Soudan and Indo-China. It was from the Far East that he was posted to Madagascar in 1896.

The French conquest under General Duchesne had effectively destroyed an organised state, and the disorder and anarchy that had broken out under Resident-General Laroche came about because no effective administration or authority had been put in its place. The problem was different from that of many African territories, where a military column of the colonising power merely imposed a central authority over a number of local chiefs or minor rulers. At the moment of the capture of Tananarive in 1896, Madagascar was an internationally-recognised state under a central monarchy exercising some kind of authority over most of the island. A relatively well-educated elite ensured a coherent administration with codified laws applied through a system of provincial administration. Communications and the beginnings of an educational system existed, as did the elements of an exchange economy.

The breakdown of these structures was due mainly to the destruction of the authority of the ruling class, the Merina aristocracy centred on the Prime Minister and the Queen. It is therefore not surprising that official French policy had envisaged a considerable measure of indirect rule and the preservation of the existing administrative structures. This policy had been applied in Tunisia and Indo-China and was later to be adopted in Morocco in 1912. It had not, of course, been the policy in Algeria; there, the Bey of Algiers was exiled immediately after the conquest of 1830, and, after a period in which the submission of local rulers such as the Bey of Constantine was sought, a uniform direct administration was substituted for what remained of local rule. Algiers had been nominally a Turkish possession; thus, French rule took the place of Turkish rule.

Although France imposed a much more coherent and uniform territorial administration on its overseas territories than did Britain, a number of local rulers were allowed to remain in their palaces, though without any powers. There was thus a vast difference between the status of the Fulani emirs of Sokoto or Kanu, with their native authority police, local courts and taxation privileges, and their French Fulani counterparts, the emirs of Zinder or Agadès, who were allowed to appear only once a year for a Muslim festival. A similar difference in status could be seen between the Yoruba obas in Nigeria and those over the border in Dahomey. There were occasional exceptions, as where France used El Glaoui, the Pasha of Marrakesh, as a Berber counterweight to divide and rule in Morocco.

The problem that faced Galliéni was that the resistance to the French conquest was primarily a resistance of the Merina people, led by members of the deposed ruling class, and that their natural rallying point was still Queen Ranavalona III. There were two kinds of officers in the French army of the period: Catholics of aristocratic descent and royalist sympathies, and anti-clerical Republicans of bourgeois families. Galliéni belonged to the latter group; his anti-clericalism had as its source a civilised neutrality developed by contact during his career with Buddhists, Hindus and Muslims, as well as with the many Christian sects. On his arrival in Madagascar, he intended to dethrone the Queen, although his official instructions were to preserve existing institutions. The tone of the new regime is indicated by his reply to the departing Resident-General, Laroche, when he offered to escort Galliéni to the palace in Tananarive to introduce him to the Queen and her family; Galliéni said: 'Ranavalona is a subject of France; I shall expect these ladies tomorrow'.[2] And, indeed, the following day the Queen, a diadem of diamonds in her long black hair, attended by the princesses and a number of nobles wearing an assortment of European-style uniforms, paid her call on the General. She is reported to have been trembling from nervousness.[3]

The resistance continued, and it became evident to Galliéni that the Queen and certain of the nobility were in contact with the rebels. He struck out at two outstanding members of the ruling class: on October 15, 1896, Prince Ratsimamanga, the Queen's uncle, and the Minister Rainandriamampandry were condemned to death by a court-martial for complicity with the rebels and publicly executed two days later by a firing-squad in Tananarive. These executions have been discussed by several writers.[4] Galliéni is said to have admitted later that the execution of Rainandriamampandry, former Governor of Tamatave, who had put up a stiff resistance to the French army, was an error, and he helped various members of the minister's family. It is now said in Madagascar of these executions that Galliéni deliberately chose from the Merina aristocracy one person who was disliked, Ratsimamanga, and one who was much respected, Rainandriamampandry. Several other members of the court were exiled to Réunion. Thus Galliéni realised one part of his programme, which was, he had stated on arrival: 'To make Madagascar French, to undermine the British influence, and to bring down the Hova [sic] pride and power.'

On February 27, 1897, Galliéni sent his Chief of Staff to the Royal Palace with a letter notifying the Queen that she had been deposed. He took this decision without any instructions from France: an indication of how freely those in command of colonial operations were able to act before the introduction of rapid telecommunications. The French government had decided to maintain the monarchy, though limiting the jurisdiction of the Queen to Imerina; but Galliéni decided otherwise and presented the government with a fait accompli, offering his resignation if his action was not accepted. France was at this time unable to undertake any extensive military operations as far away as Madagascar. The rapid expansion in West Africa brought France constantly into situations of potential conflict with Britain, and absorbed large military forces for the occupation of what Lord Salisbury described as 'vast areas of sand which we can allow the French cock to scratch'.[5] It was clear that Galliéni could not count on reinforcements in Madagascar.

It is difficult to imagine the dethroning of a monarch by any general on his own responsibility after 1900. Galliéni was fortunate that other pressing business forced the French government to leave him a free hand. The Chief of Staff had the letter presented to the Queen late in the evening and translated by a palace official. She was ordered to leave that night for the coast. A painful scene followed, since evidently she had never expected to be exiled. The aim was to get her out of Tananarive as quickly as possible, and in the greatest secrecy. She was informed that she could take her personal belongings and jewels, but not the crown and sceptre, nor, significantly enough, the Grand Cross of the Legion of Honour which the French government had awarded her. Ranavalona left at three in the morning, in a litter carried by porters and escorted by Senegalese troops, for Tamatave where she immediately put aboard a ship for Réunion. Two years later she was transferred to Algiers, where she lived in a fine villa above the town until her death in 1917. Her remains were brought back to Tananarive and placed in the royal tomb at the palace in 1938.

Galliéni survived hostile questions on this action in the French Parliament; he received unanimous support from the government and was nominated Governor-General. On March 15 he caused the remains of the Merina kings to be removed from the royal tombs at Ambohimanga, twelve miles north of Tananarive, and brought to the royal tomb at the palace; at the same time he abolished the royal Festival of the Bath* and replaced it with the French national festival of July 14. In April all feudal powers and obligations were abolished. These measures were specifically directed against the Merina oligarchy and aimed at eliminating all signs of royal and aristocratic power. The removal of the remains of the Merina kings from Ambohimanga constituted a violation of tombs, and nothing could have created a deeper impression on the Malagasy. Such a violation would be out of the question for any government today.

The resistance was not overcome for another two years, and continued in isolated areas until 1902, but with the overthrow

* A ceremony of ritual purification occurring on November 20 each year. The queen (or ruler) bathed in a stone bath still to be seen at Ambohimanga, the royal residence to the north of Tananarive. This was followed by a banquet at which all the members of the government and the notables were present.

of the Merina monarchy and his own appointment as Governor-General, Galliéni had his hands free to reconstruct the administration. He was joined in 1897 by a young officer who had served on his staff in Tonkin, Colonel Louis Hubert Gonzalve Lyautey, who was later to become a remarkable and creative governor in a similar operation of pacification and reconstruction in Morocco from 1912. Lyautey was given the command of the southern part of the island, with his headquarters at Fianarantsoa. Both he and Galliéni were voluminous writers and this period of Malagasy history is minutely documented.[6]

Galliéni's military tactics aimed at ensuring that every troop movement secured an effective occupation of territory. This put an end to the dashing 'flying columns' of his predecessor which secured nothing at all. His officers were instructed to create a frontier of military posts, which the resistants could not cross, and to reorganise and reassure the population behind this frontier, which was to be displaced gradually forward, opening schools and dispensaries behind it and re-establishing normal activities. His instructions contained this fine phrase: 'Ensure that those whom you administer tremble only at the idea of your leaving.' His second principle was that of unity of local command; his officers in the field had full military and civil powers for the districts occupied and were responsible only to their immediate military superiors. Lastly, he insisted on the political side of pacification, to secure the adherence of the population, and resorted to military action only if absolutely necessary. Reading his reports and letters, one is struck firstly by his energy but also by his constructive policies. The pacification was not carried out without killing, and certain officers left to their own responsibility certainly killed unnecessarily.[7] But there is no historical evidence for organised brutality, and such action would have been entirely contrary to Galliéni's instructions and to what he was attempting to do in Madagascar.

By the end of 1897, all the former kingdom had been occupied and was being administered by military officers from command posts afterwards transformed into districts. As part of his policy of destroying the power of the Merina oligarchy, Galliéni planned a considerable measure of indirect rule, using the *mpanjaka*, or local chiefs, among the coastal tribes. This policy failed, largely because these had not the education of their Merina counterparts and were quite unable to cope with the complexities of French administration, especially audit and financial control: Lyautey speaks of a Bara chief from whom the central audit in Tananarive demanded a justification in proper form of expenditures. The *mpanjaka* were preserved as tribal figureheads, but any idea of using them—as, for example, Britain used the Emir of Sokoto or the Litunga of Barotseland—as rulers with local administrative powers was quickly abandoned.

Most of the structures laid down by Galliéni lasted until political independence in 1960, and many of them have been taken over by the republican government. Galliéni ordered his officers to prepare monographs on each of the districts, concerning their resources, ethnography, dynasties and history. He edited a periodical called *Notes, Reconnaissances et Explorations* and in 1902 founded the Académie Malgache, which since that date has published a vast amount of first-hand scientific, economic, historical and literary material and research on Madagascar. The administrative hierarchy created by Rainilaiarivony, with governors and deputy governors, was preserved and, from the beginning, Galliéni's officers used as subordinates Malagasy officials taken over from the monarchy. These were completed by the 'clerk-intepreters' who came to occupy a key-post in the administration and to have great influence. Galliéni encouraged all French officials to learn the Malagasy language, and most district administrators spoke Malagasy, down to the last war. After 1946, few officials took the trouble to study Malagasy, as it was not compulsory for administrative staff—unlike many of the British colonies, where a knowledge of a local language was essential for promotion and examinations in it were held for officials.

The pacification was long and difficult, as it was in Algeria after 1830, and in Morocco where, as late as 1935, military operations against dissidents were still going on. Once the Merina were subdued, the outlying peoples of the coasts, who had been subject to the central Merina government only since the reigns of Radama and Ranavalona I, began a series of risings. The last big revolt took place in 1904, among the peoples of the extreme south. Galliéni acted quickly, and it must be recorded that his instructions to his officers were 'to pacify, not to exterminate'. Galliéni left Madagascar in that year, with the submission of the whole island to a central authority now completed.

The administration evolved rapidly: the military 'cercles', commanded by an officer, became provinces (twenty at first) subdivided into districts under a civilian district commissioner. These provinces were at first intended to correspond to ethnic divisions, there being nominally eighteen tribes in Madagascar. A considerable number of Malagasy officials—'cadres indigènes' (native cadres), later 'cadres spéciaux' (special cadres)—remained in their posts under the district commissioner. The districts were further subdivided into cantons under a 'chef de canton', a Malagasy, who collected local taxes, especially the capitation tax, received requests and kept the *boky*, a large book which was a simple kind of population register.

A dual judicial system was set up. There was a 'justice européenne' for Europeans and 'assimilés'—that is, Asiatics, Malagasy who had obtained French nationality, and inhabitants of the island of Ste Marie, who had enjoyed French citizenship since the island was ceded by Queen Betia in 1750. French law, both civil and criminal codes, was held to apply to this group of citizens, after promulgation. The mass of the population were not considered citizens, but 'French subjects'; the word 'subject' in French means what it says and implies submission, and thus it is different in sense from the British use of the word, which means 'citizen'. These subjects were bound under a different legal system, called the 'indigénat' and administered by the district commissioners, under which they could be arbitrarily committed to a maximum of fifteen days' imprisonment or a fine for such offences as not cultivating enough land, non-payment of taxes or refusing to give voluntary labour. The former Malagasy legal code was maintained, with certain modifications, and applied to the subjects. The indigénat was the formal recognition of the inferior status of the native population and was much resented, especially by the former ruling class in Imerina. Its abolition became a principal subject for agitation during the period of the reorganisation of nationalism from 1920 onwards.

In the fields of health and education, Galliéni moved rapidly, and the structures laid down proved as lasting as those of the administration. The role of the missions was a difficult problem in 1896, mainly because of the bitter antagonism between French Catholics, mainly Jesuits, and British Protestants, mainly of the London Missionary Society. It is unlikely that the latter were, as the French maintained, British agents, especially in view of the agreement at government level between Britain and France on action in Madagascar and East Africa. But they were patriotic nineteenth-century Britons, and their writings all reflect strong national pride and an intense disappointment that France and not Britain had finally colonised Madagascar. The French had found that the British missionaries, speaking the Malagasy language, had great personal influence with the Queen and the ruling class. In view of the traditional Franco-British antagonism of the era, which persisted, in spite of inter-governmental agreements on spheres of influence, up to the time of the Entente Cordiale of 1904, it is not surprising that, in the restricted society of Tananarive, there were bitter personal conflicts. Such personal antagonisms were a common feature of small colonial posts, where an atmosphere not unlike that on a long steamship journey (or, as some would say, a prisoner-of-war camp) has frequently prevailed. The European easily became obsessed with his own importance, because in fact he had an importance vis-à-vis the native inhabitants and could thus readily see himself as their protector against the administration. The British missionaries, all born during the reign of Queen Victoria, identified themselves closely with Queen Ranavalona III and tended to see the French Jesuits as Romish villains.

Galliéni seems to have preserved a genuine neutrality between the mutual accusations and intrigues of often excited Protestant and Catholic clergy. This was a period of intense anti-clericalism in France, during which Freemasonry had a strong grip on many French institutions. The year 1905 saw the Separation Law (Loi de Séparation des Eglises et de l'Etat) which expelled all Catholic religious orders from France, following the dénouement of the Dreyfus Affair. It was fortunate for the Malagasy that they had Galliéni, and many were to regret him during the rule of his Freemason successor, Victor Augagneur. Galliéni's chief concern was to see that the British Protestant missionaries refrained from anti-French propaganda and that they taught French in their schools. He requisitioned certain of their buildings, against compensation which even the LMS admitted to be adequate, but apart from the loss of prestige they had little to complain about. This did not prevent their expressing in their memoirs violent criticism of French policy, manners, and customs.[8] Galliéni was scarcely more indulgent to the French Jesuits; he allowed the Holy Ghost and Lazarist Fathers to set up missions, thus ending the Jesuit monopoly of Catholic influence.

Although the missions continued their important educational programmes, Galliéni appointed a Director of Education, Pierre Deschamps, under whom were rapidly created a large number of official lay primary schools ('écoles officielles laïques') with Malagasy teachers trained in regional teacher-training colleges. In 1905, at the time of Galliéni's departure, the government statistics show 23,500 pupils in the official schools and 16,000 in the mission schools, not counting 'church schools' kept by teachers who did not have the official aptitude certificate. If these latter are included, the mission schools had, in 1905, 209,000 pupils (127,000 in the Protestant schools and 82,000 in the Catholic), which shows that mission influence had actually increased, in spite of the missionaries' complaints against the French administration. The official population figure for Madagascar in 1902, when the first population census was conducted, was 2 million. The school-attendance figures given above show that, in 1905, approximately 230,000 children were receiving primary education—more than 10 per cent of the population. This is a remarkable figure when compared with the scant regard shown by other colonial powers to education, notably in African territories in which European settlement was taking place. As early as nine years after the conquest, official French policy was laying an educational foundation that has done much to promote the stability of post-independence institutions and society in Madagascar.

The regional administrative training schools, or 'écoles régionales' were created to supply Malagasy subordinate staff for the French colonial administration, and employees with a minimum technical training who were to work as overseers and accountants for the settlers and in local commercial firms. There was no intention to train Malagasy for senior posts, which were reserved for many years for French colonial servants. A very small number, drawn exclusively from the Merina elite, were enabled to study in French universities and higher schools. These included a few doctors, four veterinarians and several lawyers. Certain Malagasy who obtained professional qualifications remained in France. The profession of pharmacist was opened early on to Malagasy and was used as a means of obtaining higher education. Some of the largest personal fortunes in Tananarive are those of these early pharmacists.

The regional schools, which combined administrative training with 'trade schools' and 'vocational training', were subject to reorganisation by successive governors-general. Finally it was the regional school in Tananarive, the Ecole Myre de Villiers, which was the most successful. Most of the senior civil servants in the 1960s had begun their civil service training in this school, and continued it at the Institut des Hautes Etudes d'Outre-Mer (IHEOM) into which the old Ecole Colonaile had been transformed in France.

The French economic penetration of Madagascar occurred rapidly and concurrently with the pacification by Galliéni. This was not to be left a vast unexploited territory like certain French possessions in West Africa. There had been a long experience of European and Creole colonisation on the east coast: attempts had been made since the abortive settlement of Flacourt at Fort Dauphin in the late seventeenth century. All through the eighteenth century the Réunion settlers had looked to Madagascar as a source of food supplies and of slaves, at the same time seeing it as natural *lebensraum* for their own expansion. French writers advocated intermarriage of European settlers and Malagasy women and their establishment on legally-acquired land.[9] White settlers, usually Creoles, were established on the east coast early in the nineteenth century and many of them survived the period of xenophobia and political and economic isolation of the reign of Ranavalona I (1828–61).[10] At the time of the conquest a number of Creole settlers were established on small-holdings on the east coast, in the north near Diego-Suarez, and on the west coast on the island of Nosy-be and in the valley of the Sambirano river.

Here again French policy was decided on the spot by Galliéni, who had to choose between allowing large companies to take up extensive concessions or encouraging individual European settlers. In French West Africa, which was considered unsuitable for individual European settlement, large companies had taken over and were to remain in a position of dominance over the economy. Although Madagascar was considered more suitable for European settlement, in spite of the poor reputation it had gained as a result of the high mortality from tropical diseases among General Duchesne's expeditionary corps, it has been the large companies who have had the greatest influence.

It was hoped that a limited type of settlement would occur, similar to that which took place in Tunisia and Morocco, rather than the massive European immigration of Algeria. In spite of its size and low population density, Madagascar did not offer such favourable opportunities to European settlers as appeared at first sight. The central highland area, where an altitude of 4,000 feet gives a climate favourable to Europeans, was at first thought ideal for the small settler. A series of 'Guides to Immigrants' gave numerous details on how to set up house in Madagascar, how to deal with the 'natives' and what to grow.[11] In spite of this, no successful farms were established in the highlands like those in the not-too dissimilar climatic region of the Kenya Highlands. The comparison is not absolute, owing to the difference in latitude and the bi-modal rainfall of Kenya which gives a less severe dry season than occurs in Madagascar. But all the Kenyan crops have been tried in Madagascar and, under suitable conditions of culture, can be grown successfully. These include arabica coffee, tea, pyrethrum, maize, fruit and vegetables, conifers, and mixed farming for intensive livestock production. In the central highlands of Madagascar small areas of arabica coffee are grown, tea and pyrethrum have been established on an experimental scale by the Department of Agriculture (but only since 1961), maize appears on the edges of paddy fields, fruit and vegetables are grown in small gardens for local markets, and large plantations of conifers (*Pinus patula* and *Pinus khasya*) were established after 1955. Malagasy farmers produce small quantities of milk, and fatten pigs, cattle and poultry by traditional methods for the Tananarive market. Thus, on a small artisan scale, the central highlands of Madagascar have a production pattern similar to that of the Kenya Highlands, but no European farms remotely comparable to the Kenya coffee plantations, the milk-herds and beef ranches. By the late 1960s, the European farms on the central highlands of Madagascar were often completely abandoned, and those remaining conducted 'a mediocre mixed-farming operation'.[12]

On the east coast, European colonisation had 'a brilliant beginning followed by a profound decadence'. It is often difficult to distinguish a European or Creole plantation from that of his Malagasy neighbour. In general, the settlers appear to have had little or no capital and often little competence or aptitude. Madagascar thus appears as a land far from the centre of colonial expansion, and it would seem that the most energetic French settlers remained near the centre, in North Africa, or even Guinea and the Ivory Coast, leaving Madagascar for the less successful. A similar phenomenon can be noted in the colonisation of Central Africa, where the degree of technical competence and prosperity diminishes as one goes northwards from South Africa, and expires among the European settlers of Zambia. It can be claimed that certain regions of Zambia are more favourable ecologically for Virginia tobacco-growing than Rhodesia, but nothing comparable to the Rhodesian tobacco plantations has yet appeared in its northern neighbour. Madagascar, similarly far from the centre of the wave of settlers, does not seem to have attracted the dynamic types who operated successfully in North Africa before political independence.

The commercial companies have been far more efficient and financially successful. There had been some penetration by these companies even before the conquest, under agreements with the Merina monarchy, and by 1912 eight large territorial concessions had been granted. Of these, four were confirmed for the Compagnie Coloniale de Madagascar (64,625 acres), the Société de la Grande Ile (243,133 acres), the Compagnie Occidentale de Madagascar (220,000 acres) and the Compagnie Française et Minière de Madagascar (1,210,000 acres). As in Africa, these companies failed usually to take up or exploit the greater part of their concessions, and an official publication of 1931 lists six concessions extending over 1,360,000 acres mainly for mineral prospection, forest exploitation, extensive grazing and collection of wild products such as raphia or rubber. Only a small part of these concessions was exploited as agricultural land.

Although official figures for 1956 give 6,000 as the number of 'Europeans' having agriculture as their main occupation, these were by no means all farmers of the conventional settler type. Creoles and certain Malagasy were counted as 'Europeans', and Indians and Chinese who had acquired French citizenship would also appear as such. A high proportion of these farmers were very much part-time, either having another occupation such as trading or being retired from minor posts in government service. As late as 1956 official French policy still considered it possible to establish European farmers in Madagascar, and a few French peasants were settled in the Ankaizina, where they remained a very short time. The last attempt to settle surplus population from Réunion, always an aim of official policy, was in 1952, when a number of Réunion Creole farmers were installed at very high individual cost on the Sakay settlement scheme on volcanic soils about sixty miles west of Tananarive. The chief merit of this scheme, which has now been converted into a settlement scheme for Malagasy, was that it has enabled viable methods of mixed farming to be worked out, adapted to conditions on the central highlands.*

This European colonisation was carried out within the framework of a land system, established by the decree of February 4, 1911, which was based in its essential principles on the model of the Torrens Act of Australia. It is true that three types of land-tenure existed: the traditional system, where land was allotted by chiefs, elders or other traditional local authorities; the cadastre (central land registry), introduced in certain zones such as around Tananarive, and available for Malagasy and foreigners; and the concessions. The French administration thus, from the start, set up an orderly land-tenure system which, despite its faults, had survived with modifications into the independence period. European settlement took place on land bought from Malagasy, or on land considered 'state land', where mobile units of surveyors had marked out areas considered suitable for settlement.

There was no doubt some disturbance of traditional extensive occupation of land, but it is incorrect to speak of the 'theft' of land, as do certain emotional or politically-motivated writers. In a country with as low a population density as Madagascar, there was, and is still, room for anyone able to produce. Actual cases of displacement of population were very rare and, when they occurred, have resulted from the population's being accustomed to a very extensive use of land and being later confined to a smaller area through the installation of settlers. People practising subsistence agriculture usually consider a very large area surrounding their villages as being ancestral land over which they have rights. Some kind of shifting cultivation or bush-fallowing is practised, and extensive grazing. Only in regard to paddy fields, tree-crops and gardens around villages is property strictly defined. Dis-

*Under the direction of the Bureau pour le Développment de la Production Agricole (BDPA), a French public corporation concerned with agricultural schemes in a number of overseas territories.

turbance occurs when settlement is carried out on these under-utilised ancestral lands, and this gave rise to claims of 'theft' by European settlers.

The conflicts between European settlers and Malagasy arose mainly as a result of abuses of the compulsory labour system. Galliéni had reinstituted the corvée, or *fanompoana*, which had existed under the monarchy, largely because of the embarrassment caused to his administration by the abolition of slavery by his predecessor Laroche, which had violently disrupted the labour 'supply schedule'. These labour obligations, known as 'prestations', were considered as a payment of taxes in kind and could be discharged by cash payments. Galliéni, in common with other colonial administrators, considered the imposition of a poll tax as the best way of obliging the inhabitants to enter the monetary exchange economy, and he spoke of 'the economic and social role, the educational nature of the tax'.[13]

The grant of large concessions of land to French companies was subject to the condition of their being developed, and it was hoped that considerable investments would follow. These hopes did not materialise and the subsequent development of European-operated agriculture appears to have been characterised as much by a lack of capital as by a reliance on local monopolies and support prices for export. The majority of these undertakings appear to have aimed at a high rate of return on capital, with a rather small turnover. This continued, after independence, to be a limiting factor on many of the expatriate firms still operating in Madagascar.

While investment appears to have been limited in so far as the productive sectors were concerned, there was a rapid expansion of commerce in the early days of colonisation. Large French companies concerned with the import-export trade set up at once: the Compagnie Lyonnaise in 1897 and the Compagnie Marseillaise in 1898. Imports from France of consumer goods and raw materials rose from 5,524 tons in 1896 to 27,897 tons in 1905, the corresponding figures for exports being 1,056 tons for 1896 and 16,078 tons for 1905 (mainly primary agricultural products). This expansion of trade was facilitated by the existence of a simple exchange economy for many years before the conquest, and by the experience gained by European traders in the Mascarene region during the nineteenth century.

By the time of his departure in 1905, Galliéni had laid down structures many of which survived political independence in 1960. A uniform system of territorial administration, a land-tenure system, a communications network that included the first section of the railway from Tamatave to Tananarive, an education and health service, had all been established, to mention only his principal achievements.

His successor, Victor Augagneur, was a typical politician of the period: a deputy, a former mayor of Lyon and, above all, a Freemason. He was entirely in sympathy with the anti-clerical reaction that had passed the 1905 law separating church and state. The activities of the French lodges have always been far more political in scope than those of Britain. In the former French colonies, Freemasons were numerous and influential, especially in the Education and Public Works Departments, and, because of official policy, both these departments had considerably more power and importance than their counterparts in British colonies. Augagneur openly favoured Freemasonry and encouraged Malagasy notables to become Freemasons. In certain services, especially those of Education and Health, promotion depended on becoming a Freemason, and, since many of the educated Malagasy were doctors, this caused an important penetration among intellectuals. The corollary to this was Augagneur's attack on the missions, shown first by his energetic action in favour of lay schools and the prohibition of the non-certified church schools—which, as a result, disappeared, and several thousand children were left without schooling.

Augagneur suppressed a society of intellectuals known as the Union Chrétienne des Jeunes Gens (UCJG—Christian young people's union) which was headed by the Protestant minister Ravelojaona, one of the first nationalist political figures to emerge after the conquest and the destruction of the Merina oligarchy. Himself a Merina and the son of a Protestant minister, Ravelojaona edited a number of religious and lay periodicals in Malagasy, among them *Ny Teny Soa* (1907–15) and *Ny Mpamafy* (1911–15). Ravelojaona (1879–1956) is remembered as a moderate nationalist politician and as a man of letters. His most important work is an encyclopedia, *Firaketana ny fiteny sy ny zavatra malagasy* (Treasury of the language and things of Madagascar). He represented Madagascar from 1939 as delegate in the Conseil Supérieur de la

France d'Outre-mer and stood as candidate for the French Parliament in 1946, advocating progressive independence within the French Union. He was defeated by Ravoahangy, who advocated a policy of immediate independence. The UCJG naturally included many members of the Merina aristocracy and relatives of the former royal family and oligarchy. Madagascar differed from African territories at the time of its conquest in possessing a caste of intellectuals who had already been trained by Europeans in European thought. It was thus entirely different from the Arab or Far Eastern countries, which had an intellectual class but one trained in non-European traditions. Augagneur, in suppressing the UCJG, was also suppressing an embryonic nationalist political movement. In 1915 the UCJG became the Vy Vato Sakelika (VVS), a secret society with nationalist aspirations, which produced a violent reaction among the colonial administration.

The two groups behind the movement for political independence were the young Merina intellectuals, on the one hand, and later the ex-servicemen after their return from the First and Second World Wars. In 1912, the proposed youth organisation aimed at preserving the national culture and at the same time assimilating Western knowledge. Ravelojaona published in 1913 in one of the Malagasy-language periodicals, *Mpanolotsaina*, a series of articles concerning Japan, in which he showed how an Asiatic people could absorb Western science, and this seems to have excited considerable interest among the young Malagasy intellectuals. The French conquest was still recent, and it had reduced the former ruling class, the Merina, to the role of second-class citizens by the imposition of the indigénat. They had lost their former positions of command, their privileges and their slaves; and, though for the coastal peoples the French administration merely signified a change of masters from the Merina, these 'proud Hova' (as the British missionaries called them) could not easily forget their former status.

There was a curious ambivalence in the attitude of the Malagasy, and also of the intellectuals, towards the French administration. On the one hand there was among the Merina intense pride in their caste and traditional culture and a keen sense of loss of status. But in 1909, Augagneur, who was a man of the left, issued a decree (March 3, 1909) under which certain Malagasy who spoke French and fulfilled other conditions could apply for and receive French citizenship with full civil rights.* Most of those granted citizenship were intellectuals, professional men and minor civil servants, and many of them became fervent partisans of France and of French culture, so much so that even after independence comedians on the Tananarive radio in the programme 'Sangisangy zary tenany could always raise a laugh by imitating those of their compatriots who practise a French-culture snobbery. The majority of these citizens were assimilated into the French administration and behaved and thought as other French officials. Others, however, such as Ravoahangy, Raseta and Rabemananjara, the first two being doctors and the other a man of letters, became leading nationalists and were exiled after the 1947 Rebellion.

The assimilation of these Malagasy citizens was facilitated by the French attitude to them. A Malagasy doctor who had studied in France, and who was competent, was treated as an equal by his French colleagues. There may have been, and in fact there were, cases of slights and victimisation, but these were the exception. In bush stations, senior Malagasy officials were often received by French families in their houses in a manner that must have been very rare in British India and which was virtually unknown in British Africa. The criteria applied by French officials in judging their Malagasy colleagues were those of educational attainments and professional competence. Where these were considered to be adequate, there was no barrier to social relations, and genuine friendships existed between French and Malagasy professional and official families, occasionally leading to intermarriage. Children of such mixed marriages have risen to hold high positions in Malagasy government service.

The sporadic revolts among the coastal peoples continued. The pacification of the Antandroy, the cattle people of the extreme south, was always precarious: as late as 1946 this region was still under military control from a post at Tsihombe. Communications have always been difficult in Madagascar because of the mountainous terrain, and people could easily keep clear of the administration by following bush-tracks in empty country. Cattle-stealing was a traditional occupation which provided young men with natural training in resistance to authority.

* This decree was amplified by a second decree concerning accession to French citizenship issued by Governor-General Léon Cayla (1930–39). In 1939 there were 8,000 French citizens of Malagasy origin.

At the same time the traditional submission of the Malagasy to their chiefs or elders—*ray amandreny*—was often transferred to the French district commissioner, especially when, as was often the case, this now-vanished race of administrators showed outstanding human qualities. Such an attitude was often adopted towards British administrators in Africa in the days before centralised bureaucratic rule, but as Malagasy society was more structurally organised, this attachment to the hierarchy of command had a stronger stabilising influence.

While there may have been resentment against French rule among other peoples, it was among the Merina intellectuals that the first political organisation, as opposed to simple armed resistance, appeared. Many of those concerned with the Union Chrétienne des Jeunes Gens (UCJG), and in particular the Reverend Ravelojaona, reappeared in the secret society, Vy, Vato, Sakelika (VVS). This grouped together about 300 intellectuals and included medical students and teachers. An initiation ceremony included oaths taken on a cross and on the blood of a cock (a bird frequently used in sacrifices to the mythical Vazimba on the high mountains near Tananarive). The movement had a branch in the Betsileo province but seems to have been confined to Merina living there.

The official version, stated at the subsequent trial of leading members of the society, was that they were plotting an armed revolt for January 1916. Other writers consider that it was a student movement 'playing at conspirators'.[14] While no arms appear to have been found, there was some contact between the members of the society and the Malagasy troops being raised at this time for service in the French armies deployed on the Western Front. It is probable that the members were sincere in their desire to re-establish a Malagasy government and that they might in due course have attempted an armed revolt. It is known that certain of their leaders, including Ravelojaona and Ravoahangy, were men of outstanding personal courage.

The police learned that sections of the VVS had been formed in Fianarantsoa and Ambalavao, through which the Malagasy levies were to pass on their way to deal with unrest among the Antandroy in the south, and on December 24, 1915, a number of the leaders of the society were arrested. Within a few days 500 Malagasy, mainly intellectuals, were arrested, and 41 of these were later indicted for incitement to revolt. Their trial opened in

January 1916 in the great hall of the Palace of Andafiavaratra, the residence of the former Prime Minister, Rainilaiarivony.

The official indictment claimed that the accused had 'formed a well-organised secret society with the aim of expelling the French and restoring a Malagasy government'.[15] The administration, acting in the middle of the First World War, took this case as seriously as the British government viewed the landing of Roger Casement on the west coast of Ireland at about the same time. The Europeans living in Madagascar became very alarmed; wild rumours circulated, of a German plot, of the discovery of barrels of poison and gunpowder to kill all expatriates.[16] Heavy sentences were imposed. Eight of the defendants were sentenced to life imprisonment, four to 20 years, and nine to 15 years. Among those sentenced for life were Ravelojaona (who was later acquitted on appeal) and Ravoahangy.

It may be considered that the offences did not justify the sentences. War-time excitement certainly was partly responsible for their severity, as was the insecurity felt by European settlers in a country where local unrest had not been entirely suppressed. Certain sections of public opinion in France spoke out against the sentences, among them the governing council of the Société des Missions Evangéliques (French Protestant mission), which in its report dated May 4, 1916, declared the trial and sentences to be 'incompatible with the principles of our civilisation'. Some prisoners were freed in 1918, and the remainder under a general amnesty proclaimed in 1921.

Parallel to the abortive and embryonic nationalist movement of the vvs, and once again illustrative of the ambivalence that characterises the relationships of colonisers and colonised peoples, a large number of Malagasy were serving as volunteers in combat units of the French army on the Western Front. Approximately 46,000 Malagasy were recruited, of whom 41,000 served in combat units; 2,368 were killed in action.[17] The Malagasy units distinguished themselves especially during the final German offensive of 1918. General Gérard presented a flag of battle honours to these units in 1919 on the banks of the Rhine.[18] The return of these ex-soldiers brought a new element to the nationalist agitation. These were not intellectuals, but neither were they prepared, after fighting on terms of equality with and against Europeans in Europe, to return to inferior status. One of the Malagasy veterans,

Jean Ralaimongo, a Betsileo school-teacher who had volunteered in 1916, became a leading political figure between 1927 and 1938.

Political agitation during the period 1920 to 1930 was no longer the affair of a small band of upper-class intellectuals, but, largely due to the ex-soldiers, had spread among the salaried workers. It had two main aims at this time: equality of civil and political status with Europeans, and reform of the labour regulations.

The conditions of recruitment and employment of the labour force in colonial territories is probably one of the best-documented aspects of overseas administration. The French system, as applied in West Africa and in Madagascar, is usually described as 'forced labour' by British writers, and colonial administrators in Nigeria and the Gold Coast always attributed any migration of labour from French territories to a desire to escape such obligations. Such migration occurred also for economic motives, such as the higher purchasing power of British West African currency in the 1950s. No reliable statistics existed to show net immigration or emigration of various categories of labour from any territory, labour statistics being notoriously incomplete, even in industrialised countries.

The obligation to perform a certain number of days of voluntary labour on public works had existed under the Malagasy monarchy. Apart from slave labour, freemen were obliged by the *fokon'olona*, or rural commune, to undertake corvées (*fanompoana*). This system was immediately included by Galliéni in his new legislation, and two successive decrees of October 1896 and January 1897 obliged every fit male between the ages of 16 and 60 to give fifty days of nine hours' labour each year to the administration. Several thousand men were enrolled under military discipline and began the construction of the railway from Tamatave and the new road network radiating from Tananarive. To escape this obligation a man had to prove either that he was employed for wages or that he had his own business. Such proof in practice depended on the 'personal opinion of the administrators', to quote a former governor-general.[19]

Galliéni's decree of 1896 was the immediate reply to Laroche's abolition of slavery which disrupted the labour 'supply' and put no new relationship in its place. Before the conquest, there was an important difference in property rights and in the organisation of labour between the central highlands, where large feudal estates were worked by slave labour, and the east coast, where the inhabitants practised shifting cultivation in the forest and therefore had no settled property. In the highlands, rice was cultivated, often by slaves, on organised irrigated paddy fields; on the coast it was cultivated by bush fallowing in the forest by freemen.

French public opinion, as expressed in Parliament, demanded financial returns from what had been a costly military operation of conquest. The settlers demanded manpower to work their plantations. But the abolition of slavery had converted the serfs in the highlands into virtual owners of the land they occupied, while the shifting cultivators on the coast satisfied all their needs of food and clothing from the products of the forest. There was thus no available labour force, and the numerous decrees and orders issued by the administration from 1896 for the next forty years were a series of attempts, usually unsuccessful, to supply labour in sufficient quantity for European enterprises.

The justification of the government's measures, stated by Galliéni and repeated by many of his successors, was that such labour was not voluntarily forthcoming, that it was essential for the economic development of the colony, and that it was the duty of the administration to supply it. Marcel Olivier,* writing an apologia as late as 1930, stated categorically: 'The freedom of the worker to choose his job should only become part of the laws of a country when the obligation to work has become a customary practice'.[20] This is a very frank statement but expresses clearly the dilemma in which colonial administrators found themselves, faced with the need to force the inhabitants of a subsistence economy to enter a monetary economy. Galliéni counted, as did many other colonial rulers, on the capitation tax to force the peasant into the monetary circuit by compelling him either to produce a saleable surplus or to accept salaried employment. Galliéni also stated: 'Taxation is an indispensable stimulant to the energy of the

---

* Marcel Olivier was Governor-General from 1924 to 1930. Dynamic and intelligent, he undertook a number of administrative reforms to simplify the contacts between the administration and the population. He improved the application of the principles behind the Torrens Act, a law which is applicable primarily to the settlement of vast empty spaces, by introducing (1928) a cadastral system of land registry for Malagasy land-owners. He also began the Fianarantsoa-Manakara railway (1927) and created the SMOTIG or labour battalions, for which see below, page 162.

native'.[21] The capitation tax, today known as the 'minimum fiscal', has been vigorously applied by the Malagasy administration since independence, though for other reasons.

The regulation of the labour supply began with the suppression of the forced labour decrees of 1896 and 1897 by Galliéni himself, who established in 1900 a central labour office and regional labour offices (Office Central du Travail and Offices Régionaux du Travail). These were labour exchanges on the European model, attempting to deal with a labour situation which had nothing in common with Europe, and a series of decrees and orders between 1905 and 1910 reflect the administration's embarrassment. The settlers continued to demand a labour force which was forthcoming only sporadically and disappeared without warning. Galliéni's successor, Augagneur, abolished the labour offices and created councils of arbitration (Conseils d'Arbitrage), and the organisation of labour oscillated between absolute liberty and the drastic legal constraint sanctioned by Article 270 of the Penal Code concerning vagabondage, which could be applied by an administrator to anyone he considered not to be gainfully employed.

It is not surprising that, from 1920 onwards, nationalist agitation, and especially that led by Jean Ralaimongo, was much concerned with problems of labour, and, equally, that French administrators made numerous attempts to ensure a labour supply. The economic conference held in Tananarive in 1919 led, among other things, to a codification of the labour regulations, concerning especially contracts, inspection and arbitration, which was issued as the Code of 1920.

The situation did not improve and settlers continued to complain of labour shortages and absenteeism. By 1924, Madagascar's export crops were selling well, there was an excellent market for cattle, owing to high export prices for hides, and there was thus no shortage of money. Marcel Olivier already concluded that 'without the effective support—let us be frank, without the pressure—of the administration, nine-tenths of the European enterprises would disappear for lack of manpower'.[22] He himself admitted that salaries were low: they had doubled between 1914 and 1924, but the cost of living had multiplied by five. A labour commission was appointed by him in 1924, which re-established the labour offices of Galliéni and obliged employers to draw up contracts for all employees for more than three months.

This produced no noticeable results, and Olivier, considering that the neutrality of the administration in the absence of an adequate supply of manpower could only be 'theoretical', set up, by a decree of June 3, 1926, the much criticised Service de la Main d'Oeuvre pour les Travaux d'Intérêt Géneral (SMOTIG). This was in effect conscription for a labour battalion. The SMOTIG recruits served at first for three years with leave, and from 1929 for two years without leave. When they had been passed fit for service, they were taken to assembly camps, fitted out with clothing and sent to work camps where they put in a 48-hour week with pay, mainly on public works, including the Fianarantsoa-Manakara railway. The SMOTIG was denounced by deputies in the French Parliament and by the International Labour Office, which secured an international agreement on forced labour in 1929. Marcel Olivier argued that, if military conscription was accepted without protest, why should not civil conscription for public works be allowed in the same way? His argument has the force of logic and represents a conflict between national defence and economic development. The SMOTIG was a variety of 'capital levy' or forced capital formation, using the only capital available in quantity: manpower. In 1928 the SMOTIG effectives numbered 7,957. Military conscription was applied to Madagascar in 1929, and thereafter approximately 4,500 recruits were called up each year.

This forced labour continued in one form or another until it was officially abolished on April 11, 1946. As late as 1943 the official statistics of the Inspection of Labour give 3,810,000 man/days of forced labour for the year.[23] It cannot be denied that, apart from the Public Works Department, the beneficiaries of this labour were settlers on plantations or forest concessions, and that this guaranteed them a fairly regular and cheap labour supply. In purely economic terms, there is no doubt that this forced labour resulted in the laying down of an infrastructure for which neither the capital nor the voluntary labour would otherwise have been forthcoming. In terms of human relations, the worker was at the mercy of the district commissioner, who was himself under pressure from often influential settlers. It is not surprising that the Malagasy considered the system intolerable; the fact cannot be ignored that the 1947 rebellion broke out in its most violent form in those regions such as Ambatondrazaka and Manakara where settlers on plantations had made full use of forced labour supplies.

While in France after his demobilisation at the end of the First World War, Jean Ralaimongo came in contact with various political leaders and also with Freemasons. In 1920 he was appointed assistant secretary of the Ligue française pour l'accession des indigènes de Madagascar aux droits des citoyens français, which included Radicals, Socialists and Communists, under the patronage of Anatole France. He made the acquaintance at this time of Ho Chi Minh, with whom he shared a room in 1920; together they attended the Congress of the French Socialist Party held in Tours to consider adherence to the Third International.

The Ligue sent Ralaimongo to Madagascar in 1921, where he was received by Governor-General Hubert Garbit, who told him: 'I don't want anyone coming to upset my Malagasy under the pretext that they are unhappy, when they are not unhappy'. Ralaimongo published a report in which he exposed the application of the labour laws, and other aspects of the colonial administration.[24] While his courage and outspokenness must be admired, it must also be asked how a supposedly repressive regime allowed him to enter Madagascar, to be received by the Governor-General, to travel freely and to depart for France with his report. Many years later such actions would still have been impossible in many other colonies.

Back in France, Ralaimongo agitated for the liberation of those VVS members who were still imprisoned. They were duly amnestied, and in 1924 Garbit admitted Malagasy representatives to the economic and financial delegations, which were consultative committees set up in principle to advise the administration on the budget. The association of Malagasy, however carefully selected, with the delegations (which became later the Representative Council and finally the Representative Assembly, or Legislative Council) was an attempt at participation which can be matched in very few other colonial territories of that time.

In 1924 Ralaimongo settled in Diego-Suarez, the French naval and military base, which early on was penetrated by French left-wing influences. His main activity was the defence of Malagasy peasants apparently expropriated by settlers, and thus began a long battle with the administration, fully documented in the often nearly hysterical articles of the settler newspapers, *Le Colon* and *L'Echo de Tananarive*.

France was at this time engaged in colonial wars in Syria and in Morocco, and strikes against the Rif war were organised in France in 1925 by the left wing of the trade union movement, the Confédération Général du Travail (CGT). In Madagascar also the first recorded strike occurred in June 1925, among the dockers at the port of Tamatave. Labour agitation was occurring sporadically along the east coast.

Ravoahangy, the vvs leader, now liberated from prison, joined Ralaimongo at Diego-Suarez. A French settler, Paul Dussac, the son of a resistant of the 1871 commune who had fled to Russia, joined the two nationalists, and became director of a newspaper edited by them, *L'Opinion*, which appeared from 1927. A few months later Dussac started a newspaper in Tananarive, *L'Aurore malgache*, in which two other Malagasy nationalists (Jules Ranaivo and Emmanuel Razafindrakoto) collaborated. The aims of this movement appear modest: namely, to obtain for all Malagasy the rights of French citizens, and to denounce any abuse of power by the administration. The idea of accession to French citizenship attracted much attention among the Malagasy civil servants and intellectuals of Tananarive. The French policy of assimilation was at this time applied only to a very small minority; when, finally, citizenship was extended to all colonial subjects in 1946, the nationalists' aim had become political independence. Although the settlers' newspapers raged against the idea, Malagasy aspirations had considerable support from the French left wing, particularly from the Socialist Party (SFIO).

In May 1929 Dussac arrived in Tananarive to organise the collection of signatures demanding French citizenship for Malagasy. A public meeting was planned, to be held in the Excelsior cinema near the great market of Analakely in the centre of the city. While, as has been emphasised, official policy attached relatively greater importance to education in Madagascar than in many other colonies, and while some small steps had been taken to associate Malagasy with economic and financial aspects of government, it has been admitted that these measures were not 'a solution on a national scale'.[25] The decree of 1910, which was extended by a further decree under Marcel Olivier's successor, Léon Cayla (1930–39), did allow the accession of Malagasy possessing certain qualifications to French citizenship.* In spite of this, not only the descendants of the former Merina ruling class but also growing numbers of intellectually-active Malagasy resented their inferior status.

Mention has been made of the violent language with which the settlers' newspapers referred to any move towards racial equality for the Malagasy. Their participation in the economic and financial delegations was not on an equal footing, since these bodies were conceived as a means by which the more important traders and settlers could bring pressure to bear on the administration. Only small numbers of Malagasy passed beyond primary school level, and official policy limited the numbers admitted to lycées, ostensibly to avoid creating 'déclassés' but in fact to avoid being obliged to give them senior posts in the administration. This attitude was by no means peculiar to Madagascar, and in purely relative terms the Malagasy were considerably better off than most other colonial peoples of this time. But the literate section of the population did not see their inferior status in relative terms, and the inequality was much resented. The masses, as generally happened in early stages of nationalist movements, were unaffected: their status with regard to the only Europeans with whom they were in contact, the district commissioners, was largely a continuation of their relations with the former Merina governors.

The public meeting planned for May 19, 1929, opened its doors at the Excelsior cinema, but the strong police guard stated that only French citizens would be admitted. This sparked off a riot

* An applicant for French citizenship had to first have a thorough knowledge of the French language, only holders of the Legion of Honour and the Military Medal being exempt from this requirement. An official enquiry was then carried out concerning the background and morality of the applicant. If this was satisfactory, the Governor-General sent the file to the Ministry of Justice in Paris with a favourable note. The final decision was taken by the French President on the advice of the Ministers for the Colonies and Justice. This administrative procedure took a very long time, as may be imagined, and few Malagasy achieved French citizenship. By the Decree of April 7, 1938, issued by the Minister Marius Moutet, holders of certain diplomas and officers and non-commissioned officers of the army were admitted ex officio to French citizenship. Thus, all those coming out of the School of Medicine or the Ecole Myre de Villiers, the staff training college, received French citizenship. Even so, at independence there were only about 10,000 French citizens of Malagasy origin in Madagascar.

leading to a demonstration in front of the Governor-General's Residence. Dussac and other French and Malagasy activists were arrested, and in October sixteen of them were indicted for rebellion. Dussac and one other French citizen were sentenced to imprisonment, to which they responded by singing the *Internationale* in court and were duly sentenced to a further two years for contempt of court.

The new Governor-General, Léon Cayla, an Algerian 'pied-noir', was appointed soon after the trial. He was another outstanding man, intelligent and full of initiative; he introduced a number of economic measures which lowered the production costs of Madagascar's main export products and warded off some of the worst effects of the 1930–31 world economic crisis. He arrived, no doubt, with instructions to deal with the beginning of political unrest, which had greatly disturbed the settlers. He therefore placed Ralaimongo and Ravoahangy in restriction far from Tananarive, and, by a decree of December 4, 1930, limited the freedom of the press by making it an offence to commit 'acts and manoeuvres tending to provoke hatred of the French government'. Under Cayla's administration, the modern port of Tamatave was built, the railway from Fianarantsoa to Manakara was completed, and the road network increased from 3,125 to 15,625 miles. He opened up the first internal and external air services. He also reversed the administrative reforms of his predecessor, Olivier, and reinstalled the district commissioners with full powers. The administrative history of Madagascar, as of most other colonies, is full of such changes—provinces created and abolished, posts upgraded and downgraded. The existence of certain African states, such as Upper Volta, Niger or Mali, is the result of a sudden freezing of such actions by successive governors.

In France, left-wing strength was growing. It is not surprising, therefore, that Malagasy nationalists received active support from the Socialist and Communist Parties in the French Parliament. In 1932, *L'Aurore malgache*, Dussac's paper, which had survived the Decree of 1930, published a long letter of support from Maurice Thorez, asking why Ralaimongo was restricted and promising the support of the Ligue contre l'Impérialisme et pour l'Indépendance des Colonies and of the Secours Rouge International. The letter stated that questions concerning Madagascar were being asked by the French Communist Party in

Parliament, that a defence lawyer would be provided when needed, and that demonstrations of solidarity were to be organised in Paris, Lyon, Marseille and Strasbourg.[26] *L'Aurore malgache* commented on this letter that 'none of us can declare himself a Communist, since there are probably not two Malagasy who have studied the doctrine of Karl Marx'.[27] Evidently there was no wish on the part of the nationalists to see themselves allied too closely with international Communism, however welcome any sympathy might be. Following its success in the French municipal elections of May 1935, the Popular Front was formally established on July 14, and won the parliamentary elections of May 1936. A Popular Front government, under Léon Blum, took office. The Malagasy detainees were released from prison and from restriction and local newspapers now appeared in both French and Malagasy.*

The three years that remained before the outbreak of the Second World War saw the beginnings of an organised Malagasy trade union movement. French civil servants in Madagascar had already organised themselves in unions but rarely admitted Malagasy. Under the direction of Ravoahangy, a number of trade unions, both industrial and agricultural, were formed under the aegis of the French CGT. The first strike at an enterprise of any size occurred in the meat canning factory of the Société Emyrne in 1935 and continued as a boycott until 1938. The right to form trade unions was granted by a decree of March 19, 1937, with the proviso that members must be able to read and write French.

The Popular Front had many sympathisers among French residents in Madagascar, and demonstrations included both French and Malagasy, demanding the suppression of the 'indigénat' and the accession of all to French citizenship. Although this provoked the usual violent reaction from the more extremist settlers, it must be emphasised that henceforth nationalist aspirations in Madagascar not only had local support from a significant number of French residents, but also received substantial support from important non-Communist political parties in France itself, such as the SFIO.

The Popular Front government did not last long enough in France for it to carry out any important colonial reforms, but in 1939 the first Malagasy was elected to a metropolitan body,

* *L'Opinion* became *La Nation Malgache* (bilingual), and *Ny Rariny —La Justice* also appeared in the two languages from 1935.

the Conseil Supérieur des Colonies. The deputy elected was Ravelojaona, who had been a member of the vvs movement of 1916, who represented the Malagasy in this council until 1946. In the election he won 11,000 votes out of 14,000 cast.

The last years before the Second World War thus saw a considerable advance in political liberty, freely granted by the French administration as part of French national policy. The local press was no longer subject to censorship, the SMOTIG was abolished (although district commissioners retained powers to requisition labour for public works for a maximum of ten days per year), the formation of trade unions was permitted, and in December 1937 an amnesty was granted for political and press offences. The outbreak of war saw a reaction of attachment to France, similar to that of 1914, except that a large contingent was not at once sent overseas. Nationalist propaganda ceased for the time being.

The 1940 Armistice brought the same conflicts of opinion to Madagascar as to the other colonies. It is reported that the Governor-General, Marcel de Coppet, sent a telegram to France stating that Madagascar would continue to fight alongside the Allies; but, when he was recalled by the Vichy authorities, he handed over without resistance to his successor, Cayla, who came back for a second tour of duty. The Allied blockade forced Madagascar into some interesting experiments in the use of local materials as substitutes for what had previously been imported. There were persistent (but probably false) rumours of Japanese submarines taking on supplies in Malagasy ports, and even of an agreement by Vichy to allow Japanese forces to occupy Madagascar, which lay on the Allied route to the Far East.

The declared purpose of the Allied landing in Madagascar, which had been decided upon early in March 1942, was to occupy the naval and air base of Diego-Suarez, then held by pro-Vichy French forces. This was to forestall a possible Japanese annexation (similar to that of the French bases in Indo-China) and above all to protect vital lines of communication in the Indian Ocean. By this time Burma had been lost, and there was a strong probability of a Japanese invasion of India, where General Wavell was in command, after the monsoon.

The Madagascar operation had at first a limited objective: to occupy Diego-Suarez only, and leave the rest of the island under the control of the pro-Vichy administration. But Field-Marshal Smuts pressed from the start for an extension of Allied control of Madagascar by the capture of the ports of Majunga and Tamatave, using South African forces. The operation, known as 'Ironclad', was the first large amphibious assault undertaken by British forces, since the unsuccessful attempt to seize the Dardanelles in 1915. It preceded the Allied landings in North Africa by only a few months, and techniques were to evolve rapidly before the gigantic operations of the liberation of Europe in 1944–45. The combined sea, land and air forces were under the command of Rear-Admiral E. N. Syfret, and it will be seen that the Royal Navy played a decisive part, not only in organising the landing of the ground forces, but in extricating them from a difficult situation at a moment when the operation might well have failed.

After training in Scotland, and fitting out in Durban, a substantial force left for Madagascar on April 25, 1942. The 'Plan of the Cruising Order of the Final Approach' shows thirty-three vessels, including destroyers, mine-sweepers, troop-carriers and others. These were joined by larger naval vessels, including the *Ramillies* wearing the flag of Rear-Admiral Syfret.[28]

The harbour of Diego-Suarez is said to be roughly the size and shape of Scapa Flow and is entered by a channel from the east. To the west, it is separated from the Moçambique Channel by a narrow isthmus from two to six miles wide. The general plan of operations was to land infantry on the isthmus and assault the naval base twenty-one miles to the east by road, while the 2nd Lancashires and No. 5 Commando were to seize French gun batteries in the harbour and occupy part of the naval base.

The approach to the isthmus was made so hazardous by numerous scattered reefs and islets that the French did not consider a landing possible in darkness. The mine-sweepers exploded two mines while sweeping the channel, but the French heard nothing, and by 02.30 hours on May 5, the East Lancashires and No. 5 Commando reached Diego-Suarez with practically no opposition. They occupied a peninsula (Andrakaka) opposite the naval base but, to quote the *London Gazette*, 'attempts were made without success to find boats'. These forces found themselves unable to move further and did not take any part in later operations..

The 29th Brigade landed and set off down the road towards Diego-Suarez without any opposition. At 05.30 hours (May 5), the Fleet Air Arm bombed the airfield about six miles south of Diego-Suarez and destroyed all the French planes on the ground. The 29th Brigade captured a French officer on the road, and unwisely sent him back to Diego-Suarez with a letter demanding surrender. The effect of this letter was to inform the French command of the direction of the advance of the Allied forces and to enable them to bring up artillery and infantry forces. Thus at 11.00 hours, Allied forces came under heavy fire from French 75mm guns which knocked out five Allied tanks and forced the others to withdraw.

At the end of this first day's fighting (May 5), the 29th Brigade had advanced eighteen out of the twenty-one miles to Diego-Suarez and Major-General Sturges reported that 'lack of intelligence of enemy positions, combined with the successful advance to date, led us all to expect a good scrap which would end when we ate our breakfasts at Antsirane [the French naval base] on May 6'.[29] Unfortunately, during the night, almost everything went wrong.

The naval transport carrying fifty-four vehicles as well as guns could not find a suitable beach for landing on the isthmus, and, when it finally landed them, they found that there was no road inland from the beach. Allied forces appear to have had no information concerning the opposing French troops or their equipment. During the night (May 5–6), the South Lancashires disappeared and were assumed prisoners or casualties. In fact, they had penetrated the French lines and had taken 400 prisoners, but their man-pack radios did not allow them to maintain contact with Brigade HQ. The No. 5 Commando remained blocked on the Andrakaka peninsula, and at dawn on May 6 the French opened up with 75mm guns and mortars on the infantry, now completely exposed on the plateau south of Diego-Suarez. Major-General Sturges stated: 'It was quite clear that the attack had failed. It was an unhappy moment. The whole of the 29 Independent Brigade was deployed or being deployed, and, with the disappearance of many of the leading troops in the dawn attack, assumed casualties, units were considerably under strength.'[30]

The situation was saved by the Royal Navy. Admiral Syfret stated: 'The impression left with me after the General's visit [Sturges] was that the intended quick capture of Diego-Suarez was already a 90 per cent failure.'[31] Syfret therefore decided to land fifty Royal Marines directly in the French naval base and in the rear of the French troops. Thus, HMS *Ramilles* (a destroyer) steamed straight into the harbour at 20.00 hours, but it overshot the landing place in the dark. The commander of the destroyer put about, put his ship astern and calmly held it against the jetty long enough for the Marines to get ashore. They at once captured the artillery HQ and French naval barracks with slight opposition, while two battalions of the 29th Brigade pushed forward and occupied the rest of Diego-Suarez by 03.00 hours on May 7.

Surrender negotiations the next morning dragged on too long for the Admiral's taste, so, 'tired of these delays, which were keeping the Fleet steaming up and down in dangerous waters . . . , I informed the General [Sturges] that I intended to commence a fifteen minutes bombardment to encourage the enemy to surrender'. This he did and, after ten minutes, the French commander surrendered.

The ground forces were lucky not to have been completely defeated, out of range of the Navy's guns. The operation had been conducted against a French opposition all of whose aircraft had been knocked out by the Fleet Air Arm's strike and who had no armour for counter-attack. But it is true, as General Sturges stated, that 'the French white and Sengalese troops fought with determination, and although their armament and equipment were below first-class standards, they undoubtedly hoped to repeat the story of Dakar [1940]'.[32]

Allied forces remained in control only of Diego-Suarez, until Field Marshal Smuts finally got his way, and landings were carried out, without serious opposition, in Majunga on September 10, 1942, by the 22nd East African Brigade. On September 18, the 29th Brigade landed at Tamatave, and on September 23 Tananarive was declared an open town and occupied by the East African Brigade.

The French Governor, Annet, did not surrender but retired south to Fianarantsoa. On September 29, South African forces landed at Fort Dauphin and Tuléar in the extreme south. Annet was finally caught at Ambalavao, south of Fianarantsoa, where he signed an instrument of capitulation on November 6, eight weeks after the landing in Majunga. Allied casualties were 107 dead; French casualties about 400 dead.[33]

During the Allied occupation there occurred important changes in the political status of France's colonies, following the

Brazzaville Declaration of General de Gaulle in 1944 and the establishment of the French Union in 1946, with the accession of all colonial subjects to French citizenship with equal rights. This period must, at the same time, be considered in relation to the rebellion of 1947, which had as its object the political independence of Madagascar and the restoration of the state that had been destroyed by the French conquest of 1896.

Two factors may be considered as contributing to this revolt: one was external, the presence in France during the German occupation of a group of Malagasy students, including the future nationalist leader Jacques Rabemananjara; and one was internal, the reimposition of forced labour.

In spite of the abolition of the SMOTIG, labour was extensively requisitioned under war-time conditions. The lack of petrol meant that a great deal had to be carried by porters, as in the early days of the century. The Labour Inspection recorded 3,810,000 man/days of requisitioned labour in 1943, and this does not include days of walking to arrive on the job. The purchasing power of salaries diminished sharply between 1939 and 1945. During this period the official minimum wage was increased in Tananarive from 5·50 francs to 11 francs per day, while the official retail price index multiplied by four. This figure refers to official prices, but an extensive black market flourished, which further drastically lowered the real purchasing power. Prices of agricultural products were maintained artificially low, to stabilise the cost of living, while the peasants were obliged to sell all their surplus rice to the rice marketing board (Office du Riz) at 1,000 francs per ton (approximately $US 25). The rice marketing board had such a bad reputation twenty years later that the independent government was unable to give this name to a new rice marketing organisation created in 1963. The board appears to have brought considerable profits to the owners of rice mills and to transporters, but it was bitterly resented by the peasants and produced grave dislocations in supplies to the towns.

Churchill had officially handed over Madagascar to the Free French after the signature of an armistice in November 1942 between the Allied forces and Annet, Governor-General since 1941 and an ardent supporter of the Vichy government. Under the new Governor-General, General Legentilhomme, the exactions of the rice marketing board and the inevitable labour requisitions continued. The black market continued to flourish, and the disorganisation of life, which had resulted in the schools being closed for six months after the Allied landings and in many educated Malagasy retiring to the bush, continued. Although Madagascar was nominally under French sovereignty, Allied occupation did not end until 1946, when the last units were withdrawn. Although they did not see their district commissioners marched off to prison camps, as did the Malays and Indonesians, the Malagasy saw the defeat of French authority in their own country, and the result was to be similar to the effects on Dutch authority of the Japanese occupation of Indonesia.

While war-time conditions were not as bad as in many other countries, mass discontent and unrest built up and the rapid political evolution after 1945 opened the door to the pent-up political aspirations of the intellectual leaders. The Brazzaville Conference of 1944 established the principle of having representatives from the colonies sitting in the French Parliament. This was to prove highly important as an instrument of political education for the future leaders of these territories, both before and after independence. While future heads of state such as Kaunda, Makarios and Nkrumah were in prison or exile, Houphouet-Boigny was secretary of state in a French government and Tsiranana was a member of the French Parliament. Many other leaders and ministers received their first experience of political life alongside their French counterparts in the French Parliament and the value of such contacts can hardly be over-rated. It is certainly a contributing factor to the reality and stability of present political and cultural relations between France and many of its former colonies.

Madagascar sent four elected members to the Constituent Assembly of the Fourth French Republic. At the legislative elections held on November 18, 1945, Joseph Ravoahangy and Joseph Raseta (also a doctor, who had been restricted and disbarred from medical practice by the administration in 1935) were both elected, under the label Restauration de l'Indépendance Magache. The other two members were French residents elected by the Europeans of Madagascar. At a public meeting held on October 5, 1945, in the municipal theatre in Tananarive, Ravoahangy declared: 'France, as a signatory of the United Nations Charter, has accepted, along with other nations, to lead towards independence those colonial peoples who are still incapable of governing themselves, and to give independence immediately to those who are capable. France has therefore bound itself to give us back our independence sooner or later. It is time to demand it.' But, even at this moment, this militant, whose whole active life had been spent in resistance to French colonial authority, went on to say: 'Some of you may perhaps say that we shall break relations with France when we gain our independence. On the contrary, we shall be members of the United Nations, and we shall continue to collaborate with France, although on a higher level. It will no longer be the relationship of a master to a slave, but a relationship of brothers. Our friendship will only be stronger. Remember that to desire independence does not mean to be anti-French. We shall collaborate with other nations in a spirit of fraternity and justice.'[34]

The Malagasy members of parliament arrived in France on December 8, 1945. In Paris they met young Malagasy intellectuals who had spent the war years in France, among them Jacques Rabemananjara, and the meeting between the older activists, who had spent all their lives in Madagascar, and the young intellectuals, who had been exposed to European political thought, produced an immediate fusion. On February 22, 1946, the first Malagasy political party was formed, the Mouvement Démocratique de la Rénovation Malgache (MDRM). Raseta was elected president. It is claimed that within a few months more than 300,000 Malagasy were party members, drawn from all tribes and no longer representative only of the Merina intellectuals as in the days of the vvs. Raseta was a Merina from Tuléar, Rabemananjara was a Betsimisaraka from Maroantsetra, and Ravoahangy was a Merina of noble family, descended from the former royal family.

The first action of the MDRM was to propose to the French Parliament a bill declaring the independence of Madagascar. This appears to have been directly inspired by the agreement signed at Hanoi on March 6, 1946, between Ho Chi Minh and the French government, by which France 'recognised the Democratic Vietnam Republic as a free state having its own government, parliament, army and finances, as part of the Federation of Indo-China within the French Union'. On March 21, 1946, the two Malagasy parliamentarians introduced a bill of which the first two sections read:

Art. 1. The Law of August 6 1896, is abrogated.

Art. 2. Madagascar is a free state, having its own government, its parliament, its army, its finances, within the French Union.

Vincent Auriol, at that time President of France, refused to allow the bill to be printed and tabled, claiming that it was 'anti-constitutional', although the new constitution of the Fourth Republic was at that time being drawn up and had not yet been voted on. The bill was finally printed and distributed, but was 'sent back to committee', which was another way of saying that it was buried and would not be discussed. The First Constituent Assembly dissolved after the failure of its referendum concerning the new French constitution. The Second Assembly was elected and the same two nationalist Malagasy deputies were sent to it. The new French constitution was finally voted, and in October 1946 Madagascar became a 'Territory of the French Republic' ('Territoire de la République francaise'), and its citizens, following the official policy of assimilation, became French citizens, with equal rights with citizens of the metropolitan country. Forced labour was finally abolished at the same time.

The proposed independence bill had been widely publicised in Madagascar by the MDRM. Moreover, the Malagasy ex-servicemen, numbering about 10,000, returned to their own country with strong feelings of independence. There had been much bitterness over delays in their repatriation, leading to a 'strike' (or, as it might be called, a mutiny) among Malagasy units stationed at Djibouti. Other units had been sent to Dakar, ostensibly on their way home; but Dakar was already a centre of political activity, carried on as much by left-wing sympathisers among the large French population as by the Senegalese. The Malagasy soldiers thus returned as strong supporters of independence and were unwilling to accept anything like inferior status.

The carrying out in Madagascar of the recommendations of the Brazzaville Conference of 1944, and of the new French constitution, were entrusted to Marcel de Coppet, who returned as Governor-General in May 1946. However, Madagascar was given, by a decree of October 25, 1946, a different statute from that of other colonies. The island was divided administratively into five provinces, each with a provincial assembly and a provincial budget.

This may be interpreted in two ways. Many Malagasy and some left-wing French writers interpret it as 'divide and rule', a manoeuvre to weaken nationalist aspirations for an undivided independent Madagascar. The official explanation was that: 'In Madagascar our policy has rested on the "Hovas" (Merina) who have provided us with valuable auxiliaries. However they represent only one of the Malagasy peoples. . . . Limited suffrage has given them a majority, but there is a mass of peoples of other origins which must be allowed to voice its opinions.'[35]

A modified form of provincial structure was retained after independence, and certainly it can be justified in Madagascar, where regional climatic and topographical differences, together with difficult land communications, make some degree of regional autonomy inevitable. To the coastal peoples, the Merina were the former ruling power, which had been replaced by the French. Practically all secondary education was concentrated around Tananarive and the great majority of Malagasy civil servants were Merina. But the introduction of provincial assemblies at this time, before any central elected body had met, was to go against the spirit of national unity which inspired the MDRM, whose leaders were drawn from both Merina and coastal peoples. It was also to exaggerate the differences between the Malagasy tribes which, unlike African peoples, all speak dialects of the same language and have a clear cultural unity.

The MDRM was identified nevertheless by the colonial administration as a Merina party, aiming at re-establishing the Merina state, and thus separatist. A new party now appeared, in preparation for the elections to the new French Parliament, the Parti des Déshérités Malgaches (PADESM). This party received active support from the colonial administration, and it appears from records of correspondence between de Coppet and Moutet, French Minister for the Colonies, that it was hoped that 'the separatist party [MDRM] would hardly survive, in fact, a determined opposition to the "Hovas" (Merina) by the coastal peoples'[36] The statutes of the PADESM were approved on July 1, 1946, and they chose August 6 to publish the first number of their paper, *Voronmahery* ('Eagle'). This day, the anniversary of the Annexation Law of 1896, had been declared a day of national mourning by the MDRM and no nationalist newspapers appeared. The second number of *Voronmahery*, which appeared on August 13, carried an article glorifying the 'unforgettable date' of August 6, 1896.

Raseta had already declared before the French Parliament on May 6, 1947: 'PADESM has no roots among the population. It is a creation of the services of the High Commissioner [as the Governor-General was then styled] of Madagascar, aimed at dividing the Malagasy, and forging an instrument which will be malleable and can be made to sing hymns of fidelity at critical moments.' However, much of the membership of the PADESM was drawn from coastal peoples who had no intention of returning to Merina domination.

In spite of official support for PADESM, at the elections of November 1946 the MDRM deputies, Ravoahangy and Raseta, were reelected, and a new MDRM candidate, Jacques Rabemananjara, the young poet they had met in France on their first visit, now joined them as a third member. None of the PADESM candidates was elected. At the elections to the Provincial Assemblies in January 1947 the MDRM won all the seats in the provinces of Tananarive and Tamatave, and a majority in those of Fianarantsoa and Tuléar. Having won an absolute majority in the first elections for the newly-created National Representative Assembly, the MDRM also won all the seats of senators and councillors reserved for Malagasy as members of the French Union.

The Representative Assembly was to meet in Tananarive on March 30, 1947. For many months there had been much unrest and a number of clashes with the police. Many nationalists had been arrested, and it was clear that the application of measures of liberalisation provided for under the new French constitution was creating a considerable problem of maintaining the authority of the colonial administration. The existence of a political party which publicly and legally demanded political independence, the abolition of the inferior status of the indigénat and a general removal of the muzzling that had been applied to politically conscious Malagasy in the past, all contributed to produce a 'wind of change' that grew stronger each month.

The rapidity with which a people can seize freedom, once the door is opened, has been witnessed in many other countries. The local settlers, who had spent the war far from France, were by no means prepared to lose their privileged status. The colonial civil servants had been trained and had served under quite different principles, and many of them were out of sympathy with ideas of political autonomy. Colonial administrators who had been accustomed to the peace of paternalistic rule, under which the ruled asked no questions, often found it very hard to accept the emergence of local politicians and the consequent criticism of everything they had been trained to admire. Those serving in Madagascar were no exception.

The reasons for the Rebellion which was to break out on the night of March 29, 1947, have been widely discussed and various theories have been put forward. The leaders of the MDRM, meeting in Tananarive on March 27, sent a telegram to all their regional party chiefs, urging them 'to maintain calm and sang-froid in the face of manoeuvres and provocations of all kinds, aiming at stirring up trouble among the Malagasy people, and at sabotaging peaceful policies'.[37] During the Rebellion and at the subsequent trial of those accused of being its leaders, the MDRM strongly denied having instigated the rising. Ever since, the surviving leaders have always maintained their denial.

Three hypotheses have been put forward to account for the Rebellion, which was apparently well-organised, since it broke out in such widely-separated places as Manakara, Moramanga and Diego-Suarez. The organisation of guerrilla activity, which continued for almost a year, was militarily effective and enabled small groups with few arms and rudimentary supplies to hold out against greatly superior French military forces. The question as to who was responsible for this organisation has never been satisfactorily answered.

The first theory holds that the Rebellion was the work of agents provocateurs, who supplied arms to the rebels, and, having infiltrated the MDRM, intended to use the pretext of revolt to destroy the party and its leaders. The second theory is that within the MDRM there had appeared the elements of a split between the moderates who wished to attain political independence by constitutional means and an extreme wing who saw no other way than by violence. This is a classic situation that has been repeated within almost every nationalist or liberation movement. The official version, which was the justification for the subsequent trial and condemnation of the MDRM leaders, was that the party was solely reponsible for having organised the Rebellion.

But the MDRM had won decisive majorities not only in the Provincial Assemblies but also in the new Representative Assembly.

It had three deputies in the French Parliament as against two from the French minority. It had all the seats in the organisation of the French Union. It therefore had no obvious interest in provoking an armed rising that might lead to violent repression and its own destruction—which, in fact, is what happened. On the other hand, the Rebellion was undoubtedly organised, and the regional centres of the MDRM in the areas overrun by the rebels were active centres for the revolt.

Deschamps, writing in 1960, thought that the true history of the Rebellion would be written only when 'time would unloose tongues'. However, he pointed out that the real organisers of the 1896 rising had never been made known. It is more than probable that the surviving leaders knew facts that have never been made public, but it is also possible that none of them knew more than a small part of the organisation. Many of the most active leaders were undoubtedly killed, and the rather independent guerrilla operations carried on by local chiefs for the next year do not point to any strongly centralised command.

During the night of March 29, 1947, the French military camp at Moramanga, 100 miles east of Tananarive, was attacked by rebels and its arms were seized. A number of settlers were killed on isolated farms and plantations in the districts of Moramanga and Ambatondrazaka, and on the coast at Manakara. An attack on the armoury at the naval base of Diego-Suarez failed. In Tananarive the rebels apparently lost their nerve and dispersed, and in Fianarantsoa the leaders were arrested after cutting the electricity supply cables. At Moramanga, where the army camp had been attacked by about 2,000 men armed mainly with spears and slash-hooks, part of the Senegalese garrison was killed, but the remainder counter-attacked and massacred many of the local population. Very soon, all the coastal region between Tamatave and Fara-fangana was occupied by the nationalists, while north of Tamatave armed bands controlled most of the countryside. While the larger towns, such as Tamatave and Mananjary, remained in French hands, a number of small centres, such as Ifanadiana, Fort Carnot and Vohipeno in the forest region of the south-east coast, were taken by the rebels. About one-sixth of Madagascar was soon in rebel hands, particularly regions of European settlement where disputes over land and labour requisitions had gone on for years.

At this time, France, recovering from the German occupation

and with the reoccupation of Indo-China in progress, had few troops stationed in Madagascar. The rebels were organised in separate guerrilla units, fighting under the red and white flag of the former monarchy, to which had been added eighteen stars to represent the eighteen Malagasy tribes. Their armament was rudimentary and consisted mainly of spears and axes, the only firearms being those they had seized in military posts, apart from shotguns. But the immediate effect of the uprising was one of surprise; Tananarive was effectively isolated from the coast, except for a hastily-improvised armoured train. The railway itself was constantly cut by the rebels. Had the nationalists been armed with modern weapons and had they received supplies from abroad (as did later nationalist insurrections, notably that of Algeria seven years later), the position of the French would have been extremely difficult.

The General Staff apparently warned the High Commissioner of the impending insurrection at 22.00 hours on the night of March 29, and the town was patrolled by units of police, gendarmerie and the National Guard.[38] The French by no means lost their nerve, and the reaction of the administration, the army and individual settlers was immediate and vigorous. All civil aircraft were requisitioned and military reinforcements landed at Manakara. Simultaneously, a column disengaged the railway running north from Moramanga to Ambatondrazaka, where the settlers had already organised armed resistance. Large numbers of arrests were made, but armed clashes continued all through the dry season from May until the arrival of substantial French reinforcements, including more Senegalese troops and units of the Foreign Legion, in October 1947. Operations by the guerrillas were interrupted by the rains but began again in April 1948. By this time, many thousands of villagers had fled into the forest to escape military reprisals, and it was not until December 1, 1948, when 558,000 'submissions' (surrenders) had been registered, that the rebellion was officially ended.

The actions of the nationalist bands, the repression by units of the French army, mass arrests together with methods of extracting 'confessions', which have been seen in all wars of independence from Ireland to Algeria, produced a large number of victims—some French, but the great majority Malagasy. The exact number of victims is difficult to assess. The High Commissioner, Pierre de Chevigné (who had succeeded Marcel de Coppet), and General Garbay declared before a commission of enquiry that the number of victims was between 60,000 and 80,000.* Many villagers died of starvation or diseases in the forest, and there are few families on the east coast that cannot claim victims among their relatives.

The Rebellion was a traumatic experience for a large number of Malagasy and is rarely mentioned. A commemoration of the victims of 1947 was organised by the government for the first time in 1967. President Tsiranana preceded this by speeches in which he invited the population to remember the dead but forget the past. Twenty years after this conflict it could be said that the psychological wounds had healed, and relations between Malagasy and Europeans gave no hint of the hallucinating experiences of which both sides had vivid recollections. The settlement of the consequences of the Rebellion of 1947 are greatly to the credit of both Malagasy and French alike. It cannot have been easy to forget, and in fact the events have not been forgotten. But they are remembered with an objective dignity, and any return to extreme forms of xenophobic nationalism, as appears occasionally in fringe newspapers of small opposition groups, had been resolutely rejected by the mass of the population as well as its leaders.

In his opening address to the Representative Assembly which met for the first time in Tananarive on April 19, High Commissioner de Coppet accused the MDRM and its leaders of being solely responsible for the Rebellion. The parliamentary immunity of Ravoahangy and Rabemananjara, who were in Madagascar, was lifted, and they were arrested. Raseta was arrested in France, after his immunity had been lifted by a debate on June 6, 1947. Judicial procedures were begun against thousands of those arrested. The trial of the three members of parliament together with other leaders of the MDRM opened in Tananarive on July 22 and lasted until October 4, 1948. The prosecution held the MDRM responsible for having organised the Rebellion; the defence

---

* The commission appointed by the *Union française* was composed of Mlle Autissier and MM. Zinzou (President of Dahomey, 1966–69) and Lapart. The official figure of 11,000 dead was established later by Governor-General Bargues, on the basis of detailed enquiries in individual villages.

maintained that it had been provoked by extremist wings of the party, JINA and PANAMA.

There was probably some truth in the assertion of the defence that the rebellion was the work of extremists within the MDRM. It has been shown that, with its solid electoral majority, the party had nothing to gain by armed rebellion. But already in 1946 there had been signs of extremism in some of the MDRM newspapers. On June 4, 1946, *Ny Rariny* wrote: 'We are ready, if necessary, to have recourse to violence to reconquer our freedom by all means, even by violence.' This is not an isolated example.

The MDRM members of parliament, far away in Paris, had little possibility of guiding their following or of calming the impatient ones. The JINA and the PANAMA were more like secret societies, on the Far Eastern model, than orthodox wings of a political party. Raymond Rabemananjara, a journalist and one of the founders of the MDRM, who escaped arrest and remained for long in France, wrote that these groups represented 'a narrow nationalism, xenophobic and racist'.[39]

The leaders of MDRM misjudged the political maturity of their fellow-countrymen and underrated the explosive effect which certain ideas, and particularly newspaper articles, might have on politically uneducated people, who had never had access to normal democratic communication or means of expression. There had been virtually no press in Madagascar, except for sheets with a very limited circulation. The radio was controlled by the administration, and, anyway, few people had the cumbersome battery sets of the time. There had been no information except word-of-mouth news picked up in the market-place. Now new ideas burst upon them, together with talk of the United Nations Charter which was to set all colonial peoples free, of the liberation movements in Indonesia, Indo-China and Malaya, and of the propaganda emanating from the Soviet Union. The MDRM leaders included men who had lived in a small circle of intellectuals in Paris, and they may have judged the opinions of their friends to be those of the mass of the French public. This was not the case: the average Frenchman's ideas of the colonies were those associated with the Colonial Exhibition of 1931.

It is true that anti-colonialism was advancing rapidly in the public opinion of the colonial powers, and in particular the French left wing was at once alerted by the 1947 Rebellion, the first in a long series of post-war nationalist risings. Papers such as the Communist *Humanité*, the Socialist *Ce Soir*, and *La Défense*, attacked the methods of repression. The Secours Populaire Français sent lawyers to defend the accused. In the French Parliament, a motion proposed on May 9, 1947, by the Communist Party to send a parliamentary mission of enquiry to Madagascar was defeated by 410 votes to 197. This vote coincided with the expulsion of the Communist ministers from the government, then headed by M. Paul Ramadier.

In July 1948, before the trial of the MDRM leaders had opened, a number of sentences were passed by military tribunals in various localities. There were several executions, including that of the alleged 'generalissimo' of the nationalist forces, Samuel Rakotondrabe. Several thousand other cases were brought before magistrates' courts. The trial of the leaders, Ravoahangy, Rabemananjara and Raseta, took place in the great hall of the Palace of Andafiavaratra, the residence of Rainilaiarivony, the last Prime Minister of the monarchy. This was the second time that Ravoahangy had been sentenced in this hall. Raseta was also sentenced to death, with four others. Rabemananjara was sentenced to life imprisonment with seven others, and Senator Jules Ranaivo also received a prison sentence. A decree declaring the suppression of the MDRM was issued during the first days of the Rebellion in April 1947. With the imprisonment or execution of practically all its leaders, the activities of the party were abruptly brought to an end.

The trial of the leaders, the arbitrary lifting of their parliamentary immunity, the police methods used to extract 'confessions' and the repression carried out against the civilian population were much criticised in France itself. A number of Socialist and Communist motions, demanding suspension of proceedings against the parliamentarians, were regularly defeated. Many French newspapers attacked the trial and the sentences. A correspondent for *Le Monde*, an objective non-Communist newspaper, wrote on November 4, 1948: 'All this meanness disgusts me, but I am above all horrified by the stupidity of this policy. Is it not exactly the contrary of what we should do? If we wished to push these people into rebellion, we could hardly act otherwise.'

7—M * *

The court of Assessors (Cour de Cassation)* confirmed the sentences on July 7, 1949, but the death sentences were commuted. Trials continued to be held in Madagascar, while agitation for an amnesty continued in left-wing circles in France.

In January 1951 François Mitterand, then Minister of Overseas France and in 1967 candidate for the Presidential elections, declared: 'The future of Madagascar is within the French Republic.' This was a rash prophecy on the part of a politician who was then still a young man and it was out of line with a rapidly-evolving public opinion. Doubts concerning the permanence of existing links between France and its colonies were becoming more clearly defined among financial and business leaders, and were to be expressed with striking clarity in three articles which appeared in *Paris Match* in 1956, written by a leading journalist, Raymond Cartier. The author put the question which was beginning to be asked by many French tax-payers: 'Of what use is it to pour out huge sums of money to maintain an out-of-date colonial empire?' France's business leaders stated that the 1,400 billion francs (at that time, equivalent to $US 4,000 million) which had been spent on its colonies since 1946 would, if invested at home, have enabled the French economy to have become competitive on world markets. While pouring out these huge sums, France had had to re-equip its industry and infrastructure, devastated by the Second World War and German occupation. The European Common Market was to be created by the Treaty of Rome in 1957, and economists foresaw the great effort of investment and re-equipment which would be necessary to rescue France's industry and agriculture from the effects of two centuries of protectionism. The articles gave rise to new theories of 'cartierism', which compared the situation of an under-equipped France—the department of Aveyron in the south-west was usually cited—with the ports, roads, schools and hospitals which were being constructed in the overseas territories.[40]

In fact, the instability of the Fourth Republic and the rapid succession of French governments in the 1950s put the colonial administration in an unenviable position. The crushing of the 1947 Rebellion and the suppression of the MDRM put an end for the time

---

* Not the Court of Appeal but the Court which decides whether there has been any legal fault in the proceedings. It can either annul or confirm but not modify the sentence.

being to political activity of any kind in Madagascar. Even the PADESM, the party favoured by the administration, split up into a number of small regional parties. 'In the face of the political passivity which succeeded the tremendous shock [of the Rebellion], the administration got back power, which it shared with no-one, but at the same time it was a power without a future.'[41]

However, Malagasy political aspirations had not died. Trade unions continued to be organised, with assistance from both the CGT and the CTFC. Sensitive to popular feeling, the Catholic bishops made a joint pronouncement on December 20, 1953, declaring political independence a legitimate aspiration. During his short period as Prime Minister, Pierre Mendès-France made his influence felt in Madagascar, as in Tunisia and Indo-China. This courageous and intelligent man, who ended the Indo-China war by the Geneva agreement of 1954 and opened the way to the independence of North Africa by granting autonomy to Tunisia, appointed as Secretary of State for Overseas Territories Roger Duveau, member of the French Parliament representing the French residents of Madagascar. An amnesty was granted those condemned for the 1947 Rebellion, except those condemned to more than fifteen years' imprisonment, who were pardoned. The three MDRM leaders, Ravoahangy, Raseta and Rabemananjara, were, however, restricted to certain départements in France after their liberation from the prison of Calvi in Corsica on March 29, 1956, when the last prisoners were liberated. The former members of parliament were still detained in France and were unable to return to Madagascar to stand for re-election.

In January 1956 Duveau was elected member of parliament for the east coast of Madagascar by the Malagasy electoral college. A schoolteacher was elected to represent the west coast: Philibert Tsiranana, founder of a new political party, the Parti Social Démocrate (PSD), and future President of Madagascar.

Events now moved rapidly towards an independence which those on the spot scarcely realised was so close at hand. In 1956 a Socialist French government voted the so-called 'Loi Cadre',*

* Law No. 56–619 of June 23, 1956. In addition to René Coty, then President of the Republic, the following signatures appear on the Loi Cadre: Guy Mollet, Prime Minister and leader of the SFIO; François Mitterand, Minister of Justice (who had declared in 1951 that the future of Madagascar was as a part of the French Republic); Gaston Deferre,

concerning all the former colonies. In essence this law gave internal autonomy to the 'overseas territories', as the colonies were now called, reserving to France questions of defence, external relations, the guarantee of civil liberties and finance. It provided for the creation of a national government in each territory, elected by the legislative assembly. Elections to this assembly were to be on the basis of universal suffrage, with a single electoral roll; the European electoral roll was abolished.

Two decrees of application issued under this law[42] defined the structure of Madagascar's legislative assembly and set up in addition six Provincial Assemblies with fairly wide autonomy. This regionalisation was criticised by many nationalists as a heavy burden and as a manoeuvre to 'divide and rule'. Although the Provincial Assemblies survived independence as 'conseils généraux' they have never been given the powers and importance foreseen under the Loi Cadre, and the government, in pursuance of its policies of national unity and an end to tribalism, has not encouraged anything which might allow ambitious local personalities to take a separatist course.

At the municipal election of November 1956, moderate nationalists won control of Tananarive, Tamatave and Diego-Suarez, leaving seats for European members of the municipal councils. In April 1957 elections for the Provincial and National Assemblies took place. In the National Assembly, the representatives of the coastal peoples, headed by Philibert Tsiranana, had a numerical majority over the Merina, and included some of the more extreme nationalists and survivors of the MDRM. The application of universal suffrage meant that the coastal peoples could not democratically be dominated by the Merina, and excluded a return to the state of affairs under the monarchy. The Assembly therefore was free to pursue a policy of national unity, and at the Congress of the PSD, held in December 1957, its leader Tsiranana declared: 'Madagascar looks forward to an independence progressively acquired in a French association, the final objective being a status similar to that of a member of the British Commonwealth.'

Minister for Overseas Territories; and Felix Houphouet-Boigny, Minister of State to the Prime Minister and from 1960 President of the Ivory Coast.

The change of regime in France that brought General de Gaulle to power was to accelerate events even more. In preparation for his new constitution, which was to be put to a referendum that included the overseas territories, the General undertook a tour of all the former colonies. His first visit was to Madagascar, where he arrived on August 22, 1958, and was greeted by the Malagasy population with an enthusiasm that surprised many residents. At a public meeting held in the stadium of Mahamasina, the former military parade ground of the monarchy, which lies beneath the cliff on which stands the former royal palace, the then Vice-President Tsiranana* asked for the abrogation of the Law of Annexation of 1896 and the restoration of statehood to Madagascar. In his reply, de Gaulle first explained the meaning of the constitutional referendum which was to be held: then, pointing to the royal palace standing six hundred feet above him, he declared: 'Tomorrow you will once again be a state as you were when this palace was inhabited.' This declaration caused a tremendous sensation; and on September 28, 1958, the referendum on the new constitution gave a majority of 77 per cent for the 'Yes' vote, which meant that Madagascar had opted for gradual independence and the maintenance of links with France within the 'Community' ('Communauté'). Guinea was the only territory to vote for breaking all links with France and for immediate withdrawal from the French Community.[43]

Madagascar was the first territory to define its constitutional framework, and on October 14, 1958, the Congress of all the Provincial Assemblies met in Tananarive, where the Speaker, Norbert Zafimahova, declared: 'by virtue of the powers given to our Congress by Article 76 of the French constitution, and Article 1 of the Order of General de Gaulle . . . Madagascar is a state, and this state is a republic, as allowed for in the French constitution of October 4, 1958'. There are photographs showing Malagasy and European members of parliament embracing each other in the general enthusiasm which followed this declaration. October 14 is since celebrated as the National Day.

On October 15, André Soucadaux, High Commissioner since 1954, who had worked closely with Philibert Tsiranana to prepare for this independence, appeared before the National Assembly and

* Under the 'Loi Cadre', the French high commissioner was head of the government and presided over cabinet meetings rather as a viceroy.

declared: 'The government of the French republic solemnly recognises the establishment of the state of Madagascar, and the abrogation of the Law [of Annexation] of August 6, 1896.' On October 16, a Constituent Assembly was set up from among the members of the Congress. A new flag was adopted: red, white and green, the red and white from the flag of the monarchy and the green signifying the coastal regions.

During 1959, President Tsiranana and High Commissioner Soucadaux worked out the final phases of the transfer of power and the establishment of complete political independence. From the time of General Galliéni onwards, Madagascar had attracted a number of governors-general who were outstanding men intellectually and who made substantial contributions to the development of the country. Garbit, Olivier and Cayla all left their mark on the institutions and infrastructure of the country. Bargues (1950–54), for his preoccupation with restoring the economy shaken by the 1947 Rebellion and for his full utilisation of French development funds (FIDES), must also be mentioned.

But André Soucadaux appears as a man apart from these outstanding administrators. He belongs to the small band of governors and high commissioners who, from 1956, prepared an orderly transition to political independence in both French and British territories and who were able at the same time to win the respect and also the friendship of the nationalist leaders. The friendship between Soucadaux, a Socialist of the SFIO inspiration, and Tsiranana was a major factor in ensuring a smooth passage for the numerous affairs that had to be arranged between France and Madagascar to produce an orderly continuation of the administration, without any major disturbances of the economy. Political independence, which brought with it very considerable changes in institutions and above all in human relationships, appears to have been derived from a highly successful operation of the difficult process of decolonisation. The character of the Malagasy, the quality of *fihavanana* (that is, friendship and benevolence towards one's fellow men) which is evident to any foreigner who has lived among the country people, had a good deal to do with this smooth transition. But much credit is due to the leaders, both French and Malagasy, in whose hands the negotiations lay.

On January 5, 1959, Tsiranana and Soucadaux signed agreements placing under Malagasy jurisdiction and command the gendarmerie, the administrators ('fonctionnaires d'autorité') the security services and the police. The gendarmerie, which is an armed mobile police force spread over the whole country, became Malagasy overnight, together with its French officers, buildings and equipment. Thus the levers of power were handed over before political independence. It was clearly French policy to withdraw all civil servants in key positions of command at the earliest possible date; this was practically complete, for the territorial administration, a few months after independence in June 1960, when the great majority of district commissioners were Malagasy and only two or three French remained. The Ministry of the Interior, controlling the police, security services and the territorial administration, was the first ministry to be completely staffed by Malagasy with a handful of French advisers.

The new constitution was adopted on April 29, 1959. This was inspired by the French constitution, but with certain differences. The president of the republic is elected by universal suffrage and is also prime minister. Under its latest constitution (1965), France has also chosen to elect its president by universal suffrage, but the office of prime minister remains. The preamble to the Malagasy constitution affirms its belief in God and in man's personality, and condemns the exploitation of man by man.

The example of Mali, which had requested and obtained its independence, showed that this could be achieved while still retaining the friendship and material aid of France. Tsiranana requested the 'transfer of competence' on December 18, 1959, encouraged in his advance towards complete independence by de Gaulle who, having met Tsiranana in 1958, had had occasion to meet him again and had formed a high personal regard for his character and capabilities. Agreement was worked out with France on future relationships between the two countries: on defence, on aid, on the status of French residents in Madagascar and on that of Malagasy residents in France, and on a number of other subjects. These, the 'Accords Franco-Malgaches', were signed on April 2, 1960. On June 26, 1960, Jean Foyer, French Minister for Relations with the Community, standing on the *Vatomasina*, the sacred stone of the former monarchy at Mahamasina in Tananarive, read the joint Franco-Malagasy declaration, followed by a message from de Gaulle stating that France's 'fraternal collaboration will not be withheld from the "Great Island", an old and a new independent state'.

The red, white and green flag floated over the royal palace, almost sixty-four years after the red and white banner had been hauled down and Queen Ranavalona carried into exile on a litter escorted by Senegalese troops. The President of the new Republic of Madagascar, a Tsimihety from the north-west, rules from his office in the Palace of Andafiavaratra, the residence of the Prime Minister of the Queen, and scene of the trials where one of the republic's ministers, Ravoahangy, was twice sentenced, and another minister, Rabemananjara, was also sentenced to life imprisonment.

A former Minister of Justice, Alfred Ramangasoavina, had rightly said that it was incorrect to speak of Madagascar 'acceeding' to independence. From a legal point of view, Madagascar *recovered* its independence.[44] The ceremony of 1960 was not the liberation of a colony to form a country which had never before existed, but the restoration of a state which had been internationally recognised before the conquest of 1896. However, Madagascar was restored to sovereignty with an important and essential difference: the republic is the union of all the Malagasy peoples and not the restoration of the Merina oligarchy. On the walls of many rural buildings appears a slogan, on which, in a time of tribal dislocation in many countries, it is good to meditate:

> *Malagasy daholo, tsy misy avakavaka.*
> (We are all Malagasy; there are no more tribes.)

6. State and Politics since Independence

THE INDEPENDENCE of Madagascar was freely negotiated with France. The evolution towards full independence was greatly accelerated by the coming to power of General de Gaulle in 1958. As the author of the Brazzaville Declaration of 1944, de Gaulle has great prestige in Africa, but his determination to end the Algerian War, where fighting had been going on since 1954, undoubtedly influenced his policies towards the overseas territories. Thus, within two years of his becoming President of France, nearly all the former colonies were independent states.

The leaders of Madagascar in 1960 had not come out of prison to take over power. President Tsiranana had been a member of the French Parliament and the other ministers had been in senior civil service posts. The three exiled leaders of 1947, Ravoahangy, Rabemananjara and Raseta, were recalled to Madagascar by Tsiranana in 1960. Only Raseta refused to join the government; he persisted in a course of personal independence which has kept him apart from the main current of political activities ever since. Ravoahangy and Rabemananjara entered the government with ministerial portfolios; until his death in 1969, Ravoahangy was Minister of State for Presidential Affairs, and Rabemananjara was Vice-President and Minister of State for Foreign Affairs in 1970.

The independent government was not formed as a result of a colonial war, nor were the ministers (except for the two returned exiles) men who had suffered persecution, with long terms of imprisonment, under the colonial administration. With the exception of the two leaders of the MDRM, none had been in any way connected with the 1947 Rebellion; and these two, on their return, showed no signs of bitterness or hostility towards France in either their public or private pronouncements. Their return was a personal triumph for them and for Tsiranana, who made this one of his first acts as head of state, and they enjoyed a high degree of respect and esteem as a result of their past courage. Their attitude to France is similar to the attitude of France to Germany twenty-five years after the Second World War and occupation. The past is not forgotten, but it *is* the past and has no bearing on present relations.

There was no sudden dismantling of structures at independence, no sudden departure of French residents. Senior French civil servants, whose continuation had been agreed before independence, remained at their posts until an orderly hand-over to a Malagasy had taken place. The administrative structures were not suddenly transformed. Thus there was nothing comparable to what took place in Zambia on January 1, 1964, before independence, when there was an abrupt dismantling of provincial and district government and a sudden abolition of poll tax. In Madagascar, the chefs de district became sous-préfets, and préfectures were introduced between the chefs de province and the sous-préfets in 1960. In the same year, the sous-préfectures were subdivided into communes rurales; but the essential structure of the territorial administration, controlled by the Ministry of the Interior, remained intact and its authority was considerably increased after independence. Thus, the powers of préfects and sous-préfets are considerably greater than those of the former French district commissioners. They are responsible for the maintenance of public order, can call out the gendarmerie if necessary and can act with powers of local magistrates for offences with a maximum fine of 25,000 FMG ($US 90) or twenty-eight days' imprisonment. The object of various administrative changes has been to reinforce the direct authority of the government in the countryside. Taxation has been made a national duty, and the percentage of taxes collected by the chefs de canton in each sub-prefecture are often published and commented on by ministers in their speeches as an index of the patriotism of the inhabitants.

In 1959, there were resident in Madagascar 67,000 French citizens of 'metropolitan' origin, of whom 57 per cent were permanently resident in the country, and of these 27 per cent were Réunion islanders. (Réunion remains a department of France.) Expatriate official and contractual employees made up the remaining 43 per cent. These two groups represented 2·3 per cent of the total population. The French residents were classified by occupation as follows:[1]

	%
Commerce and industry	37
Army personnel	18
Civil servants	16
Settlers	10
Professions	8
Clergy	2
Various	9

To this figure should be added 50,000 Comoro islanders, who are French citizens since the Comoro islands have only internal autonomy. In all, 7,000 French citizens owned 220,000 acres; many of these landowners were small Réunion islander farmers, whose standard of living was indistinguishable from that of their Malagasy neighbours.

Although a number of French residents left permanently in the years following independence, this was mainly because an increasing number of responsible posts were gradually taken over by Malagasy both in administration and in the private sector. Many French decided to stay and some have taken Malagasy nationality. Those who decided to leave were able to sell their houses or businesses and repatriate their capital, as there are no restriction on movements of funds between Madagascar and other members of the franc zone. The investment code, which is an extremely elastic document and gives the Ministry of Finance very wide powers over 'taxation holidays' and repatriation of funds for investors, has encouraged a moderate amount of local capital investment by French residents and companies. Land and real estate values have remained high and have increased considerably in Tananarive. Thus, French companies and individual businesses have nearly all remained. These have not evolved as rapidly as some people might wish, and they have been an easy target for writers such as Gendarme.[2]

In the private sector of Madagascar, there are two general categories: those who carry on as before and who aim at earning a high margin of profit on a small and unexpanding turnover; and a smaller group who actively search for new fields of investment. The immobilism of local commercial houses may not have been as big an obstacle to economic development as some writers maintain. Certainly, Madagascar possessed in the late 1960s the necessary structures for a massive take-over of the economy by Malagasy entrepreneurs. There were active programmes, sponsored by the University of Tananarive, for the training of personnel to occupy senior posts in business (Section de Formation des Cadres); these training programmes have been carried out in close collaboration with the private sector. The co-operative movement has received massive official and political support, but has not appreciably modified traditional marketing structures for agricultural produce. The syndicats des communes, voluntary associations of a number of rural communes for economic purposes, have in certain cases been more successful. One instance was the complete take-over of the collection and export of the pois du cap, of which almost the entire annual production is sold to Britain to be marketed as 'Madagascar butter beans'. This crop is the main source of cash income of the population of the south-west coast, and its marketing was taken out of the hands of a small number of Pakistani traders by the Syndicat des Communes of Tuléar. The government moved similarly to control the marketing and export of vanilla, the country's second export by value, by setting up an appropriate marketing board based in the main producing area on the north-east coast, centred on Antalaha. Banana exports have multiplied more than ten times since independence, prompted by the activities of an officially-supported co-operative based in Tamatave.

Government participation in industry has been made possible by the creation of an industrial development board, the Société National d'Investissement (SNI), with a capital of 1,000 million FMG (roughly $US 4 million). The SNI participates in a number of enterprises, such as the oil refinery at Tamatave and the re-organised edible oil expressing industry (also taken over from individual private Indian traders by the government), in the hotel business and in a number of industries, such as a match factory, a pulp and paper factory, and the central milk plant of Tananarive. The SNI also moved into the field of retail trade by the establishment of a chain of low-priced shops extending into rural areas, known as the 'Magasins M'.

While these examples show that some evolution has occurred, it is, however, true that the evolution of Malagasy entrepreneurs and, above all, the emergence of efficient management personnel has delayed a more complete take-over of the inherited business structures. Retail trade in France was, until perhaps 1960, one of the most conservative sectors, although rapid evolution has taken place since. These conservative attitudes still exist among a number of individual French traders, particularly those long established in Madagascar, who are out of touch with the changes in France.[3]

Madagascar's agricultural export products had enjoyed support prices on the French market, which shielded the country's budget from the effects of world-market fluctuations for commodities such as coffee, sugar, sisal and tobacco. Vanilla, sold almost entirely on the American market, and cloves, for which Zanzibar was an important competitor and India and Indonesia the most important clients, suffered from price falls in the late 1950s and early 1960s. The support prices for a wide range of products continued after independence and were gradually aligned with world prices as part of the policy of the European Economic Community. The effects of this realignment were palliated by local stabilisation funds and by large capital grants from the Fonds Européen du Developpement (FED). These grants were applied to diversification of production patterns in main coffee-growing areas and to increasing productivity for specific crops such as rice.

The decolonisation was carried out, at the express wish of the majority party, in a spirit of friendship with France, in conformity with the affirmative vote given by the country to the constitution of the French Community proposed by General de Gaulle in 1958. Though a number of overseas territories did not join the Community, stress was laid, at the moment of independence, on Madagascar's adherence. The presence of a large and economically important French population made it necessary for assurances to be given if a sudden disruption of the economy was to be avoided. There was a temporary slowing of economic activity immediately after full political independence, which was declared on June 26, 1960, a few days before the débâcle that succeeded the independence of the Belgian Congo. At this time there was considerable alarm amongst expatriates all over Africa, which spread for a time to Madagascar. President Tsiranana made a number of public pronouncements aimed at reassuring the French residents, referring to them as the 'nineteenth tribe' of Madagascar. On their side, many of the French who remained in Madagascar have closely identified themselves with government policies. Relations between French and Malagasy are closer and more cordial than before independence, partly because the more intransigent expatriates left but also because of the relaxed atmosphere after 1960 which greatly facilitated such contacts.

Although Madagascar inherited the colonial administration, this was not left for long without structural modification. Changes have always had the effect of increasing the authority of the government. The right to strike has thus been practically forbidden to Malagasy civil servants (Ordonnance 60–149 of 1960) and salaries of ministers and civil servants were reduced by 10 per cent immediately after independence. Vigorous measures have been taken to check any tendencies to corruption among civil servants; severe prison sentences were imposed for the very few cases that have occurred, under measures introduced in 1961 (Loi 60–026 of October 9, 1961).

The replacement of French senior civil servants by Malagasy had begun several years before independence, and, after the Loi Cadre of 1957, proceeded rapidly, so that there were already many Malagasy in senior posts of the territorial administration, such as that of district commissioner, before 1960. On October 14, 1958, when the republic was proclaimed, there were 2,700 French civil servants serving in Madagascar, including a large number of teachers and doctors. In 1961 there were 1,616 French civil servants, representing 3·2 per cent of the total establishment. In 1962, 58 per cent of those remaining were teachers or doctors and only 20 per cent were technicians. In 1968 there remained 1,233 French civil servants, of whom 70 were doctors and 1,065 teachers. A further sharp reduction of French expatriate personnel occurred in 1969, as a result of French policy and not at the request of Madagascar, which protested against the reduction in the number of secondary-school teachers.

Training of Malagasy civil servants had been carried out at an advanced level in France during the years before and immediately after independence. The senior administrative staff were trained at the Institut des Hautes Etudes d'Outre-mer (IHEOM) in the buildings of the former Ecole Coloniale in Paris, which had trained several generations of French colonial civil servants. This was a two-year course, and many of the students had had some years of administrative experience and held law or other degrees. After 1960, the Ecole Nationale d'Administration Malgache (ENAM), or civil service training college, was set up as an annexe of the University of Tananarive. Here, courses were given over two years to future administrators, many of whom are today prefects and sub-prefects; the courses covered a wide range of subjects, including law, administration, economic development and finance.[4]

'Malgachisation' was rapid in key ministries. Thus, by early 1962, there were no French administrators as sub-prefects; and even in 1961 there had been only two or three ex-district commissioners, who remained in their posts when the districts were converted into sub-prefectures. The Ministry of the Interior during 1962 appointed Malgagasy to all senior posts, such as that of Director-General of the Interior and Director-General of Security. A very small number of French administrators stayed on in this Ministry as advisers on subjects such as the organisation of the newly-formed rural communes. Those French who were kept stayed on an individual basis, and were specifically requested from the French technical assistance mission in Tananarive by the Minister of the Interior. The Ministry of Finance had a French Minister until 1963, when he was replaced by a Malagasy. At the same time, all senior posts in this Ministry were taken over by well-trained Malagasy civil servants. French advisers remained in the Institut d'Emission, which performs the functions of a central bank, because of the very close ties between the Malagasy and French francs. In the Ministry of Education, senior posts were rapidly taken over by Malagasy, although in 1968 there were still over 1,000 French teachers in secondary schools and universities. By 1965, no important post remained in the hands of a French civil servant, although a number of Frenchmen remained and performed executive functions, particularly in technical ministries such as those of Public Works and Agriculture.

The close links existing between the Malagasy and French francs have meant that Madagascar has shared France's monetary problems since 1960. There has been complete freedom of transfer of funds between France and Madagascar, and Madagascar conforms to France's exchange control policy with countries outside the franc zone. In matters of internal credit policies, liquidity ratios of French-based banks in Madagascar and loan financing raised by the government outside the franc zone, there has been no clash of interests between France and Madagascar. The joint Franco-Malagasy Commission, set up under the 1960 agreements to work out common policies on financial matters of mutual interest, has met regularly and worked smoothly. French financial support to Madagascar since independence has continued in the form of capital grants, payment of expatriate personnel and military aid, and can be estimated at approximately 6,000 million FMG ($US 22 million) per annum.

Interference, or behind-the-scenes influence, would have to be looked for in the maintenance of French expatriates in key posts, in undue influence concerning the appointment of Malagasy senior staff, in financial and military matters, or in foreign policy. These sectors must be examined individually.

It can be shown statistically that French policy has been to reduce the number of expatriate technical assistance personnel more rapidly than the Malagasy government sometimes has wished. Very soon after independence, French officials were withdrawn from nearly all key posts, and particularly from those posts where policy decisions were made. In the early years after independence, when former colonial civil servants still occupied some key posts and the inherited structures had not yet undergone modifications, there was inevitably some influence on policy and appointments at the central government level. Such influence vanished very soon from provincial headquarters and was unknown lower down, in prefectures and sub-prefectures. However, the Malagasy leaders early on made it quite clear that they would not tolerate more than a certain amount of pressure, and those expatriates who over-estimated their influence soon found that they were sent on leave and not recalled. Such displacements were all carried out in the 'Malagasy manner', that is to say, with a rather tortuous oriental politeness so that the displaced expatriates never quite knew what had happened or who was responsible. But cases of French residents or officials having been declared 'prohibited immigrants' are so rare as to be highly unusual and have always been for clear breaches of law.

Financial policy might be influenced, either directly by expatriate officials within the Ministry of Finance, or by officials in the Inspection Générale d'Etat (which corresponds to the Inspection Générale des Finances in France and, roughly, to the Treasury and to the Auditor-General in Britain). The Inspection Générale d'Etat, a head of which was French until 1965, and in which a number of outstanding French civil servants have served, has carried out many useful services since independence. This service, being attached to the Office of the President, has wide powers of inspection of functions, staff, procedures and finance. It was thus able to carry out detailed analyses of many new structures and government ventures. These included co-operatives, syndicats de communes, the use of road maintenance material by the Public Works Department, the structures set up for the marketing of vanilla and a number of government economic activities. These confidential reports, being available to ministers and heads of department, were sometimes used by the President to give directives for drastic modification of procedures and for staff changes. The tradition of the French Inspection des Finances avoids anything remotely resembling a personal opinion.

The role of the French army in Madagascar has been clear from the start. At independence, all military forces stationed in Madagascar were French. The organisation of the Malagasy army was the subject of measures announced on September 30, 1960, and was carried out within the framework of the defence agreements signed between Madagascar and France on June 27, 1960. The functions of the French army are twofold: to assist in the defence of the territory and surrounding sea and airspace, and to train and equip the Malagasy army. Under the defence agreement, France maintains control over the naval and military base at Diego-Suarez and the air force base beside the international airport at Ivato, Tananarive. These bases are by no means extra-territorial or exclusive. Units of the Malagasy army form joint units with those of the French army, known as régiments inter-armes, while the navy and air force co-operate equally closely in training and periodic exercises and manoeuvres. French officers wearing Malagasy uniform served in the Malagasy army in its early days to train their successors, who passed through the military officers' colleges of St Cyr and Fréjus. France finances the equipment and arms supplies of the Malagasy army and pays the pensions of all Malagasy ex-soldiers of the French forces. The Malagasy army is directly under the control of the President of the republic, who has his own General Staff. The French forces in Madagascar are commanded by a French general, who resides in Tananarive, and by an admiral who commands the naval units at Diego-Suarez.[5]

Parallel to this, the gendarmerie has been trained and equipped by France in a similar manner. On January 25, 1961, all equipment, arms and buildings of the gendarmerie were handed over to Madagascar. This force is under a separate command from that of the army, and its head, a colonel, is immediately under the President. The command structure of the army and gendarmerie are entirely separate. The gendarmerie performs the functions of a police force outside the municipalities—that is, in all small towns, villages and rural areas. It is highly mobile and possesses an advanced communications system. Its armament includes automatic weapons, armoured cars and aircraft, and it has an important role to play in the maintenance of public order. It is a highly disciplined elite force and enjoys a good reputation among the population.

A third force has been created since independence, the Force Républicaine de Securité (FRS), also a mobile para-military unit that undertakes special police duties. This force provides a personal bodyguard for the President. The distribution of command of the army, the gendarmerie and the FRS provides a system of checks and balances in the military and para-military sectors that might well prevent an unexpected move by any single one of these units, as has happened elsewhere in recent years.

In foreign policy, Madagascar pursues an independent line, in no way aligned with France's foreign policy. Diplomatic relations have been maintained with Nationalist China, but no diplomatic relations had been established with any Communist countries except Yugoslavia and Rumania (1969), although trade missions have been exchanged with the Soviet Union, Poland, Hungary and certain other countries. These trade agreements have had very little concrete result. Certain leaders of the Antokon'ny Kongresy ho'any Fahaleovantenan'i Madagasikara (AKFM), the official opposition party, are permitted to attend international conferences behind the Iron Curtain.

Madagascar has been a member of the Organisation of African Unity (OAU) since its creation in 1963, and the President has attended a number of meetings of heads of state. Closer relations are maintained with the Organisation Africaine et Malagache de Coopération Economique (OAMCE), which groups the French-speaking members of the OAU. This economic and political grouping was formed following a meeting held in Tananarive in 1961 of twelve heads of state of former French colonies, now independent, at which common policies were worked out.

POLITICAL DEVELOPMENT

Internal politics have provided little in the way of sudden changes or startling events since independence. Madagascar had in 1970 the same head of state who was Vice-President under the first Loi Cadre government of 1957. Several of the ministers had served in the government since then and, while some portfolios had been exchanged among ministers, there had been few changes among leading government personalities. Many senior civil servants have occupied their present posts for several years. While at independence the majority of such senior staff were Merina, the accession of civil servants of coastal or Betsileo origin has been rapid since 1961. Secondary schools were opened in all provinces in the early years of independence, and training of technicians from the provinces was accelerated. These policies have already diminished the preponderance of Merina within the civil service.

Political evolution has seen the steady growth in influence and experience of the government party, the Parti Social Démocrate (PSD) founded by Philibert Tsiranana in 1956 in the province of Majunga. After the suppression of the 1947 Rebellion, the MDRM— which had substantial popular support—was suppressed; and the PADESM, which had been encouraged by the colonial administration in opposition to the MDRM, disintegrated. From 1948 to 1955 there was practically no organised political life and no distinct party activity Trade union activity took the place of party politics. In 1954 the Confédération Française des Travaileurs Chrétiens (CFTC) claimed about 35,000 members in the private sector, while the Confédération Générale du Travail (CGT)—further to the left and with Communist sympathies—was said to have 2,500 members. The CFTC figures probably indicated sympathisers and only a small number of these paid regular dues. This union was strongly supported by the missions. The Communist Party was practically non-existent in Madagascar and used the CGT as one of its agents of penetration: the secretary-general of the CGT in Madagascar in 1954 had spent some time previously in Czechoslovakia and in Poland. At this time, Malagasy trade unionists, like their African counterparts, regarded a trade union as a political party and as a means of common defence against the colonial administration as well as employers.

After visits from French members of parliament, sometimes

Communists, trade unions appeared, some of which had a very brief existence. French citizens who were organised in trade unions often were unwilling to allow any substantial Malagasy membership, regarding their union as primarily a means of defending their own position as Europeans in Madagascar. The Malagasy civil servants had organised themselves by 1954, while the French civil servants tended to organise themselves apart, especially locally recruited staff.

With the appointment in 1954 of a liberal Socialist Governor-General, André Soucadaux, political parties were reconstituted. The most important was the Front National Malgache (FNM) which included many former MDRM members. There was a split between those who wished to reconstitute the MDRM under another name—with a policy of rapid political independence—and those who desired a more gradual course. There was also an element of suspicion on the part of the inhabitants of coastal and other districts against what appeared to be movement towards a new Merina domination. The MDRM had been of Merina inspiration, although it gained popular support among coastal peoples. From 1956 the more extreme nationalists appeared to the coastal peoples to be aiming at a restoration of the Merina rule. These peoples needed time to organise themselves, and they needed support against a movement that appeared to be setting back the clock to 1895 and re-establishing, if not the Merina monarchy, certainly Merina domination.

The PSD was also a nationalist party which aimed at political independence; but it specifically desired this to be obtained by negotiation and within a policy of friendship with France. It realised that it was a friendly government headed by the leader of the SFIO, Guy Mollet, which had passed the Loi Cadre, the first step towards independence. At the Congress of the SFIO, held at Issy-les-Moulineaux in May 1961, a message was read from President Tsiranana, stating: 'I do not forget the great party which obtained the passage of the Loi Cadre and thus had a determining voice in our independence.'

The years between 1957 and 1960 saw a proliferation of small political parties, usually centring on a local personality but sometimes having not more than thirty adherents. In September 1960 there were thirty-five of such parties.

In May 1958, a Congrès de l'Indépendance was held at Tamatave. It produced a fusion of several parties, the Union des Peuples Malgaches, the Front National Malgache, the Parti Nouveau Démocratique de l'Océan Indien, and the Association des Amis des Paysans. From this fusion was created the party which has since become the official opposition in Parliament, the Antokon'ny Kongresy ho'any Fahaleovantenan'i Madagasikara (AKFM), the 'Party of the Congress for the Independence of Madagascar'. The programme of the party, which appealed to the bonds of friendship existing between France and Madagascar, was 'free negotiation for independence'.

A committee for joint action had been created in 1956 between the Front National Malgache (FNM) and the Union des Peuples Malgaches (UPM), which had Communist leanings. It was at this time that Philibert Tsiranana, disapproving of a policy of joint action with Communist sympathisers, separated from this group with a number of collaborators and founded the PSD with SFIO support.

The 1958 Congress of Tamatave saw a re-emergence of certain MDRM elements, with the support of a number of small parties having Communist sympathies. However, the AKFM which emerged from this Congress has never had support from the mass of the population. Its members are mainly intellectuals and journalists, and 90 per cent of them are Merina. The leading AKFM personalities have little influence outside the suburbs of Tananarive, and the organisation of the party is highly centralised. Because of the large number of journalists within the party, it is able to issue a number of newspapers out of all proportion to its influence. Many of these are printed by handicraft methods and have a maximum circulation of 2,000 copies. They include *Imongo Vaovao*, with Communist leanings and a circulation of about 3,000; *Hita sy Re*, read by many non-AKFM sympathisers because of the gossip it retails about personalities; and *Hehy*, a humorous illustrated weekly. They constitute a press of agitation and contain little that is constructive.

The development of the local press in Madagascar has not followed the pattern of West Africa, where for many years before independence in Nigeria and Ghana there was a vigorous and independent local English-language press, nor that of East and Central Africa, where the local press produced vigorous newspapers such as the *East African Standard*, at first entirely by and for Europeans but later taking a progressive and nationalist orientation. As late as 1961 there was no daily newspaper of international standard in Madagascar and nothing remotely resembling a national newspaper. In 1961 *Le Courrier de Madagascar*, a French language daily with one page in Malagasy, began to appear. It is discreetly and intelligently pro-government but maintains an international standard of local and foreign news coverage and of presentation. Government-inspired daily papers include *Madagasikara Mahaleontena*, *Basy Vava* (formerly an opposition paper) and *Ny Marina*. Two Catholic weeklies maintain a good professional standard of journalism, *Lumière* and *La Croix*, and are sometimes moderately critical of the government.*

The total number of copies of all dailies and weeklies is reckoned to be 54,000 per issue. The *Courrier* and main government papers are obtainable in main provincial centres, usually depending on the regularity of local air services. Opposition newspapers are received by supporters by post. Few newspapers are ever seen in the bush, where the population relies on the radio for news.

The leader of the AKFM, the head of the official parliamentary opposition and the Mayor of Tananarive (President du Conseil Municipal) was Richard Andriamanjato (1970). He is a Protestant pastor, a well-educated man descended from the Merina aristocracy. He is thus typical of the Merina bourgeoisie of Tananarive, which is far removed in way of life and sympathies from the mass of the country people, with whom they have little or no contact. At the time of the French conquest and following the liberation of their slaves, many of the Merina feudal nobles abandoned their country houses and moved into Tananarive where many of them were employed in the French colonial administration. This separation from the countryside has persisted; it is astonishing how little many of the vocal sympathisers with the common man, the intellectuals and journalists within the AKFM, in fact know about the rural people. They are seldom seen out in the bush, and it is not surprising that the political influence of the AKFM remains stationary.

* Main newspapers are *Madagasikara Mahaleotena*, *Le Courrier de Madagascar*, *Basy Vava*, *Ny Marina* (Government); *Sahy*, *Maraina Vaovao*, *Ny Feon'i Madagasikara*, *Lumière*, *La Croix* (Independents); *Imongo Vaovao*, *Hita sy Re*, *Maresaka*, *Ny Fahaleaovantenan'i Madagasikara*, *Hehy*, *Andry*, *Fanesa* (Protestant) (Opposition).

The great effort of the AKFM to win power was at the moment of the 1958 Constitutional Referendum organised by General de Gaulle.* The massive majority for the French Community (1,361,801 'Yes' votes against 391,166 'No' votes) was a direct defeat for the AKFM, which had campaigned vigorously for the 'No', meaning immediate political independence and the cutting of all links with France. In 1970, the AKFM has two members of parliament out of a total of 108. At no time have they come out with a political or economic programme differing substantially from that of the PSD.

The PSD is essentially the party of the rural masses, and in 1968 counted 500,000 card-carrying members grouped in more than a thousand local sections. It is not primarily a party of intellectuals but a number of highly-educated Merina are to be found in prominent positions within the party. These include some ex-MDRM and one or two ex-AKFM elements. The PSD Students' Federation is active and voices opinions which sometimes differ from the party line at its congresses.[6] It has been especially concerned with the government's economic policy and the execution of the First Five-Year Plan.

In its official policy statements, the PSD appears as an orthodox 'social democrat' party, resembling closely the SFIO, with which it maintains close friendly relations as with the Social Democrat Party of West Germany. Delegates from the PSD attend international Socialist conferences and are members of the Third Socialist International. Close relations were established with the Mauritius Labour Party, following that country's independence in April 1968. The programme of the PSD begins with a declaration of republican and democratic principles, with the proviso that: 'The essential condition for the preservation of democracy and in order that it may bring to the citizens the liberty and social and economic progress that they have the right to expect, is that the republican government is given the necessary authority for a sus-

---

* General de Gaulle received a mandate from the French National Assembly on June 1, 1958, for a new constitution. The draft was drawn up by a group of experts headed by Michel Debré, then Minister of Justice; it was then examined by a committee which included four African deputies—Philibert Tsiranana, Félix Houphouet-Boigny (Ivory Coast), Léopold Senghor (Senegal) and Gabriel Lisette (Chad). Houphouet-Boigny was a junior minister in the French government.

tained and effective action.' It states that there can be no democracy without social justice, and demands a just repartition of the national wealth according to the contribution and to the needs of every citizen. In the economic field it states that the development of Madagascar must be carried out within the framework of a plan which gives priority to 'satisfying the essential needs of the population'. The party is the party of the workers and depends on the workers for its support; thus it favours the evolution of collective means of production organised and run by the workers. In the international field, the PSD affirms its solidarity with other Socialist and trade union movements; it stands against reactionary xenophobic agitation of any kind.

Ideologically, the PSD has made great progress since 1960. As the government majority party, it has made an effort to define its policies and to educate the party members. A remarkable initiative was the 'Journées de Développement' organised in Tananarive in 1962. This was a gigantic seminar, with 10,000 people taking part, organised to inform the 'vital forces of the nation' of the government's intentions, but even more to carry on a discussion with these representatives of the population and to hear their wishes and opinions on development problems. The seminar opened with a mass meeting held in the covered stadium of Mahamasina at Tananarive, at which the President, in a four-hour speech, set out the economic programmes and problems of Madagascar and outlined the way the government intended to tackle them. This speech was prepared in close co-operation with ministries, and particularly with the Plan Commission, which was at that time preparing the First Five-Year Plan, 1964–68.

The 10,000 participants were drawn from the administration, from parliamentary representatives, mayors of rural communes, school teachers, private traders and clergy of all denominations. The leaders of the seminar included Alfred Sauvey (a French economist and specialist on population problems, a former French minister), Tibor Mende, and Tinbergen. These were joined by senior French and Malagasy civil servants. The seminar was addressed in plenary sessions by the guest speakers from France and by technicians from the civil service. The members were then organised in commissions set up to report on specific sectors and problems. Since attendance at this seminar had purposely been thrown open to all shades of political opinion, all were heard, and even the skeleton Malagasy Communist Party spoke at one session. This operation constituted one of the most thorough consultations which has been carried out in any country during the period of drawing up a development plan. A similar seminar was held in Zambia in January 1967 at the Kitwe Convention, which 700 representatives from all provinces and sectors attended, to discuss the implementation of the First National Development Plan, 1966–70, which had by then been adopted by Parliament in 1966.

A parallel movement to increase the participation of the rural population, not only in economic development but also in other aspects of national affairs, is furnished by the programme known as 'Animation Rurale'. This rural animation programme is carried on among the country people by means of fifteen-day courses for villagers chosen by their commune. These courses are held at rural animation centres, where the participants live in buildings constructed with local materials and eat food prepared according to their own customs. The 'animators', who are trained in national centres, give courses on the functions of government, civic duties and elementary development. The courses are simplified and adapted for people with little formal education, and allied literacy campaigns are carried out by the same service.

No organised youth movement has been created on a national scale, although the PSD has its own Mouvement de Jeunesse, as do various religious bodies. There exists, however, a parallel form of national service called the 'Service Civique', under which youths are trained under military discipline in simple development techniques of building, land reclamation, road construction and agriculture. This service has been successful in canalising several thousand youths into constructive activities after their two years' service, and few of the troubles or mistakes connected with national youth services in other countries appear to have occurred in Madagascar.

In 1965 President Tsiranana was re-elected President for a further term of seven years. More than 90 per cent of the votes cast were in favour of continuing for a further term with the same leader and with similar policies. This election was followed by a partial reshuffle within the government, which left leading political figures unchanged, but which modified the responsibilities of certain ministries.

The political history of Madagascar since 1960 was free

from major disturbances until the Rebellion in the south in March 1971. There had been no major changes in policy and no significant changes among leading political figures, except for the reshuffle caused by the untimely death of the Foreign Minister, Albert Sylla, in an air-crash in 1967, until the dismissal of the former Minister of the Interior, André Resampa from the post of Vice-President and Secretary General of the PSD, in June 1971.

CONSTITUTIONAL FRAMEWORK

The most marked structural changes since 1960 have been administrative rather than political; but they have been administrative with a political aim of securing closer ties between the rulers and the ruled and increasing the participation and responsibility of the population for its own economic development. This development is in accordance with Title VII, Articles 55 to 65, of the 1959 constitution, dealing with the Territorial Collectivities, which state that the elected bodies, including councils of rural communes and municipal and provincial councils, 'assure the association of the populations concerned by the administration of these collectivities' (Article 55).

The constitution, following its preamble affirming the belief in God and the guarantee of human rights and the exercise of democratic liberties, describes in detail the structures and responsibilities of the institutions of the republic. The President of the Republic is elected by universal suffrage for a term of seven years, and can be re-elected. The members of parliament (deputies) are elected for a period of five years. The President of Madagascar is also head of the government and thus performs the functions of a prime minister. He nominates by decree the members of the government, including the first Vice-President (who replaces him when he is absent from the country), the ministers and the secretaries of state (the latter correspond to 'junior ministers' in English-speaking African states). The President can also replace all those whom he has nominated. He presides over the 'Council of Ministers', which corresponds to a cabinet meeting in British terminology. The 'cabinet', consisting only of ministers, meets weekly, usually on Tuesdays. The Secrétaire-Général du Gouvernement performs the functions of the Secretary to the cabinet in the British system; but, unlike certain English-speaking

African countries, in Madagascar this official has no powers or responsibility for the civil service. He keeps the cabinet minutes and circulates and follows up decisions, and also performs certain other administrative functions connected with cabinet business and communications. Unlike the British practice, a concise account of cabinet proceedings and decisions is published in the press and radio by the Ministry of Information after each weekly meeting. This does not mean that confidential matters are published, however, and cabinet minutes are as secret as in the British practice. A 'Council of Government' which comprises the cabinet ministers plus secretaries of state and commissioners-general also meets regularly under the President. In his absence, a 'Council of Cabinet' is held, presided over by the first Vice-President. The President of the Republic appoints all civil servants but the administration of the civil service is the responsibility of the Secretary of State for the Civil Service (Secrétaire d'Etat à la Fonction Publique). Ministers are directly responsible for the operation of all services within their ministries.

The number of ministers is fixed by the constitution, and in 1970 comprised four Vice-Presidents, the Ministers of the Interior and of Foreign Affairs, six Ministers (Agriculture; Finance and Commerce; Education; Industry and Mines; Public Works and Communications; Justice) and a number of Secretaries of State and the Commissioners-General. The principle of collective responsibility applies to decisions, termed decrees, signed by the President. The President is commander-in-chief of the armed forces, and is responsible for national defence. He is responsible for foreign relations in nominating ambassadors and accepting the appointment of foreign diplomatic representatives. He convokes and dissolves Parliament, and promulgates laws fifteen days after their being passed by both housse. He has the right of amnesty for all offences; but there is no death penalty and no corporal punishment in Madagascar. No one has been executed since 1960.

Parliament consists of two houses—the Assemblée Nationale and the Senate. The Assemblée Nationale has a member for every 50,000 inhabitants, giving, in 1968, 108 members. They are elected for five years on a provincial basis. The candidates for each province make up a list, which must receive 55 per cent of the votes cast in order to be elected; otherwise seats are allocated proportionally to each list according to the votes cast. All eligible voters are legally obliged to cast their vote on election day. Once elected, the principal activity of Parliament is the discussion and vote on the annual budget, including capital and recurrent estimates. The constitution sets out the subjects on which Parliament is the sole arbitrator, including nationality, civil rights, national defence, organisation of the judiciary, crimes and penalties awarded by courts, civil law, the civil service rules, the Labour Code, the organisation of education and the organisation of elections.

Parliament also votes the Loi-programme, or programme-law, establishing the national plan, after discussion. Thus the development plans are given the force of law after being examined by the elected representatives of the nation. The plans have thus a far greater force than in the English-speaking African territories, where, perhaps owing to the British mistrust of planning, a plan is merely a published document which constitutes a statement of intention but whose execution is binding on no one. Parliament can delegate powers to the cabinet to pass Orders in Council (Ordonnances) concerning subjects within its competence, as listed above. These powers are given for limited periods and, while they are exercised, they have the same force as a majority vote of Parliament.

The second house, the Senate, consists of 36 senators elected (six for each province) by provincial councillors and by municipal and rural councillors; 12 senators nominated by the government, representing chambers of commerce, trade unions and cultural associations; and 6 senators designated for their special competence by the government. The Senate must examine all laws passed by the Assemblée within twenty days. It can send a law back once to the Assemblée for a second vote, but if it is again passed it becomes law.

In case of any serious difference of views between the two houses, the Constitutional Court (Conseil Supérieur des Institutions) must arbitrate. This body consists of five eminent jurists, two being nominated by the President, two by the Speaker of the Assemblée and one by the President of the Senate. The Constitutional Court examines all laws and orders to see if they are within the competence of Parliament and if the delegation to the cabinet is valid. It must also examine all bills to see whether they conform to the constitution, and, if its decision is negative, the President resubmits them to Parliament; orders are re-examined by the cabinet. The Constitutional Court watches over the regularity of presidential and legislative elections and supervises the conduct of referendums.

The judiciary is organised on the French model. The Supreme Court (Cour Suprême) deals with matters beyond the competence of lower courts and consists of three chambers. The Cour de Cassation deals with judgements against which there is no appeal (i.e., if a lower court has made a serious mistake in law, the Cour de Cassation can annul the sentence but it cannot modify it). The second is the Chambre Administrative, in which actions brought by private citizens or by civil servants against the administration are heard. The third is the Chambre des Comptes, which examines all public accounts on an annual basis. It is the guarantor of proper use of public funds.

The Court of Appeal (Cour d'Appel) examines all judgements and sentences, under both criminal and civil law, issued in Madagascar. Below this come the criminal courts, dealing with crimes punishable by more than ten years' imprisonment. For lesser offences and for minor civil cases there are the tribunaux de prémière instance. These can deal with criminal offences punishable by imprisonment for less than ten years, with certain civil cases, commercial law, land registration and labour disputes. There is one of these tribunals in each province and it is evident that it has wide responsibilities. It consists of a president of the tribunal, the procurer of the republic and an examining magistrate (juge d'instruction) who interrogate a person accused of a crime by the police or gendarmerie and either discharge him or prepare the case for the prosecution and send him up for trial.

Below these come the Tribunaux de Section, of which there are twenty-five, situated in the chief towns in each province, having much the same responsibility as the Tribunaux de Prémière Instance in the provincial capitals. The Tribunaux de Section 'filter' cases, which are judged by them if simple, and, if more complex, passed up to the higher courts. Lastly, the sous-prefet (formerly the district commissioner) is also a magistrate* and a Tribunal de Sous-Préfecture exists wherever there is no Tribunal

---

* The sous-Préfet is not a professional magistrate, but is termed a 'fonctionnaire d'autorité'. This is considered an exception to the principle of separation of the judiciary and the administration.

de Section. He judges simple cases and can inflict penalties not exceeding twenty-nine days' imprisonment or a fine of 25,000 FMG ($US 90). Appeal against these judgements can be made to the Tribunal de Première Instance.

The most marked evolution within the administration has been the rapid development of the rural commune as an instrument of economic development. The village council of elders (*fokon'olona*) existed historically in Madagascar as in many other countries. In origin, it was a large family or a group of families who appointed their leaders for defence, at a time when the villages of Imerina were isolated hill-villages surrounded by a deep moat. The Merina kings used the authority of the *fokon'olona* for local police action and to raise labour to perform essential public works, such as the canals which were dug in the late eighteenth century under Andrianampoinimerina to drain the great plain of the Betsimitatra around Tananarive. In the later years of the monarchy, the *fokon'olona* were used principally to raise forced labour for corvées (*fanompoaona*). These collectivities exist in one form or another all over Madagascar, but they are not all the same, the *fokon'olona* being essentially the collectivities of Imerina.

Municipal councils were created early on by the French administration—Diego-Suarez and Nosy-Be in 1897; Majunga, Tananarive, Tamatave and Fianarantsoa in 1898. The creation of rural communes was accelerated after the Loi Cadre, and on January 1, 1960, there were 26 municipalities and 739 rural communes. The rural communes are run by a rural council which elects a mayor. The mayor controls the registry of births, deaths and marriages, is responsible for the administration of the commune's budget, and carries out the development projects voted by the council, for which funds are provided either from his own budget or from grants from the state. The main source of revenue of the communes comes from a percentage of poll tax paid to them by the provincial administration.* The mayor and the rural communes are under the tutelage of the sous-préfet, and in fact most of the decisions of a rural council become operative only after approval

---

* Taxation, as it affects the mass of the population of Madagascar, was as follows (1970):

Impôt minimum fiscal (translated here as 'poll tax')—for all males over 20 years: 3,450 FMG, of which 2,500 FMG goes to the provincial budget, 500 FMG to the central budget and 450 FMG to the rural communal budget.

by the sous-préfet. In cases of his refusal, the council can appeal to the Ministry of the Interior.

The most important activity of the Rural Communes has been the rapid expansion of their small-scale development programmes. In May 1962 the President, on the initiative of André Resampa, Minister of the Interior and Secretary-General of the PSD, launched the programme of the 'travaux au ras du sol' (works at field level, or self help programme) with a credit for the year of 360 million FMG ($US 1,480,000). This programme has consisted from the start of projects that have been requested by the population of the rural communes. State grants are given on condition that the work is carried out with the active participation (labour) of the population. State grants or loans are paid to the rural communes and included in the communal budget, or to the syndicats des communes, groups of rural communes which join together for specific economic aims. Rural communes prepare each year lists of projects requested by the population and transmit them to the sous-préfets. The rural communes themselves establish lists of priorities. The projects are transmitted by the préfets to the Ministry of the Interior which requests the necessary capital sums from the Ministry of Finance. The Ministry of the Interior has a well-staffed Economic Bureau, the most important task of which is the organisation of priority lists of projects requested by rural communes, ordering the equipment and arranging for aid in their execution. The same Ministry conducts regular inspections of rural communes, especially concerning their use of funds. Their budgets are subject to fairly rigorous financial control, and, in the rare cases of mayors having embezzled money, heavy prison sentences have been inflicted and wide publicity given. The prefect is responsible for the preparation of an annual programme of the travaux au ras du sol, which constitutes a first list of priorities, and this list is discussed by the regional development committee over which he presides. It is he who transmits the final list to the Ministry of the Interior, which discusses the projects

---

Taxes sur les Bovidés ('cattle tax')—100 FMG per beast over one year, of which 30 per cent to the central budget and the remainder to the rural communal budget.

Impôt foncier ('land tax')—50 to 400 FMG per hectare, and 700 FMG per hectare for land owned but not cultivated.

In addition there are taxes on real estate, vehicles, firearms, dogs, etc.

with the technical services concerned and with the Ministry of Finance.

This programme was very successful during the first seven years of its operation. Certain prefectures arrived early on at 90 per cent of financial execution, while few dropped below 70 per cent. By 1965, more than 600 million FMG ($US 2,450,000) had been invested in a wide range of projects: small irrigation schemes for rice cultivation, establishment of fuel-wood plantations, construction of local roads and bridges, and so on. Many communes have bought rice-hullers (often of Scottish manufacture). Others have bought tractors, trucks for transport of produce and fertilisers for distribution to farmers.

The latest development has been the establishment of the syndicats des communes. The aim of these associations of rural communes is to group the peasants and small farmers in such a manner as to enable them to be equipped with the materials and infrastructure necessary to modernise their production. In 1963, a government order made it possible for urban and rural communes to group their resources in a body that enables the population to participate in economic development projects. After the first experience of the operation of Syndicats des Communes in the prefectures of Morondava and of Tuléar in 1963, the government decided to hand over the marketing of the pois du cap (exported to Britain as 'Madagascar butter beans') to the two syndicats des communes of Morondava and Tuléar.

In 1966 a law was passed (Loi No. 66–013 of July 5, 1966) giving the syndicats a more flexible structure and enabling them to function as industrial and commercial enterprises with financial autonomy and a management independent of administrative control. The aim of these associations of communes is to undertake and encourage projects of production, marketing and small-scale industrialisation. A syndicat is formed as a voluntary association of the urban and rural communes of a prefecture which declare their intention to join together for the purpose of executing economic projects. The syndicat is then established for a particular prefecture by government decree. It is run by its committee, composed of two delegates from the urban communes and of the rural mayors of all the rural communes making up the syndicat. This committee votes the budget of the syndicat and decides on its activities. The chairman of this committee is elected by the members. Other administrative officers, accountants, chief mechanics and buyers are appointed as necessary and are paid by funds subscribed by the communes to the common budget of the syndicat.

To increase production of local crops, the syndicat assists the peasants by making available tractors and farm machinery on hire and by carrying stocks of selected seeds, fertilisers and insecticides for sale. As a result, as much as 1,500 acres are cultivated for specific crops such as ground-nuts or maize in a given syndicat. In marketing, the syndicat tries to improve the traditional system by eliminating many of the intermediaries, just as co-operatives have done in other countries. By means of its Comptoir des Syndicats des Communes (COSICO) the syndicats' activities on the export market are grouped at a national level, and this body actively seeks new markets abroad and aids in establishing regular supplies for buyers of specific products. The industrial projects include the establishment of rice-hullers, oil-presses for groundnut oil and other small-scale processing plant.

The years following independence, showed no startling changes in the political field, and gave clear evidence of the Government's economic policy and a constant drive to push development down to the level of the peasant. This preoccupation with the rural masses was translated into concrete projects by the aid of efficient structures of territorial administration, and by the action of the former Minister of the Interior, André Resampa, who was responsible for the administrative structure of prefects, sub-prefects and rural mayors, and later for production and commerce.

Resampa who was the 'No. 2' in the government of Madagascar in power and influence, began his political career as a provincial councillor for Belo-sur-Tsiribihina on the west coast in 1952. In 1957 he was elected to the central Representative Assembly; he was appointed Minister of Social Affairs with responsibility for Education and Health in 1958; and in 1959 he became Minister of the Interior, a post he held until his appointment as first Vice-President in 1970. He headed the Malagasy delegation which negotiated the transfer of power in 1960 and drew up the Franco-Malagasy agreements before independence. He was the founder with President Tsiranana of the PSD, of which he was in 1970 secretary-general. His sudden dismissal occurred in June 1970, during the political crisis of that year.

7. The Economy

AGRICULTURE

THE ECONOMY of Madagascar was still, in 1970, based on agricultural production, which provided approximately 55 per cent of the Gross Domestic Product. This figure includes production from animal husbandry, forestry and fisheries. The Madagascar agricultural economy, however, differs in certain important ways from those of many other tropical countries. The chief particularities may be summarised as: stable and generally adequate production of the basic foodstuff, rice; diversity of production patterns due to ecological factors; wide range of export products; considerable internal exchanges of food-crops; and appearance of mixed farming in isolated areas.

Madagascar experiences neither chronic food shortages nor difficulties in producing adequate supplies of rice, the basic foodstuff consumed by the majority of the population. Rice production is maintained over the greater part of the island by irrigated paddy fields and this supplies an element of stability for the population. Adequate irrigation methods have been evolved and in many areas ploughs and harrows drawn by oxen are used. This measure of control of water supplies is aided by a generally reliable hydrology and generally reliable rainfall. The recurrent droughts experienced in East and Southern Africa are almost unknown in Madagascar, other than in the semi-arid area of Androy in the extreme south. The agricultural production of Madagascar is dominated by a reasonably stable level of rice supplies, and the annual anxiety of countries depending on monsoon rains or unreliable rainfall is absent. Massive invasions of pests such as the desert, red and African locusts, or the quelea bird, are unknown in Madagascar. Locusts exist in the country (*Nomadacris semifasciata*) and a locust control service has operated for many years in the south, but swarms encountered are now small and the damage is insignificant. The family of the quelea bird is represented by an indigenous weaver, the *fody* (*Fodia madagascarensis*). This bird, of which the male turns bright red in the mating season, constitutes a local pest and attacks paddy on the stalk. Small children are employed to scare them off. However, the *fody* never approach the catastrophic proportions of the quelea swarms over the African savannah region from Dakar to Tanzania, and south to the Transvaal.[1]

Madagascar has an unusually wide variety of production patterns, each related to one of the five major ecological regions recognised by phytogeographers in Madagascar.[2] The various types of agriculture encountered will be described as related to the vegetation, soils and climate associated with these ecological regions.

A wide diversity of products is another result of this variation in natural regions. In 1967, fifteen agricultural products accounted for over 70 per cent of total exports by value. (This wide range of products is reflected in the export pattern, as shown in the Appendix, Table VI, page 299.) Although robusta coffee and vanilla together accounted for about 45 per cent of exports by value, about 28 per cent of the remainder is made up of thirteen agricultural products, including sugar, tobacco, meat, rice, cloves, sisal, raffia and Lima beans (Pois du Cap). This is in marked contrast to mono-economies depending on groundnuts, cacao, coffee, sisal or cotton for an overwhelming percentage of their export revenue.

Dry farming is a fairly well-developed activity in all regions, favoured again by a reasonably reliable rainfall. The colluvial soils on the edges of paddy fields support a variety of food crops and fruit trees. Maize, sweet potatoes, coco-yams (*Colocasia anti-quorum*), sugar-cane and citrus are usually found, while, farther up the slopes, cassava, groundnuts and beans are the chief crops. Certain regions of the south and south-west rely almost entirely on dry-farming for food-crops, outside large river valleys such as the Mangoky or the Taheza-Onilahy. Outside these valleys rudimentary rain-fed paddy fields give meagre supplies of rice, and the food staple is maize for the Masikoro and Mahafaly in the south-west, and maize and sorgho for the Antandroy in the extreme south, where the rainfall may be as low as 14 inches per annum and droughts are not infrequent.

In spite of, or perhaps because of, the huge cattle population of Madagascar, estimated at 10 million head (1968),[3] animal husbandry and agriculture are usually unrelated activities although carried on by the same family. Mixed farming has developed to some degree among the Merina and Betsileo on the central high-lands, in the sense that ox-drawn implements are used to prepare the paddy fields and some farmyard manure is applied. In these same regions, small livestock such as pigs, sheep and poultry are extensively kept and form a staple part of farm incomes. Some part of the crop production is devoted to feeding small livestock, and the standard of living on the central highlands avoids the direct competition between humans and animals for foodstuffs which is the obstacle to rational animal husbandry in the less-advanced areas. It is significant that mixed farming appears only among the intellectually more advanced peoples, such as the Merina and Betsileo.

Such diversification as is seen is of course limited by the imple-ments available to the farmer. Rice cultivation occupies from 160 to 180 days according to the region, and is not a mere vegetation cycle but demands at least five separate manual operations, such as nursery preparation and seeding, transplanting, water control, weeding and harvesting, apart from the heavy labour of preparing the paddy fields and repairing irrigation works. Other crops tend to be residual activities and, where these interfere with rice produc-tion, their production will suffer. This applies especially to crops whose introduction has been encouraged by the administration, such as cotton or groundnuts, whose calendar may interfere, as regards time of planting and harvesting, with what are regarded as more important activities. Mechanisation of any of these activi-ties presents the usual problems encountered on small fragmented holdings, although progress is being made in introducing Japanese methods and implements for rice cultivation. The degree of diversi-fication is limited by available technology, rather than by know-ledge or physical conditions, in the more advanced areas of Madagascar.

The ecological diversity results also in an unusually wide variety of fruits cultivated in Madagascar. Apples thrive at 4,500 to 5,500 feet, while, on the coast, bananas, lychees, jakfruit and breadfruit are common. Almost all fruits, from temperate to tropical, are found in Madagascar and present a favourable export possibility. As Madagascar is south of the Equator, it enjoys the austral summer coinciding with the northern winter, which has so favoured exports of South African citrus and temperate fruits.

The diversity of products is equalled only by the wide range of technologies encountered, which include bush-fallowing in various forms at the lowest end. Some form of shifting cultivation was probably practised by the earliest immigrants to Madagascar, and the destruction of forest for crop production has certainly contributed to the wide deforestation. At the present time, bush-fallowing around permanent villages is found on the east coast, where the humid tropical forest is cut on steep slopes for planting of mountain rice, while, on the west coast, the forest is cut and burned for maize cultivation. Along the edges of remaining forest reserves, and indeed inside them, out of sight of forest guards, there is constant annual encroachment; small parcels are cut and burned for cultivation, using up the meagre fertility reserves of the forest soils which are quickly exhausted.

To summarise the favourable factors which allow present production patterns and offer considerable scope for future, development: a favourable hydrology over most of the island with a reliable rainfall and no great extremes of climate. The variety of present production, the degree of technology reached in certain regions and the existence of settled villages offer a favourable field for development. The unfavourable factors are that these communities are widely scattered and are linked by indifferent communications, which poses problems of marketing. Traditional marketing structures still result in the peasant's receiving low prices for his products and paying high prices for what he buys. Incentives are thus limited by market opportunities, while advances in technology depend on very extensive capital investments and on the availability of large numbers of technical personnel. Investment patterns in agriculture will be described more fully in Chapter 8.

Main Production Patterns

The central highlands of Madagascar, known as the Hauts-Plateaux, are inhabited by some of the most culturally advanced elements of the population, the Merina and Betsileo. Whether these peoples are more evolved because of favourable natural environment, or whether they deliberately penetrated these central highlands during the historic occupation of Madagascar because they were more dynamic, is an open question. The Hauts-Plateaux, however, enjoy a number of natural advantages which have favoured the appearance of a more organised type of agriculture, strictly comparable to levels reached by peasants in the less-developed regions of Europe.

Geologically, the Hauts-Plateaux form part of one of the two distinct structural divisions into which the surface of Madagascar is divided. There is:

> an eastern crystalline mass formed mainly of basal pre-Cambrian rocks, and a western sedimentary zone, both of these divisions stretching almost from Cap d'Ambre in the north to Cap Ste Marie in the south. The basal complex occupies the greater part of the surface, and it forms a plateau rising to 9,500 feet in the north (Tsaratanana massif), 8,500 feet in the middle (the lava plateau of Ankaratra) and a similar height farther south in the highlands of Andringitra. . . . The general character is therefore that of a plateau with maximum heights in the middle and north similar to those of the eastern highlands of Southern Rhodesia, Nyasaland and the Niassa province of Moçambique.[4]

This geological structure gives rise to a favourable water supply but is also responsible in part for the existence of soils of a low fertility and, apart from the valleys, of a low potential. The sub-structure of granite-gneiss ensures that the rivers and streams of the Hauts-Plateaux have a permanent regime through the dry season lasting from May to November. Their flow is not always sufficient to ensure double-cropping in the valleys, and many paddy fields outside the larger valleys, such as the Ikopa or the Onive, must await the first rains for transplanting of rice, as the water supply in the dry months suffices to keep only the nurseries irrigated.

Apart from artificial reservoirs such as Mantasoa or Tsiazompaniry, supplying water for Tananarive and for small hydro-electric schemes, there are no large water-storage reservoirs for irrigation purposes on the Hauts-Plateaux, although there has been much development of large and small irrigation works over the past 150 years. Irrigation works and methods are comparatively advanced but rely on seasonal rains and not on artificial water storage. The development of reservoirs for dry-season irrigation has scarcely yet been undertaken in Madagascar, and in the drier areas there is a lack even of tanks (*hafirs*) for livestock. This is due chiefly to the reliability of rainfall over most of Madagascar, and to the adaptation of production patterns to seasonal rains. There is considerable potential for complete control of available water supplies on the Hauts-Plateaux, and much could be done at low cost by encouraging the construction of small storage dams at the heads of the smaller valleys, of torrent-control works upstream from these, and, in certain cases, of cisterns on hilltops for irrigating market gardens, as is done in many countries bordering the Mediterranean.

The climate of the Hauts-Plateaux is favourable by any standards. The rainfall of Tananarive, averaging 54 inches on 154 days, almost entirely between November and May, is representative of the area.* The dry months are tempered by a kind of Scotch mist, similar to the Chiperones of Malawi and caused by the same southeast winds that prevail in the dry season. The mean annual temperatures of Tananarive vary between an average maximum of 25·1 °c and an average minimum of 12·6 °c. Thus, however warm the day, the nights are cool. Frost is not unknown but occurs regularly only in the vicinity of the highest mountain on the plateaux, Ankaratra (8,589 feet). Outside this area it is rare, and arabica coffee, which does not stand frost, may be grown successfully wherever there are suitable soil and water conditions.

Tananarive. The Hauts-Plateaux region may be subdivided into a number of ecological micro-regions. First and, economically, the most important, there is the area around the city of Tananarive, called the plain of Betsimitatatra. Two rivers, the Sissaony and the Ikopa, rise on the edge of the humid forest to the east, converge to the west of the town, and then flow on for 375 miles to enter the Moçambique Channel at Majunga. Just downstream of their junction the river Ikopa is barred by a rocksill and falls about 195 feet in 3 miles. In recent geological times, this natural dam formed a lake which had dried out to a swamp at the time of occupation by the Merina in the nineteenth century. This swamp, the Betsimitatatra, was progressively reclaimed by successive Merina monarchs and by the colonial government and forms the economic reason for the situation of Tananarive.

The plain occupies about 92 square miles and the annual pro-

* *Source:* Service Météorologique de Madagascar; all observations are average readings for the period 1931–60.

duction of rice was estimated in 1968 at 80,000 tons. It has received considerable investments from both the Fonds d'Aide et Coopération (FAC—French bilateral aid) and the Fonds Européen de Developpement (FED—Common Market Development Fund) since 1960, partly to protect the town of Tananarive, which was badly flooded in the 1959 cyclone, and also to provide new land and improved water supplies for the rapidly-expanding population. Tananarive is ringed by small towns and villages whose inhabitants are almost all farmers but with members of their families working in the city. This zone of relatively advanced and productive farming extends east towards the forest edge, entering a zone of increasing rainfall. Although rice is the main crop, the colluvial soils are usually levelled in terraces along the edge of the paddy fields and on these vegetables and fruit are grown by market gardeners, using irrigation water during the dry season. Almost all European vegetables and flowers can be seen in the Tananarive market. Strawberries are available all the year round, and peas, carrots, spinach, cabbages, beetroot, leeks and onions are also abundant. These terraces also support citrus trees, which produce high-quality fruit on the Hauts-Plateaux. Avocados, kakis and plums also fruit well, and arabica coffee will grow in micro-climates that allow it adequate protection from winter winds and a regular water supply.

The Tananarive district is one of those rare regions in tropical latitudes that produces milk in adequate quantity and of an acceptable quality. A breed of cattle known as *rana* is kept by small producers in a thirty-mile radius of the city. The *rana* has been produced as a result of successive introductions of European exotics over sixty years, and is said to contain traces of about twenty different breeds ranging from Brown Swiss to Friesian. The Norman, with its pronounced stripes down the flanks, seems to predominate, but artificial insemination with Friesian and Norman is practised according to the owner's preference. As a result, the breed of milk cattle in the Tananarive area has been upgraded within recent years and milk production is now an important farm activity. Much of the milking is still done by the cycliste-trayeurs': they go to the cows on bicycles hung with the tins into which they milk, and the proprietor is paid direct by them. But, since 1965, a modern central milk-treatment station has functioned in Tananarive, and milk from it is consumed extensively in the city.

Cattle are kept in comparatively small numbers but most farmers keep two or more beasts, especially work oxen for ploughing and for the ox-cart, still the main form of bulk transport. Poultry and pigs are kept extensively in every village and even within the city limits. Thus, farming in the Tananarive region is essentially based on the small mixed-farming unit, similar to the unit common to Japan and certainly capable of development similar to the Japanese experience. The Japanese farmer produces 20 to 25 tons of paddy per acre on 3 to 5 acres where the Tananarive farmer produces only 2 to 3 tons on the same area. The Japanese grows vegetables, fruit, chrysanthemum flowers and cuttings and raises pigs and poultry intensively without any elaborate investment but with a high productivity. Such Japanese methods and equipment as have been introduced into Madagascar, especially for rice production, have been most successful. Anyone who has visited both Japan and Madagascar is struck by the similarity between conditions in the southern regions of Japan and those in the Hauts-Plateaux and the application of Japanese methods appears well-justified. It is very probable that the Hauts-Plateaux as a whole could follow a similar pattern of development, beginning with intensification of its agriculture along Japanese lines. Already the more advanced areas of rice cultivation, especially around Tananarive, have greatly increased their production since 1964–65 through stricter control of soil fertility by increased application of fertiliser and improved cultivation practices.

Expansion of production in this region can be secured only through increasing the productivity per unit. All available valleys, except for small residual swamps, are used for paddy fields, nearly all colluvial soils are occupied, and, without massive capital investment, the potential of the bare decapped ferralitic hillsides is extremely low for anything but reafforestation. The potential for increased productivity in the form of higher rice yields, and especially in increased production of milk and small livestock, would appear to be very great.

Vakinankaratra. The second sub-division, again thickly populated, is the Vakinankaratra, situated on volcanic soils around, though mainly to the east and south of, Madagascar's second highest mountain, Ankaratra. The rainfall is higher but average temperatures are lower and frost occurs each year. The population is of Merina origin, but came to this area partly as refugees and partly because of population pressure around Tananarive since the late eighteenth century. It was forest land and bush until very recently; some fine remains of forest exist at the forest station of Manjakatompoko and higher up on Ankaratra.* The refugees lived there as bandits, and the area was considered unsafe until the end of last century. It has a wild but, in parts, almost European appearance. Production patterns are similar to those around Tananarive but methods are considerably less evolved. The peasants along the valley of the Onive have inadequate control of their water supply and practise a primitive type of mixed farming, similar to that of the poorer peasants in Spain or Italy. The district is dominated by the extinct Tertiary volcano of Ankaratra which has disturbed the granite-gneiss peneplain by basalt lava flows and local metamorphosis. This has laid down areas of soil of a higher fertility than is usually found on the Hauts-Plateaux. These unstable volcanic soils have been considerably eroded as a result of deforestation within the last two hundred years, and alluvial soils have been laid down in terraces along the main water-courses. In addition, a large lake existed in recent historical times between Antsirabe and Sambaina, which, having dried out, provides other alluvial soils and layers of turf resting on white clays containing an interesting sub-fossil fauna, including the dwarf hippopotamus, now extinct. The volcanic action has left thermal springs in considerable numbers, at Antsirabe itself, which was constructed as a watering-place on the French model in 1923, and elsewhere in the district. These springs vary in temperature from 20 °C (Ramainandra) to 51 °C (Ranoamafana, or 'hot water' in Malagasy) and contain bicarbonate, sulphates, sodium and other minerals.

The mountain mass also influences the climate. This region is the coldest place in Madagascar in winter. Frost occurs regularly, and the lowest recorded temperature at Antsirabe is − 6·6 °C. The mean annual temperature varies between 14 and 17 °C, although Antsirabe's recorded maximum is 32·9 °C. Ankaratra causes orographic rain around the village of Sambaina, south-east

* European trout, introduced in 1924 by the Service des Eaux et Forêts to the cold streams on this mountain, are still fished by enthusiasts.

of the mountain, which registers 78 inches over 170 days in the year. West of the mountain the rainfall drops to 50 inches over 100 to 105 days and frost is rare. Thus the Vakinankaratra is subdivided into a number of micro-climates, each with a slightly different cropping-pattern.

The Antsirabe area has an outstanding potential for production of all temperate crops and, in particular, for intensive livestock production. Apples* are produced in large quantities in orchards that cover a wide area around the village of Soarinandrainy, 30 miles east of Antsirabe, which sells 5–6,000 tons per year. Other fruits which are abundant in season are grapes, high-quality plums, rather inferior pears, peaches which tend to be small and sour and excellent loquats which grow on almost any soil on the Hauts-Plateaux.

Livestock are already numerous, and around Betafo, west of Antsirabe, there are two animals per head of population. Antsirabe was conceived originally as a rest-resort for Europeans, especially for those stationed on the coasts which were unhealthy places in 1923, when the new town was established. The French army kept a detachment there, and several hotels, together with the thermal springs, ensured the constant presence of European families. Externally, the main hotel resembles a late nineteenth-century Swiss mountain hotel, with huge gables and steep-pitched roofing. Thus, a good market developed early for temperate fruits and vegetables and livestock products. Butter is still made in the town, which is surrounded by small milk producers. Pigs and poultry thrive in this climate, and it would not be difficult to organise intensive production for export. Antsirabe has always had a surplus, some of which reaches the coast via Tananarive; thus, marketing structures are already established. It can grow all the crops sold by South Africa and Rhodesia and those of the Kenya Highlands. The market for such products is rapidly expanding in all the towns of tropical Africa, many of which are only two hours flight by jet from Madagascar. Intensification of the present artisan production methods and attention to grading and packing, as is practised by co-operatives in Japanese villages, could make this the most productive region of Madagascar. All high-altitude zones

* Varieties include 'Menagère', reputed to have been introduced by Norwegian missionaries, Reinette grise, Reinette du Canada, Royal d'Angleterre and Christmas.

in the tropics have a natural advantage that has been utilised to any degree only by Kenya outside Southern Africa. The area around Antsirabe thus represents a potentially 'growth-propulsive' sector.

Lake Itasy. An interesting micro-climate, also with soils of volcanic origin, but arising from much younger volcanoes, is found around Lake Itasy, about 60 miles west of Tananarive and north-west of Ankaratra. The volcanoes are held to be recent and Carbon 14 datings fix the period of the latest eruptions at approximately 5,000 years ago. Lake Itasy is itself formed in a volcanic crater and volcanic cones protrude on all sides. The soil is a structureless dark-brown, of the type one learns to avoid when driving in wet weather since, under heavy rain, its surface is like soap. Similar soils and road conditions are found on the road between Tunduma and Mbeya in the Southern Highlands of Tanzania. French settlers established tung (*Aleurites fordii*) plantations before the First World War, and tung oil and tobacco have been the chief products of Itasy. The climate is drier and warmer than that of Tananarive, although the rainfall is about the same, spread over a shorter season. This is excellent country for maize and, as a result, pig production is important, with Tananarive as the market. A French settler established intensive feed-lots for pig production near Lake Itasy before the Second World War, and his farm is now run by the Ministry of Agriculture. Following this model, a number of Malagasy farmers have established small feed-lots around the town of Soavinandriana to the south of the lake. Pigs have suffered epidemics of the 'maladie de Teschen', a form of meningitis, which has limited production, although the Veterinary Service has now produced and applies an effective vaccine.

To the west of Itasy, at a lower altitude of about 3,000 feet, is the settlement scheme of the Sakay, centred on Babetville, named after a French deputy who supported the scheme in the 1950s. This was originally conceived as an area of settlement for farmers from over-populated Réunion, and about two hundred families were installed before 1960 on small mixed-farm units. Since independence, Réunion immigration has stopped and Malagasy farmers are now being settled in the area, following the

same production patterns of organised dry farming, soil conservation and intensive livestock rearing. This scheme has clearly
demonstrated the dry-farming potential of this region of the Hauts-
Plateaux.

Moyen Ouest. The name 'Moyen Ouest' (Middle West) is
given to a very large area of open rolling grassland with an average
altitude of about 3,000 feet and a rather warmer and drier climate
than that of the eastern part of the Hauts-Plateaux. To the west,
this area is bounded by the Bongolava escarpment, from which the
ground falls sharply towards the sedimentary zone of the west
coast. Historically, this was a no-man's-land between the Merina
and Sakalava peoples and as late as 1875 accounts by missionaries
of journeys to the west read like the journals of travellers in the
Far West of the United States at the same period.[5] Today,
large numbers of cattle are driven up into the area from the west
coast, assembled for sale at Tsiroanomandidy, the biggest cattle-
fair in Madagascar, and then taken to the abattoirs in Tananarive.
The Moyen Ouest is first-class ranching country, and the first
ranch was established in 1967 by the Ministry of Agriculture at
Ambatomainty to the south of Tsiroanomandidy. The research
station of the Veterinary Service, at Kianjasoa to the south of the
town, has carried out extensive work in establishing artificial
pastures and in upgrading the local zebu by using the Texas
Brahmin, Sahiwahl and Afrikander. In 1969, the World Bank
granted a loan to the Ministry of Agriculture for the establishment
of six model cattle ranches, whose main purpose will be to regulate
the supply of cattle to the new abattoir of Tananarive, due to be
completed in 1973 with an annual capacity of 100,000 cattle.

In the late nineteenth century, the scattered villages were collections of huts inhabited by the slaves of members of the Merina
feudal nobility, charged with looking after herds of cattle for their
absentee owners. Many of the inhabitants of present-day villages,
still rare along the road to Tsiroanomandidy, are descended from
these former slaves. The existence of their ancestors was precarious,
for, although this frontier-land was nominally ruled by the Merina
monarchy, the Sakalava considered these herds of cattle their prey
and continually raided them. The villages were thus fortified cattle-
kraals:

outposts of the Imerina government, fortified by a bristling thicket of prickly pear. Each has a considerable settlement of friendly Sakalava outside. . . . Our tent is pitched in the midst of a few huts on a hill. Such hamlets are met in the 'desert' inhabited by slaves in charge of grazing cattle and are difficult of access, serving as places of safety from bands of Sakalava. . . . The inhabitants of these 'desert' villages must surely lead a wretched existence. Not a soul dares venture outside this enclosure unarmed, and hunger and thirst are enemies ever within. A day or two ago a man and a woman went down into the fields to look after their rice. They were pounced on unawares by a prowling gang and the woman carried off. The husband only escaped with his life through a gun missing fire.[6]

Fianarantsoa. The southern part of the Hauts-Plateaux, between the river Manandona to the north and Ambalavao to the south, contains approximately 750,000 inhabitants, the Betsileo, who are considered the most advanced in Madagascar for their technical mastery of irrigation works and their capacity for work. In spite of this, the region is not rich, and there is considerable emigration to other parts of Madagascar. There are Betsileo settlers on both the east and west coasts, but, unlike other ethnic groups, they appear to assimilate quickly and often merge with the local population.

Entering the Betsileo country by road, the traveller is struck by the sight of paddy fields rising in terraces up the sides of the steep valleys. Unlike Imerina, the Betsileo country possesses very few wide swamps or former lakes that could be drained and cultivated. Necessity has forced them to master water-control techniques— small canals carry water long distances to irrigate the fields high up the sides of hills. Some paddy fields cover only a few square yards but are tilled with great care. The population is scattered along the narrow valleys, living near its paddy fields. Although the names of many villages appear on the map, some of them comprise only two or three houses, perched above or below a few paddy terraces. There is only one town of any size, Fianarantsoa, the provincial capital, but even here two-thirds of the population are peasants with their main business outside the town. Ambalavao, to the south, is the assembly point for cattle coming from the south and south-west for sale to their principal market, the towns of the Hauts-Plateaux. The large and frequent cattle markets are the town's main activity. To the north, between Fianarantsoa and Antsirabe, in a thickly-wooded area, is Ambositra, where artisan wood-working activities have built up a tradition of fine marquetry work and furniture manufacture. But this handicraft and work on scattered rice-mills are the only alternatives to what is practically subsistence farming, without any important urban outlet for any surplus production.

The traditional agriculture supplies adequate staple foodstuffs but little protein. Outside this elementary security, the Betsileo peasant sells little and has very few opportunities for paid employment. Betsileo peasants are seen in their characteristic round brimless straw hats, working as seasonal labourers who prepare paddy fields around Tananarive in October and November for absentee Merina owners. The per capita income was estimated in 1962 as 8,100 FMG ($US 30) per annum,[7] which is very low by any standards, especially in a zone where more than two-thirds of the children of school age are attending school. Owing largely to early enthusiasm by the Betsileo for teaching by both Catholic and Protestant missionaries, this area is one of the most developed from the point of view of education. There is consequently a strong emigration by these young 'intellectuals', and a town such as Fandriana, near Ambositra, is conspicuous for its fine houses, all owned by those who have emigrated and made money in the administration or elsewhere.*

The limiting factors are due partly to the topography and partly to the irregular distribution of the population. The Betsileo country may be divided into four natural regions, of which the central, a 12-mile wide band, contains about 250,000 inhabitants, a third of the population living in only one-fifth of their traditional area. The eastern zone, bordering the humid tropical forest of the east, has a high rainfall (75 inches) but a small population, living in tiny valleys in the forest or on its edge. The western zones, one corresponding in climate to Itasy and the other being the southern part of the ranching country of Tsiroanomandidy, have a dry tropical climate, with about 35 inches of rain per annum, but are

---

* Fandriana is sometimes called 'the nursery of civil servants'.

purely pastoral, with a population density of less than eight per square mile.

The Betsileo country presents a curious paradox: on the one hand, a highly industrious intelligent population, with an outstanding technical mastery of irrigation in narrow valleys; on the other, a failure to go beyond this point and adapt their technology to the problems of neighbouring zones, such as the drier tropical pastoral country to the west. In the face of this inability to adapt their technique, the Betsileo emigrate to other regions, where the problem of living space does not arise. In their own region, the narrow valleys each contain the maximum of inhabitants, whose subsistence is ensured by elaborate and highly labour-intensive techniques.

Betsileo village communities are highly organised and small groups are strongly attached to tribal traditions. The customs, notably burial customs, are always kept up, even when the Betsileo immigrants appear completely absorbed within another group, such as the Masikoro in the delta of the Mangoky river on the west coast. Village elders exercise strong control and oppose change in traditional methods, especially of land distribution and production. This conservatism is understandable since, with present techniques, almost all the land cultivated is required to maintain actual standards of nutrition. Population growth, which is high, means that each year a smaller surplus is available for sale, thus diminishing still further the purchasing power of the peasants.

Development prospects for a region poor in natural resources but rich in human potential may often be good. Up to the present, the Betsileo have succeeded in maintaining an equilibrium between the resources of their narrow valleys and the growth of population. The rate of emigration shows that these resources are used to a maximum with present methods and that only rapid technological change can increase them. The populations of the Hauts-Plateaux, Merina and Betsileo, both have two alternative zones for expansion: to the east and the west. Neither, so far, has mastered the problems of the high rainfall forest domain to the east or the dry tropical grassland to the west. The Merina have the advantages of alternative employment in urban centres such as Tananarive and Antsirabe and a higher agricultural potential in the wider valleys and lake beds. To secure these advantages, the Betsileo must emigrate to other tribal areas.

The technical barriers to be overcome are the use of existing irrigation facilities and the creation of new systems, and the integration of animal husbandry and cropping. Present cropping systems allow only one crop of rice a year, and, assuming a vegetation cycle of 120 days in this zone, the paddy fields are unused, although water is available, for the remaining two-thirds of the year. While the climate of the austral winter at this altitude of 3,300 to 4,500 feet is too cold to allow double cropping of rice, other crops with a shorter vegetation cycle, such as cereals, beans, sweet potatoes, potatoes or forage crops, could be grown on the vacant paddy fields. Abundant water supplies come from the watershed at the edge of the eastern forest. The hilltops are at present used only for rough grazing, and the small mixed farms seen in Imerina hardly exist. At the same time, small livestock, such as sheep, pigs and poultry, are kept by almost every farmer and provide an important part of his cash income, since it is estimated that more than 60 per cent of this production is sold. Double cropping would allow important quantities of secondary crops to be utilised by livestock and would increase farm incomes considerably.

These are rather standard problems of the small peasant farmer in a tropical country, but stress is laid on them because the Betsileo have greater dynamism and intelligence than many of the peoples in a comparable situation. The population problem of this zone can be solved only by continued expansion, and the unoccupied western grasslands should be able to take numbers of settlers once the basic infrastructure of roads and irrigation systems, at present planned by the government, is established. The climate will be a major asset on the higher rainfall zone, which is already extensively planted with Mexican pine (*Pinus patula*) for eventual industrial use. Growth rates of pine on the Hauts-Plateaux are generally about three times the average for conifers in the northern hemisphere. The bald hills of Imerina, Vakinankaratra and the Betsileo are at present supporting one head of cattle for 25 to 50 acres, and their vanished forest cover has given place to *Aristida sp.*, a grass which is the only plant that will stand annual burning on eroded latosols but which gives little nourishment. The establishment of forests of pine—of which Mexican pine appears to give the best results among several hundreds of introductions by the Forestry Service since 1900—is already being undertaken by the government. On the upper watershed of the Matsiatra, in the Betsileo country, more than 44,000 acres are already planted and the programme extends to 132,000 acres. Other pine forests have already been laid down in the Vakinankaratra, and on the Tampoketsa, a plateau rising to 5,200 feet some 100 miles to the north of Tananarive on the road to Majunga.

Lake Alaotra. Lying about 100 miles north-east of Tananarive, between the first and second 'falaise' by which the mountains of the Hauts-Plateaux descend to the Indian Ocean, lies the basin of Lake Alaotra. This is the remains of a large Pleistocene lake, now partially silted up, which must have measured about 40 miles by 12 miles at the time of its greatest extent. Lake Alaotra thus belongs to the system of great lakes that existed in very recent geological times in Madagascar, and included the lake occupying the plain of Betsimitatra, around Tananarive, and the great lake north of Antsirabe, both now dried up. This shrinking of lakes seems to be linked with a general drying of the climate of Madagascar as it emerged from a recent pluvial period.[8]

Lake Alaotra, at the head of the valley of the Mangoro, running in a thalweg north-south, has a more favourable, drier and warmer climate than the Hauts-Plateaux and was one of the focal points of European colonisation under French rule. It was also one of the areas where this colonisation produced economic progress, and the transition to Malagasy occupation has continued the development of its productive capacity.

European colonisation began after 1920 and was aided by the construction of a rail spur from Moramanga, which linked the region to Tananarive and the east coast. Extensive surveys were carried out between 1920 and 1924* to determine how to drain the great swamps bordering the lake by controlling the outflow of the Maningoro, and thus stabilise the level of the lake at about 2,500 feet. In 1940, a number of large drainage canals were cut in the swamps, which allowed the settlers to extend their cultivated area. European farmers began extensive cultivation of rice in the swamps and of cassava on the dry ground. At the same time,

---

* The surveys were carried out by an engineer named Longuefosse who advocated piercing the rock-sill of the Maningoro to control the level of the lake. His conclusions were rejected by NEYRPIC in 1929, and the present works are being carried out as a result of extensive surveys by French engineers during the 1950s.

rice mills and tapioca factories were constructed. In 1948, the Service du Plan employed NEYRPIC as consulting engineers to carry out a complete survey of the drainage and irrigation possibilities, and the Génie Rural began the reclamation in 1950 operating over about 75,000 acres. Today the work is in the hands of the FED, while settlement has been organised by the Société Centrale d'Equipment du Territoire (SCET), a French consulting firm, acting on behalf of the Société d'Aménagement du Lac Alaotra (SOMALAC), a regional development board set up in 1962 under government auspices. Under a management-consultancy contract, the SCET assists the SOMALAC in the physical development of land and water resources, in improved cultivation practices, in all aspects of land settlement and in the management of rice-mills and farm-machinery pools.

The aim of the SOMALAC is the settlement of small farmers and work is in progress for the reclamation by 1973 of approximately 66,000 acres for irrigated paddy production on land from which the waters of the lake have receded. Over 30,000 acres had been reclaimed from swamp soils and were being cultivated in 1969. Parallel activities have endeavoured to stabilise the large cattle population of the region, estimated at about 120,000 head, by utilising parts of the cultivable land for the production of forage crops. A dairy farm, Marololo, formerly owned by a European settler, was purchased by the government in 1962 and has served as a pilot milk-production centre.

The population, although basically Sihanaka, a tribe related to the Merina, is very mixed, since the lake has acted as a magnet to immigrants from many parts of the island. In addition to agriculture, fishing is a full-time occupation for part of the population, with annual production estimated at about 3,000 tons. The lake fauna has been enriched by the introduction of two species of tilapia, which have multiplied. Most of the catch is sent fresh or smoked to the market in Tananarive.

Production of rice in the Lake Alaotra basin was about 35,000 tons in 1968, but it is estimated that by the mid-1970s, with average yields of 8 tons per acre, a production of more than 100,000 tons of paddy should be obtained. Lake Alaotra thus will be most important for the future food supply of the urban areas of the Hauts-Plateaux, and probably for eventual export of rice into deficit areas of the Indian Ocean, such as Mauritius, Réunion and

East Africa. The largest agricultural research station in Madagascar is run by the Ministry of Agriculture on the shores of the lake, and much pioneer work has been done on rice breeding and fertilisation, groundnuts, cassava and forage crops.

Ankaizina. The Hauts-Plateaux extend north of Tananarive, and a narrow chain joins them to the northern mountainous regions of the island, which is virtually uninhabited. This is the aspect of Madagascar that the traveller sees as he flies in from East Africa. Deforestation is fairly complete, though, as the altitude falls to 3,000 feet and below, gallery forests persist along the water-courses and patches have survived here and there on slopes. This region ends at the Sofia, a great river running east-west and forming the southern boundary of the northern mountain massif, dominated by Tsaratanana (9,337 feet). Immediately to the south of this mountain is the region known as the Ankaizina, inhabited mainly by the Tsimihety tribe and the country of origin of President Tsiranana. This zone has been much studied, and at one time plans for extensive European colonisation were considered by the French colonial government.

In 1937, a Polish mission visited the Ankaizina to study eventual emigration and settlement of Polish Jews and was on the point of taking up a concession in the plain of Bealanana. Although the administration considered that the establishment of a small kernel of qualified immigrants would have a stimulating effect on the population, the project was not well viewed by the inhabitants and was attacked in the local press. At the same time, a series of optimistic articles appeared in the *Gazeta Polska*, and a book was published under the title *Tomorrow Madagascar* by Arkady Fiedler. In another book, *Madagascar*, Major Lepecki alluded to the 'Polish presence' established by an eighteenth-century adventurer and pirate, Benyowsky, who made himself 'king' for a few years of a small region on the east coast. Later, in 1939, an Ethiopian mission visited the district to study the settlement of Ethiopians expelled from their country at the time of the Italian conquest. In 1941, a further mission studied the settlement of immigrants from overcrowded Réunion, but finally only five farm-pupils from France were established in 1954. All had left by 1957.

This region would appear to be one of the most favourable for intensive human occupation and for intensive agriculture production. At 3,500 to 4,000 feet, the climate is drier and warmer than on the Hauts-Plateaux and the rainfall is adequate for a wide variety of crops. In particular, arabica coffee grows well; a research station (now abandoned) existed for some years at Betankankana. Mixed farms of the type existing in Kenya would probably have been successful had immigration taken place as once planned. Instead, the entire region is dominated by extensive cattle-keeping. The total herd, estimated at more than 200,000, constitutes hardly a productive use of the land, although representing probably five head of cattle for every inhabitant, but it occupies a position of outstanding social importance which has been exhaustively studied in one of the basic books on Malagasy society, by Molet. The cattle-keepers have been responsible for the destruction of huge areas of magnificent forest, now reduced to eroded bare slopes of poor grassland subject to annual burning.

Sambirano. A few hours march over the mountains to the northwest brings a peasant from Bealanana in the Ankaizina into an entirely different climate, that of the Sambirano. Many peasants do make this trip on foot to sell raphia mats, cattle for slaughtering and other products, to the richer population of one of the five major ecological regions of Madagascar. The Sambirano, lying in the rain-shadow of Mount Tsaratanana, benefits from the orographic rain produced when the prevailing winds from the Indian Ocean reach the mountain. The river has a constant flow. In the dry season there is a temporary halt to the rains, broken by showers. Coffee and cacao are grown on both small and large plantations, and two commercial companies produce sugar cane, one on the river Mahavavy delta near Ambilobe and the other on the island of Nosy-be. Many Malagasy peasants in the Sambirano valley also grow pepper.

Nosy-be. The Sambirano micro-climate contains the island of Nosy-be (from *nosy*= island, *be* = big; it is mis-spelled on French maps as Nossi-be). Nosy-be was an early point of French occupation, ceded by Princess Tsiomeko in 1840, well before the conquest.* The island—and, indeed, much of the area—presents features of a tropical idyll. On Nosy-be the traveller finds the air truly scented and sees trees strangely bent to the ground. This is the ylang-ylang (*Camanga odorata*), the source of Macassar oil, introduced by French settlers from Indonesia;[9] the yellow flowers are distilled by the planters in large copper alembics to give an essence used in the manufacture of French perfumes. Essence of ylang-ylang sold in 1968 for $US 14·5 per kilo; the total exports of 18 tons of essence were sold for 72 million FMG, or about $US 300,000.

Pepper is also grown: an attractive vine climbing up trees, which is prepared by drying the green clusters of berries on concrete floors in the sun. Whether it comes out as black or white pepper depends on the degree of drying; white pepper is slightly more complicated to prepare and sells for a higher price. Pepper is not native to Madagascar and was introduced from Indonesia. A botanist named Poivre ('pepper') played a significant role in the introduction of this and other plants around 1770; he was also responsible for introducing the clove tree into the Mascarene islands from Molucca in 1770.

Nosy-be is volcanic and much of its surface is covered by a magnificent (probably primary) forest now held as a protected reserve. Many of the former craters are now small lakes. The climate is warm, damp and tropical. A French oceanographic station, one of the very few scientific stations working in this field in the Indian Ocean,† occupies a magnificent setting here. The island is very beautiful and, with its superb and safe beaches, clear water ideal for underwater fishing, outrigger canoes, coconut palms bending gracefully to the wind, sharks kept out of reach by coral reefs, it is understandable that the Malagasy government has placed great emphasis on the tourist development of the island. Certainly, Nosy-be offers everything that appears in the publicity

* Queen of the Sakalava from 1836 to 1843, she had appealed without success to the Sultan of Zanzibar, Seyid Said, for aid against the Merina army. She turned to the French admiral, de Hell, Governor of Réunion, who at once granted protection, and she and her chiefs ceded on July 14, 1840, their sovereignty over the coast of Madagascar from the Bay of Ampasindava to Cape St Vincent, together with the islands of Nosy-be and Nosy-komba.

† The Zanzibar oceanographic station is now defunct, since independence.

for Tahiti, including a variety of beautiful girls of partly Malayo-Polynesian extraction.

There is considerable local prosperity, and in 1970 it was estimated that the 'national income' or 'GDP' of Nosy-be, an island of 122 square miles and about 9,500 inhabitants, reached around 1,500 million FMG ($US 5.5 million). The distribution of this income is another matter, since sugar, ylang-ylang essence and much of the pepper is in the hands of large companies.

Diego-Suarez. The town of Diego-Suarez, 125 miles to the north, lies on one of the finest natural harbours in the Indian Ocean. It is named after a Portuguese navigator—according to Deschamps, in his *Histoire de Madagascar*, Diego-Suarez was 'a thief and murderer who transported Malagasy slaves to India'. It was first occupied by France in 1895, and two years later the fortifications were established by Colonel (later Field-Marshal) Joffre.

This French naval base is well known to many ex-servicemen in the United Kingdom and particularly to men of the former Northern Rhodesia regiment who occupied it after its capture from the French pro-Vichy forces in 1942. Many Zambians remember having spent two years there, some of it high up at Joffreville, built as an escape from the high temperatures of the port, on the Montagne d'Ambre. This mountain causes orographic rain, and permanent rivers stream out from it like the spokes of a wheel. Being of volcanic formation, much of the soil in the area is of basaltic origin and consequently fertile; groundnuts and maize are extensively grown, as well as rice. Diego-Suarez is a meeting place for many peoples. The majority of the population is Muslim. Swahili is spoken by the large Comorien minority, many of the shops are kept by Indians, and in 1970 a detachment of the Foreign Legion in white kepis still spent its evenings in the numerous bars of the town. Diego-Suarez is cut off from the rest of the island, except by air, during the rainy season and, even when the road is open, from June to October, it is hazardous to travel from Tananarive in anything but a four-wheel-drive vehicle.

Standing on the higher ground behind Diego-Suarez, one can see at the same time the Moçambique Channel and the Indian Ocean. The province of Diego-Suarez contains the Sambirano micro-climate, with all its diversity of cultures, and the vanilla-producing prefecture of Antalaha, which provides the greater part of Madagascar's second export by value. There are many contrasts in the province, and a considerable diversity of climate. Large numbers of cattle roam the deforested central mountains, and Vohémar has been traditionally the port of export for live cattle to Réunion and Mauritius. One of Madagascar's main meat-canning factories—the SARPA factory, established in 1890 before the French conquest, and owned by the Société Rochfortaise de Produits Alimentaires of Paris—is near Diego-Suarez and supplied meat products to the French army for many years.

Antalaha. Moving south towards Antalaha, the rainfall rapidly increases and the humid tropical forest descends to the sea. Vanilla, an orchid, is grown mainly by small Malagasy and Creole planters. It is a tricky operation: the flowers require hand pollenation and the preparation of the vanilla, which is sweated under rugs in the sun, is a skilled operation. The United States is the chief customer. The market for vanilla is highly inelastic and considerable problems of overproduction have arisen in recent years, aggravated by the difficulties of storing the aromatic pods so that they retain their aroma. Vanilla is seriously threatened both by synthetic substitutes, derived from coal, and by an extract of essence of cloves—ironically, since Madagascar is the second largest producer of cloves in the world, after Zanzibar.

Vanilla, like many other aromatic spice products, notably pepper, has always been an object of considerable speculation. Spices were brought back by the sailing-ships sent by seventeenth century merchants to the Far East, and fortunes were gained and lost by such cargoes. A number of highly respectable and (now) aristocratic families in several countries owe their present position to past speculation in spices. The situation in Antalaha is no exception. The main American buyers, owing to their important share of the world market, have held a position of near-monopoly. Collectors and exporters were numerous, including French, Creoles, Chinese, Indians and Malagasy. Antalaha in 1913 had twenty-nine intermediaries for vanilla export, handling crops worth millions of francs, but without sufficient funds to finance their operations. The government's efforts to rationalise its second most important export have battled against the tradition of speculation which is firmly fixed in the minds of all who trade in vanilla.

Immediately after independence, vanilla was exported, mainly to the United States, at an agreed fixed price of $US 13 per kilo for prepared vanilla. However, this price was obtained only by certain exporters, since vanilla is bought green from the producers, who are not those who prepare it in its dried form for export. The growers usually sell the green pod of the orchid. Others, who buy the green vanilla nominally at an annual price fixed by the government (145 FMG per kilo or $US 0.30), prepare it by drying and sweating it in the sun under varying thicknesses of covers. They then sell in turn to exporters, if they are not directly employed by them. In spite of repeated government decrees, speculation caused the 'fixed' price of green vanilla to vary in some years between 130 and 1,000 FMG per kilo. Production, stimulated by such speculation, increased until, on December 31, 1967, stocks of unsold prepared vanilla were estimated at 2,300 tons against an estimated annual production of approximately 1,400 tons.

The government has intervened to stabilise the price and to limit production by fixing annual quotas for zones and attempting to concentrate vanilla production in the prefecture of Antalaha. Production, price and export are now regulated by the Groupement Professionel de la Vanille, which associates planters, preparers and exporters. Price stability is maintained by the Caisse de Stabilisation de la Vanille—the price of green and prepared vanilla is fixed each year by government decree after consultation with the Groupement Professionel de la Vanille. Within the professional association, the Union des Coopératives de la Vanille groups many small growers, while a syndicate groups others. Although much has been done since 1964 by the government to rationalise this product, and in 1967 a single law was promulgated, superseding all the previous and numerous decrees, the basic problem remains of an over-elastic supply of vanilla in the face of a relatively inelastic market. Efforts have been made to find new customers in Europe but many of these are accustomed to using synthetics and pushing a marginal luxury is a hard task.

In spite of these difficulties, vanilla exports rose from 528 tons in 1964 to 961 tons in 1968, valued at approximately $US 6,360,000 and $US 11,532,000 respectively, which made vanilla second among Madagascar's exports by value. Thus the northern region of the east coast is fairly completely monetarised and presents few of the characteristics found in the province of Tamatave and farther south. This monetarisation gives an indication of possible changes in society that would occur among the Betsimisaraka if exposed to prosperity. The experience of the banana export production in the Tamatave prefecture has shown that such change is possible.

Antalaha is thus the richest part of the east coast of Madagascar. This coastal region contains 30 per cent of the population of Madagascar, living in a band which varies in width from twenty to sixty miles. It is in this region that food and population problems become rather acute, and where the pressure of population on resources as at present used causes considerable malnutrition and results in a generally lower standard of living than on the Hauts-Plateaux.

Tamatave. The East Coast of Madagascar is a 'faille', or the wall resulting from a rift similar to that which has formed the area of the Great Lakes in East Africa. Coming down from the mountains of the Hauts-Plateaux, which rise to 5,850 feet and even points of 6,500 feet before their rapid descent to the sea, the first zone is one of dense forest, comparatively undisturbed, with the trees in two layers and thick undergrowth. Although this is a montane forest formation, there are few lianes or epiphytes, except for lichens in the dampest areas, and palms are seen only along watercourses. In this part, rivers fall rapidly and there are numerous waterfalls. One of the waterfalls, on the river Mandraka, has been harnessed to provide electricity for Tananarive. There are few large trees at this altitude but, at lower altitudes of 2,600 to 1,600 feet, the forest becomes, where it has remained undisturbed, a fine example of the tropical rain forest, although a very high proportion are species endemic to Madagascar.[10] Valuable timbers are found in this forest—ebony, palisanders, as well as many other hardwoods quite unknown to the world markets.

Below the forest limit, and usually at about 1,500 feet, though sometimes higher, one enters the inhabited country and the forest gives way to a *savoka* or degraded secondary vegetation dominated by the travellers tree and bamboos. The forest has been destroyed by shifting cultivation of mountain rice.* The population is clus-

* In Malagasy, called 'kapa-kapa' or 'tavy', the latter term being used more frequently by agronomists.

tered in large villages, perched above the narrow river valleys, and coffee is planted around the villages.

Still lower down, the fall levels off and the rivers run among bare grass-covered sandy hills to end in lagoons, the mouth of nearly every river being blocked by a sand-bar. Sometimes the coastal forest, itself a botanical curiosity with species not found in the forest of the interior, has survived along the sea-shore and for a few hundred yards inland.

Annual rainfall here is rarely less than 120 inches, and may be locally higher. Rain falls throughout the year, with a pause, definitely not a dry season, in October, which is consequently the best month for exploring the forest on foot. January to March are the 'cyclone months' and each year, during this time, several hurricanes from the Indian Ocean, which frequently devastate Mauritius and Réunion, hit the east coast of Madagascar with varying intensity. At least every two or three years there is serious devastation—torrential rains of perhaps 15 inches in twenty-four hours, accompanied by winds of up to 125 miles per hour. The rivers, in their narrow valleys, can rise up to 75 feet in a few hours. Whole villages disappear, roads are cut, bridges swept out to sea and trees blown down in their hundreds during these hurricanes. As many rivers fall as much as 5,000 feet in 20 to 30 miles, the flooding can be catastrophic.

Thus, while a very wide variety of plants grow easily in this warm humid climate, a fact that has certainly contributed to the establishment of a dense population, the environment is not easy to master and the population, mainly Betsimisaraka, has by no means evolved techniques that enable it to do more than exist in an unstable equilibrium. Shifting cultivation occurs all over the world where the inhabitants do not have mastery over soil fertility, the basic factor in agriculture. Mountain rice is cultivated along the east coast of Madagascar by a system of bush-fallowing: the forest is cut and burned and rice is sown in pockets among the debris. This gives crops of about 720 kilos per acre with a maximum of 1,700 kilos per acre which can be maintained on the same ground for no more than one year. Ten years' forest fallow is held to be necessary to restore the original level of soil fertility.[11] However, increasing population pressure and the necessity for villages to remain near their coffee plantations has reduced the time of such fallows to seven or even five years, with consequent declining yields.

The narrow valleys among the foothills, where the greater part of the population is found, are often developed as irrigated paddy fields, but paddy production is limited to the valley-bottoms, which are restricted spaces, and this crop is only complementary to the mountain rice. There are no terraced paddy fields, such as in the Betsileo country, and in times of severe floods anything growing on the valley bottoms is swept away; thus mountain rice becomes the main crop.

The sandy hills on the coast between the foothills and the sea are largely uninhabited and the few cattle of the region graze here. Zebu cattle do not do well on the east coast, which is too humid for them, and cattle brought down from the Hauts-Plateaux rapidly lose condition. Such cattle as do survive are smaller and less productive than those on the high ground. In some places, notably near the estuaries of large rivers farther south along this coast, such as the Faraony or the Matitana, the inhabitants cultivate rice on what appear to be huge floating rafts of decaying vegetation. In flood time, the raft and the rice crop may be swept out to sea. Here and there along the larger valleys, especially towards the south, irrigated paddy fields are found, but all suffer from inadequate control of the potentially enormous water supplies.

The poorest villages, deep in the dense forest, live mainly on cooked plantains and wild yams (*ovy-anala*). Their only cash crop is wild honey, which porters carry, in a journey lasting several days, to the coast in tins containing about 50 kilos. Many of these forest villages in the prefecture of Fenerive completely disappeared after the cyclone of 1959. The villages in the foothills, although possessing uncertain rice supplies, all have a cash crop—robusta coffee, vanilla, cloves, bananas and other fruits—which enables them to buy a minimum of basic foodstuffs when needed.

Coffee was introduced probably early in the nineteenth century from Réunion, then called Bourbon, and a variety still exists, *Coffea borbonica*, reputed to contain less caffeine than *C. canephora*, known as robusta coffee. Bourbon coffee and the predominant arabica was devastated by *Hemilea vastatrix* before 1850, as was the production of Mauritius, and never regained any importance on Réunion and Mauritius. Robusta coffee, resistant to *Hemilea*, was developed on the coast, slowly until 1930, and thereafter the acreage increased rapidly until Madagascar became the world's largest producer of robusta, with 41,000 tons in 1938. Production declined during the Second World War, and especially during the 1947 Rebellion, which was particularly violent in areas where there were European coffee-plantations on parts of the east coast. It was only in 1955 that Madagascar regained its 1938 level of production, by which time it had been overtaken by the Ivory Coast, Angola and the Belgian Congo. Production has since remained static, fluctuating between 40,000 and 50,000 tons since then.

In the province of Tamatave, coffee occupies one-quarter of all cultivated land and represents half of the total value of agricultural production. Coffee accounts for 60 per cent of the tree crops in this province, cloves for 30 per cent, and coconut palms, fruit trees and bananas for the remaining 10 per cent. The chief problems are under-production and very low productivity. Given the coffee quota of 83,000 tons for 1973, the increase in production of nearly 30,000 tons provides the best, but not an easy, method of increasing incomes among this population. At present, there is a small number of European-owned plantations, usually on good alluvial soils and showing a high standard of cultivation. By far the greater part of the production comes from small planters owning a few bushes, usually on slopes. These plantations are often old and it is very difficult for the Betsimisaraka farmer to accept the idea that he should cut out a tree of thirty to forty years and plant a young tree in its place. For one thing, he will have to wait four or five years before he has his first crop.*

Much research has been carried out on coffee in Madagascar by the Institut français du café et du cacao (IFCC), whose research station is at Ilaka near Manakara.† Although this station plants mainly on alluvial soils, which are not available to most small planters, its work shows, in a striking way, what a coffee bush can produce in this environment under proper management.

---

* A coffee bush is considered past its useful life at forty years. Newly planted bushes should give their first crop at four years in Madagascar. However, Harar says: 'Who knows how long coffee trees will live and prosper and give increasing yields in a region where the environment is ideal? Single-stemmed trees and orchards are known which are thirty fifty and eighty years old and are still as good as ever.'

† The director of the IFCC for many years has been René Costes, author of the standard work, *Les Caféiers du Monde*. This station also possesses an interesting botanical collection of about thirty varieties of wild coffee found in the Mascarene islands.

While small planters are harvesting 200 to 300 grams per bush, at Ilaka and on some of the European plantations, up to 1 kilo per bush is gathered. Moreover, to produce good coffee, the berry must be properly extracted from the red cherry and then dried. This can be done either by soaking the cherries in water until the fruit ferments and falls off—the 'wet process' used for preparing arabica coffee in East Africa—or by drying the fruit on concrete floors in the sun and then extracting the coffee beans (two to each fruit) with a huller.

The Betsimisaraka dries his coffee cherries on a mat outside his house in the sun (or rain) and then pounds them in a mortar to extract the coffee beans. This does not produce good coffee. Research and extension workers have therefore concentrated on providing new plants and better processing methods, with village decorticators. The new plants are multiplied by taking leaf cuttings from proved clones and establishing local nurseries. However, there still remains the difficult problem of persuading the peasant to cut out his old bush and plant the new one on properly-prepared soil. The traditional marketing system also inhibits the change to higher quality coffee. On the east coast, the village storekeeper, usually Chinese, buys coffee from the Betsimisaraka 'tout venant' —that is, whatever quality he supplies—at a fixed price. There is no bonus for quality, since the storekeeper sees to the grading himself. The peasant will almost certainly be in debt to the storekeeper and the year's coffee crop is thus sold long before it is harvested. Growers are further hampered by the lack of roads penetrating the interior of this part of the country. Often they have to carry their coffee on their backs for perhaps ten to twenty miles, along tortuous forest paths, to the nearest Chinese store. On arrival, the grower is in no position to bargain.

There is no central processing plant and no central auction floors as at Moshi and Mombasa in East Africa. Coffee is exported by large companies, especially by the Compagnie Marseillaise and the Compagnie Lyonnaise; some of these companies have established modern processing plants, although most warehouses and equipment are ancient. Sorting methods range from one electronic grader, installed by a private company at Manakara, to the usual method: women sitting on the ground sorting the coffee beans by hand according to size and appearance.

Improvement of coffee output depends very much on better use of leached slopes. Few planters have land on the alluvial soils, which were granted to European settlers in the early days of the colonisation and which remain in their possession. The average plantation is on a hillside, unimproved and subject to continued sheet erosion and leaching. Only those coffee bushes near a house benefit from the fertilising effect of household rubbish. Cropping is simply a question of picking the berries, and no care is given to the bush at any time in its life of up to fifty years.

Many peoples of the world have mastered the techniques of achieving high levels of production on steep slopes, and their methods have been studied with a view to applying them to the conditions of the east coast of Madagascar. All around the Mediterranean peasants have established terraces held by dry stone walls that have lasted for thousands of years. High productivity has been achieved by an emphasis on tree crops—olives, carobs, citrus and other fruits—that permit intercropping for vegetables. In the Mediterranean, livestock is kept, partly extensively on the eroded mountains back from the sea, where flocks of sheep and goats graze among the maquis, and partly more intensively in stables near the terraces, fed on crops grown for them. These methods are partially applicable to the foot-hills of the east coast, where terracing for rice cultivation, on the model of the Betsileo, would remove paddy fields above flood levels. The valuable colluvial soils—formed by the leaching out of slopes higher up and found on the edge of the valley bottoms—should also be terraced, as they are on the Hauts-Plateaux, and put under tree crops. The choice of tree crops is very wide, since not only coffee but also a broad range of tropical tree-crops can demonstrably be grown profitably under the climate of this coast. The African oil-palm already grows around houses, the children picking the fruit and eating it. A project is now being financed by the FED for the establishment of a pilot plantation of 2,400 acres of oil-palm near Tamatave, and plants have been distributed by extension agents all along the coast to familiarise the population.

Many of the tropical fruits familiar to South-East Asia are seen on the east coast. In November and December lychees flood every market and are sold for low prices in Tananarive. For those who eat it for the first time in Madagascar, it is a delicious fruit, easily

peeled and tasting something like a large savoury hot-house grape.*
Other fruits include breadfruit (*Artocarpus atilis*), jakfruit (*Arto-carpus heterophyllus*), the jambolan (*Szygium cuminii*) and several varieties of annonas (*Annona spp.*), all of which appear to have been introduced to Madagascar from South-East Asia over the past few centuries.

Cloves traditionally occupied second place among tree crops on the coast and production is concentrated north of Tamatave, around Fenerive and on the island of Ste Marie. The clove tree, of the genus *Eugenia*, would grow to a fair height if allowed. The essence of cloves is extracted in artisan alembics by distilling the leaves with water. To procure the leaves, the growers hack branches off the tree; thus, clove plantations have a very battered appearance. Production has been stationary since 1940, due to competition from synthetic substitutes from coal tar. The active principle, eugenol, is used in pharmacy, and sufferers from tooth-ache may remember the smell of cloves in temporary palliatives. Cloves are also extensively consumed in India in various dishes and are contained in a cigarette that is popular in Indonesia. Balance of payments difficulties in the importing countries for some years limited these markets in Madagascar, while Zanzibar and Pemba, the world's greatest producers of cloves, are serious competitors, in spite of periodic joint meetings in Tananarive. The mysterious virus disease of Zanzibar clove plantations, 'Sudden Death', has fortunately never appeared in Madagascar.

The clove tree originated in South-East Asia, like so many of the tree crops found on the east coast, and was introduced into the Mascarene islands in 1770 by the Royal Intendant, Pierre Poivre.†

---

* This is the *Litchi sinensis*. In June/July the 'litchi chevelu' or ram-butan (*Nephelium lappaceum*) fruits. This is inferior in taste to the lychee. A practical plan for establishing terrace cultivation and soil and water conservation was worked out in detail by M. A. Drogué, formerly In-specteur-Général des Services de l'Agriculture of French Equatorial Africa, who instead of retiring in 1957 came to Madagascar and headed the provincial agricultural service at Tamatave for several years. He issued numerous mimeographed studies, among them *L'Agriculture dans la Province de Tamatave* (1957). He was also responsible for the reintro-duction of the African oil palm.

† Pierre Poivre was born to a family of silk weavers in Lyon in 1719. Having studied for the priesthood he went to China in 1745, but was captured by the English and disembarked at Batavia. It was here he saw

He obtained his plants from the island of Amboina in the Moluccas in the Dutch East Indies. In 1822, the clove tree was introduced into the island of Ste Marie by the Société Albran-Carayon-Hugot, and from there to the neighbouring coast. In 1880, production was estimated at 15 tons of cloves; at present a total of about 90,000 acres is planted with about 10 million trees.[12]

The most rapid expansion of any crop since 1960 has been on the banana plantations around Tamatave and Brickaville, operated by the members of a co-operative (now called Union des Co-opératives Fruitières, UCOFRU) and exporting to France and other countries of the European Common Market. Plantations were established from 1960–61 by some enterprising Europeans and by a larger number of Malagasy planters and a few Chinese. Concessions were granted on alluvial soils in the valleys of the Onibe and the Ivoloina, and in the lower part of the Rianila at Brickaville farther south. A number of technical and commercial staff who had helped build up the banana exports from Guinea left that country after independence and came to Tamatave. Thus the necessary management personnel was available from the start, while the Institut des Fruits et Agrumes Coloniaux (IFAC) provided planting material (the Poyo variety) and technical advice. In the absence of diseases that affect West Africa, such as Panama disease, and the plagues of eel-worms (nematodes) that infest the rich organic soils of the Ivory Coast and cost large sums in chemical control, production shot ahead, rising from 200 tons in 1961 to 20,000 tons in 1966. These figures refer to tonnages exported, nearly all to France, but quality control exercised by the co-operative meant that probably seven tons were produced for one ton of export quality.

---

for the first time the precious and then jealously guarded spice-trees, cloves, pepper and nutmeg. He had an adventurous career, being again taken prisoner during the Seven Years' War, and making various unsuccessful attempts to export spice-trees from the Philippines and the Dutch East Indies. After the Treaty of Paris (1763), which considerably reduced French trading in India, Poivre was appointed Intendant in Mauritius. Since he now controlled the French merchant ships based on the island he was able to organise an expedition to the Philippines and Dutch East Indies, which returned to Mauritius in 1770 with pepper vines, seventy clove-trees, and 400 nutmeg trees. See Alfred Lacroix, *Notice Historique sur les Membres et Correspondants de l'Académie des Sciences ayant travaillé dans les colonies françaises des Mascareignes et de' Madagascar au XVIIIème siècle*, Institut de France, Vol. 621, 1936.

The remaining six tons are sold on the local market. The proportion had been reduced by 1968 to about 1 ton of export quality bananas from every 2 tons produced.

This operation has not been without its setbacks, the first being the 'freeze' of 1964, when the winter temperature at Tamatave dropped to 8 °C, thus stopping the flow of sap in the bananas. The sap does not restart with warmer temperatures and, as a result, the bananas are woody and uneatable. The second blow was the closing of the Suez Canal in 1967, which greatly extended the transport route to Europe and put the West African countries at a considerable advantage.

Apart from these problems, the operation has shown that, when an operation is launched with obvious financial interest to the producer, a spectacular increase in output may result, thus disproving the pessimists who state that populations such as the Betsimisaraka will not respond to possibilities of technical change and economic growth. The key elements in this operation, which deserves to be more closely studied by those concerned with agricultural development, were a well-organised land-tenure system for the concessions and technical and managerial personnel who ensured correct cultural practices, proper grading for export and a marketing system that gave the producer a very fair return for his product. There is no reason, apart from the difficulties of changing an inherited system, why this procedure should not be applied to the far larger production of coffee by the intervention of an organisation similar to the UCOFRU to give the planter the same technical and economic backing and obtain a properly-graded product for export.

The replacement of the traditional commercial circuit is not as simple as it seems, unless it can be replaced by something more than this banana-producers co-operative. The banana organisation deals only with fruit for export and in no way takes the place of the small storekeeper for the supply of consumer goods and food-products or the buying of other agricultural products. While the Chinese storekeeper may be an obstacle to improvements in the quality of coffee, owing to his practices of buying 'tout venant' and of usury, it is clear that he has played also a positive role. He has traditionally enabled the peasant to sell all or any of his products, even if at prices usually well below the 'market' prices. He has supplied food and consumer goods in villages where no alternative entrepreneur existed. Finally, and very important, he has been a constant source of short and even medium-term credit, thus acting as a banker to the peasant and introducing him marginally into the monetary economy. These functions of the Chinese storekeeper have been positive, in the sense of associating peasants previously at a subsistence level with the exchange economy, and also negative, since the commercial structure is static and exploits the peasant in draining off any profit for the benefit of the storekeeper and his patrons. There is thus no room in this structure for saving by the peasant, and the 'capital formation' so desirable for technological change is rendered virtually impossible by low prices and continued indebtedness.

The Chinese storekeepers exist in all centres large and small along the east coast from Diego-Suarez to Fort Dauphin, and may be said effectively to control most of the retail trade outside the hands of a few large European companies in all the eastern half of Madagascar. In the western half, and especially on the west coast, it will be seen that this retail trade and similar functions are exercised by 'Indians', who may be Pakistanis, Ismaeli followers of the Aga Khan, Gujeratis and others. The Chinese are bound by strong family ties, although intermarriage with Malagasy is not uncommon,* and these links assist them considerably with regard to credit, supplies and manpower. Many storekeepers form part of a chain of purchase and distribution of which the head will be a wholesale trader in the nearest town or the provincial headquarters. Wholesalers may control ten or more village storekeepers by a system of loans or advances either in goods or in cash before harvest. Their relationship is thus similar, on a larger scale, to that between the storekeeper and the peasant. The products are usually collected by the wholesaler's truck from the village store.

Manakara—Mananjary—Fort-Dauphin. The south-east coast, moving southwards from Mananjary towards Fort-Dauphin, is confronted with the same problems as the Betsimisaraka, but in a more acute form owing to higher population densities. This region is inhabited by a number of smaller tribes, among them (moving south) the Antaimoro, the Antaisaka, the Antefasa, the

* It is practically unknown among the 'Indians'.

Antainosy, and, inland, the Tanala (or 'forest people').* These tribes, of which the Antaisaka are the most dynamic, live in very large villages, sometimes of two or three thousand people, and form 'closed' societies, open neither to intercourse with their neighbours nor to new ideas.

For a long period, and certainly since 1900, there has been migration towards the wide valleys of the west coast, and homogeneous villages of Antefasa (in particular) are found on the delta of the Mangoky, at Kaday at the mouth of the Tsiribihina, and even near Maintirano. In spite of this migration, population density is building up. It can be estimated that the population of the sub-prefecture of Vangaindrano, at present 500,000 people, will, at present rates, pass the million mark in twenty to twenty-five years. This will occur on 1,900 square miles in an area where techniques of cultivation on available land remain static. A similar situation prevails in other districts also. The population pressure increases fragmentation of holdings, forces down productivity, and has occasionally led to food crises in recent years—as, for example, in 1964 when rice had to be rationed in Vangaindrano.

The reasons for this economic decline are, basically, that population has outstripped available resources as utilised by existing technology. Thus, techniques of rice cultivation, which include preparation of paddy fields, by trampling—that is, by driving a small herd of cattle round and round until the soil is prepared—are wasteful both of cattle and of the paddy field itself, which would be more productive if ploughed, harrowed, fertilised and weeded. Again, sowing of rice broadcast after trampling, instead of preparing nurseries and transplanting as on the Hauts-Plateaux, leads also to low yields (less than one ton for every $2\frac{1}{2}$ acres).

Far south on the east coast, on the Tropic of Capricorn, mean annual temperatures are lower. The ideal mean annual temperature for robusta coffee is said to be 25°C: thus, the main cash crop of the east coast becomes marginal here, although a wide range of crops remain viable. The closed societies in the huge villages gathered round the *trano-be*, or 'big house', the residence of the chief, remain closed also to new techniques and new crops. In this type of society it is not well-thought-of to step out of line, and to be more prosperous than one's neighbour is to be out of line.

* As was mentioned in a previous chapter these peoples were among the most determined in the 1947 Rebellion.

The technical problems are similar to those found among the Betsimisaraka farther north: narrow valleys in the foothills of the mountains, which have not been developed by terrace cultivation, and torrential floods coming down from the forest-covered mountains which make permanent cultivation of the lower parts of the valleys hazardous. Solutions to the technical difficulties are a question of civil engineering works, together with control of soil fertility and improved cropping systems. This is a text-book solution, which applies to many other countries. The real problem, as elsewhere, is in the minds of the population. When a population such as the Antaisaka of Vangaindrano has lived for centuries in a precarious near-subsistence equilibrium, any change is a risk. For those who live near the survival level, life is already a sufficient risk, and there is no incentive to add to the risk. The 'closed' societies, disapproved of by academic sociologists, are closed to ensure survival and to present a united front to hostile surroundings.

These are some of the reasons why the population of the southeast may cause a serious food and population problem within the next fifteen years. The technical solutions are known, and alternative land is available elsewhere in this vast and under-populated island. A tradition of emigration exists, and successful communities of these coastal tribes have been established far away on the west coast. But population growth, promoted by improved medical facilities, renders urgent the rapid execution of development projects with the full participation of the population in order to provide substantially increased individual productivity.* The population density in certain valleys of this region usually exceeds 250 persons per square mile.†

Organised emigration in sufficient numbers demands costly land settlement schemes in regions that could accept the migrants. There are other problems. Already, the social and family upsets resulting from the existing exodus of young men and women can

* A UN Special Fund project, of which the FAO is the executing agency, for an agro-economic and sociological survey of the Farafangana region was started in 1966. Its conclusions are designed to orientate future government investment programmes for this area.

† At Vohipeno densities of 750 inhabitants and at Ampasimanjeva of 1,500 inhabitants per square mile were recorded in 1962. Commissariat-Général du Plan, *Etude des Regions du Sud Est*, Cinam 1962.

be observed. A massive departure would result in fertile land going out of cultivation, a diminution in the number of active workers, a lower tax income for local authorities, all leading to a further decline in economic activity of the region. These problems must be tackled but there are no simple answers.

The narrowness of the land surface available for food crops is the main factor limiting human occupation on this coast. Almost all the peoples of Madagascar have traditions of moving inland from the east coast—the Merina traditions are unusually explicit.[13] After the introduction of cash crops such as coffee and vanilla, the French administration intended that a 'complementary economy' should be developed, by which incomes would be sufficiently high on the coast to allow the population to purchase rice and meat from surplus-producing areas on the Hauts-Plateaux. But the growth of population and of purchasing power has been rapid on the Hauts-Plateaux and urban centres such as Tananarive absorb all the available surpluses. At the same time, incomes from cash crops on the east coast have declined rather than increased in buying power, and the structure of an exchange-economy with the interior has not worked out.

The economic decline of this region is strikingly paralleled in the more recent history of European colonisation of the east coast. Settlement began in the early nineteenth century, mainly by immigrants from Mauritius and Réunion who were attracted by the tropical climate, with no dry season, and the fertile soils, sheltered by the forest along the river valleys. The proximity to the sea meant easy communications, so that settlers were not cut off from the outside world, as were the first Europeans on the Hauts-Plateaux, and the cash crops to which they were accustomed in the Mascarene islands, especially coffee and sugar-cane, grew equally well here.

The proximity of Mauritius and Réunion thus played an important part in the early development of the east coast. More important still, it was the immigrants from those islands who introduced Madagascar's important cash crops—coffee, vanilla and cloves. Coffee production, which increased very rapidly between 1930 and 1940, has followed the usual cycle for this coast; after a promising start, it has remained almost stationary.

Fort-Dauphin, which marks the extreme southern limit of the east coast, was one of the earliest European settlements; here

Flacourt lived, author of one of the earliest descriptions of Madagascar, *Histoire de la Grande Isle de Madagascar*.

Androy. Driving west towards Ambovombe, one crosses not only a watershed but one of the most rapid changes in climate and vegetation imaginable. The road climbs from an area of well-distributed mean annual rainfall, passes a population of remarkable triangular palms (*Neodypsis decarii*) which grow nowhere else in the world but in these few square miles, and emerges after thirty miles into a semi-arid zone of quite a different aspect, where rain falls only during three months of the year. The vegetation has changed completely. This is the Androy, or extreme south of Madagascar, the most difficult and least-developed area but paradoxically one of the best-documented. This is partly because the military administration of General Galliéni was not replaced by civil administrators until long after the rest of the island had come under civil rule. The pacification was not completed until after the last uprising in 1915, and the military post at Tsihombe, near Cape Ste Marie, the southernmost point, existed until 1946. The military men made numerous surveys, and other scientists, such as Grandidier and Decary, devoted much time to the highly original flora.[14]

The aspect of the country is dominated by what is botanically described as 'xerophytic or sclerophytic bush', which means that the vegetation, like the Arizona cacti that it resembles, is well adapted to withstand long drought. This bush is dominated by strange single-stemmed trees covered with long thorns, the *Diderea*, and by many varieties of *Euphorbiaceae*, nearly all giving a white and poisonous latex.

The Antandroy are essentially cattle people, not, perhaps, because the country is ideally suited to cattle but because it is difficult to live from anything else. The zebu survives for long periods with inadequate forage and water, rather like the cactus. The total number of cattle in the Androy was estimated (1962) at approximately 1,740,000 head.[15] Their watering and feeding present considerable problems. For a long time, the prickly-pear (*Opuntia vulgaris*), which was probably introduced from Réunion, enabled cattle to survive, even with little water. Someone introduced the cochineal insect in 1925 and wiped out the 'raketa', as it is called locally, which caused a very serious problem. The plant has been reintroduced but has never gained the same importance as a staple for the cattle. A traditional transhumance leads the cattle, accompanied by a section of each family, to grazing farther north where conditions are less hard.

Much hydrological research has been carried out and a number of deep bore-holes have been put down across this area. The technical problems of reaching an economic equilibrium within the hard environment, in terms of water conservation and dry farming, have been defined. The disastrous famines that afflicted this region in the past no longer occur, but the population lives precariously on slender crops of maize, millet and sorgho and can look forward to one bad year of deficient rainfall every four years. Two cash crops, castor-oil plant and sisal, have known sporadic success here. The castor-oil plant appears to have grown spontaneously but has not progressed since 1939 and has one of the most fluctuating price levels of any tropical product. Sisal, ably developed by European companies, especially in the valley of the Mandrare near Ambovombe, suffers from the competition from other fibres which is adversely affecting sisal in many other countries. A small local industry of weaving carpets from the wool of angora goats, which have been introduced around Ampanihy, and a mica mine at Beraketa complete the picture of local industry. A small deposit of thorium is being exploited and exported.

The Antandroy constitute one of the largest forces of migrant labour in Madagascar; colonies of them may be found far to the north on the sugar estates of the Sambirano and Nosy-be, and almost everywhere a labour force is required.

Tuléar–Morondava. The river Onilahy provides the northern boundary of the Androy, entering the Moçambique channel just south of the port of Tuléar. Between Tuléar and Morondava the rainfall rises from an annual mean of about 14 inches at Tuléar to one of about 27 inches at Morondava. In this area is to be found a system of agriculture reasonably well adapted to a long dry season of eight months but benefiting from a rather more regular and abundant rainfall than in the extreme south. The system is one of dry-farming, often practised as bush-fallowing and using the alluvial banks or *baiboho* as they emerge in the river beds after the floods of the short rainy season. From Tuléar to the Sambirano, a number of tribes presenting significant differences appear as 'Sakalava' on ethnographic maps. While it is essentially a country of extensive cattle-keeping, many important agricultural activities centre on the numerous rivers which descend from the Hauts-Plateaux more gradually than do the rivers of the east coast.

This constitutes the second major geological division of Madagascar, the sedimentary (continental Karoo, upper marine Karoo and later sediments) as opposed to the granite-gneiss of the Hauts-Plateaux and east coast. This division is characterised by very large rivers draining considerable areas, having their sources on the watersheds of the Hauts-Plateaux. The Mangoky, for instance, drains an area of about 37,000 square miles on the Plateaux; other rivers of major importance are, moving north, the Tsiribihina, the Manombolo, the Manambao, the Mahavavy, the Ikopa and the Betsiboka (the longest rivers of Madagascar, descending from the region of Tananarive), the Mahajamba and the Sofia. All these valleys are inhabited, although sparsely-populated by Far Eastern standards, where each would probably contain several million inhabitants.

Cattle-keeping and agriculture are no more integrated here than elsewhere although practised by the same families. Traditionally, the Sakalava were the historical rivals of the Merina for the domination of Madagascar, and their subjugation, beginning with the conquests of Radama I and still in progress at the time of the French occupation in 1896, was only partially achieved. The Sakalava are still extensive cattle-keepers, with large herds and little interest in cultivating the land. Their traditional staple was maize, cultivated by bush-fallowing techniques on burned-out forest; books published before 1940 show the western area of Madagascar as maize-producing and maize-exporting.

Although the Sakalava as a whole are extensive cattle-people, the great river valleys have attracted the settlement of important groups of this tribe, who divide their activities between bush-fallowing on forest cleared by burning and cultivation of alluvial banks on the edges of the rivers. These banks, the *baiboho*, are recently deposited alluvions that remain damp at a descending level throughout the dry season. They are by no means permanent, since the beds of the rivers shift regularly and their banks have long been stripped of their protective tree-cover.

255

An important group, the Masikoro, classed sometimes as a separate tribe, occupies the area around the Mangoky, one of the largest rivers. In certain zones the Masikoro give their main attention to cattle and cultivate only on dry land during the rains. In others, particularly in river valleys and on the edge of the mangrove swamps bordering the sea, cultivation is a primary activity on land that is regularly flooded and retains some moisture throughout the dry season. Among these peoples, cattle are less of a cult and more of an economic resource than is recognised by many writers. The sentimental side of cattle-keeping should not be over-rated, especially in an area of uncertain rainfall where cattle constitute a stable reserve of value which can be realised in case of necessity. In the Mangoky valley, cattle serve as an exchange currency, much as do the copper jugs and cast-iron cooking pots that are stored in large numbers in the houses of those having some wealth— especially the *ombiasy*, or medicine-men. The economy shows a considerable instability, owing to the absence of reserves, and the uncertain rainfall, coupled with heavy flooding of the valleys during the rains, makes food-crop yields uncertain. Hence the value attached to cattle, which represent a safe reserve. The staple food of the south-west of Madagascar, as in the extreme south, was maize, not rice, but rice cultivation has been introduced progressively by immigrants from other areas and is now on the increase.

Immigration, especially of Betsileo from the Hauts-Plateaux and of Antesaka from the east coast (the latter forming homogeneous villages all along the west coast as far north as Maintirano), has introduced certain technical advances, among them irrigated paddy fields, but without substantially altering the cultivation methods of the Masikoro. The most important economic activity is the cultivation of Lima beans (pois du cap). The region between Tuléar and the Mangoky exports annually about 16,000 tons of these beans, which originated in South America but which appear to have been cultivated in Madagascar at least since the nineteenth century.[16]

The income from the pois du cap is most important for this population and constitutes their main and only cash crop, apart from irregular crops of groundnuts and the slow introduction of cotton in recent years. It is cultivated mainly in the valley of the Mangoky on *baiboho* after the annual flood, and elsewhere under dry-farming conditions but on good soils in depressions retaining some moisture. It is sown in March–April and harvested in September–October, and both operations give rise to a considerable movement of population.[17] This is one crop where government intervention since 1965 has liberated the growers from the hold of local Pakistani dealers, by handing over the collection and marketing to the Syndicat des Communes, a para-statal body under the tutelage of the Minister of the Interior. This action has given the grower a stable price, and efforts have been made to impose strict quality control as required by British buyers.

The south-west coast is the home of the chief fishing tribe of Madagascar, the Vezo, who sail Polynesian-type canoes with a single outrigger and a small square sail. The Vezo fishing fleets cover the west coast as far north as Nosy-be, and whole families migrate in canoes along the coast, using the sails of their canoes to rig make-shift tents on the shore in temporary settlements while they dry and smoke their catch for sale inland. Some of the larger (20 to 25 feet) canoes sail far out in the Moçambique Channel to Europa island to spear large sea-turtles, a much-prized delicacy.

European colonisation has not been successful along the west coast, although a very small number survive in certain of the valleys, utilising Malagasy share-croppers to grow the tobacco for them while they themselves undertake the collection, preparation and marketing. Settlement in the Tsiribihina valley was more successful; here tobacco-growing was developed by the Régie Française from 1924, and European settlers, who numbered twenty-nine at their peak in 1950, began the cultivation of Maryland tobacco. This was carried out on fertile alluvions which remain for about five months under six feet of water. Share-cropping has been extensively practised, all the operations of cultivation being left to the Malagasy *metayer*, the settler providing foremen for each group and looking after the fermentation of the leaf, sorting and sales. The traditionally-protected French market has disappeared and prices have now to be aligned with those of the European Common Market. The Malagasy Régie took over from the French Régie in 1968. The reconversion of cropping practices, and in particular the production of varieties other than Maryland in accordance with changing tastes, poses very considerable problems for the future of this crop. Similar practices and problems are also found in the tobacco-growing areas north of Majunga, in the valley of the Bemarivo, south of Port-Bergé.

ANIMAL HUSBANDRY

Madagascar possesses a huge cattle population, which approaches two beasts for every inhabitant. The exact number is difficult to estimate: cattle populations fluctuate, the animals are mobile and, where taxation intervenes, owners have every incentive to understate the numbers of their herds. Because of the national importance of cattle-keeping, and since animal husbandry is frequently not integrated with agriculture, a separate section will be devoted to it.

The regions occupied by cattle-people do not correspond to the diverse agricultural regions described above. There are two main regions: the producing region, the western half of the island and the extreme south, where large herds of zebu roam with the minimum of attention from their owners over huge expanses of grassland; and the consuming region, the eastern part of the Hauts-Plateaux and the east coast.

In 1961, a reliable estimate of the cattle population put it at 9,424,000 head. This figure is derived from the 'official' figure of 6,050,000 (declared for taxation) to which is added an estimated 26·7 per cent for fraudulent concealment from the tax-gatherer, plus 19 per cent for calves and young animals undeclared.[18]

The cattle population appears to have undergone fairly severe fluctuations between 1920 and 1960. Official figures have been published since 1904, but these are discounted before 1920 owing to the thinly spread administrative structures before that date. Although no single study of livestock in Madagascar existed before that of Lacroutz and his collaborators, the recent history of the herd has been pieced together from the study of many scattered documents, mainly from the archives of the Service de l'Elevage (Veterinary Service) and the Service des Affaires Economiques. It would appear that numbers diminished sharply between 1920 and 1937, and that from that date there has been a slow reconstitution of the herd.

The reasons for the decline are numerous and vary according to the writers. Lacroutz considers that the decline in the 1920s was due mainly to high prices prevailing for hides and skins which at that time fetched ten times (in constant 1961 francs) the price prevailing twenty years later, and to the rise in prices of coffee and vanilla prior to 1931, which automatically increased demand for cattle in the consuming area of the east coast. His study of records scattered in various government departments enabled this expert to reconstruct a 'history' of the Malagasy herd from 1920 to 1961.[19] This shows that a number of factors intervened to influence slaughterings. These include severe droughts accompanied by famine in the extreme south (the Androy) in 1921, 1930 and 1943, which may have reduced the herd of three million head in this area by more than one third. The destruction of the prickly pear (*Opuntia vulgaris*) in this area by the cochineal insect after 1924 may have caused the death of 300,000 animals. This plant was used mainly as a substitute for water and food in the long dry season.

Exports of hides and skins are estimated by this author to have varied between 700,000 and 1 million per annum for fifteen years from 1913 to 1929, while at the same time meat factories supplying mainly the French army increased their activities.* Taxation was increased after 1930 at a time when the price of hides and skins, as of all other products, fell sharply during the world economic crisis. Between 1930 and 1936 it is said that many owners sold animals to pay the tax and slaughtered cows and young stock to avoid tax. The national herd reached its lowest estimated number of 7,700,000 animals in 1937. In 1939 the administration limited the export of hides and skins to 4,000 tons or about 360,000 units per annum and forbade slaughtering of cows or animals of less than four years old, with the aim of stopping the decline in the cattle population. Since 1940, the national herd has slowly increased, aided by considerable improvements in animal disease control introduced by the Veterinary Service. These include control of bacterial anthrax by vaccination, treatment of parasites in young stock, institution of spray-races and dipping tanks against ticks and slow but effective extension of knowledge among owners.

---

* Seven companies have operated in Madagascar since 1896. Production figures are given as follows: 1917, 128,000 cattle slaughtered in five factories; 1934, 110,000 cattle and 25,000 pigs in eight factories; 1948, 114,000 cattle and 27,000 pigs. Since 1950, factories have averaged about 40,000 cattle. The British owned factory (CGF) at Bonamary shut down in 1954.

These owners are hardly cattlemen in the sense that the Masai or Fulani are in Africa. One does not see, as in Northern Nigeria and Chad, herds being led by a Fulani herdsman who scans the sky to estimate where rain may have fallen, to lead his animals to better pasture. The nomads of West Africa are expert in many things, not only in the care of their beasts but also in the constant search for good grazing. The West African zebu will stand up to long marches and will drink perhaps once in two days. The Malagasy zebu is an indifferent marcher and suffers on the track; also, he will support going without water for a day, but does not thrive. The West African zebu can arrive in reasonable condition at a market hundreds of miles from his normal grazing grounds, while the Malagasy animal loses much weight and condition on his long march to the factory or market. Under present conditions, cattle from the west coast must move up to 300 miles on foot to their eventual destination, the slaughter-houses of Tananarive or the east coast. This journey may take four or five months and the animals may change hands several times between different groups of professional drovers.

The Malagasy cattle owner leaves his herd in semi-liberty. There are no lion or large predators in Madagascar, and cattle-thieving, once a thriving business, has been more severely repressed since independence than under the French rule. The owner's 'care' is limited to a periodic count of the herd and to a seasonal trans-humance, when young members of his family take the herd out of the valleys, now under rice, to the mountains where, after the rains, young grass is coming on. He also sees to lighting grass fires. These fires have reduced the once-forested mountains of Madagascar to vast areas of poor grassland, but it must be admitted that, at present levels of development, burning is the only method that will produce anything palatable from the lateritic crusts that remain.

Livestock owners in Madagascar are never pure pastoralists like the nomadic Fulani or the Masai. Nearly all of them produce the food crops that satisfy their basic needs—rice, cassava, sweet potatoes or sorgho. Thus the cattle are not necessary for survival but serve as a store of value to be cashed when money is needed to pay taxes or buy consumer goods. Again, animals may be sold to buy heifers or young stock and thus increase the herd.

On the Hauts-Plateaux the situation is different. The Merina and Betsileo peasant cannot do without cattle, which he needs to work his land with plough and harrow, to draw his ox-cart and provide manure; but the density of population on the Hauts-Plateaux and the occupation of nearly all the valleys by paddy-fields leaves little space for extensive herds. Thus this area is a consuming, and not a producing, region. In addition, the beginning of mixed farming on the Hauts-Plateaux has enabled a start to be made in fattening cattle. An increasing number of peasants buy young stock coming up from the west and fatten them for the market with dried cassava and sometimes with forage crops. The practice of individual feed-lots, known locally as the '*dabo-kandro*' or 'boeuf de fosse', has existed traditionally in Imerina. Here an ox is kept in a hollowed-out enclosure and fattened for several months. Such animals can weigh up to 600 kilo.

The other major consumers are the peasants of the east coast. The zebu does not thrive in the humid tropical climate of this zone, but herds are kept to trample the paddy fields and for consumption. Annual rituals, funerals and other ceremonies are as important here as elsewhere and cattle are essential for sacrifice. The east coast, in spite of the fluctuations in the prices of coffee, vanilla, cloves, pepper, bananas and other crops, has a substantial cash income, and Lacroutz estimates that 75,000 head of cattle coming from the producing western region are sent each year for consumption on the east coast.

Meat consumption is relatively high in Madagascar, since beef and pork are freely available. Lacroutz gives the following two tables which show clearly that consumption-levels in Madagascar are well above those in certain countries of Southern Europe.[20]

This potential is thus not exactly what it seems. The fact that there are approximately 10 million head of cattle in Madagascar does not mean that it can rapidly become an Argentina or a New Zealand. The favourable factors are many, notably absence of rinderpest, foot-and-mouth, brucellosis, contagious pleuro-pneumonia and many of the more unpleasant tick-borne diseases such as the east coast fever of East Africa. Again, there are no large predators and animals can safely be left out all night, which is not the case in Tanzania.

Against this there is the dry season of Madagascar, lasting in the western breeding areas from April till late November. The two

		Total consumption meat and offal per head per annum
I	Meat Consumption—Madagascar (*1962*)	kgs.
	Rural population	22·1
	Small towns	28·0
	Large towns	37·3
	National average consumption	24·2
II	Comparative figures for selected countries (*1961*)	
	Madagascar	24·3
	United Kingdom	59·8
	France	59·4
	Federal Germany	52·9
	U.S.A.	72·0
	Netherlands	42·6
	Italy	21·3
	Greece	20·8
	Ivory Coast	8·3

main problems of increasing the output of the Malagasy herd are to feed the animal and enable it even to gain weight during the dry season and to reduce drastically the mortality of young animals, estimated to reach more than 50 per cent in some of the breeding areas. Young animals die either because, during the breeding season, they must remain on damp lowlands, which causes them to be infested with parasites,[21] or because, having lived with difficulty during the latter part of the dry season, the sudden change in food when the young grass comes on with the rains gives them a fatal 'scour' or diarrhoea.

Since 1900, the development of Madagascar's livestock productivity was mainly 'downstream'—that is, skimming off the available animals from the national herd and exporting them. Thus the factories worked well, and the main products, boned frozen meat and corned beef, were of a high quality. This problem has been dealt with in other places with a long dry season, such as Australia, Texas, Venezuela and Brazil. The method used has always been to intervene in the critical dry season to enable the animal not only to survive but to gain weight. To this end, considerable progress in animal nutrition has been made, necessitating the integration of crop production and animal husbandry. In Madagascar, the zebu must be fed during the six months of the dry season. At present he survives, and this is the main reason for the huge hump between his shoulders, which contains a reserve of fat to assist his survival. Since he lives but does not gain weight, the existing factories close down for at least six months of the year and reopen in March when the young grass enables the animals to regain some condition.

Ranches are a partial solution. A ranch uses the natural vegetation and some improved water supplies to maintain a given herd in reasonable condition. Ranches are essential as a holding (or breeding) ground to ensure that a fixed population of young animals is always available for fattening. The factory, however, requires animals in top condition, and the economic returns of a factory require not merely regular supplies but, even more important, supplies of a standard quality. This can be ensured only by artificial feeding, as has been done for poultry in many countries, by the 'battery' system, whereby birds are kept in cages and fed all they can take. The same system for cattle is called 'feed-lots' and is applicable with certain modifications in Madagascar. Cattle brought in from a ranch in good condition are kept in open stalls for three months and, under well-established systems of feeding and management, can gain up to 2 lb per day. All the foodstuffs necessary for this operation grow successfully in Madagascar. Maize grows well and is the staple food of the producing areas of the west coast. Cassava provides carbohydrate and calories, and 20 tons can be produced to one acre. Other products include grain legumes such as *Dolichos lablab*, which grows freely in the south, groundnut and cottoncake from oil mills, and eventually fishmeal from the extensive wastage of fish catches on the west coast.

Moving further 'upstream', a parallel operation must be carried out to bring the mortality of young animals down from 50 per cent to about 5 per cent. This can be done only by providing improved forage and utilising all available spare water supplies for irrigated forage crops and by active programmes of deparasitisation. The development of the livestock potential of Madagascar necessitates complete projects with all these elements from the cattleman to the factory, and neglect of any single phase will prevent expansion. In 1970 moves were being undertaken to implement complete projects of this nature in two widely-separated provinces, Tuléar and Diego-Suarez, while the World Bank was studying assistance to be given to ranching projects in the intermediate zone between the west and the Hauts-Plateaux.

It is fairly certain that, within ten years, Madagascar will become an important producer and exporter of meat and meat products, though, of necessity, the full development will be a long-term project and its contribution to world meat supplies will be small compared to those of countries like Argentina, Uruguay and Australia. This is, none the less, an economic proposition which the government has decided to support as a priority objective in future development programmes.[22]

INDUSTRY AND MINING

It is not yet possible to speak of industrialisation in Madagascar, and such enterprises as exist in no way form anything like a complex of secondary industries. Apart from mining, the majority of industrial activities concern the processing of agricultural products, but even this processing is not always carried very far. Other activities are scattered over the island and meet the familiar problem of transport. If they are situated on the central highlands, they may supply the local market but are unfavourably situated for export; and if they are on the coast, they are far from the main internal markets. Transport difficulties make it uneconomic to move raw materials and even finished products for any distance.

A wide variety of agricultural raw materials is available for processing, and the oldest-established industries are the rice mills and the tapioca factories, which date back to the beginning of the century. The rice mills supply the local market, and also a small tonnage of long-grained 'riz de luxe' for a traditionally protected French market, which (in 1970) was meeting difficulties in complying with the EEC price equalisation regulations. Rice mills exist around all the larger towns and at the important production centre of Lake Alaotra, but many of them have antiquated equipment, and in general much excess capacity. Rice (approximately 70 per cent extraction from paddy) production is approximately 700,000 tons per annum, of which only 200,000 tons are hulled or milled in the factories, the remainder being pounded by the producers or hulled on small machines owned by co-operatives or rural communes for local consumption. Tapioca, derived from dried cassava, is produced by European-owned factories, mainly near Lake Alaotra, but exports never exceeded 25,000 tons per annum at their height in the early 1950s and the export possibilities for this product, which is imported in large quantities by European countries such as Germany for animal feeding, have still to be exploited. Since yields of up to 20 tons of manioc per acre can be obtained, this might also have an interesting potential for the development of local intensive animal production.

The most modern and best-equipped agro-industry is the sugar industry, controlled by four French companies* operating on the east coast and in the north-west near Majunga, on the island of Nosy-be and at Ambilobe. Exports of sugar (unrefined) have varied considerably since 1960, falling from about 100,000 tons to 56,000 tons in 1968. This is essentially a plantation operation, export-orientated, in which small planters participate much less than on Mauritius, where about 15 per cent of the factory capacity is supplied by small planters. In Madagascar, the bulk of the cane used is grown by the companies on their own land with highly-developed irrigation systems, especially at Ambilobe. The sugar industry was established on the east coast long before the French conquest, and as far back as 1840 planters from Réunion and Mauritius had small sugar factories and distilleries. The capacity for sugar production is much greater but is limited by world markets. Internal consumption is limited by the price (approximately $US 0.25 per kilo), which makes Madagascar the tenth most expensive country in the world for sugar.[23] It is evident that the price is fixed to subsidise in part the cost of production and profit levels of the companies, which have monopoly powers conferred on them by the government under this arrangement.

Other processing industries include oil expressing plants, treating groundnut and cotton-seed for local consumption, and here the government has made a considerable effort since 1965 to improve the quality of edible oils produced. Madagascar produces 30–40,000 tons of groundnuts a year, and is attempting to maintain, against stiff foreign competition, an export trade in nuts of a confectionery quality.

The large cattle population began to be utilised in 1889 when the first meat factory was established at Antongombato near

* CEGEPAR: Nosy-be; SUCOMAD: Brickaville; SOSUMAV: Ambilobe; Sucreries Marseillaises de Madagascar: Namakia, Majunga.

Diego-Suarez. Other factories were established near Tananarive, Tamatave, Fianarantsoa and Tuléar, for which the chief customer for many years was the French army. Soldiers became familiar with Madagascar corned beef, which in army slang is still called 'singe' (monkey), but this preoccupation with a specialised and protected market is the main reason why Madagascar, which has neither foot-and-mouth disease, rinderpest, brucellosis, nor any of the unpleasant African pests and diseases, has not yet built up a large export trade in meat and meat products. However, the elements are there, with the large supplies of cattle and pigs and some experience in running factory and canning operations, and it is certain that present plans being carried out by the government will rapidly expand production in this sector.

Fibres treated include sisal in the extreme south, again an efficient operation run by local entrepreneurs but hampered by world fluctuations in price, and cotton, whose production has expanded considerably in the last ten years. Textile factories for local supply exist at Antsirabe and Majunga, while production of cotton is the main aim of a large (25,000 acre) irrigation project being financed by the Fonds Européen de Développement (FEB) on the Mangoky river on the west coast.

Since independence in 1960, and with considerable government support, a number of new small industries have been set up to supply the local market. Apart from the textile factories, a cigarette factory at Antsirabe supplies more than two-thirds of the Malagasy consumption and exports to Réunion and the Comoro islands. These have been followed by the establishment of breweries, shoe factories, a pharmaceutical factory and an automobile assembly plant. A small plastics factory in Tananarive is one of the few new secondary industries and nothing has yet developed equivalent to the complex of secondary industries around Nairobi or Salisbury. However it is certain that these preliminary investments will be followed by more ambitious programmes, with the expansion of local demand and continuing government support. The problems are those familiar in other developing and predominantly agricultural countries: reluctance of nationals to invest their savings other than in real estate; small inelastic local markets; high cost of transport and certain essential raw materials. This is aggravated in Madagascar by the very high cost of energy, which reached (1970) a maximum of 42 FMG (14d.) per kilowatt in Tuléar.

The high cost of electrical energy is due in part to the limited demand; in turn, the cost itself limits the demand. However, this vicious circle applies to many other goods and services in developing countries, and costs per kilowatt have been reduced in Tananarive since 1965.[24] Some economists have blamed local commercial companies, which hold equity in the private sector of the electricity supply, but the solution is not quite so simple and immediate nationalisation without further investment would not of itself reduce the cost of electrical energy.* The hydro-electric potential of large rivers, such as the Ikopa, and on the numerous falls from the central highlands to the east coast, has been calculated, by engineers of Electricité de France (French electricity board) in various surveys from 1946 to 1965, to be the equivalent of the entire electricity potential of France and is probably much greater. Present hydro-electric installations, notably that on the falls of the Mandraka which supplies Tananarive, have a considerable unused capacity.

Although an oil refinery was established by a consortium of commercial companies at Tamatave in 1965, gasoline and diesel are heavily taxed, and in 1970 petrol of ordinary grade cost 53FMG per litre (6s. 6d. per gallon). Another unused source of energy is the coal deposits of the Sakoa, south of the river Onilahy in the province of Tuléar. This coal, which belongs to the Karoo system of Southern Africa and Southern India, thus belongs to a similar geological system to the Wankie colliery of Rhodesia and the new Zambian coal mine at Mamba north of Lake Kariba. It was exploited by pick and shovel until the end of the Second World War, and small quantities are still used by the meat factory of La Société Rochfortaise at Tuléar. It is near the surface and is entered by a long sloping tunnel, on foot. It has been surveyed by Les Charbonnages de France (French coal board) and the Japanese, and at one time a project valued at $US 60 million was discussed for the establishment of a carbo-chemical complex. But the Sakoa is remote from anywhere, even by Madagascar standards, and this resource is unlikely to be exploited, more especially since the establishment of the oil refinery at Tamatave. A large quantity

---

* Electricity production and supply is furnished in Madagascar in certain regions by the Société d'Electricité de Madagascar, which is state-owned, and by a private company, the Eaux et Electricité de Madagascar.

of 'fuel' remains as a residual from the operation of the refinery, and thus petro-chemical as opposed to carbo-chemical based industries are likely to be given priority.

Mining began in Madagascar with the discovery and extraction of alluvial gold by artisan methods of panning and washing of sand in streams and rivers. Queen Ranavalona 1 (1830–62), as part of her policy to keep foreigners out of Madagascar, forbade the extraction of gold, fearing that any important discovery might attract a 'rush' from outside. Prime Minister Rainilaiarivony lifted this interdict in 1883, and concessions were given from 1885 with the aim of paying off the loan granted by the Comptoir National d'Escompte de Paris to enable the government of Madagascar to pay the indemnity demanded by France under the treaty of 1885. A French concessionnaire, Léon Suberbie, opened a number of workings along the Betsiboka and Ikopa rivers and founded a small mining centre, Suberbieville, near Maevatanana, which has today disappeared. Other French and British concessionnaires worked on the central highlands, and a minor 'gold rush' took place between 1900 and 1905 after the pacification by General Galliéni.

The prospectors worked with pick, shovel and pan, and the 'boom' consisted chiefly in their trying to resell at a profit the areas pegged out. Some more mechanised attempts at extraction were made, one by a British company from the Transvaal which introduced a mechanical drag on the Tsiribihina river near Miandrivazo in 1904. The most important of these operations was the mine at Andavoereka, which went 130 feet underground and had a small industrial plant for crushing and extraction of ore. This mine produced about 5 tons of gold over twenty years, but closed in 1921 since the mining operations were no longer economically feasible. Over the period 1900 to 1960, Madagascar produced about 70 tons of gold, and certainly there remain important unexplored and unexploited resources. However, it will be difficult to interest mining groups, unless a rise in the world price of gold occurs or accessible deposits permitting low-cost extraction are found.

Semi-precious stones, amethysts, garnets, rock crystals, zircons, citrines and tourmalines, are found in many places in Madagascar, and a minor industry has sprung up among a number of Malagasy artisans and lapidaries. It is interesting that, in Imerina, the centre of this work, the profession is largely confined to those of noble descent.

The two most important mineral export products are graphite and mica. Graphite has been mined on an industrial scale since 1907 and is exported at a rate of approximately 16,000 tons per annum. This is a difficult market, since the scale of the Malagasy operation and the high transport costs to the principal clients make it difficult to compete with more important producers, such as the United States and Ceylon. Mica requires a considerable man-power and delicate work to prepare it by splitting, and, while exports reached a maximum of 819 tons in 1928, they have never again reached this figure and were approximately 600 tons in 1966. India is also a serious competitor in this market, with Japan as an important customer.

Since 1946, the Commission d'Energie Atomique (French atomic energy agency) conducted very extensive prospections over the central highlands, the south and the west of Madagascar. Deposits of uranothorianite are exploited in the extreme south behind Fort Dauphin, at Ambovombe and Beloha in particular. Exploration for petroleum continues, and was (in 1970) concentrated on off-shore areas near Majunga. Approximately $US 50 million was spent on prospection from 1945 to 1965 by the Société des Pétroles de Madagascar (SPM).

COMMUNICATIONS

Transport problems are perhaps the biggest single obstacle to economic development in Madagascar. They arise above all from the nature of the relief, from the fact that Madagascar is a long and rather narrow island, and from the torrential rains during four to five months over two-thirds of the island. Paradoxically, it is in the area having a long dry season, rather than on the east coast where it rains throughout the year, that the principal communications problems arise. The first problem was to build roads over mountainous country and to cross numerous swamps and rivers. Madagascar is not a country in which it is sufficient to cut the bush and level the ground to make a dirt road, and road construction to adequate standards requires considerable capital and heavy machinery. The maintenance of roads, under conditions of seasonal rainfall and occasional cyclones on the east coast, is also expensive. The roads are broken up far more by the weather than by the traffic.

At the beginning of the century, all transport was by porterage along foot-paths, and important people and early colonial administrators toured by '*filanzana*', a covered litter which was carried by porters and on which they reclined. Travel by this means ceased only towards 1950 and porters are still necessary for anyone wishing to travel in the forest of the east. The first road was dug out of a footpath by squads of engineers attached to General Duchesne's expeditionary force which landed at Majunga in 1895 and set out towards Tananarive some 375 miles distant. In November 1897, Captain (afterwards Field-Marshal) Lyautey travelled from Maevatanana to Tananarive along this new road in an English dog-cart, and in 1900 General Galliéni made the same trip in the reverse direction in his motor car, a Panhard-Levassor. Regular road transport between the port of Majunga and Tananarive was opened in 1901.

The choice for the principal port of Madagascar lay between Tamatave and Majunga, and, despite various considerations that might have favoured the west coast, existing interests long established on the east coast, and especially the Réunionnais who maintained an important lobby in the French Parliament and had always considered the east coast of Madagascar as part of their 'Lebensraum', fixed the choice on Tamatave. There was already a track and, although the distance is half that to Majunga, the terrain is much more difficult. It is necessary to descend two 'cliffs', one of about 1,950 feet into the valley of the Mangoro, which runs from Lake Alaotra, and the other of 2,275 feet to sea level. This is also an area of high continuous rainfall and is covered by tropical rain forest.

The road was opened to wheeled traffic on January 1, 1901, with bridges over all the rivers except the Mangoro, where there was still a ferry. In the second quarter of 1901, official statistics show that 2,582 carts entered Tananarive coming from Tamatave and Majunga, but that only twenty of these were ox-drawn, since the former porters now pulled hand-carts, three men to a cart carrying one ton. Forage for work oxen was the main problem on these routes. The cost of transport dropped dramatically from 1,100 francs per ton in 1895 ($US 250 per ton) to 250 francs per ton in 1904 ($US 50). In 1903, General Galliéni established a 'correspondance' and 'messageries' service by automobile between Tananarive and Tamatave, which operated until 1909 when the first stage of the railway was completed.

The railway was first roughly surveyed by a member of Galliéni's forces, a commandant of engineers, in 1897. It was built, like railways in East Africa, with immigrant labour, among whom Indians and Chinese founded colonies of traders and shopkeepers, again as the Indians did in East Africa. The line is a one-metre gauge, as on nearly all the railways in former French colonies. The section from Brickaville on the east coast to Tananarive was completed in 1909, but the line from Tamatave to the capital was not opened until 1913. Its construction was not easy, partly because of the very steep gradients to be overcome in climbing from sea level to 4,225 feet in 60 miles and partly because of insecurity from bands of resistants and bandits, or *fahavalo*, who continued to operate for many years after the conquest. What are today stations on this line often began as small forts. This line was continued to Antsirabe in 1912 as the first section linking the capital with Fianarantsoa, but this was interrupted by the First World War and has never been completed, in spite of several projects. A branch line, running from Mormanga on the Tamatave line to Lake Alaotra, was opened in 1923, and a line was built from Fianarantsoa to Manakara on the east coast in 1927. Madagascar has thus two unconnected railway systems. The Manakara line was built at a time when the Betsileo country around Fianarantsoa was destined to become an area of European settlement, but the port of Manakara is an unprotected sea-shore and goods must be loaded by lighter to ships lying in a heavy swell. Lake Alaotra was also an area of European settlement and today remains one of the principal and expanding centres of rice production. A chromite mine having been opened in 1965 at Andriamena to the west of Lake Alaotra, the ore is evacuated by road to the railhead and then by rail to Tamatave for shipment.

The railway between Tananarive and Tamatave has been considerably re-equipped since 1955, although the cyclone of 1959 did considerable damage to the track, which was repaired with a grant from the FED. Although performing an essential service and efficiently run, this railway pays its way through a deliberate policy of limiting the traffic on the road which runs parallel to it. This road, which follows the same track as was formerly used by porters and was enlarged by General Galliéni, is extremely tortuous and narrow. The policy has been one of minimum maintenance to the road, with no improvement to the trajectory, in order to prevent what would undoubtedly be a very rapid expansion of road transport between Tananarive and the coast. The economics of this decision may be disputed, especially since all main railways in East Africa are doubled by a tarred road (among the lines, that from Mombasa to Kampala and that from Beira to Salisbury, both of which are profitable). It may well be that this protectionist policy towards the railway is a contributing factor to the high cost of goods on the central highlands and limits the possibilities for industrial development in this region.

By far the greater part of interior transport of goods and passengers is by automobile, of which 80,991 were registered in 1969.* A major road axis links Majunga to Tuléar via Tananarive, and this has been continued northward by a new road to Port-Berge in the centre of the main tobacco-growing region. The Majunga–Tananarive road was completely tarred by 1970, and the road from Tananarive to Tuléar is tarred to beyond Ambalavao, leaving only about 95 miles of dirt road on this length of 625 miles. The road network along the coasts is much less satisfactory. It is still not possible to motor from Tananarive to Diego-Suarez except in five months of the dry season, nor can many places on the west coast between Morondava and Majunga be reached except at this time. The east coast lacks any kind of a durable network, except for limited and isolated stretches of tarred road north of Tamatave and south of Manakara. During many months of the year, many small towns of local importance, such as Maintirano, are virtually isolated. Detailed and internally consistent plans for the establishment of a rational road-network for Madagascar already exist, but the capital sums involved are very great and the isolation of many areas may not be overcome entirely before 1980 to 1985.

Apart from the French naval base of Diego-Suarez, which is not linked to the rest of the island by an all-weather road, Madagascar has two main ports, Tamatave and Majunga, a smaller but properly-equipped port at Tuléar, and a number of so called

---

* Of this number, 40,544 were private cars. These figures are too high, since many vehicles are wrecked each year and not reported. *Source:* INSRE.

ports, such as Fort-Dauphin, Morombe and Manakara, where ships can lie offshore and be loaded from lighters. The port of Tamatave is by far the most important, and handled approximately 790,000 tons of cargo in 1969. Having a beach protected by a reef, Le Grand-Recif, Tamatave was a port from the late eighteenth century, but it was not until 1929 that construction was begun of quays and related works enabling boats with a draft of 27 to 30 feet to be unloaded alongside the quay. Further works were surveyed in 1968 and construction financed by the World Bank was scheduled to begin after 1970 to enable the port to handle more than 1 million tons per annum. Work was begun on a deep-water port at Majunga in 1939 but was interrupted by the war. Majunga has neither the swell of the Indian Ocean, which penetrates right into the port of Tamatave, nor is it struck by periodic cyclones, such as that which destroyed a good part of Tamatave in 1927 or that of 1959 which cut the railway to Tananarive in many places and swept away a railway viaduct at Brickaville. The major obstacle to the development of Majunga as a port are the enormous deposits of sand brought down by the Ikopa and Betsiboka as a result of continual erosion on the deforested mountains of the central highlands. It was estimated that, between 1939 and 1955, more than 15 feet of sand were deposited in the harbour.

From this diversified base, it is probable that the economy of Madagascar contains the elements necessary for 'take-off': that is, to achieve self-sustained growth within a reasonable time.

The agricultural production pattern is sufficiently varied to provide the possibility of self-sufficiency both in basic foodstuffs and in sources of animal protein, and also of securing increased export income from a fairly wide range of products.

Industrial potential is always an enigma in a developing country, depending on imponderables that are almost impossible to calculate, such as the expectations of foreign investors, and the ability to force an opening among world export-markets for finished or semi-finished products. Providing foreign capital and technical skill become available, Madagascar may well follow a 'modified Japanese' pattern where industries are established, preferably on the coast, importing a high proportion of their raw materials and exporting nearly all their finished products. Madagascar presents certain comparative advantages for such an operation, which will be examined in the next chapter.

Although there are a number of serious gaps in the linking up of outlying regions, the communications network is well-established in its basic elements; its completion is a question of extensions and improvements, which should all be complete by 1978–1980.

The population is a factor of primary importance and is likely to respond positively to the challenge of development prospects, as a result of present ambitious education policies. It may be reasonable to assert that the potential exists in Madagascar to create large-scale modernised production of certain crops and of livestock, and for an ambitious export-orientated industrial programme, which would provide an expanding GDP from 1975 onwards.

If, as is possible, present (1970) mineral prospection leads to the discovery of economically-exploitable petroleum deposits, the picture will become even more favourable. But it is the will of the newly educated elite, now emerging from the lycées, technical schools and the University, which alone can determine whether this undeniable potential will be realised.

8. Development Prospects

THE REVIEW of the productive resources and present production patterns of Madagascar contained in Chapter 7 shows that the country possesses many physical factors favourable to economic development. The development problems of Madagascar are those common to many other tropical countries. Approximately 80 per cent of the population is engaged wholly or partly in agriculture, largely for their own subsistence, leaving only a small proportion of the total production for cash sale. Industrialisation has always been confined mainly to small processing industries for agricultural products, but since 1960 there has been diversification into a limited number of consumer goods industries, almost entirely to supply a local market. The mountainous relief of the island, the existence of numerous large rivers and the great empty spaces separating inhabited zones make transport a major problem. To provide a modern transport network has demanded the investment of considerable capital sums and could never have been carried out without substantial foreign aid from French bilateral and the European Economic Community funds.

Against this may be placed the highly diversified agricultural production pattern, a relatively high level of artisan skills and a considerable gift for learning by which the Malagasy rapidly acquire facility as accountants, mechanical and electronic repair specialists and machine operators. The high percentage of literacy and a comparatively ancient tradition of school attendance provide the raw material for a rapid development of skilled manpower resources. Madagascar, in common with many other developing countries, has a problem of matching economic development with emerging educated young people, to create sufficient and suitable jobs to absorb school-leavers: in 1970, these included 681 'baccalauréats' and 6,785 BEPC.*

* The Baccalauréat corresponds roughly to the British 'A' level and marks the end of secondary school: the brevet élémentaire du premier cycle (BEPC) is given usually at sixteen years to those secondary school pupils who do not proceed to the 'second cycle' leading to the baccalauréat.

THE FIRST FIVE-YEAR PLAN, 1964–69

At independence in 1960, Madagascar was executing the 1958–62 Development Plan.[1] This was the third four-year plan of the post war period and was the successor to the more general development plans issued in 1946 for all the French overseas territories, which corresponded to a similar exercise carried out by the United Kingdom at that time. In 1959 the Commissariat-Général au Plan (Plan Commission) was established, in the Office of the President of the Republic, and was charged with drawing up a Five-Year Plan, 1964–1968.

The previous plans were, in fact, public expenditure programmes, which laid down certain budgetary guidelines within a broad framework of development but which did not aim at structural transformation of the economy based on detailed analysis. The objectives of the Five-Year Plan were based on an analysis of the economy of Madagascar in the ten-year period, 1950–60.[2] While this analysis is not always statistically accurate, owing to inevitable lacunas in such data as areas and crop yields in particular, it has a certain validity as a broad picture of the structure of the Malagasy economy.

The programmes contained in the Plan were drawn up by joint committees formed by the Plan Commission. These bodies contained representatives of one or more ministries and were encouraged to draw up maximum programmes, which the Plan Commission would later reduce to an internally consistent plan within the limits of foreseeable financial resources. This consultation was continued in a parallel operation at a regional level. One of the original features of the Five-Year Plan was its close attention to regional programmes as a structural element of the national plan. Regional consultation was carried out at the prefecture level. A responsible officer was appointed in each prefecture, charged with the preparation of a 'monograph' giving its physical characteristics, population data, the production pattern and development potential. This was drawn up in consultation with the responsible field technicians of each ministry and transmitted to the Plan Commission after preliminary discussion in the prefecture with officials of the Commission.

The Plan thus consisted of two volumes. The first volume contained the National Five-Year Plan, which was approved by

Parliament on June 9, 1964, as the 'Loi-Programme' (Programme Law). It defined the Plan as the framework of economic development over the period 1964–68 and set out the structures for its execution. The Programme Law also approved the level of investment proposed in the Plan, without committing the budget specifically, but stating the proportions of the capital investment proposed that were to be drawn from domestic resources and from foreign aid. The second volume, which was neither published nor submitted to Parliament, contained the regional programmes, one for each of the eighteen prefectures. This was intended to be a working document for use by the Regional Development Committees (Comités techniques régionaux du Plan et de Développement), which were defined by later decrees as the responsible bodies for execution of local projects.

The National Plan was thus mandatory and given the force of law; but, since its objectives were expressed by economic sectors and were not specifically broken down into projects, except for large elements of infrastructure such as airfields and roads, it left considerable freedom of manoeuvre by ministries and a wide field for subsequent revision. Provision was made for periodic reports on physical and financial execution to be submitted to the cabinet. These have appeared regularly, on an annual basis.

The regional presentation of the Plan and the degree of definition were thus less complete than in the development plans of certain African countries. A comparison with the First National Development Plan of Zambia, 1966–70, shows some structural similarities with the Madagascar Plan, but in Zambia the regionalisation was carried to the point where the total national plan was broken down into eight regional programmes, one for each province.[3] There was thus a complete correlation between the National Plan and the sum of the eight regional programmes. A high degree of definition is given, sectors being broken down into projects and located geographically by province. The aim of the Zambia Plan was to give a blue-print for each government official charged with the execution of the Plan. Some of the structures set up in Madagascar are similar to those in Zambia. Thus the Comités techniques régionaux du Plan et de Développement compare with the Provincial Development Committees in Zambia, with similar powers and responsibilities, but in Zambia they are presided over by the minister of state responsible for the province whereas in Madagascar they are presided over by the prefect. Internal consistency was secured in the Zambia Plan by two modified input-output tables, one for 1966 and the other for 1970, showing the expected results of total execution of the Plan. Consistency in the Madagascar Plan was hampered by the absence of National Accounts in an annual series, and an exercise was carried out by which the National Accounts for 1959 were brought up to date in 1962 and projected to 1973. The Five-Year Plan was thus drawn up within a framework of ten-year projections.

Objectives of the Plan

The Programme Law stated that the object of the First Five-Year Plan was 'economic development and the social and cultural promotion of the nation within a socialist framework'; it continued: 'with this aim in view, it seeks to raise the standard of living of the population, and particularly of the peasant'. The growth-rate for the Gross Domestic Product was set at 5.5 per cent per annum, as against a growth rate of approximately 3 per cent registered for the preceding four years.* With a population increase estimated at approximately 2·5 per cent per annum, an increase of consumption levels of approximately 2·5 per cent per annum was allowed for.

The investment programme for the five-year period appeared as follows:

Planned Public Capital Investment, 1964–69

	,000 million FMG	*million* $us
Infrastructure and transport	33·64	122·3
Agriculture	20·6	74·9
Industry	2·25	8·1
Social	10·48	38·1
Various	2·03	7·3
Total	69·00	250·7

The sources of this planned capital investment programme were estimated as follows:

* In the absence of a time-series of national accounts, it is practically impossible to estimate the rate of growth of the GDP of Madagascar.

Planned Resources, 1964–69

	,000 million FMG	*million* $US
Domestic resources	24·8	
Foreign aid	31·2	
Loans	13·0	
Total	69·0	276·2

To this was added an estimate of 14,000 million FMG ($US 56.5 million) of 'human investment', representing the mobilisation of the population; every male between the ages of twenty and fifty was asked to give ten days of labour per year to self-help projects organised by the rural communities. The Plan Commission calculated the value of such an investment on the basis of the legal daily minimum wage, 1962. The National Budget has invested annually approximately 360 million FMG ($US 1·3 million) in self-help programmes in the form of grants and material. This amount has been distributed by prefecture under the programme known as 'Travaux au ras du sol', which is administered by the Ministry of the Interior and controlled by the Ministry of Finance.

EXECUTION OF THE PLAN

The degree of execution of the Five-Year Plan, 1964–68 may be judged from the following tables:

Evolution of the Gross Domestic Product (at market prices)*

	1960	*1964*	*1966*
GDP (millions FMG)	134,000	160,000	174,000
(millions $US)	550	660	710
		(at 245 FMG = $1)	
Structure (%)			
Agriculture	38	34	32
Industry	10	10	11
Transport	9	10	11
Commerce	21	19	18
Services	8	8	9
Government	14	19	20

Source: INSRE, Tananarive.

* Because of the absence of a time-series of national accounts, the figures for 1964 and 1966 must be considered as estimates derived from the 1962 exercise.

Madagascar

Of the planned investment programme, the public sector had mobilised (1969) investment capital totalling 75,000 million FMG ($US 273 million at 275 FMG = $1, post 1969 devaluation of the franc). This represents 108 per cent of the planned investment objective for the public sector of 69,000 million FMG. The aggregate investment achieved by the major sectors is as follows:

Capital Investment: Objectives and Realisation, 1964–69 (millions, FMG)

	Objectives 1st Plan	Realisation	Percentage of Objectives
Agriculture	20,600	26,300	127·6
Industry and Mines	2,200	4,500	204·5
Infrastructure and Transport	33,700	30,600	90·8
Social (education and health)	10,500	5,200	49·5
Various	2,000	8,400	—
Total	69,000	75,000	108·6

Source: Commissariat du Plan, *Cinquième report sur l'execution du Plan Quinquennial, 1964–1968*, Tananarive 1969.

Increased levels of agricultural production have been achieved during the period of execution of the first Plan. Thus, production of paddy, the basic foodstuff, rose from 1,210,000 tons (1965) to 1,600,000 tons (1969), representing 110 per cent of the Plan target. The following table shows the evolution of the main agricultural products over this period:

Agriculture and transport were top priorities for investment under the first Five-Year Plan, as it was held important to provide self-sufficiency in rice and other essential foodstuffs and to increase export income, derived almost entirely from agricultural products. For the agricultural potential to be realised, it was important to improve rapidly the transport network. In these two fields, the financial execution of 127 and 90·8 per cent are satisfactory, even allowing for inevitable cost-push inflation.

Industrial production, manufacturing, building and energy production increased at an average annual rate of 6·5 per cent between 1960 and 1966. Manufacturing output appears to have increased more rapidly since 1966, as is shown by the table below:*

Agricultural Production (main products), 1964–69

		(*Tons*)	
Product	*1964*	*1969*	*Objectives 1968*
Paddy	1,320,000	1,600,000	1,470,000
Coffee	67,000	65,000	57,000
Sugar	105,000	98,000 (est.)	108,000
Vanilla	850	900	900
Cotton (grain)	4,910	14,000	13,300
Ground-nut (in shell)	31,000	46,000	61,000
Cassava	750,000	825,000	890,000
Lima Beans	18,000	16,000	18,600
Tobacco	4,500	5,000	6,750
Cloves	4,800	5,000	4,000
Pepper	1,750	2,600	2,500
Raphia	7,500	7,000	6,850
Banana (export)	6,054	5,125 (1968)	52,000

Industrial Production, 1967–68
(figures in tons, unless otherwise specified)

	1967	*1968*	% *Variation 1967–68*
Electricity (1,000 KW/h)	126,658	139,741	+ 10·3
Electricity consumption by industry (1,000 KW/h)	30,805	35,646	+ 34·5
Tobacco manufactures	1,796	2,039	+ 13·5
Soap	1,304	1,633	+ 25·2
Beer (hectolitres)	53,440	67,928	+ 27·1
Sugar	96,616	99,625	+ 3·1
Edible oils	4,795	8,620	+ 79·8
Cotton textiles	3,649	4,516	+ 23·8
Cement	59,585	67,743	+ 13·7
Bag manufacture	3,756	4,408	+ 17·4
Paper	3,784	4,728	+ 24·9
Matches (1,000 boxes)	24,282	48,133	+ 98·2

Source: INSRE.

* Industrial statistics are particularly inadequate in Madagascar. The first industrial census was completed in 1967 and was published by the INSRE as *Recensement Industriel, 1967*.

There are in Madagascar about 300 enterprises employing more than 100 workers each. In 1967, there were 237,042 wage-earning employees in the private sector. The Ministry of Industry and Mines estimated that capital investment in industry (to which the Investment Code was applied)[4] between 1962 and 1968 totalled 14,000 million FMG ($US 57 million) and that about 7,000 new jobs were created during this period.

The apparently rapid expansion of manufacturing must be related to its narrow base. A narrow range of industries allows many developing countries to achieve an apparently spectacular expansion in industrial output, but one which makes only a minor contribution to the GDP. The industrial development of Madagascar is a major objective of the Second Five-Year Plan, 1970–74.

In the fields of education and health, the base was considerably broader than in many countries at a similar stage of development, because of past colonial policies and continued technical assistance after independence. In 1966, there were 18,629 pupils in 60 secondary schools; in 1969, 24,600 pupils in 74 institutions, including 12 state lycées. The University of Madagascar (Tananarive) had 3,130 students in 1969, as against the Plan objective of 3,500.

EXTERNAL TRADE

External Trade by Value (millions FMG)

	1964	*1965*	*1966*	*1967*	*1968*	*1969*
Exports	22,684	22,632	24,132	25,711	28,608	29,134
Imports	33,432	34,166	35,074	35,885	42,024	46,186
% coverage imports by exports	68	66	69	72	68	63

Source: INSRE

Exports represent about 15 per cent of the GDP and about 90 per cent of these exports are agricultural products, though well-diversified. Imports represent more than 22 per cent of the GDP, but industrial equipment made up 24 per cent of imports by value in 1968 as against 22 per cent in 1964.

Exports increased during the First Plan period by volume and by value, though the terms of trade became more unfavourable as in other developing countries. The following table shows trends of Madagascar's chief exports, by volume, during the period 1964–68, listed by order of value:

Main Exports

	1964 (tons)	1968 (tons)	First Plan Objective 1968 (tons)
Coffee	37,962	53,802	50,000
Rice	27,626	69,032	50,000
Vanilla	528	961	900
Cloves	4,848	12,425	4,000
Sugar	66,796	56,053	55,000
Essential oils	916	1,188	830
Sisal	28,034	25,025	34,100
Raphia	6,807	5,941	6,550
Tobacco	3,505	3,299	7,900
Lima Beans	14,589	10,107	15,000
Bananas	14,458	12,466	52,000

Source: INSRE

BALANCE OF PAYMENTS

Importance, perhaps to an undue degree, is attached by certain writers to Madagascar's chronic balance of payments deficit. The balance of payments of a developing country, and especially of an ex-colony, is an indicator, but it is also relative to many other factors, some of them historic. A surplus or deficit cannot therefore be considered as 'good' or 'bad' in itself. What must be taken into account is the nature of the financial transactions with the outside world which bring about a balance of payments deficit. If this is caused by excessive imports of luxury goods, it is probably bad; if caused by import of capital goods to increase future productivity, it is probably good. In addition, the relationship of the currency of the country with reserve currencies, such as the dollar or sterling must also be considered.

Madagascar is a member of the franc zone, so that the metropolitan franc is the reserve currency of Madagascar, and the financial reserves of the government are in fact held in the Special Account of the French Treasury. Study of the Annual Report of the franc zone, published in Paris, reveals that a majority of the overseas territories and former colonies still belonging to this zone show a chronic balance of payments deficit. This deficit is absorbed in the overall balance of payments between France and the non-franc countries.

Monetary stability in Madagascar, as in the majority of the former French colonies still full members of the franc zone, is achieved by the fact that the former metropolitan country, France, provides a 100 per cent cover for the Malagasy franc (FMG). The assets held against the Malagasy note issue are metropolitan —i.e., held by the French Treasury—and thus an increase in the currency circulation in Madagascar results in a de facto loan to Madagascar by France. This was broadly true of all overseas currencies in colonial times, whether East African shillings or West African pounds issued by a currency board or CFA francs issued by a private bank.[5]

Madagascar's current account deficit, before transfer payments, is financed by substantial transfer payments, by long-term capital inflow and by the statistical item 'errors and omissions', which can be substantial in balance of payments accounting. The current deficit consists of payments for goods and services and of factor payments. Much of this consists of savings out of salaries repatriated to France and of commercial activities. A large portion of the public transfers are offset by private transfers towards France, of which the visible balance of payments represents only a fraction. Since there is complete freedom of banking transactions between France and Madagascar, it is almost impossible to estimate such transfers.

The transfer payments, which are large, and balance the national accounts, consist of technical assistance payments by the French government, and above all the substantial capital grants received from the Fonds d'Aide et de Coopération (FAC—French bilateral aid), and the Fonds Européen de Développement (FED— EEC multilateral aid). To these must be added declining French subsidies to the budget of Madagascar and the assessment of income tax of certain French military and other personnel.

Financial equilibrium in Madagascar is obviously very dependent on the continuation of this level of transfer payments. Government financial policy had been rather conservative between 1960 and 1969, and virtually no recourse had been made to 'deficit financing', nor to mobilising reserves for investment to any undue degree. Servicing of foreign loans outstanding still represents a modest percentage of the GDP, and during the 1970s Madagascar might well extend its indebtedness by financing feasible projects with foreign loans.

RELATION BETWEEN ADMINISTRATIVE AND ECONOMIC STRUCTURES

Structures for utilising investment funds have received much attention in Madagascar. Many countries have found that the traditional function of technical services and ministries adapted itself badly to that of utilising a massive increase of investment funds. While in Madagascar the precursors under the colonial administration of present ministries received substantial investment funds from French sources (FIDES) between 1948 and 1959, a similar problem has been encountered. There have thus been two preoccupations: firstly, to ensure a rapid and efficient utilisation of capital; and secondly, to associate elements of the population closely with government investment.

In the field of agriculture there has been a tendency towards setting up regional development organisations with a fairly autonomous financial and administrative structure; these are termed variously Sociétés d'Aménagement and Aires de mise en valeur rurale (AMVR). The co-operative movement has been similarly encouraged under government inspiration; it is controlled by the Commissariat à la Coopération.

The participation of the population has been secured by the continuation of the self-help programme, travaux au ras du sol, with a high rate of execution of small irrigation works, fuel-wood plantations and local roads. A more recent development has been the creation of the syndicats de communes, associations of rural communes for development projects and marketing of agricultural products. These associations have been equipped by the state with tractors, hangars and transport and are an important move towards 'autogestion', or autonomous bodies of socialist inspiration concerned with economic development of direct interest to the population.

The Five-Year Plan was designed primarily to define more precisely the economy of Madagascar, and, within this framework, to indicate certain priorities and objectives for development. It was a sectorial plan, for the most part, not being broken down into projects subjected to detailed costing and precise geographical location. Thus the value of this Plan lay rather with the impetus it gave the numerous bodies, public and private, charged with the development of specific sectors or activities.

It should be emphasised that planned development did not begin with the 1964–69 Plan. From 1950 to 1960 Madagascar benefited from substantial investment funds from France, with a considerable reinforcement of expatriate personnel and a rapid increase in the training of Malagasy to fill responsible posts. With the advent of independence, and particularly during the period covered by the first Five-Year Plan, marked progress has been made in securing the participation of the rural masses and in orienting the administration towards economic development as its most important function.

The importance of a close relation between the administration and programmes of economic development is often neglected by academic economists. The paternalistic approach of colonial administrations enabled dynamic district commissioners to lay down much infrastructure, and even to modify local production patterns. The role of the administration of an independent country is no longer to compel but rather to animate the population. It is this animation, if wisely carried out, which creates the 'capacity for absorption' of capital investment funds, without which these funds remain unspent or are wasted.[6]

In Madagascar, the setting up of the rural commune as the basic unit, not only of administration, as in France, but also of development, and putting it under the tutelage of the prefect has provided a most important link between government programmes and the population. It is the villages making up the rural communes who themselves propose projects later included in the programme of travaux au ras du sol, carried out with government funds entrusted to the rural mayor, under the supervision of the prefect and the sub-prefect. It is the prefect, sitting as chairman of the regional development committee, who is charged with the co-ordination of representatives of technical services and with ensuring the execution of the National Plan within the prefecture. Development thus comes from above, with national programmes executed within the prefecture, and from below, with a mass of small projects—irrigation, local roads, fuel-wood plantations, buildings —proposed and executed by the rural population themselves.

The role of the Ministry of the Interior is thus paramount in development as it is seen by the mass of the population. The territorial administration—prefects, sub-prefects and chefs de canton—depends directly from this Ministry, while the rural mayors are under their supervision. The Ministry approves the programmes au ras du sol and secures the grants from the Ministry of Finance. In addition, the Ministry of the Interior supervises the programmes of the syndicats de communes and assists them by providing equipment and funds and by giving advice on the marketing of their produce.

EFFECTS ON THE STANDARD OF LIVING OF THE POPULATION

What are the concrete results of these programmes and structural innovations as they affect the rural masses whom they are designed to benefit? Here it would be convenient to quote statistics based on detailed family budget surveys which showed specific increases in individual consumption and income levels. Speaking in broad aggregate terms, private and government consumption levels for the years 1960 to 1967 appear as follows:

	1960	*1964*	*1965*	*1966*	*1967*
Population (millions)	5,300	5,940	6,070	6,200	6,330
GDP (,000 FMG)	128,600	161,700	168,200	176,800	187,500
Total private and government consumption (,000 FMG)	109,400	126,300	133,300	139,900	145,200

Source: INSRE

It is true that these figures mean little in themselves. They indicate modest expansion, which must be deflated by the increase in population, rise in retail prices and variations in the terms of trade as regards export prices of principal products. A detailed analysis would be possible only if we possessed information enabling us to assess movements in income and in purchasing power of much smaller groups of people rather than the broad aggregate represented by the total population.

Per capita income figures for any region must be treated with similar caution. They will be higher, relatively, for the extreme south of Madagascar, owing to the presence of a few large sisal plantations, than for more densely-populated regions (near Tananarive) containing mainly small peasant farmers with a relatively high level of individual productivity. Economists have put us on guard against facile acceptance of aggregate national income or per capita income figures.[7] Estimates of changes in standards of living in Madagascar must often rest on subjective observations, and on the opinions of those who have lived for many years in close contact with specific populations.

What truth is there in the views of those who argue that development is sluggish and that there are major obstacles to the expansion of the economy?[8] Gendarme's arguments, repeated in Balogh's *Unequal Partners*, examine the 'pacte coloniale' or the economic relations between a colony and the metropolitan power. The facts are true, but they are true not only of Madagascar. Unequal partnerships exist between almost all economically active countries and also within those countries themselves. Thus the United States and the European Economic Community have their underdeveloped regions: for instance, the southern states of the United States, Brittany and the Massif Central in France. Indeed, an 'unequal partnership' exists in the economic relations of the United States and Western Europe.[9]

The metropolitan-inspired structures were certainly designed for the profit of individuals and companies based outside the colony. But, at that particular time, these were the only sources of capital and entrepreneurship available to the colonies. There was never any surge of capital and entrepreneurial settlers towards the tropical colonies similar to the tremendous development of temperate 'empty' lands such as Canada, New Zealand, Argentina and parts of Australia in the late nineteenth century. Neither were the products of the tropical countries those which found an immediate market in the expanding economies of the industrial countries, such as the wheat of Canada, the wool of Australia and Argentine meat.

ECONOMIC PROSPECTS, 1970–80

If the economic structures of Madagascar have been slow to evolve, this is mainly because nothing had emerged to take their place. Entrepreneurship among individual Malagasy is slowly evolving and will undoubtedly make rapid progress before 1980. But skilled management personnel, capable of conducting complex investment and commercial operations, are still rare in Madagascar, though less so than in many countries in Africa.

The obstacles to development in Madagascar, apart from the transport difficulties already referred to, lie in the capacity to mobilise resources and productivity in the modern sense of 'management'. The potential for such a mobilisation is certainly to be found in the human capital represented by the Malagasy population, in its capacity for education and in the dynamism it has always shown towards accepting and utilising knowledge introduced from outside.

A cautious evaluation of the development prospects of Madagascar up to 1980 would perhaps begin by assessing the role of the human potential in such an evolution. It is highly probable that the Malagasy can absorb skills at a rate comparable to certain populations of the Far East, such as those of Japan and Taiwan. The geographical position of Madagascar, with the gradual eclipse of the Suez Canal and especially with the evolution of very large ships which cannot pass through any canal, has put Madagascar back on the main shipping routes, where it was before 1867. Before the Canal was opened, ships from Europe called at Madagascar to take on supplies on their way to and from the Far East. Now, once again, the major shipping routes pass along its west coast, through the Moçambique Channel. The country is thus well-placed for the establishment of industries for re-export, based on imported raw materials and the comparative advantages offered by the quality of manpower available and the economies offered by large shipping units.

The rapid development and lowering costs of air freight

transport will radically alter trade patterns and reduce former disadvantages of distance from supplies and markets. Energy will be no problem to Madagascar, which possesses an enormous hydro-electric potential on the 'rift' mountain range which runs along its east coast and in the great rivers with permanent flow which descend more gradually to the west.

Specific sectors appear as likely to provide important growth points in the Malagasy economy. In 1970 Madagascar had not yet reached the stage when agricultural supply of major products becomes elastic, so that production expands and new methods are adopted in response to greater price incentives. However, it is possible that this stage is not far off for certain products and that a breakthrough may be achieved during the 1970s.

The demand for certain products which Madagascar is well-equipped to supply may well provide the necessary price-incentive during this decade. World consumption of meat is rising more rapidly than supplies, and this was already evident in 1969 price trends. The rapid expansion of wage- earning urban populations in many countries will accelerate demand for meat and certain livestock products during the 1970s. Madagascar possesses a cattle population estimated at approximately 10 million head, and this resource can, if modern methods of animal husbandry are applied (as are at present being undertaken on a pilot scale), result in exports in meat and by-products from one million animals per annum, at a modest utilisation rate of 10 per cent, and of two million if a rate approaching that of Uruguay, at 25 per cent, were to be aimed at. It can be seen that the export of 150,000 to 200,000 tons of meat per annum is an attainable objective for which the technical methods are already known.

Rice is consumed by a large majority of the world's population, including those countries having in 1970 the highest birth-rate. A recent survey predicts a world shortage of 5 million tons in 1975 to be experienced by the major importers, and states: 'the most urgent problem concerning rice is that of production'.[10] The survey predicts a regular expansion in world trade in rice, in which Madagascar could certainly benefit, making use of its inherited techniques and skill, its favourable water-resources, and the vast unused potential of the great river-valleys such as the Mangoky and the Tsiribihina on the west coast.

Coffee, which is Madagascar's major export, is still hampered by world over-production. However, many countries which now consume hardly any coffee or where consumption is artificially limited by high internal taxation could substantially increase their imports in response to national fiscal adjustments. This may well be included in future arrangements for aiding developing countries by trade rather than aid, which has been the aim of the UNCTAD conferences in the 1960s.

The highlands of Madagascar present important climatic advantages for the production of fruit and vegetables for tropical urban societies, and the development of air freight might aid a rapid expansion of markets in neighbouring tropical Africa. There are also a series of 'special crops', such as pimentos and dwarf maize, for which Europe and the United States provide an expanding and unsatisfied market. Urbanisation in Madagascar is unlikely to approach in any way the creation of such a megalopolis as Calcutta, and is likely to be confined to Tananarive. However, the population of the Malagasy capital, which will be approaching one million towards the end of the century, will provide a substantial market for agricultural products.

Mention has already been made of the scope for industrial development in Madagascar, whereby raw materials would be imported and the greater part of the product exported. Attention has been focused during the 1960s on the implantation of United States companies in Europe. On December 27, 1969, the London *Economist* published an article that foresaw the possibility of an equivalent trend in the implantation of large international firms in the developing countries.

> There is tentative reason to hope that, just as American companies flooded to Europe in the 1960s in order to take advantage of lower European wage rates, so these multi-national companies in the 1970s might begin to spread a significant proportion of their investment projects to the poorer countries in order to take advantage of their lower wage rates still.

Madagascar offers to such enterprises a number of comparative advantages which include a stable political scene, available and teachable man-power and proximity to the new sea-routes following the indefinite closure of the Suez Canal.

The mineral resources of the complicated geology of Madagascar have been mapped in detail as they occur on the surface, but prospecting by remote-sensing techniques and using modern geo-chemical, seismic and other methods was in 1970 beginning to indicate mineral deposits of economic potential. Considerable activity was taking place among oil-companies with concessions off-shore and on the west coast, particularly in the Majunga area where drilling was in progress. Within the period 1970–80, Madagascar may export petroleum, chromite, nickel, copper, and rare minerals such as those derived from ilmenite, rare earths, and perhaps also radio-active materials. All these are known to exist.

Madagascar has a great tourist potential in the vast sandy beaches of the west coast. Here the climate is dry for nine months of the year and summer sunshine occurs just when North America and Northern Europe are plunged into their long winter. The 'winter' in this region of Madagascar, with its day temperatures of 20 °C, is warmer than many northern summers. The airfields at Tuléar, Morondava and Majunga will either take small jet aircraft already or, as they lie on flat land, could easily be expanded to do so. The development of mass air transport by the giant airliners which will be in service in the 1970s may well be important for the development of tourism, and especially of collective tours, to Madagascar. Its long white beaches will probably not remain undisturbed for long.

Statistical Appendix

TABLE III shows the evolution of the economy of Madagascar between 1958 and 1967—that is, during the period of transition from French colonial administration to independence, during the first years of political independence and during the initial execution period of the First Five-Year Development Plan. The National Income figures, or Gross Domestic Product (GDP), represent an estimate of the sum of the gross products of goods and services in Madagascar. The gross product is the gross output, or gross value of all goods and services produced during the year from which is deducted the value of goods and services consumed in the production processes in the same period.

While such figures are an indicator of change, at the same time they may give a misleading picture of a country whose economy is mainly determined by a large rural population, only a small fraction of whose production enters the exchange economy—that is, is sold for money. The normal definition of GDP excludes specifically such items as farmers' and fishermen's consumption of their own products. Thus an increase in autoconsumption would not be reflected in national income figures, yet at the same time contributes substantially to the individual well-being of the rural population. Other figures which escape national income statistics include: local trading of goods and services between families and villages; local transport services; improvements in rural housing carried out by the people themselves; and benefits arising from government investment in rural areas, in new schools, dispensaries roads (the 'feed-back' effect of investment in social and physical infrastructure). Since little is known statistically about changes in the subsistence sector of agricultural production, the rate of growth of the economy may well be higher than would appear from the GDP figures which assume that subsistence output is stationary.* The application of national income figures designed for developed economies, where by far the greater part of goods and

---

* Colin Clark, *The Economics of Subsistence Agriculture*, London 1964, examines in detail the contribution of subsistence agriculture to the monetary economy and to welfare.

services produced are paid for in money, may thus be misleading.

However, to detect, and perhaps measure, growth in an economy such as that of Madagascar, where almost all the rural population touch the monetary economy at certain points, although only occasionally, one may seek other indicators and deduce rates of change from these. For example, a high proportion of the monetary expenditure of the rural population will go on two items—textiles for clothing, and transport equipment. They do not directly purchase transport equipment, except for bicycles, but their use of such equipment determines its purchase by entrepreneurs.

The rate of change in expenditure on these two items is shown by the following Table I.

Table I

Million FMG

	1966	*1967*	*1968*	% *increase* over 3 yrs
Textiles	2,256·2	2,895·1	3,843·9	+ 70
Transport equipment	2,557·2	3,693·5	4,565·5	+ 81

Source: INSRE

These figures, taken from the external trade returns, do not include local production of textiles, whose value was approximately 2,000 million FMG for the three-year period. Although an important proportion of these two items is consumed by the urban population, they also serve as a significant indicator of rural consumption.

Tables VI and VII, showing the pattern of external trade over three years, indicates the wide variety of Madagascar's exports, due to the climatic diversity of the country.

From the trade figures (Table VIII) one might deduce an important negative trade balance; however, the main positive items in the balance of payments are the large transfer payments mainly made on public account. These include foreign capital grant aid payments from the Fonds d'Aide et de Coopération (FA—French) and the Fonds Européen de Développement (FED—European Economic Community Development Fund), payment of French technical assistance personnel and of a number of technical and scientific institutes maintained by France for Madagascar, income tax paid by French civilian and military personnel, and similar items. These transfer items balance out the balance of payments, of which the trade balance is a major element.

In addition, by belonging to the franc zone, Madagascar enjoys considerable benefits, in common with other franc zone countries whose issuing institute (corresponding in certain functions to a central bank) is linked to the French Treasury by a convention covering a joint operating account. To such countries France guarantees the unlimited convertibility of their money (in this case the FMG or franc malgache) through the machinery provided by the joint operating account. France also provides assistance in running the instituts d'emission of these countries.

As a reciprocal obligation, franc zone countries allow free and unlimited transfer of funds between themselves and France and align their exchange control regulations with those in force in France. Franc zone countries all have equal rights of access to the foreign exchange market of Paris, while the greater part of the foreign exchange reserves held by their instituts d'emission are held in French francs.*

* Franc zone countries (1968) were Ivory Coast, Dahomey, Upper Volta, Mauretania, Niger, Senegal and Togo, with a single Institut d'Emission of the 'Union monétaire ouest-africaine'; Cameroun, the Central African Republic, Congo-Brazzaville, Gabon and Chad (Zone d'Emission de la Banque Centrale des Etats d'Afrique équatoriale et du Cameroun); Madagascar (Institut d'Emission malgache); Mali (since March 30, 1968). Algeria, Morocco and Tunisia have a looser monetary association with France but are included in the franc zone of economic and monetary co-operation.

Table II Population: Distribution by Province and Nationality (January 1, 1970)

Province	Malagasy	French*	Comorians	Indians†	Chinese	Other foreigners	Total
Tananarive	1,716,265	12,054	2,893	1,500	1,748	1,427	1,735,887
Fianarantsoa	1,760,157	3,289	214	928	2,204	239	1,767,031
Tamatave	1,131,354	4,110	886	1,214	3,291	308	1,141,163
Majunga	827,699	3,315	14,761	5,402	105	943	853,223
Tuléar	1,106,552	2,075	1,024	4,207	203	599	1,114,642
Diego-Suarez	558,062	7,135	16,716	2,643	1,931	1,205	587,692
Total	7,100,089	31,978	36,494	15,894	9,482	4,721	7,198,640

Source: Institut de la Statistique, INSRE. Some figures are provisional, and the total should be regarded as an upward limit, subject to errors up to minus 7 per cent.

* Includes French citizens of Réunion Island origin.

† The term "Indians" includes a majority of Moslems of Pakistani affiliation.

Table III Evolution of Leading Indicators of the Economy: 1958–67

	1958	*1967*
Population	4,976,000	6,330,000*
GDP (market prices)	114,000 million FMG	187,500 million FMG*
	414 million $US	765 million $US
Wages and salaries, public and private sectors	16,000 million FMG	53,000 million FMG
	58 million $US	216 million $US
Total gross capital formation	10,000 million FMG	19,000 million FMG
	40 million $US	77 million $US
Imports	26,600 million FMG	35,800 million FMG
	108 million $US	146 million $US
Exports	20,500 million FMG	25·700 million FMG
	84 million $US	97 million $US
Electricity production	70 × 10⁶ KW	127 × 10⁶ KW

Source: INSRE
* = estimate

Table IV Agricultural Production

	1965–66	*1966–67*	*1967–68*
Paddy	1,141,000	1,350,000	1,470,000
Ground-nuts	28,700	32,000	47,000
Lima beans (Pois du Cap)	15,000	8,200	10,000
Bananas (export)	18,000	32,000	46,720
Coffee	43,000	53,000	71,000
Vanilla	650	1,000	1,000
Pepper	1,300	2,200	2,500
Cloves	6,500	500	13,000
Cacao	410	500	643
Cashew-nuts	700	700	700
Tobacco (chewing)	556	763	1,046
Tobacco (leaf-cigarette)	3,875	2,579	3,344
Sisal	27,717	23,332	22,500
Raphia	7,000	7,000	8,000
Cotton (seed)	5,800	5,374	9,155
Castor oil seed	1,065	1,565	1,200
Tung oil seed	10,400	6,400	6,400
Wine (hectolitres)	15,126	12,500	10,769

Source: Projet de Loi des Finances, 1969, INSRE

Table v Industrial Production

	Unit	1965	1966	1967	1968	1969
Electricity production	1,000 kT	102,167	110,273	126,658	139,800	150,300
Electricity (industrial consumption)	1,00 kT	16,073	19,411	23,593	34,600	35,800
Tobacco (plug)	Tons	1,071	1,185	920	n.a.	n.a.
Tobacco (manufactured)	Tons	116	111	83	n.a.	n.a.
Cigarettes	Tons	705	738	793	n.a.	n.a.
Soap	Tons	3,322	1,268	1,304	2,034	4,084
Beer	Hectolitres	34,611	49,939	53,440	67,928	79,398
Sugar	Tons	105,002	109,175	106,616	99,625	98,050
Groundnut oil	Tons	4,380	2,410	4,957	5,284	n.a.
Cotton cloth	Tons	2,613	3,030	3,649	4,516	4,144
Sacks	Tons	2,742	2,723	3,756	4,408	3,907
Cement	Tons	39,192	50,714	59,585	67,743	77,079
Tapioca	Tons	4,409	3,851	6,477	5,348	5,620
(fecule)	Tons	901	971	1,271	1,685	1,646
Graphite	Tons	17,015	16,411	16,484	16,071	17,114
Mica	Tons	630	712	738	838	1,182
Cattle (factory slaughterings)	Head	77,000	78,571	59,979	67,539	67,594
Cattle (manufactured products)	Tons	11,500	11,598	9,276	9,730	9,473
Pigs (factory slaughterings)	Head	6,700	5,881	4,554	4,092	4,862
Pigs (manufactured products)	Tons	450	369	327	325	406

Table VI Composition of Main Exports (28 Products) at Current Producers' Prices

	(*million* FMG)			% Varia-tion '68/69
	1967	*1968*	*1969*	
Coffee	8,121·9	8,803·3	8,270·2	− 6.1
Vanilla	1,672·0	2,529·9	3,012·6	+ 19·1
Rice	1,854·2	3,047·2	2,438·3	− 20·0
Sugar	2,137·8	1,575·0	1,656·0	+ 5·1
Petroleum products	982·6	984·8	1.023·2	+ 3·9
Canned meat	799·5	664·6	915·0	+ 37·7
Clove essence	369·2	723·3	907·1	+ 25·4
Sisal	721·3	748·5	875·1	+ 16·9
Meat	528·0	575·1	663·2	+ 15·3
Pepper	259·3	491·9	565·2	+ 14·9
Tobacco	482·7	382·5	541·6	+ 41·6
Lima beans	340·3	487·6	521·2	+ 6·9
Raphia	918·4	698·3	515·9	− 26·1
Graphite	423·3	432·7	508·9	+ 17·6
Hides and skins	372·3	311·9	466·6	+ 49·6
Fish, shell-fish	159·5	282·1	460·1	+ 63·1
Cinnamon	67·5	66·7	408·7	+512·7
Cloves	875·6	1,958·2	497·2	+123·6
Mica	259·6	303·1	390·3	+ 28·8
Live cattle	295·8	277·2	300·1	+ 8·3
Groundnuts	363·7	301·1	247·2	− 17·9
Oil-cake and bran	152·7	286·7	238·6	− 16·8
Beans	196·7	152·2	224·3	+ 47·4
Timber, wood mfgs.	122·7	168·1	221·8	+ 31·9
Chromite ore	—	—	205·9	—
Tapioca	240·0	245·4	198·9	− 18·9
Cigarettes	228·3	167·9	184·1	+ 9·6
Bananas	263·6	159·5	183·8	− 15·2
Total	23,277.6	26,824·8	26,551·0	
Total exports	25,711·9	28,607·9	29,134·0	+ 1·8

Source: INSRE, Tananarive

Table VII Composition of Imports at Current Prices (*million* MG) F

	1967	1968	1969	% Variation '68/69
Raw materials	7,376·6	9,082·0	10,712·0	+19·9
Petroleum (crude and oil products)	1,527·8	1,951·6	2,289·7	+17·3
Capital goods	8,681·5	9,885·0	11,982·4	+21·3
Food and food products	3,759·5	4,372·6	5,795·2	+32·5
Consumer goods	14,539·9	16,732·9	15,408·3	− 7·9
Total	35,885·3	42,024·1	46·187·6	+ 9·9

Source: INSRE, Tananarive

Table VIII. External Trade Summary: 1964–68

	1964	1965	1966	1967	1968
Imports					
Quantity (tons)	435,953	540,606	602,746	624,010	792,170
Value					
('000,000 FMG)	33,452	34,166	35,074	35,885	42,024
('000 $US)	136,000	139,000	143,000	146,000	172,000
Exports					
Quantity (tons)	303,649	287,345	378,728	489,402	561,507
Value					
('000,000 FMG)	22,654	22,632	24,132	25,711	28,608
('000 $US)	92,000	92,000	98,000	105,000	117,000

Source: Commissariat au Plan, *5ème Rapport*, September 1969

Table IX Money and Banking

	(million FMG*)*			
	1965	*1966*	*1967*	*1968*
Total money supply	40,598	44,201	46,015	51,553
('000 $US)	148,000	160,000	167,000	189,000
Currency in circulation	15,392	16,506	18,939	19,097
Bank deposits and post office cheques (CCP)	16,932	19,237	21,312	25,528
Deposits with savings bank (Caisse d'Epargne)	1,298	1,377	1,431	1,735
Commercial banks—Advances				
short-term loans	28,890	31,520	37,156	38,043
medium-term loans	1,932	2,904	3,182	4,677
long-term loans	1,710	2,201	2,560	3,679

Source: Rapport de l'Institut d'Emission, 1969

Notes and References

INTRODUCTION

1. See Alexander Wetmore, "Recreating Madagascar's Giant Extinct Bird", *National Geographic Magazine*, October 1967.
2. The full title is *Tantara ny Andriana eto Madagasikara*, collected by Father Francois Callet, sj, 1875–83, published Tananarive 1908.
3. Etienne de Flacourt, *Histoire de la Grande Isle de Madagascar*, Paris 1661; Mayeur, "Voyage au pays d'Ancove, 1785", *Bulletin de l'Académie Malgache*, Tananarive 1913 ('Ancove', from Hova—thus, Imerina); Mayeur, "Voyages dans le Nord au pays des Séclaves, 1774", *Bulletin de l'Académie Malgache*, Tananarive 1912 ('Seclaves', from Sakalava); Dumaine, *Mémoires sur Madagascar*, Paris 1792.
4. Alfred Grandidier, *Histoire physique, naturelle et politique de Madagascar*, Paris 1908–28.

1. THE LAND

1. J. H. Wellington, *Southern Africa*, Cambridge 1955.
2. *National Geographic Magazine*, Vol. 132, No. 4, October 1967: Special Supplement, "Indian Ocean Floor".
3. Ronald Good, *The Geography of the Flowering Plants*, London 1953.
4. M. Hachiuska, *The Dodo and Kindred Birds, or the Extinct Birds of the Mascarene Islands*, London 1953.
5. Wellington, op. cit.
6. Much of this chapter is derived from published material of the Service Géologique de Madagascar, and in particular of H. Besaire, who created this service and has contributed a vast mass of published material. Geological maps covering the whole country have been published at 1 : 200,000, 1 : 500,000 and 1 : 1,000,000. Besaire has also published a tectonic map of the Island at 1 : 2,500,000 (1957) and a geomorphological sketch-map at 1 : 1,000,000 (1957).
7. H. Besaire, *Considérations sur le Socle ancien de Madagascar: comparison avec l'Afrique Orientale*, Service Géographique de Madagascar, Tananarive 1900; C. Robequain, "Géologie et Morphologie à Madagascar", *Annales de Géographie*, Paris 1953.
8. C. Robequain, *Madagascar et les Bases Dispersées de l'Union Française*, Paris 1958.
9. R. P. C. Poisson, "Accidents tectoniques et tremblements de terre à Madagascar", *Bulletin Géologique de Madagascar*, Tananarive 1949. Of forty-seven earth tremors recorded between 1929 and 1949 at the Observatory of Tananarive, nineteen had their centre on the upper part of the Mangoro, which drains the southern portion of the valley in which Lake Alaotra is situated.

10. Meteorological data quoted in this chapter is taken from the publications of the Service Météorologique de Madagascar. Other valuable data and analysis will be found in P. Duverge, *Principes de Météorologie dynamique et types de temps à Madagascar*, Publications du Service Météorologique de Madagascar, Tananarive 1949; J. Ravet, *Atlas Climatologique de Madagascar*, Publications du Service Météorologique de Madagascar, Tananarive 1948; and "Notice sur la Climatologie de Madagascar et des Comoros", *Mémoires de l'Institut Scientifique de Madagascar*, Tananarive 1952.

11. R. Jalu and A. Viaut, "La Circulation générale dans le Sud-Ouest de l'Océan indien méridional", *Comptes-rendus de l'Académie des Sciences*, Paris 1952.

12. Robequain, op. cit.

13. H. Humbert, *Les Territoires phytogéographiques de Madagascar: leur cartographie*, Paris 1954.

14. Ravet, op. cit.

15. A. Aubreville, *Contribution a la Paléohistorie des Fôrets de l'Afrique Tropicale*, Paris 1949.

16. A. Aubreville, *Climats, Forêts et Désertification de l'Afrique Tropicale*, Paris 1949.

17. H. Perrier de la Bathie, *Biogéographie des Plantes de Madagascar*, Paris 1936, estimates the African element as 27 per cent of the total flora, the Asiatic at 7 per cent. These percentages are confirmed by H. Humbert, "Origines de la Flore de Madagascar", *Mémoires de l'Institut Scientifique de Madagascar*, Tananarive 1959.

18. R. Good, *Madagascar and New Caledonia: a problem in plant geography*, Blumea No. 6, London 1950.

19. See "Upper Chalk Zone" in Lake and Rastall, *Textbook of Geology*, London 1958.

20. Humbert, op. cit.

21. P. E. Richards, *The Tropical Rain Forest*, Cambridge 1952.

22. Philip J. Darlington, Jr., *Zoogeography: The Geographical Distribution of Animals*, New York 1957.

23. P. J. Darlington and A. L. Rand, "The Distribution and Habits of Madagascar Birds", *Bulletin of the American Museum of Natural History*, New York 1936.

24. Darlington, *Zoogeography*, op. cit.

25. David Attenborough, *Zoo Quest to Madagascar*, London 1961. This popular and quite accurate account of a collecting expedition gives much information in an easily assimilable form on the Madagascar fauna.

26. D. A. Hoojer, "Pygmy Elephant and Giant Tortoise", *Science Monthly*, 1951.

2. THE PEOPLE: ORIGINS TO 1800

1. Dr Albert Rakoto-Ratsimamanga, "Tâche pigmentaire congénitale et Origines des Malgaches", *Revue Anthropologique*, Paris 1940;

303

Marie-Claude Chamla, *Recherches Anthropologiques sur l'Origine des Malgaches*, Mémoires du Museum, Paris 1958.

2. Hubert Deschamps, *Histoire de Madagascar*, Paris 1960.

3. P. M. Vérin, *Les recherches archéologiques a Madagascar*, Azaniz 1, 1966; P. Gaudebout and E. Vernier, "Notes sur une Campagne de Fouilles à Vohémar, Mission Rasikajy, 1941", *Bulletin de l'Académie Malgache*, Tananarive 1941.

4. Father François Callet, *Tantara ny Andriana eto Madagasikara*, Tananarive 1908; Emile Birkeli, "Les Vazimba de la Côte Ouest", *Mémoires de l'Académie Malgache*, Tananarive 1936.

5. John Layard, *The Stonemen of Malekula*, London 1946.

6. G. Ferrand, "L'Origine africaine des Malgaches", *Journal Asiatique*, Paris 1908.

7. E. Ralaimihoatra, *Revue de Madagascar*, 1948; and *Histoire de Madagascar*, Tananarive 1965.

8. Cabot L. Briggs, *The Living Races of the Sahara Desert*, Peabody Papers, Harvard University 1958.

9. Callet, op. cit.

10. Ibid.

11. Samuel W. Matthews, "Science Explores the Monsoon Sea", *National Geographic Magazine*, October 1967; US Navy Hydrographic Service, *Atlas of Surface Currents*, Washington 1950.

12. C. D. Darlington, *Chromosome Botany and the Origin of Cultivated Plants*. London 1963: 'The hexaploidy of the sweet potatoe, *Ipomoea batatas*, both in Peru and Polynesia . . . demonstrates the spread of the sweet potatoe from Peru to Polynesia. . . . It was later from Tahiti, as Burkill and Barrau have pointed out, that the Polynesians carried the sweet potato to the less equatorial regions where it became indispensable, namely Hawaii and New Zealand.' See also I. H. Burkill, *A Dictionary of the Economic Products of the Malay Peninsular*, London 1935.

13. Such as Edrissi in the twelfth century and Ibn-al-Mudjawir in the *Tarik al Mustanir* in the thirteenth century; see G. Ferrand, "Les Iles Ramny, Lamery, Waq-Waq, Komor des géographes arabes, et Madagascar", *Journal Asiatique*, Paris 1907, and "Le Kouen-Louen et les anciennes navigations dans les Mers du Sud", *Journal Asiatique*, Paris 1919.

14. Alfred and Guillaume Grandidier, *Collection des Ouvrages Anciens concernant Madagascar*, 9 vols., Paris 1903–20.

15. Deschamps, op. cit.

16. An early but thorough attempt was made by a Norwegian missionary in *Madagascar Land og Folk*, Christiana 1876.

17. Etienne de Flacourt, *Relation de la Grande Isle de Madagascar*, 1642–1660, Paris 1661.

18. A long list of miscellaneous words which appeared to the author to be the same in Malagasy and Arabic is contained in L. Dahle, "The influence of the Arabs on the Malagasy Language", *Antanararivo Annual*, 1876. The Reverend Lars Dahle wzs one of the founders

of the Norwegian Mission in Madagascar. His most important work is *Le Folklore malgache* (1877) of 457 pages, containing 300 proverbs and 84 tales. He was evidently a considerable Arabic scholar also. G. Ferrand, *Les Musulmans à Madagascar et aux Comores*, Publications de l'Ecole des Lettres d'Alger, 3 vols., Paris, 1891, 1893, 1902, is the most detailed and authoritative study of the Muslim influences on Madagascar.

19. Deschamps, op. cit. The comparative study he refers to is Curt Sachs, *Les Instruments de Musique à Madagascar*, Institut d'Ethnologie, Paris 1938.
20. Roland Portères, *Vieilles Agricultures de l'Afrique inter-tropicale: Agronomie Tropicale*, Paris 1950.
21. Albuquerque, in Grandidier, op. cit.
22. Henri Lavondes, *Bekoropoka: Quelques aspects de la vie familiale et sociale d'un village malgache*, Paris 1967.
23. Ibid.
24. Reverend T. T. Matthews, *Thirty Years in Madagascar*, Religious Tract Society, London 1904.
25. Deschamps, op. cit.
26. Walter Hammond, *A Paradox proving that the Inhabitants of Madagascar are (for temporal things) the Happiest People of the World*, London 1640.
27. Richard Boothby, *A Brief Discovery or Description of the most famous Island of Madagascar or St Laurence, in Asia Near unto the East Indies*, London 1646.
28. Quoted in translation in Grandidier, op. cit.
29. See François Martin, *Mémoires*, Paris 1665–68; and Souchu de Rennefort, *L'Histoire des Indes Orientales*, Paris 1668.
30. Hubert Deschamps, *Les Pirates à Madagascar aux XVII*ᵉ *et XVIII*ᵉ *siècles*, Paris 1949.

3. THE SOCIETY

1. Henri Lavondes, *Bekoropoka: Quelques aspects de la vie familiale et sociale d'un village malgache*, Paris 1967.
2. Raymond Decary, *La Mort et les Coutumes Funéraires à Madagascar*, Paris 1962.
3. The material in this section is taken from Alfred Ramangasoavina (Minister of Justice of Madagascar, 1960–69), "Du Droit Coutumier aux Codes Modernes Malgaches", *Bulletin de Madagascar*, Tananarive October 1962.
4. Hubert Deschamps, *Histoire de Madagascar*, Paris 1960.

4. STATE AND POLITICS: 1800–1896

1. Hubert Deschamps, in his *Histoire de Madagascar*, Paris 1960, claims that Andrianampoinimerina furnished 1,500 slaves a year.

2. Father François Callet, *Tantara ny Andriana eto Madagasikara*, Vol. IV, Tananarive 1907, p. 106.

3. Hastie's diaries were published in French in the *Bulletin de l'Académie Malgache*, Tananarive, in 1903, 1904, 1918 and 1919.

4. Ibid., 1918–19.

5. Reverend T. T. Matthews, *Thirty Years in Madagascar*, London 1904.

6. Ibid.

7. Pierre Boiteau, *Madagascar: Contribution à l'Histoire de la Nation Malgache*, Paris 1958.

8. Deschamps, op. cit.

9. Ibid.

10. Details are given in Fontoynont and Nicol, "Les Traitants Français sur la côte est de Madagascar", *Mémoires de l'Académie Malgache*, Vol. XXXIII, Tananarive 1940. The contract concerned mainly sugar plantations, factories and distilleries with an important turnover. A photocopy of the contract signed by the Queen appeared in the *Bulletin de l'Académie Malgache*, Tananarive 1939.

11. G. Mondain, "Documents historiques malgaches", *Mémoires de l'Académie Malgache*, Vol. VII, Tananarive 1928.

12. The diary of Raombana gives their names; see "Manuscript de Raombana et Rahaniraka", *Bulletin de l'Académie Malgache*, Vol. XIX, Tananarive 1936.

13. Matthews, op. cit.

14. Mondain, op. cit., for "Report of the Malagasy ambassadors".

15. Deschamps, op. cit.

16. Ibid.

17. A letter from Lastelle to Rainiharo, dated April 14, 1850, on this subject, is reproduced in the *Bulletin de l'Académie Malgache*, Tananarive 1937.

18. Deschamps, op. cit.

19. Reverend Father Boudou, "Une lettre du Prince Rakoto", *Bulletin de l'Académie Malgache*, Tananarive 1932.

20. Boiteau, op. cit., quotes the Journal of Rahombana: 'Prince Rakotoseheno [sic] confided to me this morning that M. Laborde has written to Prince Louis Bonaparte *in his name*, asking him to send troops to deliver Madagascar from the cruelty and oppression of Her Majesty, adding that he, the prince, had signed the letter.' The letter is published in the *Bulletin de l'Académie Malgache*, Tananarive 1911. Rahombana was one of the young men sent by Radama I in 1820 to study in England. He had remained there till 1829 and on his return became the friend of Prince Rakoto.

21. R. Rajemisa-Raolison, *Dictionnaire Historique et Géographique de Madagascar*, Fianarantsoa 1966.

22. Deschamps, op. cit.

23. Especially the Reverend T. T. Matthews, op. cit., and the *Antananarivo Annual*, LMS, Tananarive.

24. Ida Pfeiffer, *The Last Travels of Ida Pfeiffer, inclusive of a Visit to*

Madagascar, London 1861, contains a fanciful account of the journey and of Tananarive society.

25. Ellis was accused of having instigated the assassination of Radama II in 1863, but a Jesuit historian, Father Adrien Boudou, has exonerated him in "Le Meutre de Radama II", *Bulletin de l'Académie Malgache*, Vol. XXVI, Tananarive 1938.

26. Rajemisa-Raolison, op. cit.

27. Lovett, *History of the London Missionary Society*, Vol. I, p. 714.

28. Boiteau, op. cit., quotes an article by H. Galos in the *Revue des Deux Mondes*, October 1863, which specifically states this renunciation.

29. A detailed study of Rainilaiarivony is contained in G. S. Chapus and G. Mondain, *Rainilaiarivony, un Homme d'Etat malgache*, Paris 1953.

30. Ibid.

31. An eye-witness account by a Malagasy Christian who participated in the burning, is given in the *Antananarivo Annual*, Tananarive 1875.

32. Lavondes, op. cit.

33. Deschamps, op. cit.

34. For the history of the development of medicine in Madagascar, see the account given by Dr Randriamaro entitled "La Médicine à Madagascar", in *Comptes-Rendus du XIIe Congrès international d'Histoire de la Médicine*, Nice-Cannes-Monaco 1952. The *Bulletin de la Société mutuelle du Corps Médical Malgache* (1933–1939) published the biographies of the outstanding Malagasy doctors of this historic period.

35. Figures quoted by Boiteau, op. cit.

36. Deschamps, op. cit. See also G. Julien, *Institutions Politiques et Sociales de Madagascar*, Paris 1908.

37. Deschamps, op. cit.

38. Original documents, including exchanges between the British and French governments, are quoted in G. S. Chapus and G. Mondain, "Quelques rapports de Gouvernment Malgache avec les etrangers", *Bulletin de l'Académie Malgache*, Vol. XXXI, Tananarive 1940.

39. Deschamps, op. cit.

40. A contemporary account, with English translations of original documents, is given in Captain Oliver Pasfield, RA, *The True Story of the French Dispute in Madagascar*, London 1885.

41. Jean Valette, "Introduction" to *Histoire de la Monnaie* (a catalogue of an exhibition on Malagasy money), Tananarive 1968. One piastre was held to be the equivalent of 5 gold francs during the latter half of the nineteenth century, and contained 25 grams of silver at 9/10 es; or 22.5 grams of pure silver. The Royal Edict of Marly (France) of January 1726 fixed the legal relationship between gold and silver at the ratio of 1 : 15.5, which ratio was confirmed by the law of Germinal 17, An XI, or April 7, 1805. The conversion of these nineteenth-century currencies to contemporary values in pounds and US dollars presents considerable problems. Throughout this book a conversion system suggested by Boiteau, op. cit., has been adopted, as follows: A conversion to 1955 French francs is first obtained by

multiplying the sum to be converted by a coefficient based on the French wholesale price index, base 1901–1910, published by the Annaire Statistique de la France, 1954, 2nd part, pages 47–51 and 69. Using coefficients derived in this manner, franc values have been obtained as follows:

Year	francs 1955	francs 1970
1780 x 137		minus 25%
1825 x 128		minus 25%
1880 x 156		minus 25%

Two devaluations and annual inflations since 1955 are estimated conservatively as having reduced the purchasing power of the franc by 25 per cent. Thus, to bring 1955 franc values to 1970 post-1969 devaluation francs, the values obtained for 1955 francs by using the conversion coefficient are deflated by 25 per cent. This obviously gives only the roughest idea of comparative money values.

42. *Tacchi's Money Table for use in the Island of Madagascar, giving the native names of money values, and showing the method of writing according to Malagasy notation. By this table any sum from a cent to a dollar, or from a halfpenny to a shilling, can immediately be written down in the Malagasy form*, printed in Tananarive about 1890; in the Collection Rabary, Bibliothèque Nationale, Tananarive.

43. Deschamps, op. cit.; and G. S. Chapus, "Quatre-vingt années d' influences européennes en Imerina", *Bulletin de l'Académie Malgache*, Tananarive 1925.

44. *Ten Years Review of the Mission Work in Madagascar*, 1891/1900, London Missionary Society, Tananarive 1903.

45. Matthews, op. cit.

46. Ibid.

5. STATE AND POLITICS: 1896–1960

1. Reverend T. T. Matthews, *Thirty Years in Madagascar*, London 1904.

2. General J. Charbonneau, *Galliéni à Madagascar*, Paris 1950.

3. Report of Lieutenant Boucabeille, ADC to Galliéni, quoted in ibid.

4. Jean Carol, *Chez les Hova*, Paris 1898; E. F. Gautier, *Trois Héros* (Rainandriamampandry), Paris 1949.

5. Quoted by E. F. Gautier in *Le Passé de l'Afrique du Nord*, Paris 1950.

6. General J-S. Galliéni, *Neuf Ans à Madagascar*, Paris 1908; Pierre Lyautey, *Dans le Sud de Madagascar*, Paris 1902; C. Savaron, "Contribution à l'histoire de l'Imerina", *Bulletin de l'Académie Malgache*, Tananarive 1928.

7. O. Hatzfeld, *Madagascar*, Paris 1952, puts the number killed during the pacification at 100,000, but this figure has no better statistical basis than similar figures given for the 1947 Rebellion.

8. Matthews, op. cit.

9. G. T. Raynal, *Histoire Philosophique et Politique des Etablissements et du Commerce des Européens dans les deux Indes*, 10 Vols., Geneva 1781; A. Billiard, *Voyage aux Colonies orientales*, Paris 1822.

10. Fontoynont and Nicol, "Les Traitants Français de la côte est de Madagascar", *Mémoires de l'Académie Malgache*, Vol. XXXIII, Tananarive 1940.
11. Gouvernement-Général de Madagascar, *Guide de l'Immigrant à Madagascar*, 3 Vols., Paris 1899, and subsequent editions.
12. Charles Robequain, *Madagascar et les Bases dispersées de l'Union française*, Paris 1958.
13. H. Deschamps and P. Chauvet, *Galliéni, Pacificateur*, Paris 1949.
14. Hubert Deschamps, *Histoire de Madagascar*, Paris 1960.
15. The text of the official indictment and sentences—acte d'accusation et jugement—was published as a brochure by the Imprimerie d'Imerina, Tananarive 1916 (58 pp.).
16. Deschamps, op. cit.
17. Hubert Garbit, *L'Effort de Madagascar pendant la Guerre*, Paris 1919; A. Sarrault, *La Mise en Valeur des Colonies Françaises*, Paris 1900.
18. The battle honours were Bois du Chatelet, Dommiers, Terny, Sorny and Allemant and are listed in the General's proclamation, as quoted by Garbit, op. cit.
19. Marcel Olivier, *Six ans de politique sociale à Madagascar*, Paris, 1930.
20. Ibid.
21. Galliéni, op. cit.
22. Olivier, op. cit.
23. Pierre Boiteau, *Madagascar: Contribution a l'Histoire de la Nation Malgache*, Paris 1958.
24. J. Ralaimongo, *Compte-rendu d'un voyage effectué à Madagascar de Juillet à Décembre 1921*, Paris 1922.
25. Deschamps, op. cit.
26. Quoted in Boiteau, op. cit.
27. *L'Aurore malgache*, No. 113, January 13, 1933.
28. The ground forces commanded by Major-General Sturges, Royal Marines, included the 29th Independent Brigade, consisting of the 1st Royal Scots Fusiliers, 2nd Royal Welch Fusiliers, 2nd East Lancashire and 2nd South Lancashire Regiments, 455th Light Battery R.A., and 236th Field Company R.E. The 17th Brigade group, with the 2nd Royal Scots Fusiliers, 6th Seaforth Highlanders, 2nd Northamptonshire Regiment, 9th Field Regiment R.A., 38th Field Company R.E., 141st Field Ambulance R.A.M.C., and No. 5 Commando. *Source:* Supplement to the *London Gazette*, March 4, 1948.
29. Ibid.
30. Ibid.
31. Ibid.
32. Ibid.
33. Ibid.
34. This speech was made in Malagasy and published as a pamphlet. It is quoted in French by Boiteau, op. cit.
35. Interview entitled "M. Marius Moutet nous dit" which appeared in *Climats* of February 28, 1946.

36. Reply of Minister Moutet, dated September 30, 1946, to Report No. 380 of de Coppet; quoted by Boiteau, op. cit.
37. Quoted by Deschamps, op. cit.
38. Address of the High Commissioner to the Representative Assembly meeting in Tananarive on April 19, 1947.
39. Raymond Rabemananjara, *Madagascar sous la Rénovation malgache*, Paris 1953.
40. Five years later the same arguments were being put forward in an article entitled "La décolonisation de M. Fabre" in *Combat*, July 29, 1961.
41. Deschamps, op. cit.
42. Decrees Nos. 57–463 and 57–464.
43. G. Chaffard, *Les Carnets secrets de la Décolonisation*, Paris 1968, contains a very full account of this period but comparatively little on Madagascar.
44. Introduction to E. P. Thebault, *Traité de Droit Civil Malgache moderne*, Tananarive 1962.

6. State and Politics since Independence

1. The figures come from the Inspection du Travail and the Service de la Statistique.
2. René Gendarme, *L'Economie de Madagascar*, Paris 1961.
3. The great success of J-J. Servan-Schreiber, *Le Défi Americain*, Paris 1967, which sold nearly a million copies in one year, and of Roger Priouret, *La France et le Management*, Paris 1968, indicate the intense interest in modern industrial management techniques which are bringing profound changes to the structure of French industry and commerce.
4. Nigel Heseltine, "Le Rôle de l'Agriculture dans le Développement Economique", ENAM 1965, lectures given between 1961 and 1965.
5. P. Coutant, "Les Accords de Defense avec la République Malgache", *Revue Administrative*, Paris 1960, examines in detail the execution of the agreement of June 27, 1960.
6. *Jeune Afrique*, April 1968, reported debates of the PSD Students' Federation concerning government economic policy.

7. The Economy

1. Nigel Heseltine, *The Quelea Bird*, London 1960.
2. H. Perrier de la Bathie, *Biogéographie des Plantes à Madagascar*, Paris 1936.
3. M. Lacroutz et al., *L'Elevage et la Commercialisation du Bétail et de la Viande à Madagascar*, Ministère de le Coopération, Paris 1962.
4. John H. Wellington, *Southern Africa*, Vol. 1, Cambridge 1955.
5. Reverend W. C. Pickersgill, "From Twilight to Gross Darkness. Being chiefly a narrative of what happened on the Way on a Journey to Ankavandra and Imanandaza", *Antananarivo Annual*, No. 1,

1875. Pickersgill was a missionary of the London Missionary Society. He and Sewell of the Friends' Foreign Mission Association carried letters of introduction from the Prime Minister, and appear to have been the first Europeans to have seen west of Tsiroamandidy.

6. Ibid.

7. *Programme d'Etudes pour la Mise en Valeur de 7 Regions*, Commissariat-Général au Plan, Tananarive 1962.

8. See R. Battistini, "Les Transformations écologiques à Madagascar à l'époque proto-historique", *Bulletin de Madagascar*, No. 244, Tananarive 1966, on the correlation between the East African pluvial periods (Gambian) and those, far less well-defined, of Madagascar.

9. J. C. Willis, *Dictionary of Flowering Plants and Ferns*, Cambridge 1960.

10. Perrier de la Bathie, op. cit., estimates 6,000 endemic species out of 6,865 species of *Phanerogamae* (those plants that produce seeds).

11. Bulletin Technique des Eaux et Forêts et de la Conservation des Sols, *Monographie de la Côte Est de Madagascar*, Tananarive n.d.

12. For an exhaustive bibliography on the clove tree and its cultivation in Madagascar, see R. Dufournet, "Le Girofle à Madagascar", *Bulletin de Madagascar*, Tananarive March 1968.

13. Father François Callet, *Tantara ny Andriana eto Madagasikara*, Tananarive 1908. The sagas of the Merina have them move inland from the Bay of Antongil, to the Plateaux, then southwards to Lake Alaotra, and finally towards Antananarivo and the Betsimitatra plain.

14. Alfred Grandidier, *Histoire physique, naturelle et politique de Madagascar*, Paris 1875–97; Raymond Decary, *L'Androy*, 3 Vols., Paris 1930–33. R. Battistini, *Etude Géomorphologique de l'Extrême-Sud de Madagascar*, 2 Vols., Paris 1964.

15. Lacroutz et al., op. cit.

16. H. Perrier de la Bathie, "Les Phaseolus de Madagascar", *Bulletin Economique de Madagascar*, Tananarive 1924, states that the pois du cap was seen in cultivation in the Bay of Saint-Augustin, one of the first points of contact of Europeans, south of Tuléar, in 1620.

17. Paul Ottino, *Les économies paysannes malgaches du Bas-Mangoky*, Paris 1963. The lower valley of the Mangoky is the site of one of the largest irrigation schemes in Madagascar, in progress since 1959, and financed by the FED. The objective is to secure 25,000 acres of irrigated cotton with associated cultures; 2,200 acres produced 2,769 tons of cotton in 1969. Total cotton production in Madagascar in 1969 was 14,000 tons as against 4,910 tons in 1964.

18. Lacroutz et al., op. cit. In this report, the cattle population is calculated according to the formula $X = \dfrac{100\,N}{100 - Y}$

where X is the real total population
  N is the 'official total' + fraud
  Y is the percentage of young animals.

19. Ibid., Table 3, p. 17, "Variations de l'Effectif Bovin, en relation avec divers éléments, prix des animaux, exportations des cuirs, etc.".
20. Ibid.
21. E. Hopfen, *The Pastoral Fulani Family in Gwandu*, Oxford 1958, states that the Fulani never leave animals more than four weeks at a time on damp lowlands for this reason.
22. Commissariat-Général au Plan, *Plan Quinquennial, 1964–1969*, and *Programme des Grandes Operations*.
23. FAO, *World Sugar Consumption Trends*, Commodity Monograph No. 32.
24. Notably René Gendarme, *L'Economie de Madagascar*, Paris 1961.

8. DEVELOPMENT PROSPECTS

1. *Plan de Développement Economique et Social: Programme 1958–1962: Territoire de Madagascar:* Haut-Commissariat de la République Française; Ministère de l'Economie: Bureau des Investissements du Plan; Tananarive 1958.
2. *Le Livre Blanc de l'Economie Malgache: 1950–1960*, Tananarive 1967.
3. *First National Development Plan, 1966–1970*, Office of National Development and Planning, Lusaka, Zambia, 1966.
4. *Code des Investissements*, Ordonnance No. 62/024 of September 9, 1962; see also the *Guide de l'Investisseur*, issued by the Bureau de développement et de la promotion industrielle.
5. This is fully discussed by Thomas Balogh, "The Mechanism of Neo-Imperialism: The economic impact of monetary and commercial institutions in Africa", *Bulletin of the Institute of Statistics*, No. 24, Oxford, August 1962. The writer has not seen this very important consideration discussed so frankly elsewhere.
6. Nigel Heseltine, "The Role of Administration in Economic Development", *Journal of Administration Overseas*, London 1967, gives a brief comparative study of the influence of administration on development in Madagascar and in Zambia.
7. Hla Myint, "The Gains from International Trade and the Backward Countries", *Economic Studies*, Vol. XXII, No. 2; "The Classical Theory of International Trade and the Underdeveloped Countries", *Economic Journal*, June 1958; Nigel Heseltine, "Problems of Investment in Agriculture", *World Crops*, London 1966.
8. René Gendarme, *L'Economie de Madagascar*, Paris 1961; René Dumont, *L'Evolution des Campagnes malgaches*, Paris 1959, and *False Start in Africa*, London 1964 (originally published as *L'Afrique est mal partie*, Paris 1961); T. Balogh, *Unequal Partners*, London 1963.
9. J-J. Servan-Schreiber, *Le Défi Americain*, Paris 1967.
10. FAO, *Produits agricoles: Projections pour 1975 et 1985*, Rome 1967.

Bibliography

Note: An asterisk (*) indicates the basic works which, in the writer's opinion, make an original contribution to the knowledge of Madagascar. The Bibliography has been divided into two parts: Archives; and Sources. The second part has in turn been divided into eight categories: General and Administrative; Statistics; Maps; History; Ethnology; Malagasy Language; Scientific Studies; and Agriculture.

1. ARCHIVES

French and European official archives are listed in Guillaume Grandidier, *Bibliographie de Madagascar*, Vol. II, Tananarive 1906, pp. 676–827; however, the archives of the French Ministère des Colonies have been reclassified since that date.

A list of British official archives concerning Madagascar is contained in R. I. P. Wastell, "British Imperial Policy in relation to Madagascar", unpublished thesis, University of London 1944.

Alfred Grandidier was the first explorer to describe the structure of Madagascar. He was a wealthy traveller and a many-sided scholar, geographer, naturalist, ethnographer and historian. Between 1864 and 1870 he made more than twenty journeys to the interior of Madagascar; his reconnaissance maps and his triangulation of Imerina enabled him to establish in 1871 the first general map of the island. He devoted the rest of his life (1836–1921) to the publication of 38 volumes of his *Histoire Physique, Naturelle et Politique de Madagascar*. His work was contined by his son Guillaume (1873–1957) who collaborated throughout twenty-five years in the compilation of the encyclopedic *Histoire*; a number of other scientists also contributed, among them Milne-Edwards, Sauvage de Saussure and Baillon.

*Grandidier, Alfred, *Histoire Physique, Naturelle et Politique de Madagascar*.
Géographie: Vols I and II, Texte, Vol. III, Atlas. Ethnographie: I Les Habitants, II Les Etrangers, III La Famille Malgache, rapports sociaux, Vie matérielle, Les Croyances et la Vie religieuse.
Histoire de la Géographie de Madagascar (1885). Agriculture, Elevage, Industrie et Commerce, Travaux Publics, Transports, Education, Médecine (1928).
Histoire Naturelle:
Mammifères (4 vols), Oiseaux (5 vols), Mollusques, Poissons (2 vols), Reptiles (2 vols), Lépidoptères (2 vols), Hymenoptères, Formicidae, Coléoptères (2 vols), Orthoptères, Myriapodes, Botanique, Mousses (2 vols).

A classified alphabetical index of the publications appearing in the *Bulletin de l'Académie Malgache* has been published by the Académie Malgache in two parts:

1re *Série, Volumes 1 à 12, Annés 1902 à 1913*, by A. Dandouau, Imprimerie Officielle, Tananarive.
Années 1914 à 1967, mimeographed, Académie Malgache, Tananarive 1969.
Mémoires de l'Academie Malgache, Fascicules 1 to XXXVIII (1967).

II. SOURCES QUOTED FROM, OR REFERRED TO, IN THE TEXT

1. General and Administrative

Annales de l'Université de Madagascar: Lettres, Toulouse from 1965; *Droit*, Tananarive from 1964; *Médecine*, Tananarive from 1963; *Sciences*, Tananarive from 1963.
*Antananarivo Annual and Madagascar Magazine, London Missionary Society, Tananarive 1875 to 1900.
Automobile Club de Madagascar, *Guide Routier et Touristique, Madagascar, Réunion, Maurice, Comores*, Tananarive 1969.
Brunschwig, H., *La Colonisation française*, Paris 1944.
Budget Général de l'Etat, Ministère des Finances, Imprimerie Nationale, Tananarive, annually.
*Bulletin de l'Académie Malgache, Tananarive from 1902.
*Bulletin de Madagascar, Tananarive, monthly from 1950.
Comte, J., *Les Communes à Madagascar*, University of Madagascar 1967.
Coutant, P., "Les Accords de Défense avec la République malgache", *Revue Administrative*, Paris 1960.
Duignan, Peter, "Madagascar. A list of materials in the African collections of Stanford University and the Hoover Institute of War, Revolution and Peace", mimeo., Stanford University 1962.
Encyclopédie Coloniale et Maritime, "Madagascar et la Réunion", Paris 1947.
Guide Bleu, *Madagascar et les Iles Mascareignes*, Paris 1968.
Guide de l'Immigrant à Madagascar, 3 Vols., Tananarive 1899.
**Grandidier, Alfred, *Histoire de la Géographie de Madagascar*, Paris 1885; *Histoire Physique, Naturelle et Politique de Madagascar*, Paris 1905–28.
**Grandidier, Guillaume, *Bibliographie de Madagascar*, 4 Vols., Tananarive 1905, 1906, 1935, 1957.
Heseltine, Nigel, *Remaking Africa*, London 1962; "The Role of Administration in Economic Development", *Journal of Administration Overseas*, London 1967.
Isnard, H., "Madagascar, colonie d'exploitation. Diagnostique économique et sociale", *Economie et Humanisme*, No. 18, Paris 1950.
Journal Officiel de la République Malgache, Tananarive 1883–96.
Journal Officiel de Madagascar et Dépendances, Tananarive 1896–1958.
Journal Officiel de la République Malgache, Tananarive since 1958.
Julien, G., *Institutions Politiques et Sociales à Madagascar*, Paris 1908.

La Loi Cadre du 23 Juin 1956, portant réformes des institutions politiques, économiques et sociales de Madagascar; et les textes d'application: décrets, arrêtés, délibérations, Tananarive 1957.

Madagascar: Recoeuil des textes constitutionels, législatifs et réglementairs de la République Malgache, Tananarive 1960.

Mannoni, O., *Psychologie de la Colonisation,* Paris 1950.

Massiot, Michel, *Les Institutions Politiques et Administratives de la République Malgache,* University of Madagascar 1967.

Masseron, J. P., *La Justice administrative à Madagascar,* Tananarive 1963.

Raharijaona, Henri, *Le Droit foncier à Madagascar; La Protection de l'Enfant dans le Droit traditionnel malgache,* Tananarive 1963.

*Rajemisa-Raolison, Régis, *Dictionnaire Historique et Géographique de Madagascar,* Fianarantsoa 1966.

Ramangasoavina, Alfred, *Du Droit Coutumier aux Codes modernes malgaches,* Tananarive 1962.

Rapport sur l'Activité du Gouvernement, du 1er Juillet 19.. au 30 Juin 19.., Présidence de la République, Imprimerie Nationale, Tananarive, annually.

Réformes d'Outre-Mer, *Loi No 56–619 du 23 Juin 1965 et Décrets d'Application* ("*La Loi-cadre*"), *Journal Officiel de la République française,* Paris 1957.

Sala, G., *Les travaux au Ras du Sol,* University of Madagascar 1966.

Thebault, E. P., *Code des 305 Articles promulgué par la Reine Ranavalona II le 29 Mars 1881* (Complete malagasy text, with French translation, notes, bibliography), Tananarive 1960; *Traité du Droit Civil malgache moderne,* Tananarive 1962; *Constitution et Lois Organiques,* Tananarive 1964.

Tyack, Maurice, ed., *Madagascar, Continent du Futur,* Lausanne 1965.

*Valette, Jean, *Les Archives de Madagascar,* Abbéville 1962.

2. Statistics

Publications of the Institut National de la Statistique et de la Recherche Economique (INSRE), Ministére des Finances, Tananarive.

(i) Monthly publications

Bulletin mensuel de la Statistique.

(ii) Annual publications

Situation Economique.
Population de Madagascar.
Notes sur la Conjoncture (twice yearly).
Statistiques du Commerce Extérieur de Madagascar.
Parc automobile de Madagascar.

(iii) Census and Surveys

Enquête budgétaire en milieu assistance technique à Tananarive, July 1962: family budgets.

315

Madagascar

Enquête rizicoles dans la Province de Tananarive, 1962: paddy, acreages and yields.

Enquête agricole, 1961–62: elements of agricultural census.

Enquête sur les budgets familiaux malgaches en milieu urbain, 1961–62: family budgets.

Enquête sur le rendement des rizières dans 23 zones, 1965.

Recensements démographiques urbains pour les villes de plus de 5,000 habitants: Provinces de Tananarive, Fianarantsoa, Majunga, Tamatave, Tuléar.

Recensements démographiques des six chefs lieux de Province, 1961–62.

Enquête budgets et alimentation des ménages ruraux en 1962:
  i. Données sur la population.
  ii. Nutrition et sociologie alimentaire.
  iii. Ressources agricoles et budgets familiaux.

(iv) Occasional Publications

Essai de Prévision de la Population malgache.

Etat-Civil, naissances et décès, 1964.

Séries chronologues et graphiques sur l'économie malgache, 1949–64.

Comptes Economiques de Madagascar, 1962, 1964 and 1966.

Dénombrement des Etablissements, 1963.

Le travail à Madagascar, 1964.

Note sur la Concentration du Commerce à Madagascar, n.d.

Recensement Industriel, 1967.

Code officiel géographique de Madagascar, 1965.

3. Maps

1 : 100,000—the basic topographical map of Madagascar—in approximately 420 sheets.

1 : 1,000,000 and 1 : 1,500,000 in 3 sheets.

1 : 2,000,000—administrative and showing population density.

There are a number of maps and plans of special development areas and town plans at scales between 1 : 1,000 and 1 : 50,000.

Special maps issued by various government departments include geological maps, soils maps and forest maps.

The topographical maps, of a high standard of definition, are published by the Institut Géographique National.

Atlas de Madagascar, Laboratoire de Géographie, University of Madagascar, BDPA.IGN, 1969.

4. History

*Ackermann, Dr Paul, *Histoire des Révolutions de Madagascar de 1642 à nos jours*, Paris 1833.

André, E., *L'Esclavage à Madagascar*, Paris 1899.

Benyowski, Maurice-Auguste, *Memoirs and travels of Maurice-Augustus, Count de Benyowski*, London 1904.

Billiard, A., *Voyage aux Colonies Orientales*, Paris 1822.

*Boiteau, Pierre, *Contribution à l'Histoire de la Nation Malgache*, Paris, 1958.

Boothby, Richard, *A Brief Discovery or description of the most famous Island of Madagascar or St. Laurence, in Asia near unto the East Indies*, London 1745.

Boudou, Reverend Adrien, SJ, "Une Lettre de Prince Rakoto", *Bulletin de l'Académie Malgache*, Tananarive 1932; "Le Meutre de Radama II", *Bulletin de l'Académie Malgache*, Tananarive 1938; *Les Jésuites à Madagascar au XIX siècle*, Paris 1940.

*Callet, Reverend François, SJ, ed., *Tantara ny Andriana eto Madagasikara*, translated as *Histoire des Rois*, 4 Vols., Tananarive 1953–58.

Carol, Jean, *Chez les Hova*, Paris 1898.

*Chapus, G. S., "Quatre-vingt années d'influences européennes en Imerina", *Bulletin de l'Académie Malgache*, Tananarive 1925.

Chapus, G. S. and Mondain, G., "Quelques Rapports du Gouvernement Malgache avec les Etrangers", *Bulletin de l'Academie Malgache*, Tananarive 1940; *Rainilaiarivony, un Homme d'Etat malgache*, Paris 1953.

Chaffard, G., *Les Carnets Secrets de la Décolonisation*, Paris 1968.

Charbonneau, General Jean, *Galliéni à Madagascar*, Paris 1950.

Copland, Samuel, *A History of the Island of Madagascar*, London 1822.

Cousins, Reverend W. E., *Madagascar of Today*, London 1895.

*Deschamps, Hubert, *Les Pirates à Madagascar au XVIIᵉ et XVIIIᵉ Siècles*, Paris 1949; *Histoire de Madagascar*, Paris 1960.

Deschamps, Hubert and Chauvet, P., *Galliéni, pacificateur*, Paris 1949.

Drury, Robert, *Madagascar, or Robert Drury's Journal during Fifteen years of Captivity on that Island, 1702–1717*, London 1729.

Dumaine, *Mémoire sur Madagascar: la côte ouest entre Ankoule et Morondava, 1792*, *Annales des Voyages*, Vol. XI, Paris 1810; *Rapport sur l'utilité de cette partie de la côte, peut-être au Commerce français, 1792*, in British Museum, Department of Manuscripts.

Duchesne, General Charles, *Rapport sur l'Expédition de Madagascar*, Paris 1897.

*Ellis, Reverend William, *History of Madagascar*, 2 Vols., London 1838; *Three visits to Madagascar during the years 1853–1854–1856, including a journey to the Capital*, London 1858; *Madagascar revisited, describing the events of a new reign, and the revolution which followed*, London 1867.

Faublée, Jacques and Orbain-Faublée, Marcelle, *Madagascar vu par les auteurs arabes avant le XIᵉ sièck*, Studia II, Lisbon 1963.

Ferrand, Gabriel, *Les Musulmans à Madagascar et aux Iles Comores*, 3 Vols., Paris 1891–1902.

*Flacourt, Etienne de, *Histoire de la Grande Isle de Madagascar, par le Sieur de Flacourt, Directeur-Général de la Compagnie Française de l'Orient, et Commandant pour Sa Majésté dans la dite Isle et les Isles adjacents*, Paris 1661. The 'Dictionary' of the Malagasy language forms part of this work.

Fontoynont, Victor, *Les Traitants Français de la côte est de Madagascar, de Ranavalona I à Radama II*, Tananarive 1940.

*Freeman, J. J. and Johns, D., *A Narrative of the Persecution of the Christians in Madagascar, with Details of the Escape of the six Christian Refugees now in England*, London 1840.

*Froberville, Barthélémy Huet de, *Le Grand Dictionnaire de Madagascar*, edited by Flavien Ranaivo and Jean Valette, published in instalments in the *Bulletin de Madagascar*, Tananarive from 1963.

*Galliéni, General Joseph-Simon, *Rapport sur la Pacification, l'Organisation, et la Colonisation de Madagascar, Octobre 1896 à Mars 1899; Madagascar de 1896 à 1905: rapports et annexes*, 2 Vols., Tananarive 1905; *Neuf Ans à Madagascar*, Paris 1908; *Lettres de Madagascar, 1896-1905*, Paris 1928.

Gautier, E. F., *Trois Héros* (Rainandriamampandry), Paris 1931.

Garbit, Hubert, *L'Effort de Madagascar pendant la Guerre*, Paris 1919.

*Grandidier, Alfred, *Collection des Ouvrages anciens concernant Madagascar*, 9 Vols., Paris 1913-30.

Grandidier, Guillaume, *Galliéni*, Paris 1931.

Goodall, Norman, *A History of the London Missionary Society: 1895-1945*, London 1954.

Hardyman, J. T., *Madagascar on the Move*, London 1950.

*Hastie, James, *Journaux* (Diaries), *Bulletin de l'Académie Malgache*, Tananarive 1903-04 and 1918-19.

Historique du 1er Régiment de Chasseurs Malgaches, Paris 1920.

Howe, Sonia, *The Drama of Madagascar*, with foreword by Lord Lugard, London 1938.

Hué, Ferdinand, *La France et l'Angleterre à Madagascar*, Paris 1885.

Huet, Barthélémy, *Histoire de Madagascar ou Mémoires pour servir à l'Histoire de l'Ile de Madagascar*, rédigés, mis en ordre, et publiés sur les notes manuscrites de M. M. Mayeur, Dumaine et autres, et enrichis des extraits de plusieurs voyages anciens et modernes; 2 Vols., Ile de France 1809.

Lyautey, Pierre, *Dans le Sud de Madagascar*, Paris 1902; *Lettres de Tonkin et de Madagascar, 1894-1899*, Paris 1921.

Mayeur, *Voyage au pays des Seclaves, 1774; Voyage au Nord de Madagascar, 1774; Voyage à Ancove (Imerina) par Ancaye (Bezanozano), 1785;* in British Museum, Department of Manuscripts.

*Matthews, Reverend T. T., *Thirty Years in Madagascar*, London 1904.

Mondain, G., "Documents historiques malgaches", *Mémoires de l'Académie Malgache*, Tananarive 1928; "Report of the Malagasy Ambassadors", *Mémoires de l'Académie Malgache*, Tananarive 1928.

Olivier, Marcel, *Six Ans de Politique Sociale à Madagascar*, Paris 1931.

Pascal, Roger, "La Décolonisation de Madagascar: Cause—Moyens—Effets", thesis for doctorate, Faculté de Droit, University of Madagascar, 1963.

Pasfield, Captain Oliver, RA, *The True Story of the French Dispute in Madagascar*, London 1885.

Pfeiffer, Ida, *The Last Travels of Ida Pfeiffer, inclusive of a Visit to Madagascar*, London 1881.

Rabemananjara, Jacques, "Témoignage malgache et Colonialisme",

Présence Africaine, Paris 1956; *Nationalisme et Problèmes malgaches*, Paris 1958.

Rabemananjara, Raymond, *Madagascar sous la Rénovation malgache*, Paris 1951; *Madagascar: Histoire de la Nation malgache*, Paris 1952.

Ralaimihoatra, E., *Histoire de Madagascar*, Tananarive 1965.

*Raombana, "Manuscript de Raombana et Rahaniraka, 1853–1854", *Bulletin de l'Académie Malgache*, Tananarive 1930, extract of 12 pages; complete MS in English in library of Académie Malgache.

Ralaimongo, J., *Compte-rendu d'un Voyage effectué à Madagascar de Juillet à Décembre 1921*, Paris 1922.

Raynal, G. T., *Histoire philosophique et politique des Etablissements et du Commerce des Européens dans les deux Indes*, 10 Vols., Geneva 1781.

Sibrée, Reverend James, *Madagascar and its people*, London 1870; *The Great African Island: chapters on Madagascar*, London and Westport, Conn. 1880; *Fifty Years in Madagascar: personal experiences of mission life and work*, London 1924.

Spacensky, Alain, *Madagascar, 50 ans de vie politique*, Paris 1970.

Wastell, R. I. P., "British Imperial Policy in relation to Madagascar", unpublished thesis, University of London 1944.

5. *Ethnology*

*Andriamanjato, Richard, *Le Tsiny et le Tody dans la Pensée malgache*, Paris 1957.

Arabes et Islamisés à Madagascar, University of Madagascar, Tananarive 1967.

Birkeli, Emil, "Marques de boeufs et traditions de race. Documents sur l'éthnographie de la côte occidentale de Madagascar", *Mémoires de l'Académie Malgache*, Tananarive 1936.

Chamla, Marie-Claude, "Recherches anthropologiques sur l'origine des Malgaches", *Mémoires du Muséum*, Paris 1958; "Les Origines du Peuple malgache", *La Nature*, No. 3297, Paris 1960.

Condominas, Georges, *Fokon'olona et collectivités rurales en Imerina*, Paris 1960.

Decary, Raymond, *Moeurs et Coutumes des Malgaches*, Paris 1951.

*Deschamps, Hubert, *Les Migrations intérieures passées et présentes à Madagascar*, Paris 1959.

*Dubois, Reverend P. H., SJ, *Monographie des Betsileo*, Paris 1938.

Faublée, Jacques, *L'Ethnographie de Madagascar*, Paris 1946; *Les Esprits de la Vie à Madagascar*, Paris 1954.

Ferrand, G., "Les Iles Ramny, Lamery, Waq Waq, Komor, des géographes arabes, et Madagascar", *Journal Asiatique*, Paris 1907; "Les Origines africaines des malgaches", *Journal Asiatique*, Paris 1908; "Le Kouen-Louen et les anciens navigations dans les mers du sud", *Journal Asiatique*, Paris 1919.

*Decary, Raymond, *La Mort et les coutumes funéraires à Madagascar*, Paris 1962.

Dez, J., "L'apport lexical de l'Indonésien commun à la langue malgache", *Bulletin de Madagascar*, Tananarive 1963; "De l'influence arabe à Madagascar à l'aide de faits de linguistique", *Revue de Madagascar*, Tananarive 1966.

Ferrand, G., "Les Voyages des Javanais à Madagascar", *Journal Asiatique*, Paris 1910.

Gaudebout, P. and Vernier, E., "Notes sur une Campagne de Fouilles à Vohémar", *Bulletin de l'Académie Malgache*, Tananarive 1941.

*Grandidier, Alfred and Guillaume, *Ethnographie de Madagascar*, 5 Vols., Paris 1908 to 1928.

Lavondès, Henri, *Bekoporopoka. Quelques aspects de la vie familiale et sociale d'un village malgache*, Paris 1967.

Molet, Louis, *Le Boeuf dans l'Ankaizina*, Tananarive 1953; *Le Bain Royal à Madagascar*, Tananarive 1956.

Ottino, Paul, *Les Economies paysannes malgaches du Bas-Mangoky*, Paris 1963.

Rakoto-Ratsimamanga, Dr Albert, " Tache pigmentaire héréditaire, et Origines des Malgaches", *Revue Anthropologique*, Paris 1940.

Saches, Curt, "Les Instruments de Musique à Madagascar", *Mémoires de l'Institut d'Ethnographie*, Paris 1938.

Urbain-Faublée, Marcelle, "L'Art malgache", *Les Pays d'Outre-Mer*, 5th Series, Paris 1963.

Vérin, Pierre, "L'Origine Indonésienne des Malgaches", *Bulletin de Madagascar*, Tananarive 1967.

6. *Malagasy Language*

Boky Firaketana ny Fiteny sy ny Zavatra malagasy, edited by Raveljaona and Gabriel Rajaona, 5 Vols, ABA to LOK published Tananarive 1937–67, remainder in progress: a Malagasy encyclopedic dictionary of *fiteny* (words) and *zavatra* (things).

Dahl, Otto, "Les Convergences phonétiques entre le malgache et le manjaan de Borneo", *Bulletin de l'Académie Malgache*, Tananarive 1938; *Malgache et Manjaan, une comparison linguistique*, Oslo 1951.

Froberville, Barthélémy Huet de, *Le Grand Dictionnaire de Madagascar*, edited by Flavien Ranaivo and Jean Valette, published in instalments in the *Bulletin de Madagascar*, Tananarive from 1963.

*Gerbinis, Ernest, *La Langue Malgache*, Paris 1949.

Houlder, Reverend J. A., *Oholobolona, or Malagasy proverbs, illustrating the wit and wisdom of the Hova of Madagascar*, Tananarive 1916.

*Malzac, Victorin, SJ, *Grammaire Malgache*, new edn., Paris 1950. Malzac, Victorin, SJ, and Abinal, Albert, SJ, *Dictionnaire Malgache-Français, Français-Malgache*, 2 Vols., new edn., Paris 1963.

Rajaobelina, Prosper, *Parlez Malgache*, Tananarive 1960.

Ralaivola, Clovis, "Notes de Philologie", *Bulletin de l'Académie Malgache*, Tananarive 1967.

Razafintsalama, *La Langue malgache et les Origines malgaches*, 2 Vols., Tananarive 1928.

Richardson, Reverend John, *A New Malagasy-English Dictionary*, LMS, Tananarive 1885; reprinted London 1967.

7. *Scientific Studies*

*Aubreville, A., *Contribution à la Paléohistoire des Forêts de l'Afrique tropicale*, Paris 1949; *Climats, Forêts et Désertification de l'Afrique tropicale*, Paris 1949.

**Atlas of Surface Currents*, US Navy Hydrographic Services, Washington 1950.

Attenborough, David, *Zoo Quest to Madagascar*, London 1961.

Battistini, René, *Etude Géomorphologique de l'Extrême-Sud de Madagascar*, 2 Vols., Paris 1964.

Battistini, R. and Verin, P., "A propos d'une datation au radio-carbon du gisement de sub-fossiles à Itampolo", *Bulletin de la Société Préhistorique Française*, Paris 1964–65; "Les Transformations écologiques à Madagascar à l'époque proto-historique", *Bulletin de Madagascar*, No. 244, Tananarive 1966.

Besaire, Henri, "Bibliographie géologique de Madagascar, 1940–1950", *Bulletin Géologique de Madagascar*, Tananarive 1951; "La Géologie de Madagascar et ses grands problèmes", *Bulletin de la Société géologique de France*, Paris 1956; *La Géologie de Madagascar en 1957*, Service Géologique de Madagascar, Tananarive 1957; *Considérations sur le Socle ancien de Madagascar, comparisons avec l'Afrique orientale*, Service Géologique de Madagascar, Tananarive 1956.

Burkill, I. H., *A Dictionary of the Economic Products of the Malay Peninsular*, London 1935.

Capuron, R., *Essai d'Introduction à l'Etude de la Flore forestière de Madagascar*, Inspection Générale des Eaux et Forêts, Tananarive 1957.

Darlington, C. D., *Chromosome Botany and the Origin of Cultivated Plants*, London and Darien, Conn. 1963.

Darlington, P. J. and Rand, A. L., "The Distribution and Habits of Madagascar Birds", *Bulletin of the American Museum of Natural History*, New York 1936.

*Darlington, Philip J., Jr., *Zoogeography. The Geographical Distribution of Animals*, New York 1957.

Decary, Raymond, *L'Androy*, 3 Vols., Paris 1930–33; *La Faune Malgache*, Paris 1950.

*Dumont, René, *Evolution des Campagnes malgaches*, Tananarive 1959.

Duverge, P., *Principes de météorologie dynamiques et types de temps à Madagascar*, Tananarive 1949.

Drogué, A., *L'Agriculture dans la Province de Tamatave*, Service de l'Agriculture, mimeo., Tananarive 1959.

Dufournet, R., "Le Girofle à Madagascar", *Bulletin de Madagascar*, Tananarive 1968.

*Gendarme, René, *L'Economie de Madagascar*, Paris 1961.

Good, Ronald, *Madagascar and New Caledonia: a problem in plant geography*, Blumea No. 6, London 1950; *The Geography of the Flowering Plants*, 2nd edn., London and New York 1953.

Grandidier, Alfred, "Les Animaux disparus de Madagascar", *Revue de Madagascar*, Tananarive 1905.

Grandidier, Guillaume, "Les Lémuriens Disparus de Madagascar", *Nouvelles Archives du Muséum*, 4th Series, Vol. VII, Paris 1905.

Hachiuska, M., *The Dodo and Kindred Birds, or the extinct birds of the Mascarene Islands*, London 1953.

Hoojer, D. A., "Pygmy Elephant and Giant Tortoise", *Science Monthly*, New York 1951.

Humbert, H., "La Déstruction d'une flore insulaire par le feu: principaux aspects de la végétation à Madagascar", *Mémoires de l'Académie Malgache*, Tananarive 1927; *Les Territoires phytogéographiques de Madagascar: leur cartographie*, Paris 1954.

Jalu, R. and Viaud, A., *La Circulation générale dans le Sud-Ouest de l'Océan Indien méridional*, Académie des Sciences, Paris 1952.

Lacroutz, M., et al., *L'Elevage et la Commercialisation du Bétail et de la Viande à Madagascar*, Ministère de la Coopération, Paris 1962.

Lake and Rastall, *Textbook of Geology*, London 1958.

Matthews, Samuel W., "Science explores the Monsoon Sea", *National Geographic Magazine*, Washington 1967.

Minelle, Jean, *L'Agriculture à Madagascar*, Paris 1959.

National Geographic Magazine, Vol. 132, No. 4: Special Supplement, *Indian Ocean Floor*, maps, Washington 1967.

Paulian, Renaud, *Les Animaux protégés à Madagascar*, Institut de Recherche scientifique, Tananarive 1955.

Pernet, R., *Pharmacopée de Madagascar*, Institut de Recherche scientifique, Tananarive 1967.

*Perrier de la Bathie, H., "La Végétation malgache", *Annales du Musée colonial de Marseille*, Marseille 1920; "Les Plantes introduites à Madagascar", *Revue de Botanique appliquée et d'Agriculture tropicale*, Paris 1931–32; *Biogéographie des Plantes de Madagascar*, Paris 1938.

Poisson, Reverend Charles, SJ, "Accidents tectoniques et tremblements de terre à Madagascar", *Bulletin Géologique de Madagascar*, Tananari~ 1949; *Météorologie de Madagascar*, Paris 1950.

Portéres, Roland, *Vieilles Agricultures de l'Afrique Inter-tropicale* *L'Agronomie Tropicale*, Paris 1950.

Ravet, Jacques, *Atlas Climatologique de Madagascar*, Tananarive 1948.

Randriamaro, Dr, "La Médecine a Madagascar", XIIe *Congrés International de Médecine*, Nice 1952.

Richards, P. W., *The Tropical Rain Forest*, Cambridge and New York 1952.

Standing, Dr Herbert F., "Of recently-discovered Sub-fossil Primates from Madagascar", *Transactions of the Royal Zoological Society*, Vol. XVIII, Part II, London May 1908.

Straka, H., *C–14 Datierung zweier Torfproben aus Madagascar*, Die Naturwissenschaft, Vol. II, 1961.

Terre Malgache, annual publication of the Ecole Nationale Supérieure Agronomique, University of Madagascar, Tananarive from 1966.

*Wellington, J. H., *Southern Africa*, 2 Vols., Cambridge 1955.

Wetmore, Alexander, "Recreating Madagascar's Giant Extinct Bird", *National Geographic Magazine*, Washington 1967.

Zolotarevsky, B-N., "Le Criquet Migrateur à Madagascar", *Annales des Epiphyties*, Paris 1929.

8. *Agriculture*

There is no single work covering adequately the agricultural sector of the economy of Madagascar, similar to Tothill, J. P., *Agriculture in the Sudan*, Oxford 1948, and *Agriculture in Uganda*, Oxford 1952, which are models of concise analytic description of patterns of agricultural production. Apart from the specific studies mentioned below, some of which are of a high technical standard, but usually unpublished and thus inaccessible for research, such general works as have appeared are compilations of often undigested material.

The best concise general descriptions of agriculture in Madagascar are found in Robequain, Professor Charles, *Madagascar et les Bases dispersées de l'Union française*, Paris 1958; and Dumont, Professor René, *Evolution des Campagnes malgaches*, Paris 1958; and in a more controversial but none the less interesting and provocative work by Dumont, "Les principales conditions d'un rapide développement de l'agriculture malgache", 1961, which remains in mimeographed form.

A large number of articles and special studies have been written by R. Dufournet (whose study on cloves appears in the present Bibliography). This author also produced a general study, "Madagascar et sa Production agricole, 1960–61", which was issued in mimeographed form with a printed cover by the Institut de Recherches Agronomiques de Madagascar (IRAM). Many other special studies by this author have appeared in the *Bulletin de Madagascar*, and in general he is the most consistently interesting writer on agriculture in Madagascar. Montagnac, P., "Cultures Fruitières à Madagascar", IRAM 1960, and numerous monographs on the soils of Madagascar by P. Riquier are among other outstanding publications.

General descriptive and statistical material concerning the agricultural sector can be found in two publications of the Commissariat-Général du Plan (Planning Commission of the Government): *Plan Quinquennial, 1964–69;* and *L'Economie Malgache, 1960*. The Second Five-Year Plan will appear in 1971.

A large number of special surveys and studies of specific regions and crops have been prepared since 1960. These have been compiled by government consultants or 'Bureaux d'Etudes'. These include the following:

Institut de recherches agronomiques de Madagascar (IRAM).
Institut de recherches scientifiques de Madagascar (IRSM), now Office de recherche scientifique d'outre-mer (ORSTOM).
Institut français du café et du cacao (IFCC).

Madagascar

Institut de recherche cotonnière et du textile (IRCT).
Institut de recherche des huiles et des oléagineux (IRHO).
Institut des fruits et des agrumes coloniaux (IFAC).
Station de Recherche Océanographique, Nosy-be.

Of these, all except IRAM are wholly financed by France under bilateral agreements; IRAM is financed partly by the Malagasy government and partly by France.

Other 'Bureaux d'Etudes' whose activities in the field of survey and design are important are:

Bureau pour le développement de la production agricole (BDPA).
Société centrale d'equipement du territoire (SCET).
Société grenobloise de l'aménagement hydraulique (SOGREAH).

Index